Microsoft *Press*

Web Applications with
Microsoft®
Visual
InterDev® 6.0
MCSD
Training Kit

For Exam
70-152

PUBLISHED BY
Microsoft Press
A Division of Microsoft Corporation
One Microsoft Way
Redmond, Washington 98052-6399

Library of Congress Cataloging-in-Publication Data
Web Applications with Microsoft Visual InterDev 6.0 MCSD Training Kit / Microsoft Corporation.
    p. cm.
  Includes index.
  ISBN 0-7356-0967-5
  1. Microsoft Visual InterDev. 2. Web sites--Design. I. Microsoft Corporation.

TK5105.8885.M55 W43   2000
005.7'2--dc21   99-055181

Printed and bound in the United States of America.

1 2 3 4 5 6 7 8 9 QMQM   5 4 3 2 1 0

Distributed in Canada by Penguin Books Canada Limited.

A CIP catalogue record for this book is available from the British Library.

Microsoft Press books are available through booksellers and distributors worldwide. For further information about international editions, contact your local Microsoft Corporation office or contact Microsoft Press International directly at fax (425) 936-7329. Visit our Web site at mspress.microsoft.com.

Acquisitions Editor: Eric Stroo
Project Editor: Wendy Zucker

Contents

About This Book

Welcome to *Web Applications with Microsoft Visual InterDev 6.0 MCSD Training Kit*. By completing the lessons and associated exercises in this course, you will acquire the knowledge and skills necessary to develop Web bases solutions using Microsoft Visual InterDev 6.0.

This book also addresses the objectives of the Microsoft Designing and Implementing Distributed Applications for Microsoft Visual InterDev 6.0 (70-152) exam. This self-paced course provides content that supports the skills measured by this exam.

Note For more information on becoming a Microsoft Certified Solutions Developer, see the section titled "The Microsoft Certified Professional Program" later in this chapter.

Each chapter in this book is divided into lessons. Most lessons include hands-on procedures that allow you to practice or demonstrate a particular concept or skill. The lessons in each chapter end with a short summary. Each chapter ends with a hands-on lab and a set of review questions to test your knowledge of the chapter material.

The "Getting Started" section of this chapter provides important setup instructions that describe the hardware and software requirements to complete the exercises and labs in this course. Read through this section thoroughly before you start the lessons.

Intended Audience

This course is designed for students interested in developing Visual InterDev solutions at an intermediate and advanced level, and will teach experienced developers how to create custom solutions and enterprise-level Web sites using Visual InterDev 6. More complex topics, such as creating Microsoft Transaction Server components, are included in this course.

Prerequisites

Before beginning this self-paced course, you should:

- Have a basic understanding of the Internet
- Be able to deploy Web sites using Microsoft Internet Information Server
- Define client/server application architecture
- Be able to write simple client-side script with Microsoft Visual Basic Scripting Edition (VBScript) or JavaScript
- Develop ActiveX DLLs and describe their use
- Create Web sites using programs such as Microsoft FrontPage
- Have a general understanding of the HTML programming language
- Have an understanding of Microsoft SQL Server and Structured Query Language syntax
- Have a basic understanding of Microsoft Windows NT Server and SQL Server

Getting Started

This self-paced training course contains hands-on procedures to help you learn Visual InterDev. To complete the exercises, your computer must meet the following hardware and software requirements.

Hardware Requirements

All hardware should be on the Microsoft Windows 98 or Microsoft Windows NT Hardware Compatibility List.

Computer/ Processor	PC with a Pentium-class processor; 166 MHz or higher processor recommended
Memory	32 MB of RAM for Windows 95 or later (48 MB recommended); 32 MB for Windows NT 4.0 (48 MB recommended)
Hard Disk	Visual InterDev 6.0: 81 MB typical, 98 MB maximum
	IE: 43MB typical; 59MB maximum
	MSDN: 57MB typical; 493MB maximum
	SQL Server 7.0 Enterprise Edition; 180MB maximum; 170MB typical
	Windows NT 4.0 Option Pack: 200MB Windows NT 4.0
Drive	CD-ROM drive
Display	VGA or higher-resolution monitor; Super VGA recommended

Operating System	Microsoft Windows 95, Windows 98, or Windows NT Workstation operating system to be used as a client computer. Microsoft Windows NT Server operating system version 4.0 with Service Pack 4 or later to be used as a Web and database server.
Peripheral/Miscellaneous	Microsoft Internet Explorer 5
	Microsoft Mouse or compatible pointing device
	A sound card and speakers or headphones for the multimedia clips

Software Requirements

The following software is required to complete the procedures in this course:

- Visual InterDev 6.0
- Microsoft Visual Basic 6.0
- Microsoft Transaction Server 2.0
- SQL Server 7.0, Enterprise
- Windows NT 4.0 Option Pack
- Windows NT Server 4.0 with Service Pack 4 or later

Course Overview

This self-paced course combines text, graphics, hands-on procedures, multimedia presentations, and review questions to teach you Visual InterDev. The course is designed for you to work through the book from beginning to end, but you can choose a customized track and complete only the sections that interest you. If you choose to customize your study, see the "Before You Begin" section in each chapter for important information regarding prerequisites.

The self-paced training book is divided into the following chapters:

- "About This Book" contains a self-paced training overview and introduces the components of this book. Read this section thoroughly to get the greatest educational value from this self-paced training and to plan which lessons you will complete.

- Chapter 1, "Developing Web-Based Solutions," discusses how to plan a Web site that uses a service-based application model. You will also learn about architectural concepts, various development models and resources, and available technologies and their implications. In preparation for the labs to be used in this course, you will be introduced to the members of a Web site development team and the development tools available to them.

  With these design principles in hand, you will begin planning and developing a Web site for a fictitious hotel named the Chateau St. Mark. Building this Web site with Visual InterDev will be the focus of the labs for each chapter.

- Chapter 2, "Creating a Web Site," discusses how to create a site diagram, and how to add and organize the pages that will make up the site. You will create cascading style sheets to customize the look and feel of individual pages. You will then begin assembling a service based application model for their Visual InterDev project. This includes developing the conceptual and logistical design. Using the Visual InterDev tools, you will then construct an HTML page and an HTML form.

- Chapter 3, "Using Dynamic HTML," discusses how to use the Chateau Web site created in Chapter 2 to begin incorporating dynamic HTML (DHTML) script. This includes incorporating browser objects, document objects, and scriptlets into the Web site. As a result, the Web site will be much more interactive.

- Chapter 4, "Using Active Server Pages," discusses how to create active server pages (ASP) to further improve functionality. With ASP you will be able to design pages that will read requests and send responses. You will also be able to save state data and use COM components and page objects.

- Chapter 5, "Accessing Databases," discusses how to add a data environment to a Visual InterDev project. You will learn how to view and use data from the database in the Data View window. Additionally, you will be introduced to Database Designer, a tool for creating and manipulating database tables, and Query Designer, a tool for creating SQL queries.

- Chapter 6, "Understanding Data Access Technologies," discusses how to create Web pages that retrieve and update information in a database by using ActiveX Data Objects and the Remote Data Service. Specifically, you will be writing ADO code and using the Remote Data Service.

- Chapter 7, "Creating COM Components," discusses the business service aspect of the Web site, which can run on a Web server. You will also learn how to use Microsoft Visual Basic 6.0 to build COM components that contain business rules, and how to call these COM components from a Web page.

- Chapter 8, "Using Microsoft Transaction Server," discusses how to use the Microsoft Transaction Server (MTS), which provides transaction and resource management for COM components. You will also learn how to create MTS components, which are COM components that work within the MTS architecture.

- Chapter 9, "Implementing Security," discusses how to implement controls and security on a Web site. To practice these concepts, you will authenticate users and control access to files and resources on the Chateau St. Mark Web site.

- Chapter 10, "Integrating Other Server-Side Technology," discusses how to use the Simple Mail Transport Protocol (SMTP) service of IIS 4.0 to send e-mail from a Web site. You will learn how to enable custom search capabilities for a Web site. You will also add media delivery capabilities to the Web site, such as Java applets, Microsoft NetShow, and embedded MPEGs. You will also be able to deploy updated pages, graphics, sound, and ActiveX controls.

Features of This Book

- Each chapter opens with a "Before You Begin" section, which prepares you for the completion of the chapter.

- Each chapter is divided into lessons. Most lessons include hands-on exercises that allow you to practice an associated skill or procedure. Some lessons also contain references to animations included on the companion CD that further explain conceptual material.

- Most lessons contain procedures that give you an opportunity to use the skills presented or explore the part of the application described in the lesson. All procedures are identified with an arrow symbol at the left margin.

- Some lessons also contain Practices that allow you to try the new procedure on your own. The icon shown in the left margin identifies the Practices.

- Each lesson ends with a short Lesson Summary of the material presented.

- The Review section at the end of the chapter lets you test what you have learned in the lesson. The icon shown in the left margin identifies the Reviews.

- Appendix A, "Questions and Answers," located at the end of this book, contains all of the book's lab and review questions and corresponding answers.

- Appendix B, "Creating Client Script," provides an overview of developing script that executes within an HTML page. Understanding basic scripting techniques is required before learning the concepts of Dynamic HTML.

Conventions Used in This Book

Before you start any of the lessons, it is important that you understand the terms and notational conventions used in this book.

Notational Conventions

- *Italic* in syntax statements indicates placeholders for variable information. *Italic* is also used for book titles and new terms.

- Names of files and folders appear in Title Caps. Unless otherwise indicated, you can use all lowercase letters when you type a file name in a dialog box or at a command prompt.

- File name extensions appear in all lowercase.

- Acronyms appear in all uppercase.

- MONOSPACE type represents code samples, examples of screen text, or entries that you might type at a command prompt or in initialization files.

- Square brackets [ ] are used in syntax statements to enclose optional items. For example, [*filename*] in command syntax indicates that you can choose to type a file name with the command. Type only the information within the brackets, not the brackets themselves.

- Braces { } are used in syntax statements to enclose required items. Type only the information within the braces, not the braces themselves.

Keyboard Conventions

- You can choose menu commands with the keyboard. Press the ALT key to activate the menu bar, and then sequentially press the keys that correspond to the highlighted or underlined letter of the menu name and the command name. For some commands, you can also press a key combination listed in the menu.

- You can select or clear check boxes or option buttons in dialogs with the keyboard. Press the ALT key, and then press the key that corresponds to the underlined letter of the option name. Or you can press TAB until the option is highlighted, and then press the spacebar to select or clear the check box or option button.

- You can cancel the display of a dialog by pressing the ESC key.

About the CD-ROM

The companion CD contains files required to perform the hands-on lab exercises for the Chateau St. Mark Hotel Web site. These files must first be copied onto your hard disk using the setup program located on the CD.

You can compare your work with the Lab solutions located on the companion CD in the \Labs\Solution folder.

Using the Multimedia Presentations

The multimedia presentations supplement some of the key concepts covered in the book. You should view these presentations when suggested, and then use them as a review tool while you work through the material. The animations are denoted with the icon that appears in the left margin.

To play the animation, open the Animations folder on the CD, and double-click the appropriate file. The animation contains controls that can start, pause, and stop the animations, control the volume, and toggle on or off the sound and associated text.

Using This Book to Prepare for Certification

Where to Find Specific Skills in This Book

The following tables provide a list of the skills measured on the certification exam 70-152: Designing and Implementing Web Solutions with Microsoft Visual InterDev 6.0. The tables provide the skill, and the location in this book where you will find the lesson relating to that skill.

Note Exam skills are subject to change without prior notice and at the sole discretion of Microsoft.

Skill Being Measured	Location in Book
Analyze the scope of a project	
Identify the purpose of a Web site.	Chapter 1 Lesson 2
Identify the target audience; for example, an audience on the Internet, an extranet, an intranet, or any combination of these three.	Chapter 1 Lesson 2
Review the functionality and design of existing applications.	Chapter 1 Lesson 3
Examine anticipated changes in the current environment.	Chapter 1 Lesson 2
Estimate an expected lifetime of the solution.	Chapter 1 Lesson 2
Estimate the scope of the solution.	Chapter 1 Lesson 3
Quantify tradeoffs among time, cost, budget, and benefits.	Chapter 1 Lesson 2
Analyze the extent of a business requirement	
Specify the planned platform and infrastructure.	Chapter 1 Lesson 3
	Chapter 2 Lesson 2
Identify business requirements based on customer input.	Chapter 1 Lesson 2
	Chapter 2 Lesson 2
Identify which type of business problem exists.	Chapter 1 Lesson 2
Analyze security requirements	
Identify the need for roles of specific types of users, including administrators, groups, guests, and clients.	Chapter 9 Lesson 4
Identify requirements for access to components on a Web site.	Chapter 9 Lesson 4
Specify auditing capabilities.	Chapter 9 Lesson 4
Specify logging capabilities.	Chapter 9 Lesson 4
Identify the level of security required.	Chapter 9 Lessons 2, 3

Skill Being Measured	Location in Book
Analyze performance requirements.	
Identify the impact of components that affect performance. Such components include bandwidth, which includes maximum page size and modem speed; multimedia; and browser capabilities.	Chapter 1 Lesson 2
Identify the impact of customer response-time expectations on an application.	Chapter 1 Lesson 2
Identify the impact of scalability on the solution.	Chapter 1 Lesson 2
Identify tradeoffs between performance requirements and available technology.	Chapter 1 Lesson 2
Identify tradeoffs between performance and portability in the selection of a Web browser and a Web server.	Chapter 1 Lesson 2
Analyze maintainability requirements.	
Identify the requirements for ongoing updates and distribution of the application.	Chapter 1 Lesson 2
Analyze extensibility requirements.	
Identify the impact of an increase in the number of end users, the growth of an organization, and an increase in the functionality of the application.	Chapter 1 Lesson 2
Identify the impact of an increase in data.	Chapter 5 Lesson 1
Analyze availability requirements.	
Identify the level of availability required.	Chapter 1 Lesson 2
Identify the geographic area to be covered.	Chapter 1 Lesson 3
Assess the impact of downtime on end users.	Chapter 1 Lesson 3
Analyze requirements that include such human factors as target audience, localization, accessibility, roaming users, online Help, and special needs.	
Identify localization requirements, including target languages.	Chapter 1 Lesson 2
Identify accessibility needs, including alternate text site, tab order, and text-only links.	Chapter 2 Lesson 2
Analyze documentation and online Help requirements	Chapter 2 Lesson 2
Identify the impact of various connectivity solutions on the application.	Chapter 2 Lesson 2
Identify constraints due to the environment; for example, 640 x 480 screen resolution and Internet versus intranet.	Chapter 1 Lesson 2

Skill Being Measured	Location in Book
Analyze the requirements for integrating a Microsoft Visual InterDev solution with existing applications.	
Identify the location of existing data.	Chapter 5 Lesson 6
Identify the format of existing data.	Chapter 5 Lesson 6
Identify all migration considerations.	Chapter 5 Lesson 6
Identify data conversion requirements.	Chapter 5 Lesson 6
Analyze Web site development requirements.	
Identify the number of Web developers and content authors needed to develop and initially implement the solution, and identify how the team will be staffed.	Chapter 1 Lesson 2
Identify the security levels needed for each type of development role.	Chapter 9 Lesson 2
Identify hardware and software needs for the development team	Chapter 1 Lesson 2
Given a business scenario, identify which solution type is appropriate. Solution types are single-tier, two-tier, and *n*-tier.	Chapter 1 Lesson 2
Identify which technologies are appropriate for implementation of a given business solution.	
Select the appropriate development tools to use.	Chapter 2 Lesson 1
Identify which products and technologies are appropriate for implementation.	Chapter 2 Lesson 1
	Chapter 9 Lesson 1
	Chapter 5 Lesson 1
Choose a data storage architecture. Considerations include volume; number of transactions per time slice; number of connections or sessions; scope of business requirements; extensibility requirements; reporting requirements; and number of users.	Chapter 8 Lesson 1
Test the feasibility of a proposed technical architecture.	
Demonstrate that business requirements are met.	Chapter 1 Lesson 2
	Lab 1
Meet existing technology constraints.	Chapter 5 Lesson 1
	Chapter 1 Lesson 2
Assess the impact and tradeoffs that result if a specific requirement is not met.	Chapter 1 Lesson 3
Construct a conceptual design that is based on a variety of scenarios and that includes context, workflow process, task sequence, and physical environment models.	Chapter 2 Lesson 2

Skill Being Measured	Location in Book
Given a conceptual design, apply the principles of modular design to derive the components and services of the logical design.	Chapter 7 Lesson 3
Incorporate business rules into object design.	Chapter 7 Lesson 3
Identify an appropriate navigational scheme for a Web site that reflects the information flow.	Chapter 2 Lesson 2
Identify input validation procedures that should be integrated into the user interface.	
Identify which type of script to use: server-side or client-side.	Chapter 3 Lesson 1
Compare VBScript and JavaScript	Chapter 3 Lesson 1
Evaluate methods of providing user assistance.	Chapter 1 Lesson 2
Use the Visual InterDev WYSIWYG page editor to construct a prototype user interface that is based on business requirements, user interface guidelines, and the organization's standards.	Chapter 2 Lesson 1 Lab 1
Assess the potential impact of the logical design on performance, maintainability, extensibility, scalability, availability, and security.	Chapter 1 Lesson 2
Evaluate whether access to a database should be encapsulated in an object.	Chapter 5 Lesson 4 Chapter 6 Lesson 1 Chapter 7 Lesson 1
Design the properties, methods, and events of COM components and Microsoft Transaction Server (MTS) components on a server.	Chapter 7 Lesson 2 Chapter 8 Lesson 2
Install and integrate Microsoft Visual InterDev with Microsoft Visual SourceSafe.	Chapter 2 Lesson 1
Install Visual InterDev development tools. Development tools include Visual InterDev client components and Visual InterDev server components.	Chapter 2 Lesson 1
Install and configure server services. Services include Active Server Pages (ASP) on a Web server; the Microsoft FrontPage Server Extensions; Web servers; and other servers or services such as MTS, SMTP service, Microsoft Index Server, and NetShow.	Chapter 8 Lesson 2 Chapter 10 Lesson 3
Configure a client computer to use an MTS component.	Chapter 8 Lesson 2
Implement the sequence of flow for the user interface.	
Apply consistent site navigation within a page and between pages.	Chapter 2 Lesson 3
Use components such as HTML tags, text hyperlinks, graphics, tables, and frames.	Chapter 2 Lesson 3

Skill Being Measured	Location in Book
Create an HTML form.	Chapter 2 Lesson 3
Validate user input.	
Validate user input by using an HTML form.	Chapter 2 Lesson 3
Validate server-side code.	Chapter 2 Lesson 3
Process user input from an HTML form.	Chapter 2 Lesson 3
Add Microsoft ActiveX controls to a Web page.	Chapter 5 Lesson 2
Add a Java applet to a Web page.	Chapter 2 Lesson 3
Create dynamic Web pages by using Active Server Pages.	
Create server-side scripts.	Chapter 4 Lesson 1
Create client-side scripts.	Chapter 4 Lesson 1
Add a scriptlet to a Web page.	Chapter 3 Lesson 4
Use scripting and DHTML to create a Web page that dynamically changes attributes of elements, changes content, changes styles, positions elements, and uses visual filters and transitions.	Chapter 3 Lessons 2, 3, 4
Dynamically return different Web pages based on a user ID.	
Identify authentication methods.	Chapter 9 Lesson 3
Display data by using ActiveX Data Objects (ADO).	Chapter 6 Lesson 1
Add error handling to server-side and client-side scripts.	Chapter 6 Lesson 1
Implement a client-side solution or a server-side solution that enables users to send e-mail from a Web page.	Chapter 10 Lesson 1
Create a Web page that is dynamically constructed from data in a database.	Chapter 6 Lesson 3 Lab 6
Enable a Web page to author a channel.	Chapter 4 Lesson 1
Add search capabilities to a Web site.	Chapter 2 Lesson 1
Apply a consistent look and feel to a Web site.	
Apply linked cascading style sheets to Web pages.	Chapter 2 Lesson 1
Use themes.	Chapter 2 Lesson 3
Use layouts.	Chapter 2 Lesson 1
Add media delivery capabilities to a Web site. Components include animation, sound, push content, NetShow, Java applets, plug-ins, and embedded MPEG.	Chapter 10 Lesson 3
Create a Web page that includes tables, graphics, and animation.	Chapter 2 Lesson 3
Create a Web site that allows membership.	Chapter 4 Lesson 3
Use ODBC and ADO to access or manipulate a data source.	Chapter 6 Lesson 2
Write ADO code that accesses data by using the Execute Direct model.	Chapter 6 Lesson 2

Skill Being Measured	Location in Book
Write ADO code that accesses data by using the Prepare and Execute model.	Chapter 6 Lesson 2
Write ADO code that accesses data by using the Stored Procedure model.	Chapter 5 Lesson 4
Manipulate data by using client-side cursors.	Chapter 5 Lesson 4
Manipulate data by using server-side cursors.	Chapter 5 Lesson 4
Given a database error, handle the error.	Chapter 6 Lesson 1
Manage transactions to ensure data consistency and recoverability.	Chapter 6 Lesson 1
Write SQL statements that retrieve and modify data.	Chapter 6 Lesson 1
Write SQL statements that use joins to combine data from multiple tables.	Chapter 6 Lesson 1
Create a stored procedure that returns information.	Chapter 5 Lesson 3
Create triggers that implement rules.	Chapter 6 Lesson 1
Create a test plan.	Chapter 1 Lesson 3
Debug a Web application by using Visual InterDev debugging tools.	
Set breakpoints on client-side and server-side scripts.	Chapter 4 Lesson 1
Inspect and manipulate variables.	Chapter 4 Lesson 1
Create a connection to remote server processes.	Chapter 4 Lesson 1
Use the MTS Explorer to track availability and performance of MTS middle-tier components.	Chapter 8 Lesson 2
Publish and distribute Web content and components across multiple servers.	Chapter 2 Lesson 1
	Chapter 8 Lesson 3
Replicate Web content and components across multiple servers.	Chapter 9 Lesson 3
	Chapter 8 Lesson 3
Establish mechanisms for posting content on a Web site.	Chapter 1 Lesson 2
	Chapter 4 Lesson 2
Deploy updated pages, graphics, sound, ActiveX controls, and COM components on a Web site.	Chapter 7 Lesson 3
Verify hyperlinks.	Chapter 2 Lesson 1
Maintain streaming media on a Web site.	Chapter 10 Lesson 3

The Microsoft Certified Professional Program

The Microsoft Certified Professional (MCP) program provides the best method for proving your command of current Microsoft products and technologies. Microsoft, an industry leader in certification, is on the forefront of testing methodology. Our exams and corresponding certifications are developed to validate your mastery of critical competencies as you design and develop, or implement and support, solutions with Microsoft products and technologies. Computer professionals who become Microsoft certified are recognized as experts and are sought after industry-wide.

The Microsoft Certified Professional program offers five certifications, based on specific areas of technical expertise:

- *Microsoft Certified Professional (MCP).* Demonstrated in-depth knowledge of at least one Microsoft operating system. Candidates may pass additional Microsoft certification exams to further qualify their skills with Microsoft BackOffice products, development tools, or desktop programs.

- *Microsoft Certified Professional - Specialist: Internet.* MCPs with a specialty in the Internet are qualified to plan security, install and configure server products, manage server resources, extend servers to run CGI scripts or ISAPI scripts, monitor and analyze performance, and troubleshoot problems.

- *Microsoft Certified Systems Engineer (MCSE).* Qualified to effectively plan, implement, maintain, and support information systems in a wide range of computing environments with Microsoft Windows 98, Microsoft Windows NT, and the Microsoft BackOffice integrated family of server software.

- *Microsoft Certified Solution Developer (MCSD).* Qualified to design and develop custom business solutions with Microsoft development tools, technologies, and platforms, including Microsoft Office and Microsoft BackOffice.

- *Microsoft Certified Trainer (MCT).* Instructionally and technically qualified to deliver Microsoft Official Curriculum through a Microsoft Authorized Technical Education Center (ATEC).

Microsoft Certification Benefits

Microsoft certification, one of the most comprehensive certification programs available for assessing and maintaining software-related skills, is a valuable measure of an individual's knowledge and expertise. Microsoft certification is awarded to individuals who have successfully demonstrated their ability to perform specific tasks and implement solutions with Microsoft products. Not only does this provide an objective measure for employers to consider; it also provides guidance for what an individual should know to be proficient. And as with any skills-assessment and benchmarking measure, certification brings a variety of benefits: to the individual, and to employers and organizations.

Technical Support

Every effort has been made to ensure the accuracy of this book and the contents of the companion CD. If you have comments, questions, or ideas regarding this book or the companion CD, please send them to Microsoft Press using either of the following methods:

E-mail:

tkinput@microsoft.com

Postal Mail:

Microsoft Press
Attn: Web Applications with Microsoft Visual InterDev 6.0 MCSD
Training Kit
One Microsoft Way
Redmond, WA 98052-6399

Microsoft Press provides corrections for books through the World Wide Web at the following address:

http://mspress.microsoft.com/support/

Please note that product support is not offered through the above mail addresses. For further information regarding Microsoft software support options, please connect to http://www.microsoft.com/support/ or call Microsoft Support Network Sales at (800) 936-3500.

About the Authors

This course was developed for Microsoft Press by Training Associates, Inc., an Arizona-based corporation founded in 1995. Training Associates has developed a number of MCSD- and MCSE-related courses for Microsoft. These include traditional instructor-led courses, self-paced kits, and computer-based (CD-ROM) multimedia titles. In addition, Training Associates offers complete conversion services for existing courses that will be used in an online training environment.

As a Microsoft Certified Technical Education Center (CTEC), Training Associates is one of the first Microsoft-approved online training organizations. Training Associates has delivered courses to thousands of students worldwide that are interested in obtaining all levels of Microsoft certification (MOUS, MCSD, and MCSE). All Training Associates' online instructors and authors are Microsoft Certified Trainers with both traditional classroom and online training experience.

In addition to developing technical curriculum and delivering online instruction, Training Associates has also created the edCenter online learning system. This Web-based, client/server application can be used by training organizations that want to deliver curriculum via a local network or over the Internet. Training Associates has designed edCenter to support all forms of technical and non-technical curriculum.

For more information about the products or services offered by Training Associates, please contact us at:

- E-mail: curriculum@trainingassociates.com
- Web site: www.trainingassociates.com

The Training Associates staff that developed this course includes:

Project Lead	Dave Perkovich, MCT, MCSD
Subject Matter Experts	Sean Chase, MCT, MCSD
	Wade Harding, MCSD
Instructional Designer	Jim Croasmun, M.S.
Video	Sean Chase, MCT, MCSD
Graphic Designer	Stephanie Polhamus
Indexer	Laura Laurie

CHAPTER 1

Developing Web-Based Solutions

About This Chapter

This chapter will discuss Web solution design principles, architectural concepts, various development models and resources, and available development technologies. With an understanding of the design principles covered in this chapter, you will begin planning and developing a Web site for a fictitious hotel named the Chateau St. Mark. To help you prepare to work through the labs in this course, you will be introduced to the members of a Web site development team and the development tools available to them. Building the Chateau St. Mark Web site with Microsoft Visual InterDev 6.0 will be the focus of the labs for each chapter.

Before You Begin

To complete the lessons in this chapter, you must have done the following:

- Installed Visual InterDev 6.0.
- Installed the lab files from the companion CD.

Lesson 1: Web Site Overview

When planning a Web-based solution, you should base the Web site's design on the site's architectural implementation as well as on the tools and technologies you will be using.

In this section, you will learn about the architecture of a generic client/server Web-based solution and available Microsoft tools and technologies. In addition, you will learn which programming tasks, concepts, tools, and technologies are specific to Web site development.

After this lesson, you will be able to:

- Describe the types and purpose of Web servers.
- Describe the functionality provided by Web browsers.
- Identify Microsoft Web client, server, and development technologies and products.

Estimated lesson time: 20 minutes

Web Site Architecture

The World Wide Web was originally a platform for sharing and publishing documents over the Internet. Currently, the Web is being used for much more than simple document publishing. In fact, most commercial and corporate Internet sites can be more accurately described as Web applications. This is because they use complex processing to create a more compelling, informative experience for users. Web technology is also experiencing widespread growth as an effective platform for deploying corporate intranet applications.

Web Browsers

A World Wide Web client is called a Web browser, or simply a "browser." A Web browser, illustrated in Figure 1.1, is a program that displays HTML pages. The Web browser requests a page from a server based on its Internet address. It retrieves the document from the server and displays the contents to the user.

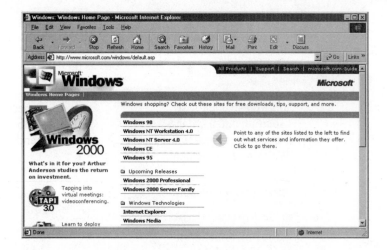

Figure 1.1 The Internet Explorer Web browser

As more advanced functionality is included in HTML, Web browsers evolve to support it. For example, Microsoft Internet Explorer displays ActiveX controls and runs Microsoft Visual Basic Script programs and Java applets. There have been three general phases in the evolution of Web browsers:

- Static content, which primarily consisted of static HTML and embedded media.

- Dynamic content, which includes scripting and client-side active components such as Java applets, ActiveX controls, and plug-ins.

- Integration, which includes XML, Dynamic HTML, and scriptlets. There is also better integration between the host user interface and the operating system.

An HTML page contains embedded commands to present the text to the user. These commands are called HTML tags. Different types of Web browsers interpret HTML tags and their attributes differently. Although the appearance of the elements on a page, such as text or graphics, may differ from Web browser to Web browser, the structural relationship between elements is consistent.

Web Servers

Internet protocols and technologies have advanced rapidly since the World WideWeb's inception in 1993. There have been three distinct generations of Web servers during this time period:

- First-generation Web servers delivered mostly static content—Hypertext Markup Language (HTML) pages with embedded graphics, sound files, and other basic features.

  Originally, both the Web server and Web client were nonintelligent. The server sent HTML files, which provided formatted text to a client. (This arrangement is still often used.) In this scenario, a user sends a request for a particular HTML file to a Web server via the hypertext transport protocol (HTTP). The server receives the request and sends the HTML file back to the client's browser. The browser reads the HTML and displays it accordingly. While this model provides instant access to formatted pages of information for employees or potential customers, interaction between the user and the Web server is limited. In addition, the information is only as up-to-date as the last time someone manually edited the files.

- Second-generation servers supported dynamic content through server-side extensions such as Common Gateway Interface (CGI) and application programming interfaces (API).

  CGI programs, or scripts, execute based on requests from Web browsers. CGI scripts run on the server and return dynamic HTML pages for the Web browser to display. For example, suppose a user is registering for a service on a Web site. When the user fills in a form on a page, the form is often processed by a CGI script that enters the user's name and other information into a database on the server. The script composes an HTML page that thanks the user by name for the information. The page is then sent back to the Web browser to be displayed. This functionality is in contrast to first-generation web servers that return only static pages.

- Third-generation servers support Web-based applications that integrate with other enterprise services such as transaction support. Optimally, these Web-based applications can be developed in popular programming languages such as Microsoft Visual Basic and can make use of the existing object technologies and services for the platform.

  With third-generation servers, you can take advantage of component technology and transactions to provide greater scalability and fault tolerance (the ability to recover from severe errors) for mission-critical Web applications.

Microsoft Web Technologies and Products

Microsoft has a full range of products and technologies for creating advanced Web-based solutions. To meet the needs of developers, Microsoft has created Visual InterDev for building dynamic Web applications for corporate intranets and the Internet. As a member of the Microsoft Visual tools family, Visual InterDev was designed for developing HTML-based Web applications. In addition, Visual InterDev fully interoperates with the Microsoft FrontPage Web authoring and management tool. Most Web sites are created by teams of people with different skills (such as programmers, content experts, graphic artists, and user interface design specialists). The combination of Visual InterDev and FrontPage offers organizations an effective enterprise development environment for both programmers and nonprogrammers alike.

In addition, almost all new Microsoft products and technologies now contain some Internet capability. For example, as illustrated in Figure 1.2, you can now insert Internet-based hyperlinks (pointers to external documents that reside on a network) into Microsoft Word documents.

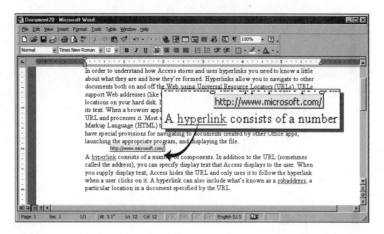

Figure 1.2 A hyperlink pointing to a Web location from Microsoft Word

Lesson Summary

Although the World Wide Web was originally a platform for sharing documents over the Internet, most commercial and corporate Internet sites include complex Web applications.

Originally, Web servers delivered mostly static content. Today's servers support robust applications that integrate with other enterprise services such as transaction support. Scripting and client-side active components such as Java applets, ActiveX controls, and plug-ins allow Web browsers to be more robust.

Visual InterDev 6.0 allows you to develop Web applications for corporate intranets and the Internet. Visual InterDev interoperates with Microsoft FrontPage Web authoring and management tools.

Lesson 2: The Web Development Process

Web site development technology, such as Visual InterDev, is becoming more complex, so you must carefully consider how a Web site's content will be supported. You must also consider how the content will be used and presented. Content management and graphic design are also critical in any Web development project. Quality production in all of these areas helps ensure that your site is useful and usable to the audience that you define.

Whether you'll be doing all the development tasks yourself or coordinating the work of people across multiple departments, clearly defining objectives and goals ultimately saves time, money, and effort. Although requirements can change as a project progresses, creating a comprehensive plan from the start enables you to know how any change or compromise will affect the design, budget, functionality, and launch date of the project.

After this lesson, you will be able to:

- List and describe the phases of the Web development process.
- Identify the components of the service-based application model.
- Describe the differences between single-tier, two-tier, and three-tier applications.

Estimated lesson time: 45 minutes

The Web Life Cycle

Developers should understand the Web site life cycle because they are playing increasingly important roles in creating, maintaining, and improving sites. Although this course is primarily written for developers who focus on developing creating active content and database services, topics such as Web site security and maintenance are also addressed because increasingly they are becoming integrated with development.

Businesses measure the success of the technology implementation by its impact on the bottom line. Return on investment is of the utmost importance, whether a business Web site is focused internally on employees or externally on customers or business partners. The return on investment for a Web site is evaluated based on two main factors: the ability to increase the business value of the site, and effective management.

As intranet and Internet business sites have become more sophisticated, the costs of creating and maintaining them have risen. The business-critical nature and complexity of sites has increased the demands on business managers, site developers, and site administrators. Today, business sites are corporate assets that need to be managed, measured, and enhanced to take advantage of new business opportunities. They are constantly evolving to meet the changing demands of consumers and organizations.

This management and evolution process defines the life cycle of an intranet or Internet business Web site. Companies that can effectively address the challenges of managing the life cycle and that can continuously and strategically improve their sites will have a significant competitive advantage. The Web life cycle represents the cycle of events involved in creating, managing, and maintaining a typical business Web site. These events include:

- Analyzing customer requirements and available technologies.
- Designing the site architecture and content areas.
- Developing content including:
  - Static HTML, media elements, Active Documents, and links to outside resources.
  - Dynamic elements such as client-side and server-side script and server components.
  - Integrated database information.
- Staging and deploying new and updated content quickly and securely.
- Applying and managing site security.
- Managing and troubleshooting the site environment.
- Measuring and analyzing site usage.
- Incorporating site enhancements that drive business value.

The illustration in Figure 1.3 represents the Web site life cycle.

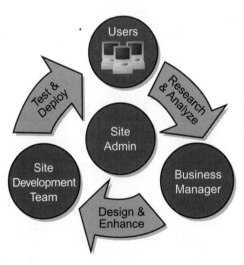

Figure 1.3 How the Web site life cycle works

Phases of the Web Development Process

To plan an effective Web-based solution, you must first understand several Web-related concepts and processes. You should be familiar with the application models used in client/server architecture, and you should be aware of the roles of the development team members.

The Web development process consists of five phases:

1. Planning Phase

2. The Analysis and Design Phase

3. Implementation and Testing Phase

4. Production Phase

5. Support Phase

Planning Phase

Creating a project plan is essential to the success of a Web development project. Project goals should be identified before actual implementation begins. When planning the project, the following questions should be considered:

- What is the project timeline?

- Who is the target audience?

- What company departments will participate?

- What are the hardware requirements?

- Do we have the resources to build and maintain a Web site?

- What are the customer response-time expectations on the Web application?

During the planning phase, you should perform a feasibility study to quantify tradeoffs among time, cost, budget, and benefits. This is a very simple process of determining whether the cost of the project is greater than the benefits, and whether the timeline is acceptable to the organization. This will provide you with feedback its impact to the organization in areas such as:

- Finances

- Budget

- Total Cost of Ownership (TCO)

- Return on Investment (ROI)

You also need to determine what content will be presented. When you do this, you should consider issues such as the politics of the organization, people's technical acceptance level, and any training that may be required. One technique that will help you decide what content will be included is to compose a short mission statement for the site. This statement should clearly state the goals of the site and the target audience.

Content for your Internet site could include:

- Information about company products or services

  Using a Web site to provide basic information about your company is a common use of corporate web sites. Effective use of a Web site to provide product and service information can reduce costs associated with presale support.

- Product manuals or frequently asked customer questions

  Using a Web site to publish product manuals and provide a frequently asked question list can also reduce presale, and post-sale, support costs. In addition, unless your company provides 24-hour phone support, the Web site may be the only tool your customers have for support at certain times during the day.

- Online catalogs and ordering information

  Web sites that support e-commerce, such as a "shopping cart" feature, are becoming quite common. Providing customers the ability to order products and services 24 hours a day is becoming an expectation of today's consumer. In addution, providing your existing customers access to their order status via a live Web site can further reduce costs for your organization. Besides providing an online catalog and ordering system, consider implementing advanced features into your catalog, such as cross-selling additional products. For example, when a customer selects a book to purchase, your Web site can suggest additonal books the customer may be interested in reading.

- Press releases or a lists of partners and clients of your company

  A Web site can be a powerful tool to aid potential, and current, customers decide if they will use your services or your competitors. Providing testimonials and current corporate information can help customers make informed decisions. As the amount of information on the World Wide Web increases, customers can become overwhelmed. Therefore, your Web site needs to be selective in what information is included and how efficient that information is presented.

International Issues

In the past, Web content was mostly in English because of the Web's popularity in the United States. However, today the Web is used around the world; Japan, Germany, and China have a large number of users, and the Spanish-speaking population on the Web is increasing rapidly. This makes the Web a multicultural and multilingual medium. Web sites are becoming available in the native languages of the audiences they are targeting. On the global market, there are now plenty of opportunities for English-speaking companies to port their Web sites to local markets. If your customer demographics include multiple regions of the world, you should consider localization in when planning your Web site.

There are many localization issues such as different address conventions and money or date formats. The types of issues you encounter depend on the format and complexity of your site. To ensure that idiomatic expressions, symbols, and other content is appropriate for a particular market, you need to have your content reviewed by someone in that market. Having a native or expatriate review your content can be critical, especially in politically or culturally sensitive areas of the world.

You need to carefully research the Internet connection speeds that are available to your target audience in those markets. Although a Web server is centrally located in your company, information from that Web server could travel thousands of miles over semi-reliable phone lines. You should ensure that your Web site provides a good experience to these users. For example, you could develop international versions of your site, or limit the size of graphics that are used.

Analysis and Design Phase

The analysis and design phase follows the planning phase. In this phase, you define the structure of the Web site, navigation, application tasks, and data requirements. You can use a service-based application model to detail and categorize these components of your Web site.

The Services Model

The term service-based means that the functionality of an application is specified as collections of services that meet specific user needs. A service-based application is typically comprised of three categories: user services, business services, and data services.

User services provide an application with its user interface. The user of a service can be a person or another service. Therefore, the interface for a service can provide a graphical user interface or a programmatic interface, respectively.

Business services enforce business rules and handle transactions. These services can impose constraints or apply transformations to change user input or raw database information into usable business information. A business service does not need to know where data is located, how it is implemented, or how it is accessed, because data services handles these tasks.

Data services, which are used by business services, provide storage and low-level manipulation of data in a database. Examples of data services include create, read, update, and delete.

The illustration in Figure 1.4 shows the services model.

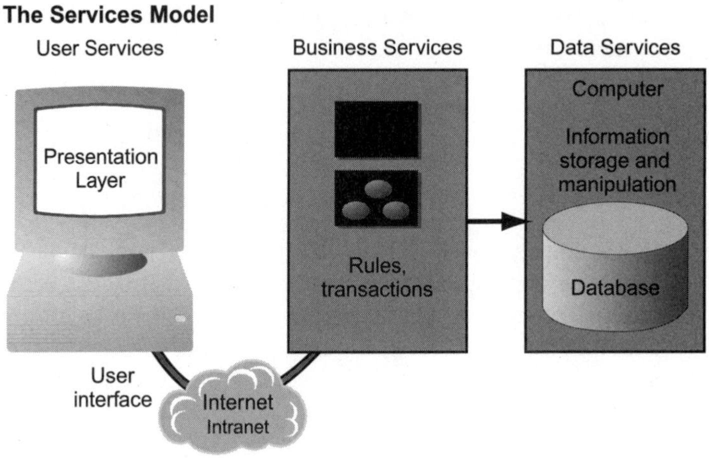

The Services Model

Figure 1.4 Designing a Web site using the Services Model

Benefits of Using the Services Model

After determining what capabilities you need for your Web site, you can decide how to implement the site. Using services to define the division of functionality in your Web site provides the following benefits:

- Clear and consistent development goals

  By dividing your Web site into services, you enable a Web development team to easily envision the direction of development. The functionality of each service, implemented as a component, is clearly defined.

- Better manageability

  Because services divide the functionality of your Web site into distinct tasks, any changes in the implementation of one service will not introduce changes to another service component.

- Isolation of functionality

  The functionality of a specific service is encapsulated, so any error in the implementation of a service can be easily traced to the corresponding component.

- Division of labor

  Identifying services enables you to determine which member of the Web development team is best suited to build and complete the corresponding component.

Application Models

The system architecture is an important feature in application design since it defines how elements in the application interact and what functionality each element provides. The three types of system (or application) architecture are:

- Single-tier (or monolithic)
- Two-tier
- Multi-tier

In this course, you will focus on creating Web applications that are multi-tier. Multi-tier applications have three or more tiers that can be implemented using multiple computers across a network. This type of application is also referred to as a distributed application, or an *n-tier application*. An n-tier application represents a special instance of a three-tier application, in which one or more of the tiers are separated into additional tiers, providing better scalability.

Single-Tier Applications

A single-tier application is simply a monolithic, stand-alone program that runs on the user's computer. It may communicate with a database, but that database resides on the same computer (or perhaps on a mapped network drive). The key point to know about a single-tier application is that all three services—user, business, and data—are architecturally combined into a single program. Typically, only a single person uses a particular installation of a single-tier application.

Two-Tier Client/Server Applications

The simplest type of distributed computing is the two-tier client/server application. In this type of application, the database (and perhaps a portion of the data services) is separated from the user interface and business logic. Typically, the database is placed on a dedicated server.

Two-tier client/server applications are the most common type of client/server applications built today. They offer significant benefits over single-tier applications because data processing is centralized and becomes a shared resource among potentially many users.

Note There is not necessarily a perfect mapping between the corresponding physical and logical tiers. For example, whereas business logic is generally placed on a separate application server, some business services such as validation code may map to a client computer or be partially implemented in stored SQL procedures on the database server. Likewise, data services may be distributed on either the application server or the database server.

Multi-Tier Client/Server Applications

The two-tier client/server model is not flexible or powerful (scalable) enough to handle many larger applications. For example, maintaining a connection between many client workstations and the central database server can result in high network traffic and poor performance.

Three-tier (and multi-tier) client server applications help address these issues by implementing an additional layer between the users and the database—the application service. This type of central application service can manage network traffic and database server loads more efficiently.

Typically, the application layer handles most of the business services and may be implemented on its own server computer, separate from the database. One of the main advantages of a multi-tier architecture is the extraction of business logic from the user and data tiers. This logic is then placed into the middle tier where it is easier to maintain.

Microsoft Solutions Framework

The Microsoft Solutions Framework (MSF) was created in 1994 based on best practices within Microsoft product development and IT organizations. The MSF was implemented into standardized training courses to promote consistency and effectiveness within the Microsoft Consulting Services (MCS) organization.

The MSF is a flexible, interrelated series of concepts, models, and best practices that lays the foundation for planning, building, and managing technology projects. MSF principles and practices can guide an organization through assembling the resources, managing the people, and implementing the processes necessary for technology solutions and infrastructure to meet changing business objectives.

Furthermore, MSF provides thorough project guidance that is flexible enough to be adapted to meet the needs of various projects and organizations. There are six models that comprise the MSF:

- The Enterprise Architecture Model
- The Team Model
- The Process Model
- The Risk Management Model
- The Design Process Model
- The Application Model

MSF models promote principles such as risk-driven scheduling, a fixed release date mind-set, versioned releases, visible milestones, and small peer-based teams. By following these models, you can expose critical risks, important planning assumptions, and key interdependencies required for successfully planning, building, and managing a technology infrastructure or a business solution. In addition, MSF models use a services paradigm to describe an application, and include standards and guidelines for designing distributed, multi-tier client/server applications.

Defining Technical Requirements

When the content for your site is defined and an application model is selected, you can determine the technical needs of the Web site relatively easily.

First, you should identify tradeoffs between performance requirements and available technology. For example, if your Web application involves streaming multimedia and your clients use 28.8 Kbs Internet connections, the performance requirements may not be met. In this case, you must assess the impact and tradeoffs that result if a specific requirement is not met. If you have clearly identified the impact of customer response-time expectations on your application, then you can decide which requirements can and can't be met.

Determining technical requirements also involves figuring out whether the Web application ties into other systems, such as an existing corporate database, and what user data needs to be collected and used. For example, you could create an online customer registration service. For an intranet application, information could be tied to a corporate database or existing application. To sell products or gather information on the Internet, you need to either build a database infrastructure or tie into an existing one.

Another consideration is setting up a Web server. The Web server needs enough processing power to support all of the following:

- The operating system
- The Web server service
- Web server processes (such as those that generate dynamic Web pages)
- Other processes (such as file and print services)

The Web server will run more effectively if it is not also a file server, print server, application server, RAS server, or domain controller.

Implementation and Testing Phase

In the implementation and testing phase, you should already have a working prototype of your Web site, and your company or client should have approved it. You can then create HTML pages, COM components, ActiveX controls, scripts, and databases. You can use your design specification to create graphics, sound, video, and text files for your Web application.

At this point, you should also create a test plan. For example, you can create step-by-step instructions for testing Web site functionality, and you can populate a test database with test data. To ensure data integrity and to prevent the loss of data, you should frequently back up any databases. In addition, you should test the Web site to ensure that each component is functioning properly.

Web Site Development Team

In the early days of Web development, a single person, the Webmaster, often developed, authored, published, and administered the site. However, a specialized Web site development team, which consists of a minimum of three people, typically performs modern Web development. These members include a Web developer, a programmer, and an HTML author. Additional team members are required when developing advanced Web sites. The following list describes the functions of these team members:

- Web developer

  Analyzes and designs Web site architecture and creates all necessary client-side and server-side scripts.

- Programmer

  Creates and maintains the applications and components used for a Web site. These include: server components, ActiveX controls, Java programs, and SQL stored procedures.

- HTML author

  Authors Web site content; creates HTML files; gathers appropriate graphics and other media.

- Graphic artist

  Designs and creates the graphic and multimedia elements.

- Test/documentation specialist

  Documents the Web site for maintenance; tests the content, navigation, and active content.

- Web administrator

  Installs the content and maintains server processes.

- Database administrator

  Installs and maintains the database management system (DBMS) and data sources used by the Web solution.

The content-driven nature of the Web requires that developers interact seamlessly with a wide range of other contributors while building the application. Visual InterDev contains the tools most team members will use for Web site development, enabling team members to collaborate. These tools provide the following benefits and features:

- Independence for programmers

  During a team-based development process, individual developers need to build and test pages. This can interfere with other developers working on different parts of the site. Visual InterDev improves the development process by allowing individual developers to isolate themselves from the rest of the team.

Developers can create and debug their pages locally before checking them back into the master Web project.

- Source code control

  Large development efforts often require source code control that allows check-in/check-out functionality with file locking. This also includes version control and rollback. Visual InterDev integrates with Microsoft Visual SourceSafe to provide these features. Developers can compare differences between two versions of the same file, and accept or reject specific changes to merge the files into a single, new master file. Visual InterDev also extends Visual SourceSafe to allow versioning of database scripts and stored procedures.

- Interoperability with other development tools

  Web developers need to be able to cooperatively work on files and projects with a range of other authors and developers. Visual InterDev allows developers to work seamlessly with the broadest range of tools, from page editors such as FrontPage to component creation tools such as Visual Basic.

Testing Hardware and Software

You should test required hardware for your Web site to evaluate how well it meets your needs. You can set up a test using one server and a few clients as a small pilot group. You can also use the Web Capacity Analysis Tool to run simulated workloads on an Internet Information Server (IIS). By using this tool, you can test the responsiveness of your pages. After you run the tests, you can decide how you want to fine-tune your Web site. You can also take advantage of third-party testing tools to determine the performance of your Web site.

Production Phase

Deployment of your Web application in the production phase can be very challenging for you and your development team. This phase is an opportunity for you to thoroughly evaluate the result of your work and to see your design in action. The goal of the production phase is to implement a working Web application on a production server. The Web application should be fully tested at this point.

Support Phase

Once a Web site has been released to production, the project life cycle is not yet complete. Outdated content will need to be removed from the site, and changes and updates need to be posted. When updated content is posted from different groups in your corporation, make sure style is consistent throughout the Web site. You will also need to optimize or rework code as you receive feedback from customers.

Consider the following questions about the continuing life cycle of your Web site when determining how to maintain it on an ongoing basis:

- Are you responding appropriately to what customers are saying?
- Are you ensuring that the corporate message is communicated clearly without grammar or syntax errors?
- Is the Web site always fresh with new content?
- Are you making sure that editorial standards are in place to help maintain consistency across the site?

A condition often overlooked is the *bottleneck*. In a bottleneck, the limitations in one component prevent the whole system from achieving optimal performance. The device with the lowest maximum throughput is the most likely to become a bottleneck if it is in demand. All the factors that affect server performance change, and most are hard to predict, but the following have clear trends that lead to future performance problems:

- The total number of clients will increase.
- The bandwidth of the average client's connection will increase.

Over time you should expect demand on the server to increase. Bottlenecks on static HTML pages usually reside in network components, slow hard disks, and lack of memory, which can all be gradually upgraded. In Chapter 4, you will learn that one of the potential bottlenecks in ASP application performance is connection management. If not managed properly, the opening and closing of connections can happen too frequently, causing reduced server performance. By continually checking for bottlenecks, you can often see changes coming and diminish their impact.

Lesson Summary

The Web life cycle involves creating, managing, and maintaining a Web site. Each Web site development team member should understand the Web life cycle so they understand their role in creating, maintaining, and improving sites. The Web development process consists of five phases:

1. Planning Phase
2. Analysis and Design Phase
3. Implementation and Testing Phase
4. Production Phase
5. Support Phase

A service-based application is typically comprised of three categories: user services, business services, and data services. User services provide an application with its user interface. Business services enforce business rules and handle transactions. Data services provide storage and low-level manipulation of data in a database.

Most Web applications have a multi-tier application architecture. Multi-tier applications have three or more tiers that can be implemented using multiple computers across a network. In addition to multi-tier applications, there are two other types of application architectures: single-tier (or monolithic) and two-tier.

In the early days of Web development, one person did all of the development, authoring, publishing, and administration. However, modern Web development requires many team members with varying skills.

Lesson 3: Overview of the Chateau St. Mark Hotel Lab

Throughout this course, you will develop a Web site for a fictitious company called the Chateau St. Mark Hotel. In this lesson, you will learn about the services and business needs of the hotel.

After this lesson, you will be able to:

- Identify the business objectives of the Chateau St. Mark Hotel.
- Plan the Chateau St. Mark Hotel Web development project.
- Determine the scope the Chateau St. Mark Hotel Web development project.
- Define development and performance requirements for the project.

Estimated lesson time: 15 minutes

Description of the Chateau St. Mark Hotel Web Site

The Chateau St. Mark Hotel Web site application provides an electronic means for customers to view different types of information and perform various activities such as making a reservation or planning a meeting. An outline of the Chateau St. Mark Web site is illustrated in Figure 1.5.

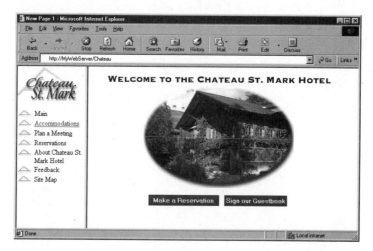

Figure 1.5 The Default.htm page of the Chateau St. Mark Web site

In the Chateau St. Mark Web site, customers can view the following types of information:

- Chateau St. Mark Hotel information

  This includes the home page and related pages with general information about the hotel and guidance to subtopics.

- Meeting room and service information

  This includes a design layout with descriptions for each meeting room, and availability. Descriptions include a room classification, an associated price, and a list of services provided for meeting rooms. Customers need to be able to look at this information to make a reservation.

- Hotel information

  Customers view room types and the number of beds each room has, select dates, and provide reservation information. To verify a reservation and prevent unauthorized access to private information, security considerations require a valid logon password.

Chateau St. Mark Services

The user services for the Chateau St. Mark Web site enable a customer to enter reservation information. The user services are implemented through the user's Web browser with HTML files and Active Server Pages (ASP) files. These files contain inline scripts that execute on the client or the server.

The business services for the Chateau St. Mark Web site implement business logic when a reservation is added or verified. An example of this business logic would be a business service that verifies room availability before adding a new reservation. Server-based COM components installed on the Web server provide the business services for the Chateau St. Mark Web site.

The data services for the Chateau St. Mark Web site perform the actual update of the Chateau St. Mark Hotel database, based on commands issued by components of the business services. Microsoft SQL Server provides the data services. The database is installed on the Chateau St. Mark Web server but can also be installed on a separate server computer.

Your Role in Web Application Development

Web site development involves building rich, dynamic content and applications designed to improve the user experience and deliver the information necessary for analysis. Content and application development on the Web today includes programming as well as developing graphics and multimedia. When creating labs for this course, you will assume the role of the Web developer, programmer, and HTML author. As a Web developer and HTML author of the Chateau St. Mark

Web site, you will use Visual InterDev to create HTML and ASP files. As the Web programmer, you will use Visual InterDev 6.0 to create COM components that implement business services. You will also use Microsoft Transaction Server (MTS) to provide transaction and resource management for server-based COM components.

Lesson Summary

The Chateau St. Mark Web site application provides customers with the ability to view hotel information make reservations on line. In the Chateau St. Mark Web site, customers can view:

- Chateau St. Mark Hotel information
- Meeting room and service information
- Hotel information

Throughout this course, you will assume the role of the Web developer, programmer, and HTML author. You will implement user, business, and data services for the Chateau St. Mark Web application project.

Lab 1: Tour of the Chateau St. Mark Web Site

In this lab you will create a prototype of the Chateau St. Mark Hotel Web site. You will start by creating a new project, and will add new files to the Web project to view the Chateau St. Mark Web site.

To see a demonstration of this lab, run the Lab01.exe animation located in the Animations folder on the companion CD-ROM that accompanies this book.

Before You Begin

In order to complete this lab, you must first install the partial and lab solution files from the companion CD-ROM included with this course. In future labs, you can optionally use the partial files to update your Chateau St. Mark Hotel Web project, and use the solution files to check your work.

Estimated lab time: 30 minutes

Exercise 1: Creating a New Project

In this exercise, you will create a new Visual InterDev project for the Chateau St. Mark Web site. You will then add files to the site.

➤ **Create a new Visual InterDev Web project**

1. Start Microsoft Visual InterDev 6.0.

2. If the New Project dialog does not automatically appear, from the File menu, click New Project.

3. In the left pane of the New Project dialog, select Visual InterDev Projects node.

4. In the right pane of the New Project dialog, select the New Web Project icon.

5. Change the name of the project to "ChateauDemo".

6. Optionally, specify a location different than the default for the project files. Since you will be using these files in future labs, you may want to place the project in a central location. Consider creating a new folder C:\My Documents\Visual Studio Projects\ChateauDemo. Do not create the project folder in the Internet publishing directory, typically C:\InetPub\WWWRoot.

7. Click Open when you have entered your changes.

   The Web Project Wizard will appear.

➤ Use the Web Project Wizard

1. The Web Project Wizard has four steps. In step one, where you specify a server and mode dialog, supply the name of the server that will be hosting the Web site.

   Since it is assumed you are hosting the site on your current, virtual root, the local machine name should be supplied here. If Visual InterDev does not automatically display the name of the local Web server, enter its name manually.

2. Since you are the only developer working on this site, select Master Mode.

   It is not recommended that you connect using secure sockets layer.

3. Click Next.

4. In step two, where you specify your Web, the default options Create A New Web Application and Create Search.htm To Enable Full Text Searching should remain checked.

5. Click Next to proceed to the Apply A Layout dialog.

6. In step three, where you apply a layout, verify <none> is selected and then click Next.

7. In step four, where you apply a theme, verify <none> is selected.

8. Click Finish and both the base Web site and a set of project files will be created.

9. Click the Save All button on the Standard toolbar to save the project files.

➤ **Add existing files to the project**

1. In Visual InterDev, highlight the <server-name>/Chateau node in the Project Explorer window.

2. From the Project menu, click Add Item.

   The Add Item dialog appears.

3. Click the Existing tab, and then navigate to the \Labs\Labs01\Partial directory.

4. Change the file mask to All Files (*.*).

5. Select all of the files located in this folder, then click Open.

   The files are added to the list of project files in the Project Explorer window. (Expand the ChateauDemo project node if necessary.)

6. From the Project menu, click Add Item.

7. Navigate to the Labs\Labs01\Partial directory. Select the \images subdirectory and then click Add Folder. Click Yes in response to any confirmation messages.

8. In the Project Explorer window, right-click the Default.htm node and choose View In Browser from the context menu.

Review

The following questions are intended to reinforce key information presented in this chapter. If you are unable to answer a question, review the appropriate lesson and then try the question again. Answers to the questions can be found in Appendix A, "Questions and Answers."

1. Describe the functionality of the three generations of Web servers.

2. What are the main differences between single-tier, two-tier, and three-tier applications?

3. Briefly describe the five phases of the Web development process.

4. Currently your organization provides goods and services in the United States. However, your business plan calls for an increase in revenue generated from International customers. In which phase of Web site development should localizing your site to foreign languages be discussed?

5. List three benefits of using Visual InterDev to develop a corporate Web site.

6. List three team members typically associated with advanced Web site development.

C H A P T E R   2

Creating a Web Site

About This Chapter

In this chapter, you will learn how to use Microsoft Visual InterDev 6.0 to build and manage Web sites. You will also learn how to author static Hypertext Markup Language (HTML) pages.

Before You Begin

- Install Visual InterDev 6.0.
- Install the lab files from the companion CD-ROM included with this course.

Lesson 1: Introduction to Visual InterDev

Microsoft Visual InterDev is for developers who are designing and deploying component-based Web applications. Visual InterDev can also manage database connectivity used by advanced Web sites. Specifically, Visual InterDev is used to create:

- Data-driven Web applications using data sources supported by ODBC or OLE DB.
- Broad-reaching Web pages by using HTML and script in Web applications that take advantage of the latest advances in browser technology.
- Integrated solutions that can include applets or COM components created in Microsoft Visual Basic, Microsoft Visual C++, Microsoft Visual J++, and Microsoft Visual FoxPro.

Visual InterDev provides a robust development environment with a scripting object model, design-time controls, and an extensible toolbox that enable rapid design, testing, and debugging.

After this lesson, you will be able to:

- Create Web projects in Visual InterDev.
- Create a site diagram.
- Use Visual InterDev version-control tools.

Estimated lesson time: 45 minutes

Working With Projects

This lesson will focus on creating Web projects with Visual InterDev. The project wizard can be used to create all types of related Visual Studio projects:

- Database project

   Allows direct manipulation of the database objects and data.

- Distribution unit

   Any one of three software distribution methods can be created: cabinet files, self-extracting setup files, and ZIP files.

- Utility project

   A container for files that you want to build, such as a master project for several subprojects, or a list of custom build rules.

- Visual Studio Analyzer project

   Contains performance data from all the components and systems.

Developing Web Projects

A Web project contains the files and information needed to create and publish a single Web application. These Web application files can consist of several different file formats that can be modified during design time, including:

- HTML pages
- Active Server Pages (ASP)
- Image files
- Layouts
- Themes

Web pages can be either static or active. A static Web page is an HTML page that can have hyperlinks to other pages and files, but it does not update server data and is not updated by the viewer's actions or information on the server. Most Web pages are static.

An active Web page allows the user to interact with a server by changing data, usually in a database, that is located on the server. For example, an active Web page is usually a form, such as an online order or purchase form, through which the user enters and submits information to a Web server. An active Web page can also contain ActiveX controls or scripting that provides the page with information-processing capabilities. One example is a Web page that welcomes a user, by their name, on each subsequent visit to the site. In this course, you will learn to create both static and active Web pages that you can use in your Web projects.

Creating a New Web Project

To create a new Web project in Visual InterDev, you can use the Web Project Wizard. The Web Project Wizard walks you through five steps that create and set default properties for the new project. The Web Project Wizard helps you complete the following tasks:

Task	Description
Start a new project	Creates the project and sets its default values
Open an existing project	Presents a list of Visual Studio projects that exist on the developer's workstation
Open a recent project	Presents a list of recently opened Visual Studio projects

To create a new project, use the New Project dialog to specify a new project. The Web Project Wizard will open and generate a set of starter Web directories and pages as illustrated in Figure 2.1.

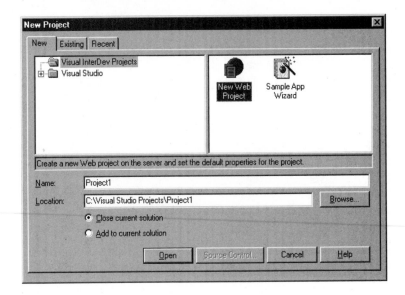

Figure 2.1 Creating a new project using the New Project dialog

The Web Project Wizard includes four steps, each having its own dialog. The following list outlines the your choices in each of these dialogs:

- Create a new project. (See Figure 2.1.)
  - Enter a project name.
  - Enter a project location.
- Specify a server and development mode. (See Figure 2.2.)
  - Enter the name of the server that you will be using.
  - Select whether you want to connect to that server using Secure Socket Layer.
  - Select the mode that you want to work in. Master mode updates the master Web application automatically. Local mode lets you control when updates are made.

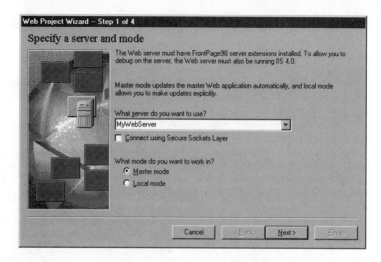

Figure 2.2 Specifying a server and mode for your Web project

■ Specify the name for your Web application. (See Figure 2.3)

  • Create a new application with the same name as that of the project.

  • Connect to an existing Web application on the server that you connected to in the first step.

  • Enable or disable site searching.

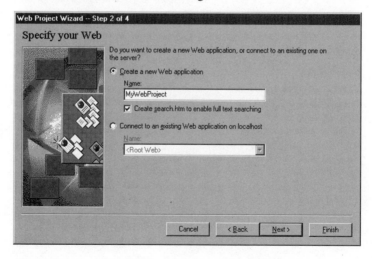

Figure 2.3 Specifying your Web for your Web project

- Apply navigation control layout to your project. (See Figure 2.4.)
  - Specify the location for navigation bars on the pages you will create. The Apply a Layout dialog is illustrated in Figure 2.4.

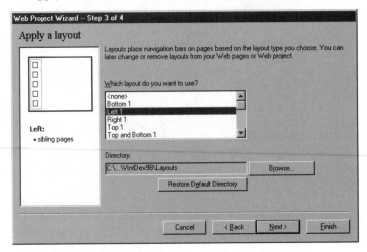

Figure 2.4 Setting the navigation control layout for your Web project

- Apply a visual theme to your project. (See Figure 2.5.)
  - Specify default backgrounds, headings, and list styles to the pages that will be created in this project.

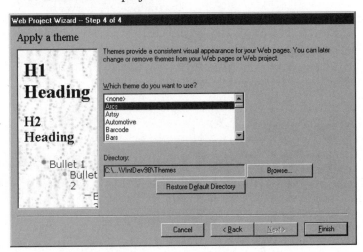

Figure 2.5 Applying a theme to your Web project

Web Server and Site Structure

There are different types of Web servers that you can connect to for your applications:

- Microsoft Internet Information Server (IIS)

    IIS is an Internet file and application server included with the Microsoft Windows NT Server and the Windows 2000 Server operating system. IIS version 4.0 is shipped with the Windows NT 4.0 Option Pack; IIS 5 ships with Windows 2000 Server.

    IIS can be used alone as a Web server, or in conjunction with compatible technologies to set up a complete Internet commerce server. It is also used to access and manipulate data from a variety of data sources, and to build Web applications that take advantage of server script and component code.

- Microsoft Personal Web Server

    Personal Web Server is designed for small-scale peer-to-peer or small Web server usage. Personal Web Server is ideal for developing, testing, and staging Web applications as well as for peer-to-peer publishing because it supports sharing files over HTTP and FTP protocols.

- Microsoft Peer Web Services

    Peer Web Services make it easy for users to create personal Web pages and also share information on their corporate intranets so that others can easily access the information from a browser. Peer Web Services is a subset of IIS. It enables you to test content and applications developed for IIS without requiring you to run the Windows NT Server or the Windows 2000 Server operating system on the computer used to create the content.

When a team builds a Web site, files can be hosted in three different locations. These locations are illustrated in Figure 2.6.

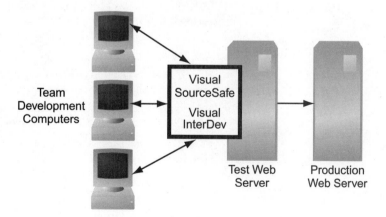

Figure 2.6 Locations where a Web site can be hosted

These project site locations are described in the following table:

Project site location	Description
Team development computers	Team members edit files on their local development computers and save them to the test server. When a master file is available on the test server (no one has a working copy of the master), any team member can retrieve and edit a copy of the master file.
Test Web server	When a Web development process begins, a team member creates a project in Visual InterDev on a test Web server. This is where the master files for a site are hosted until the site is fully developed and tested.
Production Web server	Once the files for the Web site are finished, the Web team publishes the files to a secure Web server. This ensures that files are not arbitrarily changed. The team can also provide the appropriate security on the production web server.

Web Project File Types

Web applications are composed of a number of different files. The following table lists those that are commonly used. Each file type is described in further detail later in this chapter.

File type	Description
Global.asa	This Active Server Application file contains global data and scripts for the Web application—global variables, database connections, and initialization and termination code. Each project may contain a single Global.asa file.
.asp	Active Server Pages files, which contain static text as well as data-bound controls that display data from a database.
.css	Cascading style sheet files, which contain information on customizing page element appearance.
.gif, .jpg, .jpeg, .bmp	Graphic files of various types that can be displayed in a Web application.
.htm or .html	HTML pages, which can contain forms and controls, static text, images, and links to other pages.
.sln	Solution files, which contain references to project, page, and other files that compose a Web application.
.vip	Project definition files, which contain Visual InterDev–specific information about the project.

Understanding Directory Structures

The Web Project Wizard creates the following folders for a new Web project:

Folder name	Description
<root>	Named after the project; contains the default home page and the top-level pages for the site.
_Layouts	Contains the template HTML files for your selected layout, if you chose to apply a layout to the project.
_private	Contains miscellaneous internal project files.
_ScriptLibrary	Contains the source for script objects used by Visual InterDev controls.
_Themes	Contains the bitmaps and the cascading style sheets for a selected theme, if you chose to apply a layout to the project.
Images	Created empty, this folder contains bitmaps added to the site's HTML pages.

By default, the Web Project Wizard creates two pages in the root directory: Search.htm (the Web site search page) and Global.asa (the Active Server Pages application-wide script file).

Note Search.htm will be included only if search functionality was selected when creating the new Web project.

Project Modes

The files for your Web application reside in two places: in the project directory on your computer and in the virtual directory on the master Web server. When you are working in your project, you are working on the local files. The way in which your changes are made to the master Web server depends on one of two project modes—local mode or master mode.

In local mode, changes made to the files are not immediately saved to the master Web server. The new versions are sent to the master Web server only when you explicitly request that the server be updated. In master mode, changes are saved to the local version and the master version at the same time. All master Web application files are stored on the master Web server, allowing the files to be accessible to multiple developers and authors.

Before editing files, files are retrieved from the server so that working copies are placed into your local Web application. In a multiple-developer scenario, each member of the development team has his or her own project, which can refer to the same master Web application.

Note When you import an existing page into your project, Visual InterDev adds the page to the master Web server and then locks the page. In order to edit the page, you must first request a working copy.

➤ **To get working copies of the Web application files**

1. Right-click the project icon in the Project Explorer window.

2. Click Get Working Copy on the context menu as illustrated in Figure 2.7.

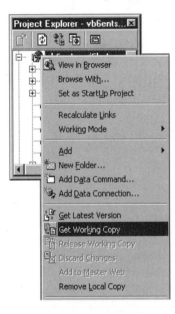

Figure 2.7 Getting a working copy of all files in a Web project

---

Note Although you can get working copies of all Web application files by right-clicking the project icon, you can also retrieve individual files by right-clicking each file.

Working With Files

As mentioned earlier in this lesson, the pages of a Web application in a Visual InterDev project are stored in two places. A copy is stored locally in the Visual

InterDev project folder, and the master copy is stored in a folder on the development server.

Members of the development team create their own local Visual InterDev projects. Each project contains copies of the Web application's files. Visual InterDev allows team members to modify project files through its developer isolation feature. To work with an existing file in a team setting, you use the following four basic steps, which can be performed in Visual InterDev:

1. Retrieve a working copy of the file from the Web server to your local development computer.

2. Edit the local copy of the file.

3. Preview and confirm the changes in a Web browser. If the page has dynamic content such as script code, test and debug this content as well.

4. Submit the files back to the Web server (release the working copy).

Note An individual developer working in master mode can use this same process. However, it is not strictly necessary to release working copies after each edit since the server files are updated automatically when the local version is saved.

➤ **To get the latest version of a file from the server**

1. Right-click the file node in Project Explorer window.

2. Click Get Latest Version on the context menu.

Notice that the icon next to the file node in the Project Explorer window changes from a lock to a pencil to indicate you have an editable, working copy of the file. If other team members subsequently try to get working copies of the same file, they will receive a warning that it is already checked out. Note that they can choose to ignore this warning and still get their own working copies.

➤ **To release the working copy of a file on your computer**

1. Right-click your local copy of the file.

2. Click Release Working Copy on the context menu.

Only when you release the file does Visual InterDev update the master copy of the file located on the Web server. If a team member has also changed the master copy during this period, Visual InterDev automatically displays the Merge Local Version dialog. This dialog allows you to integrate the changes to the file made by both team members.

The procedures for getting and releasing working copies allow a developer to update changes in the master project. However, because multiple developers can concurrently update the project files on the master Web server, it is important that a developer's local project maintain up-to-date information. Visual InterDev provides the following two mechanisms for updating local machines. These are illustrated in Figure 2.8.

■ Refresh Project View

Refreshing the view causes the file list in the local project to be synchronized with the master list. Files added or deleted from the master project by other developers will now appear in your local Project Explorer window.

■ Synchronize Files

Synchronizing the project will refresh the file list with the master Web project and update the contents of existing files that have been changed by other developers.

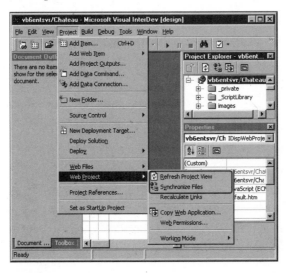

Figure 2.8 Refresh Project View and Synchronize Files menu items

Adding a Site Diagram

In order to create an effective design for your Web application, you must research, carefully plan, and thoroughly test your ideas. Consider the organization of the information on your Web site and how users will navigate that information.

To help you plan your site, you can create a site diagram, which is a graphical representation of the navigation structure of a Web site. In a site diagram, you create hierarchical relationships among pages by grouping them into trees. A tree contains one or more parent pages and one or more child pages. Each Web application can have multiple site diagrams, and each site diagram can have multiple trees.

To create parent, child, and sibling relationships, you drop pages beside or beneath one another in a site diagram. Use the dashed link lines to aid you in creating relationships.

Site diagrams use layouts to create and maintain the links between pages.

➤ **To add a site diagram to a project**

1. From the Project menu, click Add Web Item.

2. Click Site Diagram.

3. Assign a name to the diagram in the Name text box and click Open.

When you create a site diagram, a home page with a file name of default.htm for the site is automatically created for you and placed at the top of the diagram.

The illustration in Figure 2.9 shows you what a new site diagram looks like.

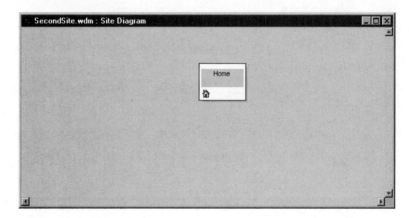

Figure 2.9 A new site diagram

Site diagrams provide a way for you to rapidly design and populate a Web application. You can create new pages for your project directly in a site diagram.

➤ **To add a Web page to a site**

1. Place the mouse cursor anywhere on the site diagram and right-click.

2. From the context menu, select the type of page that you want to add: a new HTML page, a new ASP page, an existing page, or another home page.

   A new page with a default name is added to the site diagram. You can then drag the page to position it in the diagram.

3. Apply the appropriate layouts for the pages at the various levels of the site.

You can add pages to your site diagram by dragging files from the Project Explorer window into the site diagram. You can also drag files from other applications, such as Microsoft Internet Explorer or Microsoft FrontPage.

When you save the site diagram, the site structure file is updated and all new pages are created and added to the project. The new pages are named according to the label names you entered in the site diagram, as illustrated in Figure 2.10.

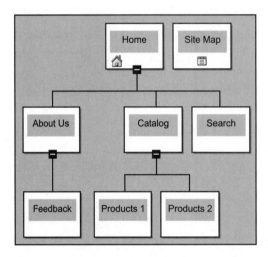

Figure 2.10 An example of a site diagram structure

If you have applied themes or defined a layout for the Web application, the new pages are created using those defaults. The navigation structure for the site is also automatically incorporated and updated for each page. You can add either HTML or ASP pages to the site diagram.

Understanding Layouts

Before you begin using site diagrams, you should understand what layouts are and how they are related to site diagrams. Layouts define how the navigation controls of a site are arranged on a page. They depend upon setting parent, children, and sibling relationships among pages on a site. Layouts make use of different combinations of regions on a page.

Figure 2.11 shows you the five possible regions of the page that can be controlled by a layout.

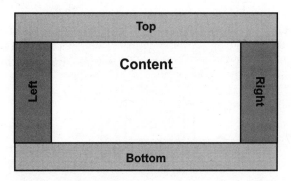

Figure 2.11 Regions used by layouts

Generally, layouts make use of the top, left, and bottom portions of a page. Because users typically read from top to bottom, left to right, use of the right region for navigation is not advised. However, this rule is solely dependent on your users. You will need to decide which layout to use based on your specific audience. Visual InterDev creates these regions by using HTML tables, and each layout is based on a unique HTML template. The template contains the source text for the layout. When the layout is applied to the page, Visual InterDev inserts header and footer information into the page.

Changing Layouts

You can specify a layout for a site when you create the project. You can also change layouts for individual pages while you are creating the site diagram. In addition, you can change the layout and theme for a page at any time during the development process. To change the theme and/or the layout for a page, select the page from the Edit menu (or the context menu) and then click Apply Theme And Layout.

Note Although you can use the layout templates available in Visual InterDev, you can also create a custom layout template by modifying an existing template and saving it with a new name to the _Layouts directory.

Understanding Cascading Style Sheets

Cascading style sheets (CSS) let you define a set of styles that override a browser's standard HTML styles. For example, you can use a cascading stylesheet to set a specific font style, face, and color attribute for all H1 tags. Cascading style sheets also let you adjust layout and formatting—for example, line spacing, justification, and border properties—for HTML elements and the entire document. This allows you to give your pages a unique and consistent design.

You can implement style sheets in three ways:

- Linked

  Style definitions are stored in a document that is separate from the HTML pages to which it applies. A single style sheet can be linked to many different HTML pages.

- Embedded

  Style definitions are stored in the header section, using the <STYLE> tag, within an HTML document. The style definition applies to all instances of that style within that HTML page.

- Inline

  Style definitions, created for individual elements within an HTML page, are added as properties to the elements to which they apply.

Of these three implementations, linked CSS allow for the highest degree of reuse and site consistency. Remember, if you use all three methods listed above, the inline styles take precedence over the embedded <STYLE> block, which overrides the linked styles.

➤ **To link a style sheet to a page**

1. Create a new CSS file for the style (or use an existing one).

   Typically, these files have an extension of .css. Visual InterDev contains a CSS Editor that allows you to create and modify CSS files.

2. Apply the style sheet to a page by adding a <LINK> tag in the HTML document heading section (between <HEAD> and </HEAD> tags).

   You can do this by manually inserting a statement such as the following into your page:

   ```
   <LINK REL="stylesheet" TYPE="text/css" HREF="YourStyles/COLOR0.CSS">
   ```

In Visual InterDev you can also simply drag the name of the style sheet from the Project Explorer window and drop it in within the head tags of the HTML or ASP page whose styles you want to set.

Understanding Themes

Themes are comprised of sets of graphics and one or more cascading style sheets that control the styles, fonts, and graphics. There are two advantages to using themes:

- They provide your pages with a consistent look and feel.
- You can change themes without changing content.

You can set a default theme for an entire project so that each page you create in that project will have the same theme applied. You can also override the default theme for a project on particular files where you might want to apply a different theme or no theme at all. The illustration in Figure 2.12 shows the same content rendered with two different themes.

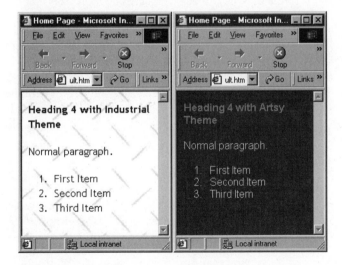

Figure 2.12 Two different themes with the same content

Using Visual InterDev Tools

Once you have created a Visual InterDev project, you are ready to use the tools offered by Visual InterDev. This section focuses on the individual windows that make up the Visual InterDev interface.

The Project Explorer Window

The Project Explorer window displays a hierarchical list of all the projects within a solution, and all of the items contained within each project. Typically, you use the Project Explorer window to:

- View the contents of a project.
- Open files within a project.
- Synchronize local files with files on the master Web server.
- Remove files from a project.
- Copy files.
- Display the Properties window for a given file.

To fully understand the architecture of Visual InterDev and the Project Explorer window, it is important to understand the concepts defined in the following list:

- Solution

  A collection of Web projects and dependent projects that makes up a Web application.
- Local Web application

  The collection of Web pages that resides on the developer's workstation. These pages are used for creating, developing, and testing prior to propagation to the master Web server.
- Master Web application

  The collection of Web files that is saved and stored on the Web server. The master Web application is accessible to multiple developers and authors. It can also be made available to intranet or Internet users.
- Web application

  A collection of elements that makes up a Web site or a distinct portion of a Web site. Web applications are built from Web projects.
- Web project

  A collection of files that specifies elements of a Web application.

The illustration in Figure 2.13 shows a sample solution within the Project Explorer window.

Figure 2.13 Viewing Web application project files in the Project Explorer window

Toolboxes

The Toolbox contains groups of related tools that you will use to build Web pages. The names and purposes for each of the tool groups in the default Toolbox (illustrated in Figure 2.14) are described in the following table.

Tool group	Purpose	Examples
Server objects	Objects available from a Web server	Dictionary, File system, My Info
ActiveX controls	Reusable components that provide added functionality to your Web page	Calendar, Toolbar, Treeview, Slider
Design-time controls	Reusable, primarily data-bound components that provide a graphical user interface for run-time activities such as connecting to a database	Label, Textbox, Checkbox, Grid
HTML	Standard graphical controls that are available within HTML	Form, Textbox, Listbox, Submit button
General	A place to collect objects to which you want easy access	Fragments of HTML code

Figure 2.14 The default Toolbox

Typically you use the mouse to select and drag a toolbox item onto pages. Double-clicking an item will have the same result, but the item will be placed in the center of the active designer window.

When you write code or create your own set of tools, you will want to make the tools readily available. You can add more tabs to the Toolbox and add items to them.

➤ **To add a tab to the Toolbox**

1. Right-click on any blank area of the Toolbox and click Add Tab.

2. Enter a name for the tab.

There are two methods for adding items to a tab. The method that you use depends upon the item that you want to add.

➤ **To add either a design-time control or an ActiveX control**

1. Right-click on any blank part of the Toolbox.

2. Click Customize Toolbox on the context menu.

3. Click the appropriate tab and locate the control that you want to add.

4. Select the control by clicking the check box.

5. Click OK.

Note: You can also browse to other sites to locate controls that you want to add to the project.

➤ **To add fragments of HTML code or script to a tab**

1. Select the fragment of code to save.

2. Drag it onto the appropriate tab.

Properties Window

The Properties window lists the design-time properties for the selected object or objects and their current settings. The elements of the Properties window show you what object currently has focus in the editor, and let you list those properties either alphabetically or by category as illustrated in Figure 2.15.

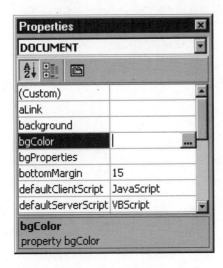

Figure 2.15 Setting document properties using the Properties Window

---

Note To display the Properties window for an HTML element, you must be in Design view to see a list of the element's properties.

HTML Editor Window

The HTML Editor offers three separate views of files: Design view, Source view, and Quick View. Each view provides you with different functionality. The illustration in Figure 2.16 shows a sample HTML file in Source view.

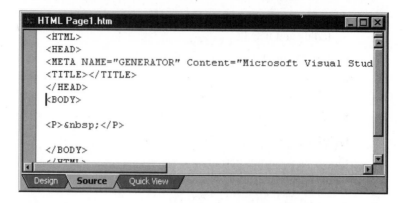

Figure 2.16 The Source view in the HTML Editor Window

Source View

Source view allows you to work directly with the underlying HTML and scripting code on a page. Source view also enables you to:

- View and edit text and HTML tags.
- View and edit scripts in the page.
- Work with design-time controls, Java applets, and most other objects using the visual representation they will have in the browser.
- Use the Properties window and custom properties dialogs to edit the appearance and behavior of HTML text and controls on the page.
- Use the HTML Outline window to jump to any element on the page.
- Use the Script Outline window to view and create scripts for elements on the page.
- Perform debugging functions, such as setting breakpoints and viewing the current line indicator.

Design View

Design view allows you to view and edit a page in a WYSIWYG environment. Design view also enables you to:

- Work with HTML controls such as buttons and text boxes, Java applets, and most ActiveX controls, using the visual representation they will have in the browser.
- Use menu and toolbar commands to apply certain types of formatting, such as paragraph alignment, that are not available in Source view.

- Use menu and toolbar commands to add and edit certain elements, such as tables and lists that you must edit as HTML text in Source view.
- Use the drag-and-drop operation to reposition absolutely positioned elements.
- Use the Properties window and custom properties dialogs to edit the appearance and behavior of HTML text and controls on the page.
- Use the HTML Outline window to jump to any element in the page.

Quick View

Quick view allows you to quickly test the look and feel of a page, as it will be displayed in Internet Explorer. Quick view also enables you to:

- View .htm files in a manner similar to how they will look in your browser.
- View the client elements in an ASP page, such as HTML intrinsic controls.
- See the results of your most recent changes instantly, without saving the document.
- Test client run-time elements of your page such as links, bookmarks, marquees, and client scripts.

Note   Server-side script, such as in ASP files, will not execute within the Quick view window because there is no Web server supporting this window. To fully preview a page, including the execution of code on an ASP page, right-click the file in the Project Explorer window and select View In Browser from the context menu.

Getting Help

Online help is always available while you are designing and developing Web sites. Help is available in HTML-style format with Previous, Next, Back, and Forward buttons for easy navigation.

Online help contains a wide variety of materials:

- Individual product documentation
- Knowledge Base articles
- Platform SDKs
- Resource Kits
- White papers

- Backgrounders
- Online help offers you four separate views of the documentation. The following table outlines those views:

View	Description
Contents	A table of contents of the entire Visual Studio library.
Index	An alphabetical index of the library. Enter a word in the text box and the tool displays a listing of related topics.
Search	A ranked listing of all topics related to a query.
Favorites	A location for pointers to commonly used resources.

➤ **To start MSDN Library Visual Studio 6.0**

1. Click Help.

2. Select the appropriate view command: Contents, Index, or Search.

The Task List Window

The Task List window helps you customize, categorize, and manage work associated with your project. The Task List window, illustrated in Figure 2.17, contains:

- Specially marked comments and tasks.
- Named shortcuts in files.
- Warning errors detected while you type in the Text Editor window.
- Errors detected while you are compiling a project.

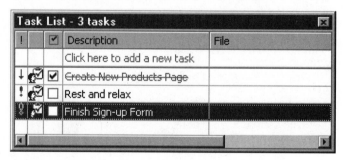

Figure 2.17 Using the Task List Window

➤ **To display the Task List window**

1. From the View menu, click Other Windows.

2. Click Task List.

Using Visual SourceSafe

Visual InterDev's management of local and master copies works well for small teams. If two developers have the same file checked out, Visual InterDev gives them the option of merging, overwriting, or discarding differences. However, with larger teams, a more robust version control, such as that provided by Microsoft Visual SourceSafe (VSS), is preferable.

Visual SourceSafe, like most modern version control management systems, enhances file-based development projects through the following features and capabilities:

- Version archiving of text-based and binary files (version control) enables developers to recall any past versions of a file. If desired, changes to a file can be rolled-back by restoring a previous version of the file.

- File access management allows the project administrator to determine team member access to files and folders within the SourceSafe project. In addition, by default, only one member of a team may check out an individual file at a time.

- Flexible interface to user and administrative functions is provided through the GUI Visual SourceSafe Explorer, through command-line arguments and utilities, or programmatically through COM interfaces.

- Integration with Visual Studio lets developers access the main version control functionality from within their main development environment.

Visual SourceSafe can be purchased as a separate product or as part of Microsoft Visual Studio Enterprise Edition. You first install Visual SourceSafe on the master Web server for a project and then enable the source control system for an individual Web site. You can then open files just as you did without Visual SourceSafe. When you want to check out a working copy of a file that has not been checked out by someone else, Visual SourceSafe provides you with a local, write-enabled copy of the file.

After you have a write-enabled copy of the file, Visual SourceSafe marks the file as checked out so no one else can edit it. When you check in the working copy, Visual SourceSafe marks the file as checked in so other developers can now check out and edit the file.

If you request a working copy of a file that another user has already checked out, Visual SourceSafe will display a warning message. If you still want the file, SourceSafe will provide you with a read-only version. Multiple users can have read-only copies of the file, but only one user can have a write-enabled copy. (Because Visual InterDev supplies all team members with local versions of Web project files, there is little reason to request read-only versions of Web project files.)

Lesson Summary

Developers who are designing, building, testing, debugging, deploying, and managing component-based, data-intensive Web applications can use Visual InterDev 6.0. The first step in developing a Web application is to create a new Web project. Once you've created a new project, you can begin designing the site. You do this by creating a site diagram, then adding and organizing the pages that will make up the site. You can also create or add cascading style sheets to customize the look and feel of individual pages. After you have created a Visual InterDev project, you can use the tools that it contains:

- The Project Explorer window
- Toolboxes
- The Properties window
- The HTML Editor window
- The Task List window

Version control is an issue for any team development environment. Visual InterDev offers two levels of version control support. For smaller development teams, Visual InterDev Professional Edition provides integrated version control. For larger teams, Visual InterDev Enterprise Edition includes the advanced Visual SourceSafe control system.

Lesson 2: Developing a Conceptual and Logical Design

Projects created in Visual InterDev are often pieces of a larger distributed application. The requirements of the many different kinds of enterprise applications make distributed application development a challenging task. Improvements are constantly being made to computer hardware and software. In addition, competition has created an environment that requires solutions to deliver high levels of performance. Because these demands are continuous, businesses need to be automated and software must be developed more quickly to serve more users and to process an increasing amount of data.

The changes in technology for Web-based solutions make efficient development increasingly more complex. For these reasons, it is important to follow a structured approach to designing and developing your Web applications.

After this lesson, you will be able to:

- Define the scope of a Web development project.
- Describe the importance of conceptual and logic design when developing a solution.
- Identify the relationship between a conceptual, logical, and physical design.

Estimated lesson time: 15 minutes

Defining the Project Scope

As you learned in Chapter 1, a project scope document expands on the vision statement with specific details, including business reasons for deployment, features, resources, and a schedule framework. As with the vision statement, the project scope presents a high-level view, but it also provides sufficient detail to direct and guide deployment.

Vision specifications in the scope document will be expanded during deployment. The scope document should be no more than three pages long. Be sure your project scope document includes:

- Identification of business needs and constraints

  Determine the high-level requirements.

- Identification of critical dates

  It's important to identify any fixed deployment dates in the vision/scope document and record the business reasons for them.

- Statement of assumptions

  A statement of project assumptions includes constraints, dependencies, and anything else that is required or assumed necessary for successful deployment.

It is essential to have a clear understanding of the business needs behind the deployment of your Web application. Here are some examples of business needs that apply to creating a Web application:

- Increase marketing as a result of broader audience.
- Reduce support costs by providing online assistance.
- Increase business flexibility by leveraging intranet capabilities.
- Reduce customer service response times by 25 percent.
- Decrease cycle time for problem resolution by 50 percent.

Creating a Conceptual Design

Conceptual design facilitates complete and accurate business requirements by involving both developers and users to determine the following:

- The problem
- The needs and technological capabilities of the business and users
- The desired, future state of the work
- Whether upgrading an existing solution is viable

Team members present scenarios to enhance understanding and express the problems and visions for the future state of the solution. The purpose of scenarios is to think of the solution in the business environment, and to answer the who, what, when, why, and how questions. When you develop a conceptual and logical design for your solution, you base the design on business requirements including:

- Workflow process
- Task sequence
- Physical environments
- Customer requirements
- Business goals

Conceptual design is an analysis activity that leads to determining which processes and activities will go into the new system, how the objectives of those processes and activities will be met, and what the user's experience of those activities will be. A complete understanding of business processes will help to create a complete model that encompasses all requirements and definition of these activities. For the Chateau St. Mark Hotel, we know that customers need information about hotel services, and they also must have the ability to reserve rooms.

A reservation is made in this sequence:

1. The customer requests information about room availability.

2. Based on availability, the information about rooms, including number of beds, smoking preferences, and price are provided.

3. The customer finalizes a reservation based on a room selection and by providing a credit card number.

4. The reservation system is updated with the customer's information.

Creating a Logical Design

Once the conceptual design is in place, you then derive a logical design that includes the data, user interface, components, and services of the application. The logical design describes how the solution is based on business rules and describes the structure and relationships between the different parts of the application. Tools such as Microsoft Visual Modeler can help create the logical application design by allowing a high-level view of the components.

Furthermore, logical design activities are integrated directly with the resulting scenarios from conceptual design and provide the basis for physical design. Logical design describes the organization of the elements that make up the solution and how they interact. You assemble the elements for optimum efficiency, performance, and reuse.

A logical design presents questions and answers very specific to the business for which you are writing your application. For the Chateau St. Mark Hotel, these questions could include:

- When should a customer be given a discount?

- When can a reservation be cancelled?

- How many people are allowed per room?

When you are creating a logical design, you should include a specification document to be approved before development begins. This will allow the development team and application users (or your client) to know what the end result will be. Once everyone is in agreement regarding the business rules addressed in the design, you can develop visual representations and prototypes of the application. Creating prototypes is part of the design process, not part of the development phase. By having a working prototype that becomes a part of the design, the application can undergo a live test phase prior to delivering the final product.

Remember that the logical design of a system is evolutionary, and the design should be updated and changed as the system develops. It is unlikely that a project team will arrive at the perfect design the first time out, and it's even less likely that the perfect design will remain in place as the needs of the business change.

Eventually, a physical design is derived from the logical design to translate the application into an actual system made up of the specific technologies, databases, networks, and other tangible elements of the real world. This describes a solution in a way that allows developers to construct it. Physical design communicates the necessary details of the solution, including its organization, structure, technology, and the relationships between components.

Lesson Summary

Because projects created in Visual InterDev are often components of a large distributed application, it is important to follow a structured approach to designing and developing your Web applications. First, create a conceptual design that addresses the objectives to be included in the solution. While it should be non-technical, the conceptual design should also be detailed regarding the functionality in the proposed solution, how the existing technology infrastructure will react to the introduction of this functionality, how the solution will interact with the user, and what is included in the performance criteria.

The logical design process is discovering the services that are required to deliver to solve a business problem. A logical design describes how the solution is based on business rules and is updated as the solution is developed. As you develop a logic and physical design, you should pay attention to the scope of the project. This will help you to maintain focus on requirements as you design your application.

Lesson 3: Working With HTML

This lesson shows you how to author a simple, static HTML page. You will learn how to set global attributes for individual pages such as background and link color. You will also learn how to add text, graphics, and hyperlinks to a page as well as how to use tables and frames to arrange items on a page. The goal of this lesson is to show you how to hand code some of the typical HTML tags. Larger sites will use style sheets, themes, and layouts to handle layout and formatting issues.

After this lesson, you will be able to:

- Add text and images to an HTML page.
- Create tables on an HTML page.
- Use frames and create hyperlinks in frames.
- Use DIV and SPAN tags.

Estimated lesson time: 30 minutes

Creating an HTML Page

Pages displayed on the Web are contained in an ASCII file format known as HTML. Hypertext makes the Web easy to navigate, and allows you move from one Web page to another through hyperlinks. HTML pages can contain images, movies, and sounds. The pages and files themselves can reside anywhere on the Internet. When you use HTML to create a Web page, you "tag" portions of text. Tags are embedded commands that supply the Web browser with information about the page's structure, appearance, and contents. HTML enables a variety of browsers to display the same file; the Web browser can then format the page for each client.

Each HTML page has properties that you can set in the HTML Editor. These properties affect the appearance of the page and provide information about the scripting language and model to use with the page.

➤ **To display the property page for an HTML page**

1. Double-click the file name in the Project Explorer window.
2. Click the Source tab at the bottom of the HTML Editor window.
3. Place the mouse cursor on the page and right-click.
4. Select Properties from the context menu.

The Property Pages dialog contains the General and Color and Margins tabs. The following table lists and describes some of the common visual properties you can set:

Property	Description	Tab location
Background color	The color that appears behind the contents of the page	Color and margins
Background image	The image that appears on a page behind the contents of the HTML page	General
Link text color	Default color for link text	Color and margins
Page margins	Default settings for the top, bottom, left, and right margins for the page	Color and margins
Page title	A descriptive word or phrase that appears in a browser's title bar when the page is displayed	General
Text font color	Default color of the text font used on the page	Color and margins
Default Scripting Language	Default client and server scripting language used if not specifically overridden by the code author.	General

The HTML editor makes it easy for you to add text and graphics to an HTML page. You can format text portions using the HTML toolbar, and design the look and feel of the individual page using the Design toolbar. Figure 2.18 shows the Design and the HTML toolbars, which are only enabled for Design view.

Figure 2.18 Design and the HTML toolbars in Visual InterDev

You use the HTML editor to apply formatting to an HTML page the same way that you apply formatting to a Microsoft Office document. For example, you can cut and paste text or use the drag-and-drop feature to move text to a new location. In addition, you can change the font and paragraph properties using the HTML toolbar or menu.

Some of the available formatting options include:

- Centering the style of a paragraph to make it centered or right aligned.
- Changing the text font to make it bold, italic, or underlined.
- Changing text to a bulleted or numbered list.

Adding Images to a Single Static Page

Adding images to your Web pages can make them more interesting and enhance how well they communicate your message. Two different graphics formats are commonly used in Web pages: the graphics interchange format (.gif) and the joint photographic expert group (.jpg or .jpeg). A .gif file is an encoded and compressed file for images of up to 8 bits of color. A .jpg or .jpeg file is an encoded and compressed file for images of up to 24 bits of color. The HTML Editor includes a library of clip art for commonly used buttons, icons, and backgrounds.

➤ **To insert an image**

1. Add the image to the images folder.
2. Open the page where you want to insert the image.
3. Drag the image file from The Project Explorer window onto the page.
4. To set properties for the image, such as alternate text, or alignment and size, right-click the image, and then click Properties on the context menu to display the Property Pages dialog.

Although images can enhance your web pages, many users turn off image display to download Web pages faster. Therefore, you should always provide alternate text for images on your Web pages. The following HTML uses the ALT attribute to display "textbooks" when a browser does not display images:

```
<P><img border="0" src="Textbooks.wmf" alt="textbooks" width="417"
height="364"></p>
```

Creating Tables

Tables can be used on HTML pages to display information in a tabular format, or to make images and text appear in an exact location on a Web page. This means that tables can contain any valid HTML text, images, forms, or controls. By setting various attributes you can control absolute positioning of content on your page. These attributes include:

- The width and height of cells
- Whether or not a border is displayed
- The amount of padding around content or between cells

➤ **To create a table**

1. Click on the location where you want the table to appear on the page.

2. On the Table menu, click Insert Table.

3. In the Insert Table dialog shown in Figure 2.19, do the following:

    a. Select the number of rows and columns.

    b. Select an alignment.

    c. Select a border size.

    d. If you want the table to use a specific percentage of the page, or if you want it to be a fixed pixel size, modify the Width setting in the Table Attributes option group.

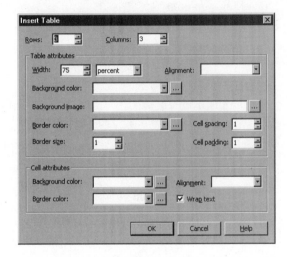

Figure 2.19 The Insert Table dialog, available from the HTML Editor

After you have inserted a table, you can customize it using the Table menu. You can also change the properties for individual table cells by right-clicking the cell, then clicking Properties on the context menu. A dialog will appear as illustrated in Figure 2.20.

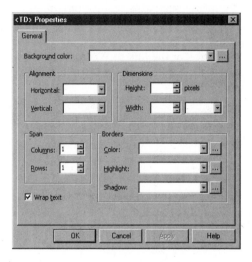

Figure 2.20 Customizing a table using the Table menu

In addition to setting table properties, you can also set properties for individual cells. The following table describes some of the cell properties you can set:

Property	Description
Background color	Sets the background color of the cell.
Cell alignment	Sets vertical and horizontal alignment of cell content.
Rows spanned	Sets the cell to span down more than one row.
Columns spanned	Sets the cell to span across more than one column.

Note Understanding how Visual InterDev builds and uses tables is very important, as tables are the primary element used for constructing multi-column layouts on Web pages.

Adding Hyperlinks

HTML lets you link text or images to another document. The browser highlights these elements to indicate that they are hyperlinks. You can add hyperlinks from pages in your current project to a page either on an intranet or on the Web. You can also create hyperlinks that allow clients to send e-mail or download files.

➤ **To create a hyperlink with the HTML Editor**

1. Select the text that will identify the hyperlink.

2. On the HTML menu, click Link, or click the Hyperlink button on the toolbar.

3. In the Hyperlink dialog, specify the relative or absolute URL to which you want to link, then click OK.

When you specify the URL for the link to Web pages, specify the server, path, and full file name (including the extension), in the format //Server/Path/File.ext, as in the following example:

```
//Myserver/Myproj/Startpage.htm
```

For e-mail, specify the e-mail name of the person to send to, as in the following example:

```
webmaster@mysite.com
```

The single hyperlink-related tag for HTML is <A>, which stands for anchor. The following example shows the HTML that the HTML Editor adds to a Web page when you create a hyperlink:

```
<A HREF="finance.htm">ABC Co. Financial Statement</A>
```

In this example, the syntax makes the text "ABC Co. Financial Statement" a relative hyperlink to the page Finance.htm, which is located in the same folder.

Using Frames

A frames page divides a Web browser's window into sections known as frames. Each frame in a frames page displays a separate Web page. Web pages that use frames include two main elements:

- Main frame HTML file

  This file contains the tags necessary to implement each frame on a page, along with references to the HTML files for each frame. The file does not contain a <BODY> tag.

- Source HTML files

  Each frame on a page contains its own source HTML file.

➤ **To create an HTML page with frames**

1. Create one source HTML file for each frame on a Web page. The source files can contain any HTML tags.

2. Create a new HTML file that contains <HTML> and <HEAD> tags, but not a <BODY> tag.

   This is the main frame file that users open with a Web browser.

3. In the area of the document that typically contains the <BODY> tag, add a <FRAMESET> tag for each group of frames.

4. For each frame on a page, add a <FRAME> tag, and set the SRC (source) attribute to the name of the HTML file that you want to appear in the frame.

The <FRAMESET> Tag

The <FRAMESET> tag defines the location, size, and orientation of frames on an HTML page. This tag has two attributes: ROWS and COLS. You can create a frameset with either rows or columns.

The following code creates two vertical frames:

```
<FRAMESET COLS="*, 2*">
    <FRAME SRC="Cell_1.htm">
    <FRAME SRC="Cell_2.htm">
</FRAMESET>
```

The left frame will be half as wide as the right frame because of the relative size attributes given in the <FRAMESET> tag. If you change the code in the first line to <FRAMESET COLS="*. 3*">, the left frame will be one third the size of the right frame. Figure 2.21 shows what you will see in the browser if you use these <FRAMESET> tags.

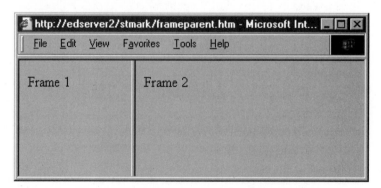

Figure 2.21 A browser displaying HTML with a FRAMESET tag

The ROWS attribute defines horizontal frames. It is followed by a comma-delimited list of the sizes for each frame on the page. The following code defines a page with two horizontal frames:

```
<HTML>
<FRAMESET ROWS="100, *">
</FRAMESET>
</HTML>
```

You can specify actual pixel sizes, percentages, or relative sizes. In the following code, the first frame is 120 pixels, the third frame is 20 percent of the total height, and the second frame occupies the remainder of the height:

```
<FRAMESET ROWS="120, *, 20%">
```

You can also create vertical frames by using the COLS attribute. You specify the frame in the same way as the ROWS attribute. The following example code creates two vertical frames in which the left frame will be twice as wide as the right frame:

```
<FRAMESET COLS="2*, *">
```

Browsers That Do Not Support Frames

Not all browsers support the frames feature in HTML 3.0. As a consideration to users of these browsers, you can supply alternate HTML by placing it in the <NOFRAMES> tag of the main frame HTML file. The <NOFRAMES> tag appears after the <FRAMESET> tag, as shown in the following example code:

```
<HTML>
<FRAMESET COLS="*, 2*">
    <FRAME SRC="Cell_1.htm">
    <FRAME SRC="Cell_2.htm">
</FRAMESET>

<NOFRAMES>
<BODY>
<P>Your browser does not support frames.</P>
</BODY>
</NOFRAMES>
</HTML>
```

Creating Hyperlinks in Frames

When a user clicks a hyperlink in a frame, the link loads in the target frame. When you create a hyperlink, you can change the default target frame where a link should be loaded by using the TARGET attribute of the <A> tag. The following bullet list describes the values of the TARGET attribute.

Attribute	Description	Example
"frame_name"	Sets the link to load the specified page into a named frame. In the <FRAMES> tag, this is the NAME attribute of the frame you want to load. In the sample code, the sample.htm will be loaded into the target frame named "frame1."	<A TARGET="frame1" HREF="sample.htm">
"_blank"	Sets the link to load into a new blank window. The window is not named.	<A TARGET="_blank" HREF="sample.htm">
"_parent"	Sets the link to load into the parent window of the window in which the link is located.	<A TARGET="_parent" HREF="sample.htm">
"_self"	Sets the link to load into the same window in which the link was clicked. This is the default.	<A TARGET="_self" HREF="sample.htm">
"_top"	Sets the link to load into the entire window.	<A TARGET="_top" HREF="sample.htm">

You can also specify that the target frame for loading all hyperlinks on a page should be in the same location. To set this location, you use the <BASE> tag with the TARGET attribute. In the following example code, the <BASE> tag specifies that all links should be loaded in the body of a window:

```
<BASE TARGET="_top">
```

Note With the HTML editor, you set the target frame in which a link should be loaded by using the Hyperlink dialog. To set the base target frame for all hyperlinks on a page, you use the Property Pages dialog.

Using DIVs and SPANs

DIV (short for division) and SPAN are HTML tags that group elements of an HTML page when you want to perform an action on all of them. You use these tools to apply style or absolute positioning information.

The illustration in Figure 2.22 shows a Web page that uses DIV and SPAN tags.

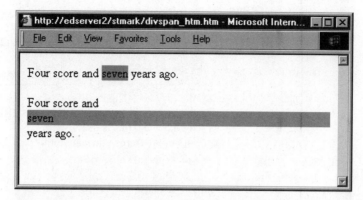

Figure 2.22 SPAN and DIV tags used on an HTML page

Both DIVs and SPANs are used to group HTML elements together so that an action can be uniformly applied. Examples include a cascading style sheet or dynamic HTML operation. Although both DIVs and SPANs act as containers for other elements, the difference between these two tags is that after the closing DIV tag, an implicit line break is inserted.

➤ **To create a DIV**

1. Switch to Design view.

2. Select the portion of the HTML document that you want to include in the DIV.

3. From the HTML menu, choose DIV.

4. In the Insert DIV dialog, choose a positioning option, either Absolute or Inline.

➤ **To create a SPAN**

1. Switch to Design view.

2. Select the portion of the HTML document that you want to include in the SPAN.

3. From the HTML menu, choose SPAN.

Note You will learn about how DIVs are used in Dynamic HTML in Chapter 3.

Creating HTML Forms

A form is a set of data-entry fields, called form fields, on a Web page. You can use a form to display dynamic data to a user or to gather input from a user and send the data to a Web server for processing. Typical uses for forms include:

- Providing data from a database on request.
- Registering users for membership or events.
- Gathering feedback about your site.

An HTML form contains standard HTML controls, which are also referred to as intrinsic controls. All Web browsers support these controls, which include text boxes, command buttons, radio buttons, and drop-down list boxes. Standard HTML controls reside within forms on an HTML page. On a form, controls are also known as form fields. Figure 2.23 shows an HTML form that contains standard HTML controls.

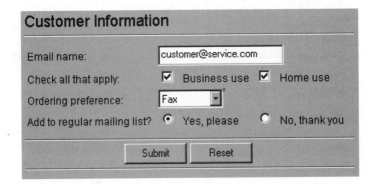

Figure 2.23 Gathering customer information using an HTML form

Note Internet Explorer does not require standard HTML controls to be contained on forms, but other browsers do. Therefore, you should always place standard HTML controls on forms.

You can add an intrinsic control by dragging it from the HTML tab of the Toolbox to its desired position on the page. You can then set the control's properties by clicking the control and providing values in the Properties window.

The following list contains the name of each of the controls that are available on the HTML toolbox.

- Button
- Checkbox
- Drop-down list box
- File field
- Listbox
- Password
- Radio button
- Reset button
- Submit button
- Text Area
- Textbox

Note This tab also contains entries for the following HTML elements: Button, Horizontal Rule, Line Break, Paragraph Break, Label, and Space.

Handling Control Data Using HTML Forms

When you use the HTML editor to add standard controls to an HTML document, you must also add a form control. The following code shows how to create a form that contains a text box, two check boxes, and two buttons.

```
<FORM METHOD=POST>
    Email name: <INPUT NAME="txtEditBox" VALUE="My Name"><P>
    Check all that apply:
    <INPUT TYPE="CHECKBOX" NAME="chkBusinessUse"> Business use
    <INPUT TYPE="CHECKBOX" NAME="chkHomeUse"> Home use<P>
    <INPUT TYPE=SUBMIT VALUE="Submit">
    <INPUT TYPE=RESET VALUE="Reset">
</FORM>
```

Forms can contain any HTML elements except other forms. You can add more than one HTML form to a document; however, forms cannot be nested.

HTML forms package the names and values of each control, and then send them to the location specified by the ACTION attribute. The location can be a CGI application, an ISAPI application, or an ASP page. In the following code, the form will send information to the file Events.asp.

```
<FORM ACTION=events.asp METHOD=POST>
```

In HTML, the ACTION attribute is referred to as a form handler. You can set a handler for a form by right-clicking the form and opening the Properties dialog.

Sending Control Values to a Server

To send values of a control to the Web server, place a Submit button on the form. Only controls with the NAME attribute will be sent to the server.

Note Internet Explorer does not require that all standard controls be placed on forms. However, if you want to send the information from controls to the server, you must use a form.

Only standard HTML controls are submitted with a form. To submit the value of an ActiveX control or Java applet with a form, set the VALUE attribute of a standard HTML control to an appropriate property of the ActiveX control or Java applet. Typically, you use hidden controls to submit values of ActiveX controls or Java applets with a form. You create a hidden control in the form, and then add client-side script to the onsubmit event procedure for the form.

In the onsubmit event procedure of the form, you set the VALUE attribute of the hidden control to an appropriate property of the ActiveX control or Java applet. A hidden control is a standard HTML control, so the value of the control will be submitted with the other HTML controls on the form.

For more information about adding client-side script for controls, see Appendix B.

Lesson Summary

Pages displayed on the Web are contained in an ASCII file format known as HTML. You can add images, sounds, tables, hyperlinks, and frames to your Web pages. You can also use DIV and SPAN tags to group elements of an HTML page when you want to perform an action on all of them.

In addition, HTML forms can be used to display dynamic data to a user or to gather input from a user and send the data to a Web server for processing. An HTML form contains standard HTML controls, which are also referred to as intrinsic controls. All Web browsers support these controls, which include text boxes, command buttons, radio buttons, and drop-down list boxes. Standard HTML controls reside within forms on an HTML page.

You can send control values to the Web server by placing a Submit button on the form. Standard HTML controls are submitted with a form. You can also submit the value of an ActiveX control or Java applet with a form, but you must set the VALUE attribute of a standard HTML control to a corresponding property of the ActiveX control or Java applet.

Lab 2: Developing a Web Project

In this lab you will create the Chateau St. Mark Hotel Web site. You will start by creating a new project, and will continue to develop the site by editing existing files as well as adding new files. You will use the results of this lab in subsequent exercises for other labs.

To see a demonstration of this lab, run the Lab02.exe animation located in the Animations folder on the companion CD-ROM that accompanies this book.

Before You Begin

In order to complete this lab, you must first install the partial and lab solution files from the companion CD-ROM included with this course. In future labs, you can optionally use the partial files to update your Chateau St. Mark Hotel Web project, and use the solution files to check your work.

Estimated lab time: 40 minutes

Exercise 1: Creating a New Project

In this exercise, you will create a new Visual InterDev project for the Chateau St. Mark Web site. You will then add files to the site.

➤ **Create a new Visual InterDev Web project**

1. Start Visual InterDev 6.0.

2. If the New Project dialog does not automatically appear, from the File menu, click New Project.

3. In the left pane of the New Project dialog, select Visual InterDev Projects node.

4. In the right pane of the New Project dialog, select the New Web Project icon.

5. Change the name of the project to "Chateau".

6. Optionally, specify a location different than the default for the project files. Since you will be using these files in future labs, you may want to place the project in a central location. Consider creating a new folder C:\My Documents\Visual Studio Projects\Chateau. Do not create the project folder in the Internet publishing directory, typically C:\InetPub\WWWRoot.

7. Click Open when you have entered your changes.

    The Web Project Wizard will appear.

➤ **Use the Web Project Wizard**

1. The Web Project Wizard has four steps. In step one, where you specify a server and mode dialog, supply the name of the server that will be hosting the Web site.

Since it is assumed you are hosting the site on your current, virtual root, the local machine name should be supplied here. If Visual InterDev does not automatically display the name of the local Web server, enter its name manually.

2. Since you are the only developer working on this site, select Master Mode.

   It is not recommended that you connect using secure sockets layer.

3. Click Next.

4. In step two, where you specify your Web, the default options Create A New Web Application and Create Search.htm To Enable Full Text Searching should remain checked.

5. Click Next to proceed to the Apply A Layout dialog.

6. In step three, where you apply a layout, verify <none> is selected and then click Next.

7. In step four, where you apply a theme, verify <none> is selected.

8. Click Finish and both the base Web site and a set of project files will be created.

9. Click the Save All button on the Standard toolbar to save the project files.

➤ **Add existing files to the project**

1. In Visual InterDev, highlight the <server-name>/Chateau node in the Project Explorer window.

2. From the Project menu, click Add Item.

   The Add Item dialog appears.

3. Click the Existing tab, and then navigate to the \Labs\Labs02\Partial directory.

4. Change the file mask to All Files (*.*).

5. Select the four files located in this folder: Feedback.htm, Sidebar.htm, Default.htm, and Main.htm, then click Open.

   The files are added to the list of project files in the Project Explorer window. (Expand the Chateau project node if necessary.)

6. From the Project menu, click Add Item.

7. Navigate to the Labs\Labs02\Partial directory. Select the \images subdirectory and then click Add Folder. Click Yes in response to any confirmation messages.

8. In the Project Explorer window, right-click the Default.htm node and choose View In Browser from the context menu.

Exercise 2: Creating a Static HTML Page

In this exercise, you will modify the Sidebar.htm file to provide a menu to users of the Chateau St. Mark Hotel Web site.

➤ **Edit the Sidebar.htm file**

1. Open the Sidebar.htm file for editing.

2. Place the insertion point below the Chateau St. Mark image at the top of the page.

3. From the Table menu, choose Insert Table.

4. In the Insert Table dialog, select 7 rows and 2 columns, set the Width to 100 percent, and then click OK.

5. Add the following items to the second column of the table:
   - Main
   - Accommodations
   - Plan a Meeting
   - Reservations
   - About Chateau St. Mark Hotel
   - Feedback
   - Site Map

6. Place the insertion point on the first column of the first row of the table.

7. On the HTML menu, click Image.

   The Insert Image dialog appears.

8. For the picture source, enter or browse to the images/hotel_icon.gif file.

9. Repeat steps 7 and 8 for the rest of the rows in column 1.

10. Switch to Source view for Sidebar.htm.

11. Locate and highlight the following HTML code:

```
<TABLE Border=1 cellPadding=1 cellSpacing=1 width="100%">
```

12. Replace it with the following HTML code:

```
<Table Border="0" width="100%" cellspacing="0" cellpadding="0">
```

13. Click the Save Sidebar.htm button on the Standard toolbar.

14. In the Project Explorer window, right-click the Default.htm node and choose View In Browser from the context menu.

Notice that the table you created is used as a sidebar menu for the Chateau Web site.

Exercise 3: Creating Dynamic Content

In this exercise, you will add HTML controls to an HTML form, write client-side validation script, and include ASP script to display user entries.

➤ **Edit feedback.htm to add dynamic elements**

1. Switch to Design view.

2. On the Toolbox, select the HTML tab.

3. Drag and drop a Text Area control below the text that reads, "Enter your comments in the space provided below:"

    You can adjust the size of the Text Area control as you feel appropriate.

4. Use the Properties window to change the Id and Name properties of the Text Area control to Comments.

5. Add a Button control on the line below the FAX textbox.

6. Change the Id and Name properties of the Button control to btnSubmit1.

7. Change the Value property to Submit.

8. Drag and drop a Reset button next to the Submit button.

9. Change the Value property of the Reset button to Clear Form.

10. Switch to Source view.

11. Place the insertion point below the HTML script that reads, "<!-- Client-side form validation code -->"

12. Type the following VBScript to validate entries made on the HTML form on Feedback.htm:

```
<SCRIPT Language="VBScript">
Sub btnSubmit1_onclick ()
    Dim ErrorString

    ErrorString = CheckFields()
    If Trim(ErrorString) = "" Then
        ' No Errors
        frmFB.submit
    Else
        MsgBox ErrorString
    End If
End Sub

Function CheckFields
    Dim strMissing

    If Trim(frmFB.comments.value) = "" Then
        strMissing = "Please enter your comments."
    ElseIf frmFB.CommentType.selectedIndex = 5 _
    And Trim(frmFB.Other.value) = "" Then
        strMissing = "You have selected (Other)" & _
            " as a comment type. Please specify a type of comment."
    ElseIf Trim(frmFB.name.value) = "" Then
        strMissing = "Please enter your name."
    ElseIf Trim(frmFB.email.value) = "" And _
        Trim(frmFB.telephone.value) = "" And _
        Trim(frmFB.fax.value) = "" Then
        strMissing = "Please specify either your email" & _
            " address, telephone number, or fax number."
    End If
    CheckFields = strMissing
End Function
</SCRIPT>
```

13. From the Standard toolbar, click Save Feedback.htm.

14. Open Feedback.htm in your Web browser and click the Submit button without entering any information on the form.

Notice that a message box is displayed notifying you of an invalid entry.

➤ **Create a simple ASP page**

1. From the Project menu, click Add Item.

2. In the right pane of the Add Item dialog, select ASP Page, set its name to Feedback.asp, and then click Open.

3. Below the BODY tag, type the following script:

```
<!-- Server-side script to echo user response -->
<%
Response.Write "<P>The feedback we received was: </P>"
Response.Write "<P><STRONG>Thank you " & _
    "for your feedback " & Request.Form("name") & "!"
Response.Write "<BR>Your comments were: " & _
    Request.Form("Comments")
Response.Write "</STRONG>"
Response.Write "<P>It was received at: " & Now
%>
```

4. From the Standard toolbar, click Save Feedback.asp.

5. Open Sidebar.htm for editing.

6. Create a hyperlink to the Feedback.htm page to allow the user to navigate from the sidebar.

7. Open Default.htm in your Web browser and click the Feedback hyperlink on the sidebar.

8. On the Feedback.htm page, click the Submit button after entering a comment, your name, and your email address.

   Feedback.asp is loaded in your Web browser containing your name and the time of your response.

Review

The following questions are intended to reinforce key information presented in this chapter. If you are unable to answer a question, review the appropriate lesson and then try the question again. Answers to the questions can be found in Appendix A, "Questions and Answers."

1. How are conceptual, logical, and a physical designs related to each other?

2. List the Visual InterDev version-control tools.

3. Why is the conceptual design of a solution so important?

C H A P T E R   3

Using Dynamic HTML

About This Chapter

Hypertext markup language (HTML), the underlying language for creating Web pages, is a standard for delivering document-oriented content across the Internet. It is supported by browsers and authoring tools on numerous operating systems. Dynamic HTML (DHTML) extends HTML, allowing developers and Web page designers to bring more creativity, control, and sophistication to their Web sites. DHTML pages use scripting language such as Microsoft Visual Basic Script (VBScript) to provide this functionality.

In this chapter, you will learn how to use objects exposed by the Document Object Model (DOM), and how to handle errors and debug scripts and scriptlets.

Before You Begin

To complete the lessons in this chapter, you should have read Chapter 2.

Specifically, you should be able to:

- Create a static Web page using HTML tags.
- Create a static Web site using frames and framesets.
- Create and use cascading style sheets to customize the look of text items on a Web page.
- Explain the purpose of methods, properties, objects, and events.

Lesson 1: Introduction to DHTML

In this lesson you will learn about a powerful feature in Web technology called dynamic HTML (DHTML). Microsoft and Netscape have collaborated on a proposed standard for DHTML and together they have presented this to the World Wide Web Consortium (W3C). Most new versions of Web browsers will support DHTML and this standard.

After this lesson, you will be able to:

- Describe the Document Object Model (DOM).
- Explain the features provided by DHTML.

Estimated lesson time: 30 minutes

Overview of Dynamic HTML

DHTML is one of the most powerful features in Web technology. Microsoft has proposed a standard for DHTML to the World Wide Web Consortium, and most new versions of Web browsers will support these new technologies. DHTML functionality in the browser allows you to create Web pages and other documents that automatically adapt to specific users, user requests, and to the changing state of data from sources on the Web and other locations. Scripting is the primary tool that enables dynamic pages. However, scripting is more than a language because it combines a language, an object model, and event handling.

Note For more information on creating Web pages that use scripts, see Appendix B, "Creating Client Script."

DHTML is an extension to the basic capabilities HTML. That is, DHTML includes all the elements that make up a traditional Web page. However, with DHTML, all of those elements are now programmable objects because you can assign each element an ID and then use scripting to alter the elements after the page has been downloaded. The following table describes the four Web page features that you can set dynamically to control the look and content of a Web page.

Language	Description
Dynamic styles	Changes element styles on a page.
Dynamic positioning	Changes the position of an element on the page.
Dynamic content	Adds new text or HTML content to a page.
Data binding	Binds elements to records in a database.

By first specifying an ID attribute of an HTML tag, you can then dynamically change the appearance of the item. For example, once the ID has been added, you can specify what code should be executed when certain events for the object are fired. In the following example, an H1 object is created with an ID of MyHeader. Code is associated with the onmouseover and onmouseout events to dynamically change the appearance of the MyHeader object.

```
<HTML>
<SCRIPT LANGUAGE="VBScript">
<!--
Sub ChangeColor()
    MyHeader.style.color = "red"
End Sub

Sub ChangeBack()
    MyHeader.style.color = "black"
End Sub
-->
</SCRIPT>
<BODY>
<H1 ID="MyHeader" onmouseover="ChangeColor()"
onmouseout="ChangeBack()">Hello, world!
</BODY>
</HTML>
```

Note   When you add the ID attribute to the H1 tag and assign it the value "MyHeader," you are creating a programmable object whose properties can then be manipulated in script.

The Document Object Model

Both Microsoft and Netscape have worked closely with the World Wide Web Consortium (W3C) to create a standard for DHTML. Both models propose the following items:

- A Document Object Model (DOM) to provide a way to control elements on the page using scripting
- Multimedia controls for animations and other effects
- A way to bind data to an HTML page

Note   This course will focus on the Microsoft DOM.

The DOM is an interface that permits script to access and update the content, structure, and style of a document. The DOM includes a model for how standard sets of objects representing documents are combined, and an interface for accessing and manipulating them. The key advantages of the DOM are the ability to access everything in the document, to make numerous content updates, and to work with content in separate document fragments. You can use the DOM interface in Microsoft Internet Explorer to take advantage of this dynamic model.

Objects exposed by the DOM provide all of the functionality that DHTML exploits. In this chapter, you will focus on two content areas:

- Writing script to handle routine page-level issues.
- Adding dynamic features to your page.

Benefits of the DOM

Working together with the DHTML Object Model, the DOM enhances your ability to build and manage complex documents and data. Many tasks, such as moving an object from one part of the document to another, are highly efficient and easy to perform using DOM members. The primary differences between the Microsoft and Netscape DOM are in the extent of the object model and the scripting language to be used. The DOM proposed by Microsoft is both browser- and language-independent. Figure 3.1 shows you the structure of the Microsoft DOM.

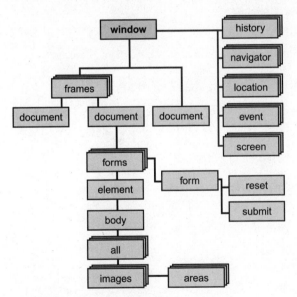

Figure 3.1 Structure of the DOM

Using Object Collections

Object models are composed of two different types of entities—objects and collections of objects.

An object model is the set of rules and organization devised to make that object do something in particular. For example, if the object is a car, the object model is the specification for the car that is used for routine maintenance and repairs. The air pressure would be a property and the air inflator would be akin to a method. Using the same car analogy, an event might be the car starting.

A collection is a feature of DHTML and object-oriented programming that makes it easy to organize and access similar objects. For example, just as a window can contain one or more frames, a document can contain one or more images or forms. There are two methods for accessing members of a collection—you can use either the index of the collection member or its name. For example, in the following example code, the first line accesses the second member of the images collection using the index 1 (collections are zero-based). The second line accesses the member of the images collection that is named myimage.

```
document.images(1)
document.images("myimage")
```

Every collection in DHTML has two properties:

- Item

  The Item property allows you to retrieve an element or a collection of elements from the current collection.

- Length

  The Length property contains the number of elements in the collection.

Working with Objects in the DOM

In the DOM, the top-level object in the hierarchy is the Window object. Objects in the DOM are referenced in order with the parent object before the child, separated by periods. For example, the Document object is a child of the Window object, and can be referenced as follows:

```
<SCRIPT Language=VBScript>
Sub window_onload()
    MsgBox Window.Document.Title
End Sub
</SCRIPT>
```

The Document object is a container for other objects in a particular Web page, and represents the HTML page the user views in the Web browser or Web browser control. The Document object can be used to access or modify elements in the document. In the previous example, the Document object accesses the Title element in the document.

In addition, you use events in the Document object to access the DHTML object model and handle user actions in the browser. The Document object also contains a number of collections, including anchors, frames, forms, links, and scripts. Both the Window and Document objects will be covered in greater detail later in this chapter.

Lesson Summary

DHTML allows you to create Web pages and other documents that automatically and instantly adapt to specific users, user requests, and to the changing state of data from sources on the Web and other locations. Unlike ASP, a page that has DHTML script can change without requiring the user to return to the server.

Lesson 2: Using the Window Object

The DOM exposes several important browser objects and collections that you will access on a regular basis. In this lesson, you will learn how to use the Window object and the objects it exposes (such as the Navigator object, the Frames collection, the Location object, and the Event object.)

After this lesson, you will be able to:

- Describe the purposes of four commonly used objects.
- Define an event.
- Explain event bubbling.

Estimated lesson time: 30 minutes

Programming a Web Browser

The Window object represents the browser window that contains the HTML document the user is viewing. For example, the Window object can represent Internet Explorer itself and give you control over the browser. It is the top-level object in the object model hierarchy illustrated in Figure 3.2. You can use the Window object to retrieve information about the state of the window. You also can use this object to gain access to the document in the window, to the events that occur in the window, and to features of the browser that affect the window. In addition, you can use methods and properties of the Window object to modify the appearance of a window and retrieve information about the browser. The Window object has several subobjects and collections as properties, including the Navigator object, the Frames collection, and the Location object.

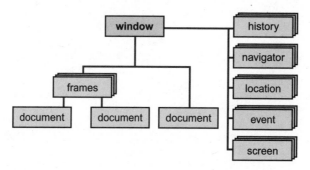

Figure 3.2 Window child objects in the DOM hierarchy

The Window object has an onload event that is called to initialize a page when the browser has finished loading the page. The object also has an onunload event that is called when the page has been unloaded. When an HTML page loads, the onload event of the Window object will run. To use this event, you can either create a subprocedure named window_onload or add the onload attribute to the <BODY> tag.

In the following example, the window_onload event procedure uses the Window object's Navigate method.

```
<SCRIPT LANGUAGE="VBScript">
Sub window_onload
    Window.Navigate "http://www.microsoft.com"
End Sub
</SCRIPT>
```

The following example code sets the onload attribute of the <BODY> tag to navigate to www.microsoft.com when the page loads:

```
<BODY LANGUAGE=VBScript
onload=window.navigate("http://www.microsoft.com")>
```

Displaying and Retrieving Information

To retrieve and then display information from a user, you use the Prompt and Alert methods of the Window object, respectively. The Prompt method prompts a user for input. The Alert method displays a message. The following example code prompts the user for a name with the Prompt method, and displays the name to the user with the Alert method:

```
<SCRIPT Language=VBSCRIPT>
Sub window_onload
    strName = Window.Prompt ("Enter your name")
    Window.Alert "Hello " & strName
End Sub
</SCRIPT>
```

Navigator Object

The Navigator object contains information about the browser application being used to view the HTML document. It includes the browser name and version number. You can use the Navigator object to detect the browser and use other objects in the object model to load an alternate document that was specifically authored for the browser. Different browsers have different capabilities, so by using the Navigator object, you can ensure that the user gets the appropriate content. The following table describes the properties of the Navigator object that expose the browser name and version:

Property	Description
appCodeName	Mozilla, for both Internet Explorer and Netscape Navigator.
appName	Either Internet Explorer or Netscape Navigator.
appVersion	Version number of the browser.
userAgent	Contains the HTTP user-agent string that was specified in the HTTP request. It is a concatenation of the appCodeName and appVersion properties.

The following example code illustrates using the Navigator object to display the name and version of the browser:

```
<HTML>
<HEAD><TITLE>Displaying the all collection</TITLE>
<SCRIPT LANGUAGE="VBScript">
Sub DisplayBrowserVer()
    Dim strName, strVersion

    strName = window.navigator.appName
    strVersion = window.navigator.appVersion

    Alert("The browser is " & strName & _
        ", version " & strVersion)
End Sub
</SCRIPT>
</HEAD>
<BODY onload="DisplayBrowserVer()">
</BODY>
</HTML>
```

Frames Collection

The Frames object represents a collection of frames in a window. This collection allows you to access all the frames in any frameset currently displayed in the browser. Each frame is also a Window object with its own properties, including a Document property that returns a Document object. The Frames collection allows you to control each frame in a frameset as though you are controlling a separate window.

Scope of Script in Frames

The scope of scripting code is at the frame level of a document. If you want to write script in one frame to access an object in another frame, you must navigate the object model to retrieve the parent window, and then use the Frames collection to retrieve the frame you want to access.

To access a different frame with script, refer to the Frames collection of the parent window of the current frame by using one of these syntax methods:

```
Parent.Frames("FrameName")
Parent.FrameName
```

For example, if the frameset with an index of 1 was named frame1, we could also access it with this code:

```
window.frames("frame1").navigate "http://www.microsoft.com"
```

Location Object

The Location object represents the URL of the current document. To load a document, you set the HRef property of the Location object. The following example code loads the default document from the Microsoft Web site:

```
Location.HRef = "http://www.microsoft.com/"
```

One use for this object is to direct the browser to different pages from the same hyperlink (HREF tag). To do this, you must first define the hyperlink as an object. Then, you can add script to the associated events of this tag. To define a hyperlink as an object with events, set the HRef and ID attributes of the hyperlink object. If you then set the HRef attribute of the Location object to a URL, the script will run and display the new document. If you set HRef to an empty string, the script will run but will not display a new document.

The following example shows a hyperlink defined as an object with associated code in the onclick event using the Location object:

```
<A HREF="" ID="JumpNext">Next Page</A>

<SCRIPT LANGUAGE=VBSCRIPT>
Sub JumpNext_onclick()
    If Navigator.appName = "Microsoft Internet Explorer" Then
        Location.HRef = "IEPage1.htm"
    Else
        Location.HRef = "OtherPage1.htm"
    End If
End Sub
</SCRIPT>
```

In the onclick event procedure, the script determines which browser type is currently being used. The Location object is then used according to the browser type. This allows your Web site to contain specific pages that leverage the unique capabilities of multiple browsers. However, the primary reason for creating an event procedure for a hyperlink is to perform more than one action, such as changing a document in multiple frames, in response to one user event.

Figure 3.3 shows a document with three frames. The hyperlink in the links frame has an event procedure that changes the documents contained in all three frames.

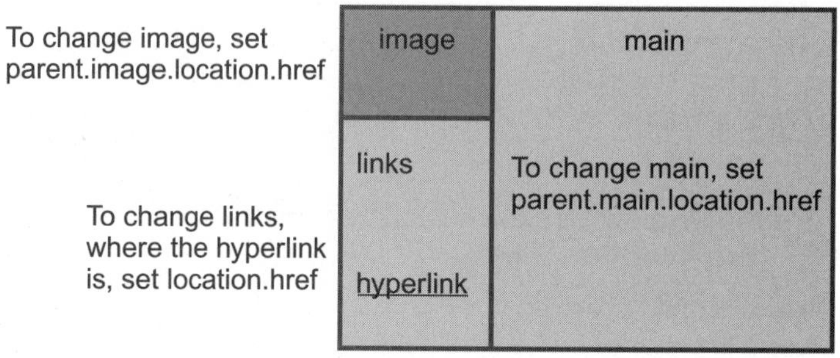

Figure 3.3 A document with three frames

The following example code shows this hyperlink event procedure discussed in the previous illustration:

```
' Change the source of the frame the hyperlink is in
Location.HRef = "Page1.htm"
' Change the source of the frame named "main"
Parent.main.Location.HRef = "Page2.htm"
' Change the source of the frame named "image"
Parent.image.Location.HRef = "Page3.htm"
```

Handling Events Using the Event Object

An event is a notification that occurs in response to an action, such as a change in state, or as a result of the user clicking the mouse or pressing a key while viewing the document. An event handler is code, typically a function or routine written in a scripting language, which receives control when the corresponding event occurs.

Events and event handling form the basis of DHTML. For example, an event fires when the user clicks a Submit button or rolls the mouse pointer over an element on a Web page. DHTML provides the mechanism for capturing and handling these events. Internet Explorer contains an Event object, which provides your Web application with detailed information about a user's actions.

The following terms are associated with handling events in DHTML to create interactive Web applications:

- Event object

  Exposes the information related to an event to the script.

- Event binding

  The association of a script with a notification from a document, or an element in a document.

- Standard user events

  Mouse, keyboard, focus, and help events that are available on almost every element in a document.

The Event object is a language-independent mechanism for accessing information related to an event and controlling whether the event bubbles (moves up to the parent element in the hierarchy) and the default action for the event occurs. The Event object is also a property of the Window object and exposes the properties discussed in the following table:

Property	Description
cancelBubble	A value that determines whether to cancel event bubbling. By setting cancelBubble to *False*, you prevent the parent element from receiving the event.
srcElement	The element that originated the event sequence.
returnValue	The default action for the event. By setting returnValue to *False*, you prevent the default action for that event.

The following example code shows you how to use the srcElement property to determine where an event occurred:

```
<HTML>
<BODY>
<SCRIPT for="document" event="onmousedown()" language="VBScript">
    msgbox "The click event happened in the " & _
    window.event.srcElement.tagName & " element."
</SCRIPT>
</BODY>
</HTML>
```

Writing Event Procedures

After creating and naming the objects on a Web page, you create event procedures and bind them to elements on the page. There are four different ways to create an event procedure for an object:

- Create a separate <SCRIPT> block for the event procedure.

  You can create a separate <SCRIPT> block that contains script that runs for a specific event of a control. You can use either JavaScript or VBScript to create event procedures for ActiveX controls and standard HTML controls. The following example code shows script that will run when the click event of the Calendar1 control occurs:

  ```
  <SCRIPT LANGUAGE="VBScript" FOR="Calendar1" EVENT="Click()">
      ' Code goes here.
  </SCRIPT>
  ```

- Assign the event procedure in an HTML tag for the object.

  You can specify an event name and the procedure to be invoked when that event occurs in the HTML tag that defines an object. You must include a <SCRIPT> block that includes the procedure declaration before the HTML tag that defines the object. This technique is useful if you want events from different objects to invoke the same procedure and to assign event procedures for standard HTML controls. Additionally, this technique is supported by both VBScript and JavaScript. In the following example code, the ProcessOrder procedure is called when the user clicks the option button:

  ```
  <SCRIPT LANGUAGE=VBScript>
  Sub ProcessOrder ()
      ' Code goes here.
  End Sub
  </SCRIPT>
  <INPUT TYPE=RADIO NAME=RadioGroup onclick="ProcessOrder">
  ```

- Include the script in the HTML tag that defines the object.

  You can specify an event name and the script to run when that event occurs in the HTML tag that defines the object. You can use this technique with VBScript or JavaScript to assign event procedures for standard HTML controls. The following example code displays the message "Hello World" when a user clicks the Hello button:

  ```
  <INPUT LANGUAGE="VBScript" TYPE=button VALUE="hello" onclick="Msgbox
  &quot;Hello World&quot;">
  ```

- Name a procedure objectname_event.

  If you name a procedure objectname_event, the procedure will run automatically when the event for the object occurs. This naming convention is the same as the convention used to define event procedures in Visual Basic.

This technique is supported only by VBScript. In the following example code, the procedure runs when the user clicks Button1:

```
Sub Button1_onclick ()
    ' Code goes here.
End Sub
```

Event Bubbling

When an event occurs, it fires the source element first and then on the parent of the source element through a process known as *bubbling*. It continues to fire on successive parent elements until it has reached the top element, the document. For example, when the user clicks a button on a Web page, the onclick event is first fired on the button itself, then on the form that contains the button, then the document, and so on. Figure 3.4 shows event bubbling through the browser object hierarchy.

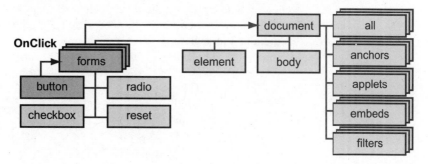

Figure 3.4 Event bubbling

The Life Cycle of an Event

An event has a life cycle that begins with the action or condition that initiates the event and ends with the final response by the event handler or Internet Explorer. The life cycle of a typical event has these steps:

1. The action associated with the event occurs.

2. The event object is updated to reflect the conditions of the event.

3. The event fires, causing the actual notification in response to the event.

4. The event handler associated with the source element is called to carry out its actions and returns.

5. The event bubbles up to the next element in the hierarchy, and the event handler for that element is called. This step repeats until the event bubbles up to the window object or a handler cancels bubbling.

6. The action in response to the event is executed unless an event handler has canceled the action.

Advantages of Event Bubbling

For events that bubble, if there is no event handler bound to the source element, the event handler for the next element up the hierarchy is called. When an event handler carries out its actions, it uses the Event object to retrieve information about the event, such as the position of the mouse, the state of the keyboard keys, the element in which the event occurred, and so on. Event bubbling is useful because:

- It allows multiple common actions to be handled centrally.
- It reduces the amount of overall code in the Web page.
- It reduces the number of code changes necessitated by changes in the document.

In the following example code, when the user clicks on the text "Click on this text to see the OuterSpan example." a dialog appears with the text "You clicked OuterSpan." When the user clicks on the second span, another dialog appears with the text "You clicked InnerSpan".

```
<HTML>
<BODY>
<SPAN ID=OuterSpan style="color: red" language=vbscript
onclick="Alert('You clicked ' & window.event.srcElement.id)">
Click on this text to see the OuterSpan example.<BR><BR>
<SPAN ID=InnerSpan style="color: blue">
Click on this text to see the InnerSpan example.
</SPAN>
</SPAN>
</BODY>
</HTML>
```

The onclick event for the InnerSpan element is handled even though it does not have an event handler. The onclick event from the InnerSpan element bubbles up to its parent element, which is the OuterSpan element. OuterSpan has an event handler registered for the onclick event, so it fires.

Every time an event is fired, a special property on the Window object is created. This special property contains the Event object. The Event object contains context information about the event that just fired, including mouse location, keyboard status, and most important, the source element of the event.

Note Set the cancelBubble property of the Event object to *True* when you want to prevent an event from bubbling to the element's parent.

Lesson Summary

You will be incorporating many browser objects and collections into your Web page as you use DHTML. Four common objects include the Navigator object, the Frames collection, the Location object, and the Event object.

The Navigator object includes information about the browser application being used to view the Web page. It includes the browser name and version number. The Frames object represents a collection of frames in a window. This collection allows you to access all of the frames in any frameset currently displayed in the browser. The Location object represents the URL of the current document. The Event object exposes the information related to an event to the script

An event is a notification that happens when an action occurs, such as a change in state. It can also be triggered as a result of the user clicking the mouse or pressing a key while viewing the document. An event handler is code, typically a function or routine written in a scripting language, that executes when the corresponding event occurs.

When an event occurs, it first executes the appropriate code associated the source element. It then fires on the parent of the source element and continues to fire on successive parent elements until it has reached the top element, the document. This is known as event bubbling. Event bubbling is advantageous because it allows multiple common actions to be handled centrally and it reduces the amount of code in the Web page.

Lesson 3: Using the Document Object

As you learned in Lesson 2, you can use the Document object to retrieve information about the document, to examine and modify the HTML elements and text within the document, and to process events. In this lesson, you will learn how to use the Document object to create dynamic content, styles, and positioning.

After this lesson, you will be able to:

- Use DHTML to dynamically add content to the page.
- Create a dynamic outline.

Estimated lesson time: 45 minutes

Using Element Objects

Every HTML tag and HTML tag attribute is represented in the object model as an element object. An element object exposes methods and properties that enable you to get information about and change the attributes of the corresponding element.

Element objects are referenced through document collections, such as the All, Children, and StyleSheets collections. Most element properties have the same name and take the same values as the corresponding attributes. Some properties do not correspond to element attributes. These properties typically give additional information about the element that is not available through attributes. The following table describes the commonly used properties of element objects. You can use three of these properties—tagName, ID, and className—to identify elements in code.

Event	Description
children	Gets the collection of child elements in the element hierarchy.
className	Sets and gets the style sheet class name of the element.
ID	Gets the string identifying the element.
parentElement	Gets the parent element in the element hierarchy.
style	Subobject used to set and get styles associated with the element.
tagName	Gets the name of the HTML tag of the element.

The following code illustrates how the className property of an element object can be used in a procedure:

```
Sub doclick()
    If (window.event.srcElement.className = "parent") _
        Or (window.event.srcElement.className = "image") Then
            ExpandCollapse
    End If
    window.event.cancelBubble = True
End Sub
```

When you want your code to apply to a particular element, use the ID property to reference a single element. However, if you want your code to apply to all the elements of the same type, use the tagName property to reference all elements of a single type. Additionally, you can use the className property to reference any set of elements that you define when want your code to apply to a set of elements with the same style sheet class name.

Using Document Collections

The DOM contains several collections that enable finding and adding different types of elements in an HTML document. You can access individual element objects within collections with their index, name, or ID as you learned in Lesson 1. Three important document collections are the All, Children, and styleSheets collections.

Using the All Collection

An HTML document is a hierarchical construct of tags that define the contents of the document. The All collection on the document object represents all the elements in the document hierarchy in the order that they appear in the HTML source code. It can also include comments, elements not in the document, and unknown or invalid tags. The reason for including these other elements is to give you accurate information about the document. Each element is represented as a programmable object appearing within the collection in source order. You access individual element objects by index or identifier (unique name). The All collection is automatically updated to reflect any changes in the document such as when elements and their content are added or removed.

Because each item in the All collection is an element object, you can apply properties and methods to these items. For example, you can use the tagName property to retrieve the HTML tag name of the element. Similarly, you can access properties and methods of the respective element by accessing this through the document.all collection.

The following code uses the all collection to display a list of all the tags in the document:

```
<HTML>
<HEAD><TITLE>Displaying the all collection</TITLE>
<SCRIPT LANGUAGE="VBScript">
Sub ShowElements()
    Dim i, tagNames
    tagNames = ""

    For i = 0 To document.all.length-1
        tagNames = tagNames & document.all(i).tagName & " "
    Next
    Alert("This document contains: " + tagNames)
End Sub
</SCRIPT>
</HEAD>
<BODY onload="ShowElements()">
<!-- A comment -->
<P>This document has an <ZZZ>unknown</ZZZ> and an invalid</B> tag.
</BODY>
</HTML>
```

The all collection is much like an array in that it contains one or more items of the same type—in this case, element objects. You can access the items by using zero-based index value or by name or identifier, and determine how many items are in the collection by using the length property.

Using the Children Collection

Each element exposes a Children collection, which contains only the elements that are direct descendants of the element in the HTML hierarchy. The Children collection contains only those elements whose parentElement property would return that element.

In the following example, the Children collection for the <DIV> tag with the ID parentDiv will contain the image and the <DIV> tag with the ID childDiv. The Children collection for childDiv will contain the hyperlink.

```
<DIV ID=parentDiv>
<IMG SRC="images/blue.gif">
<DIV ID=childDiv>
<A HREF="home.htm">General Information</A>
</DIV>
</DIV>
```

In the following example, the B tag would be in the DIV object's All collection but would not appear in the DIV object's Children collection. Similarly, the DIV tag is a member of the BODY object's Children collection, but the P tag is not.

```
<HTML>
<BODY>
<DIV>
<P>Some text in a <B>paragraph</B>
<IMG ID=image1 src="mygif.gif">
</DIV>
<IMG ID=image2 src="mygif.gif">
</BODY>
</HTML>
```

Using the styleSheets Collection

The styleSheets collection contains all the style sheet objects corresponding to each instance of a <LINK> or <STYLE> element in the document. The following example code uses the styleSheets collection to add a style sheet to a document:

```
Sub AddStyleSheet(strUrl)
    ' pass URL for .css file
    ' containing the style sheet
    document.stylesheets(0).addImport(strUrl)
End Sub
```

Dynamic Styles

DHTML offers Web designers the ability to alter the style for elements dynamically, in response to interaction with the user. Changing styles on a Web page entails completing the following three steps:

1. Changing elements in an HTML document

    You define two styles with class names and attributes.

2. Dynamically changing a section of text

    You first create an object with the ID= attribute and then add a style class name to the section using the CLASS= attribute. Then you add a script function name to the event attribute for the section.

3. Creating a style-changing function

    You create a separate script function that changes the style to one of those defined in the style tags.

An example of altering a style dynamically would be to change the font family or font color of an item when the cursor is over it to show users their immediate choices. This approach is often found in tables of contents for a Web site. Using static HTML, you would need to download a new page in order to change the size of the font, which means that the server would have to reload the page. However, with DHTML, you can change font size without having to reload the page as shown in the following example:

```
<HTML>
<HEAD>
<TITLE>Dynamic Styles Example</TITLE>
<SCRIPT LANGUAGE=vbscript>
Sub div_onmouseover()
    div.style.fontSize = 16
End Sub

Sub div_onmouseout()
    div.style.fontSize = 12
End Sub
</SCRIPT>
</HEAD>
<BODY>
<DIV ID=div>Place the mouse cursor over this text to change font
size.</DIV>
</BODY>
</HTML>
```

There are a number of reasons to dynamically change the styles for elements on a page:

- To make the page visually interesting.
- To provide feedback to users as they interact with the page.
- To customize the appearance of the content for users who might not otherwise be able to use the page.

Changing Styles Using the Style Object

You can also change styles using the Style object for the element. Each cascading style sheet (CSS) style is a property of the Style object for the element. The following code shows how to change an element's style inline:

```
<H1 ID=myStyle onclick="this.style.color=blue">This text will change to
blue when clicked </H1>
```

Dynamic Positioning

Dynamic positioning enables you to change the placement of elements in the document. The Positioning attributes for an element determine how it is affected by changes in the flow of the document, such as when the user resizes the browser window, or when content is added or removed.

The concepts of dynamic positioning are based on the following principles of DHTML:

- A document has a default flow in which elements are consecutively placed on the page, with the spacing depending on the type of element and the content of the element.

- Elements can contain other elements (i.e., be parents of other elements). If an element is not contained by another element, its default parent is the <BODY> tag.

- Absolute positioning takes the element out of the default flow, and allows you to specify exact x-, y- coordinates relative to the parent of the element.

- Relative positioning leaves the element in the default flow, but allows you to specify exact x-, y- coordinates relative to the previous element in the document flow.

- When using absolute positioning and two or more elements occupy the same x,y-position in the document, their z-order determines which is displayed on top of the other.

The following table describes the concepts of dynamic positioning:

Concept	Description
Absolute positioning	The x- and y-coordinates for the element are relative to the parent element, regardless of the position of any other elements.
Display	Setting the Display attribute to none means that an element does not appear in the document, and no space is reserved for it on screen. The element is completely removed from the flow of the document.
Relative positioning	The x- and y-coordinates for the element are relative to the preceding element in the document.
Visibility	Setting the Visibility property to hidden means that an element has a reserved space on the document but its contents are not visible on screen. Setting visibility to visible means that an element appears in the document.
z-index	The z-index affects how elements positioned in the same place in the document are displayed. Positive z-index values are positioned above a negative (or lesser value) z-index value. Two elements with the same z-index value are stacked according to the order in which they appear in the HTML source code.

Dynamic Content

Dynamic content enables you to add or remove text or HTML content in an HTML document, without having to reload the page from the server. The Web browser will automatically reflow the document when you add or remove content. The process for adding dynamic content is the same as for adding dynamic styles.

➤ **To add content to an element**

1. Add an ID= attribute.

2. Add event attributes and assign them function names.

3. Add script for each of the functions and assign the additional content to the ID= attribute.

4. Use the appropriate text or HTML property to add the content.

You add content using two different kinds of properties—text properties and HTML properties (described in the table below). Text properties insert text, including HTML tags, as text. For example the browser will read <H3> as the string <H3>, not as the HTML tag to render the following text as an H3. In contrast, the browser will read any tags within the HTML properties with the correct format.

The following tables list dynamic content properties and methods that you can use:

Text Properties	HTML Properties
InnerText	InnerHTML
OuterText	OuterHTML

Text Methods	HTML methods
InsertAdjacentText	InsertAdjacentHTML

The following example code will add dynamic content to a Web page when a user positions the mouse cursor over the text.

```
<HTML>
<HEAD>
<SCRIPT LANGUAGE=vbscript>
Sub div_onmouseover
    div.innerHTML = div.innerHTML & " more content"
End Sub
</SCRIPT>
</HEAD>
<BODY>
<DIV ID=div>more content</DIV>
</BODY>
</HTML>
```

You can also use the insertAdjacentText and insertAdjacentHTML methods to add to the existing text in an element. These methods take two parameters— *where* and *text*. The following table describes the values for the parameter where:

Parameter	Description
BeforeBegin	Inserts the text immediately before the element.
AfterBegin	Inserts the text after the start of the element but before all other content in the element.
BeforeEnd	Inserts the text immediately before the end of the element but after all other content in the element.
AfterEnd	Inserts the text immediately after the end of the element.

Note   These parameters are case sensitive.

Using the insertAdjacentHTML Method

In this practice, you will create an HTML page and use DHTML to dynamically add content to the page. To accomplish this, you will use the insertAdjacentHTML method of the document.body object.

➤ **To create a new Web page**

1. Start Visual InterDev.

2. If the New Project dialog appears, click Cancel.

3. From the File menu, choose New File.

   The New File dialog appears.

4. Click HTML Page, and then click Open.

5. Switch to Source view and replace the existing code with the following code:

```
<HTML>
<HEAD>
<TITLE>Dynamic Content: Inserting Elements</TITLE>
<SCRIPT LANGUAGE="VBScript">
Sub AddText()
    document.body.insertAdjacentHTML
    document.body.insertAdjacentHTML "BeforeEnd", _
        "<P>" + oText.value + "</P>"
End Sub
</SCRIPT>
</HEAD>
```

(continued)

```
<BODY>
<P>
<INPUT TYPE=text ID=oText VALUE="Here is some text.">
<INPUT TYPE=button VALUE="Add" onclick="AddText()">
</P>
</BODY>
</HTML>
```

6. Click the Quick View tab to test the page.

   A textbox and button appear on the Web page.

7. Click the Add button.

   The text "Here is some text" appears dynamically on the page.

8. Close the page. You do not need to save your changes.

Creating a Dynamic Outline

You can create a dynamic outline using DHTML. A dynamic outline is a list of items that you add to or remove items from. You can also expand and collapse items in the outline at any time using parent items and child items. A parent item is associated with a graphic and a name and can contain zero or more child items. A parent item consists of a DIV element and contains an IMG element and another DIV element. The inner DIV is a container for all the child items for the parent. This nesting structure makes it easier to insert child items, and to control the appearance of all the child items for a parent as a group.

The DIV for the parent item also has an ID. The ID is used to uniquely identify the parent and make it easy to locate it within the document. It also allows you to add new child items to a specific parent at any time. The following example code illustrates the HTML structure of a parent item:

```
<DIV ID=Id CLASS="parent">
<IMG CLASS="image" SRC="images/blue.gif" ALT="*" ALIGN=MIDDLE BORDER=0
WIDTH=11 HEIGHT=11>Parent Name
<DIV CLASS="child">
</DIV>
</DIV>
```

In this example, a child item is a hyperlink that is inserted within its parent, and has the following HTML structure:

```
<A HREF="Url" CLASS="link">Child Name</A><BR>
```

Expanding and Collapsing the Outline

In addition to adding and removing items, the dynamic outline supports expanding and collapsing items. The following example code is a VBScript procedure that expands and collapses all of the child items for a parent:

```
Sub ExpandCollapse()
    Dim objElement
    Dim objTargetDiv
    Dim imgIcon

    Set objElement = window.event.srcElement

    ' Did the user click the image or the parent name?
    If objElement.className = "parent" Then
        Set objTargetDiv = objElement.children(1)
        Set imgIcon = objElement.children(0)
    Else
        Set objTargetDiv = objElement.parentElement.children(1)
        Set imgIcon = objElement
    End If

    ' If the parent has children, expand or collapse them
    If objTargetDiv.children.length > 0 Then
        If objTargetDiv.style.display = "none" Then
            objTargetDiv.style.display = ""
            imgIcon.src = "images/red.gif"
        Else
            objTargetDiv.style.display = "none"
            imgIcon.src = "images/blue.gif"
        End If
    End If
End Sub
```

This procedure expands or collapses all the child items of the element the user has clicked. It first checks the class name of the object to see whether the user clicked the image or name of a parent item. It does this so that it can get the element object for the inner DIV of the parent (which contains all its child items) and the element object for the image associated with the parent.

If the parent does have child items, it expands or collapses them and changes the image associated with the parent depending on the current state. If the child items are currently expanded, it sets their style to display:none to hide them, and changes the image to a blue triangle. If the child items are currently collapsed, it sets their style to display:"" to make them visible, and changes the image to a red triangle.

Lesson Summary

The Document Object Model (DOM) is an interface that allows script to access and update the structure, style, and content of a document. This can be done using dynamic positioning, dynamic content, and dynamic styles. The DOM includes a model for how a standard set of objects representing documents are combined, and an interface for accessing and manipulating them. The key advantages of the DOM are the abilities to access everything in the document, to make numerous content updates, and to work with content in separate document fragments.

The DOM contains several collections that enable finding and adding different types of elements in an HTML document. You can access individual element objects within collections with their index, name, or ID.

You can also create a dynamic outline using DHTML. A dynamic outline is a list of items that you can add item to or remove items from. You can also expand and collapse items in the outline at any time using parent items and child items.

Lesson 4: Creating DTHML Scriptlets

Scriptlets were originally implemented with Internet Explorer 4.0 for creating user-interface components for HTML pages. They are advantageous because all you needed to know is HTML and script to create a scriptlet. If you know Dynamic HTML (DHTML), then with a few simple naming conventions you can create a component for use in your HTML pages. Since scriptlets are based on DHTML and used within HTML documents, they are called DHTML scriptlets.

Scriptlets allow Web page authors to create reusable components with script without having to harness the full power of C, C++, or other control-building environments.

After this lesson, you will be able to:

- Identify the advantages of using scriptlets.
- Add a scriptlet to a Web page.

Estimated lesson time: 20 minutes

Overview of Scriptlets

Microsoft Scripting Components (scriptlets) provide a way for you to create reusable controls and components. You create scriptlets using a scripting language such as JavaScript or VBScript. A scriptlet is a complete Web-ready .htm file but includes information that allows you to work with it as a control—for example, you can set its properties and call its methods. Scriptlets provide the following four advantages:

- They allow Web page authors to create reusable user interface components without having to harness the full power of C, C++, or other control-building environments.
- The allow developers using Visual Basic, Visual InterDev, and other development environments that support controls to make use of features built into Web pages.
- They are easy to create and maintain.
- They are small and efficient.

You use a scriptlet like a standard control. You create any properties, methods, or events that you want using languages such as JScript or VBScript. The scripts rely on the scripting capabilities of DHTML, which gives you a complete object model for elements on the scriptlet. For example, a scriptlet that moves and resizes text on a page might be a Web page that contains animations based on DHTML. You can write scripts to expose properties that allow another application to set the text, speed, and direction of the animation text, as well as methods that allow another application to start, stop, and pause the animation.

Scriptlets also provide other capabilities that allow you to:

- Use the graphical and hypertext capabilities of Web pages as a visually rich interface for an application (such as a calendar control that you can display in a Web page) in Visual Basic or in another environment.

- Create components that incorporate business rules that you can call from a Web server, a browser, or any other type of application.

- Prototype controls that you intend to write in other environments. Because writing a scriptlet is quick and easy, you can test ideas. When you have completed your design, you can implement the control in another environment, such as Visual C++, Visual Basic, or Visual J++, if you want greater performance or a different means of packaging your control.

Types of Scriptlets

There are two kinds of scriptlets—DHTML and server scriptlets. DHTML scriptlets are used in the browser, while server scriptlets are used in external applications or on a Web server. DHTML scriptlets typically display a user interface, while server scriptlets do not. A skeleton scriptlet looks like the following:

```
<HTML ID=MyPage>
<HEAD>
<TITLE>Our First Scriptlet</title>
</HEAD>
<SCRIPT LANGUAGE="JScript">
public_description = new CreateFirstScriptlet;
function CreateFirstScriptlet() {
    this.TellMeSomething = HelloWorld;
}
function HelloWorld() {
    alert("Hello, World!");
}
</SCRIPT>
<BODY>
</BODY>
</HTML>
```

The scriptlet outlined above has just one method named TellMeSomething. This method is implemented via a JavaScript function named HelloWorld.

Exposing Properties, Methods, and Events

By default, the browser exposes standard methods and properties to scriptlets. Scriptlets expose standard properties, methods, and events to the browser. The following table describes some of the methods and properties that the browser exposes.

Properties and Methods	Description
Frozen property	Indicates whether the browser window containing the scriptlet is ready to handle events. Syntax *boolean = window.external.frozen*
BubbleEvent method	Sends event notification from the scriptlet to the browser window when a standard event has occurred. Syntax *window.external.bubbleEvent( )*
raiseEvent method	Passes a custom event notification from the scriptlet to the browser window. Syntax *window.external.raiseEvent(eventName, eventObject)*
setContextMenu Method	Constructs a context menu that is displayed when a user right-clicks a scriptlet in the browser window. Syntax *window.external.setContextMenu(menuDefinition)*

The following table describes some of the properties that scriptlets expose:

Properties and Methods	Description
Event property	Provides state information about a standard DHTML event passed from the scriptlet to the browser window. Syntax *value = ScriptID.event.member*
readyState property	Returns information about the load state of the scriptlet from the browser. Syntax *ScriptID.readyState = integer*

In addition to standard properties and methods, you can also expose any number of custom properties and methods in VBScript by using the keywords described in the following table:

Scenario	Solution
To create a read/write property	Declare a variable scoped at the page level, and assign it the prefix public_.
To create a readable property function	Define a function with the prefix public_get_.
To create a writeable property function	Define a function with the prefix public_put_.
To create a method	Define a function with the prefix public_.

The following example code creates a property function that imports the style sheet from a URL and makes it the style sheet for the current document.

```
Sub Public_Put_StyleSheet(strUrl)
    document.stylesheets(0).addImport(strUrl)
End Sub
```

Using Scriptlet Events

When you use a DHTML scriptlet in your Web page, you can be notified about events that occur in the scriptlet. A scriptlet can expose two types of events:

- Standard DHTML events such as the onclick event and the onkeypress event.
- Custom events, which are events that you define or DHTML events that are not provided as standard events. For example, a scriptlet can fire an event when a property value changes. You can expose custom events in either DHTML or server events.

A DHTML scriptlet can expose the following standard DHTML events:

- onclick
- onkeypress
- onmousemove
- ondblclick
- onkeyup
- onmouseup
- onkeydown
- onmousedown

Standard events are triggered for the scriptlet container object. Use a custom event to pinpoint which control in the scriptlet triggered the event. To work with standard events in the host application, you must write handlers in two places: one in the scriptlet to send the event, and another in the host application to capture the event. The following list outlines the procedures for passing a standard event from a scriptlet to a host application.

➤ **To pass a standard DHTML event from a scriptlet**

1. Attach an event handler script to the event that you want to pass.

2. Within the event handler script, call the bubbleevent method to send the event to the host application.

3. Check the scriptlet's frozen property to be sure that the container object is ready to handle events.

The following example code shows how you can pass a textbox's onkeyup event to the host application:

```
<INPUT TYPE=text onkeyup="passKeyUp" NAME="t1" VALUE="">

<SCRIPT LANGUAGE="VBScript">
Sub passKeyUp
    ' Script statements here if required
    window.external.bubbleEvent
    ' Further script statements here if required
End Sub
</SCRIPT>
```

You can also create custom events to allow you to:

- Notify the hosting page about nonstandard changes in the scriptlet, such as when the value of a property changes.

- Send more detail about a standard event that occurred—for example, which of several buttons in the scriptlet was clicked.

- Notify the host page about DHTML events that are not among the standard events handled by the bubbleEvent method.

As with standard DHTML events, you must send the event from the scriptlet and capture the event in the host page. The following listings show you how to send a custom event in the scriptlet to a host page.

➤ **To send a custom event in the scriptlet to the host page**

1. Check the scriptlet's frozen property to make sure that the host page is ready to handle events.

2. Call the scriptlet's raiseEvent method.

➤ **To handle a custom event in the host page**

Create an event handler for the onscriptletevent event.

For example, the following example code shows how you can send a custom event called oncolorchange whenever the scriptlet's backgroundcolor property is reset:

```
<SCRIPT LANGUAGE="VBScript">
Sub public_put_backgroundColor(value)
    window.document.bgColor = value
    window.external.raiseEvent "event_onbgcolorchange",window.document
End Sub
</SCRIPT>
```

The following example code (in Visual Basic) shows how you can determine what control triggered an event:

```
Sub myscriptlet_onscriptletevent(txtTitle, eventData)
    objName = eventData.srcElement.ID
    MsgBox "The event " & txtTitle & " occurred in " & objName
End Sub
```

Adding a Scriptlet to a Page

After you have created a DHTML scriptlet, you can use it in your applications. Using DHTML scriptlets is similar to using other controls and components.

If you are working with a Web page, you can use the <OBJECT> tag to reference the scriptlet. You can add a scriptlet to the Microsoft Visual InterDev Toolbox.

➤ **To add a DHTML scriptlet to the Toolbox**

In the Project Explorer window, right-click the scriptlet's .htm file, and then choose Mark As Scriptlet from the context menu.

An <OBJECT> tag containing a pointer to that scriptlet is added to the Scriptlet tab of the Toolbox. (If this is the first scriptlet on the Toolbar, the Scriptlet tab is created.) You can then drag the scriptlet from the Toolbox onto another page and automatically create the <OBJECT> tag necessary to implement the scriptlet.

Note   When you add a scriptlet to the Toolbox, it includes the scriptlet's absolute URL. After you drag a scriptlet onto your page, you might need to modify the <OBJECT> tag's URL property in the Properties window or in Source view to make the link relative.

Alternatively, you can create an <OBJECT> tag yourself that references the scriptlet.

➤ **To refer to a DHTML scriptlet in an <OBJECT> tag**

Create an <OBJECT> tag with the following syntax, substituting the scriptlet's
URL and name for url/scriptletName:

```
<OBJECT ID="MyScriptlet" TYPE="text/x-scriptlet" WIDTH=300 HEIGHT=200>
    <PARAM NAME="url" VALUE="url/scriptletName">
</OBJECT>
```

After creating an instance of the DHTML scriptlet, you can write scripts for it as
you would for any other control. The object you are using to work with properties
and methods is the scriptlet host page; the exact properties and methods you can
use are defined by the scriptlet identified in the container's URL property.

Before getting a scriptlet's properties or calling its methods, you must be sure that
the scriptlet has been fully loaded. For details, see the container object's
onreadystatechange event and readyState property, and the scriptlet's frozen
property.

Lesson Summary

A scriptlet is a.htm file, but it allows you to work with it as a control. For instance, you can get and set its properties, call its methods, and so on. Scriptlets are useful because Web page authors can create reusable interface components without having to draw upon control building environments. You use a scriptlet just like a standard control. You can create any properties, methods, or events that you want by creating scripts in languages such as JScript or VBScript.

There are two kinds of scriptlets—DHTML and server scriptlets. DHTML scriptlets are used in the browser, whereas server scriptlets are used in external applications or on a Web server.

Lab 3: Working with DHTML

In this lab, you will create items for the Sidebar.htm file dynamically. You will also use DHTML to alter the appearance of text as a result of mouse events.

To see a demonstration of this lab, run the Lab03.exe animation located in the Animations folder on the companion CD-ROM that accompanies this book.

Before you begin

You should have already completed Lab 2. If you have not, follow the steps in Lab 2 to create the Chateau Web project and use the files in the Labs\Lab02\Partial folder to obtain the necessary files to complete this lab.

Estimated lab time: 45 minutes

Exercise 1: Creating Sidebar Items Dynamically

In this exercise, you will create sidebar items using DHTML. To do this, you will create several sub and function procedures, and use the onload event of the window object to load the sidebar items.

➤ **To add and remove items on the sidebar**

1. Open the Chateau project in Visual InterDev.

2. Open the Sidebar.htm file for editing.

3. Click the Source tab on the HTML Editor window.

4. Delete the table entry below the following HTML code:

   ```
   <p><IMG border=0 height=77 src="images/chateauLogo.gif"
   width=148></p>
   ```

   Note that the table entry begins with a <TABLE> tag and ends with the </TABLE> tag.

5. Below the IMG tag shown in step 4, insert the following DIV tag:

   ```
   <DIV ID="outlineDiv" LANGUAGE="VBScript" onclick="DoClick">
   </DIV>
   ```

6. Below the <base target="main"> tag, make the following style tag entry.

   ```
   <STYLE>
   <!--
       .parent {font-size: 12pt;
               font-weight: bold;
               margin-top: 10;
               text-indent: -14;
   ```

(continued)

```
            margin-left: 14;
            cursor: hand;}
            .child   {font-size: 10pt;
            font-weight: normal;}
      .image   {}
-->
</STYLE>
```

7. Create a script tag in the HTML heading, and declare a variable named oldColor and inCount.

8. Initialize the value of inCount to a value of zero.

   Your code should look similar to the following:

```
<SCRIPT ID=clientEventHandlersVBS LANGUAGE=vbscript>
<!--
Dim oldColor
Dim intCount
intCount = 0
</SCRIPT>
```

9. Create the following sub procedures and functions within the same script tag to load a table of contents dynamically:

```
Sub window_onload
    Dim intParentID

    intParentID = AddParent("Hotel Information")
    Call AddChild(intParentID, "General Information", "")
    Call AddChild(intParentID, "Provide Feedback", "")

    intParentID = AddParent("Reservations ")
    Call AddChild(intParentID, "Reserve a Room", "")

    intParentID = AddParent("Site Services")
    Call AddChild(intParentID, "Search the Site", "")
    Call AddChild(intParentID, _
        "Email the WebMaster", "mailto:webmaster@chateau.com")
End Sub

Function AddParent(strName)
    Dim strID
    Dim strTemp

    strID = "ID" & intCount
    intCount = intCount + 1
    strTemp = "<DIV ID=""" & strID & """ CLASS=""parent"">" & _
        "<IMG CLASS=""image"" SRC=""images/hotel_icon.gif""" & _
        "ALT=""*"" ALIGN=MIDDLE BORDER=0 WIDTH=11 HEIGHT=11>" & _
        strName & "<DIV CLASS=""child""" & _
        "STYLE=""display:none""></DIV></DIV>"
```

```
            outlineDiv.insertAdjacentHTML "BeforeEnd", strTemp
            AddParent = strID
        End Function

        Sub DeleteParent(strParentID)
            Dim objTemp
            Set objTemp = document.all.item(strParentID)
            objTemp.outerHTML = ""
        End Sub

        Sub AddChild(strParentID, strName, strUrl)
            Dim strTemp
            Dim objTemp
            strTemp = "<A HREF=""" & strUrl & """ CLASS=""link"">" & _
                strName & "</A><BR>"
            Set objTemp = document.all.item(strParentID)
            objTemp.children(1).insertAdjacentHTML "BeforeEnd", strTemp
        End Sub

        Sub ExpandCollapse()
            Dim objElement
            Dim objTargetDiv
            Dim imgIcon

            Set objElement = window.event.srcElement
            ' Determine if the user clicked the image or the parent name
            If objElement.className = "parent" Then
                Set objTargetDiv = objElement.children(1)
                Set imgIcon = objElement.children(0)
            Else
                Set objTargetDiv = objElement.parentElement.children(1)
                Set imgIcon = objElement
            End If

            ' If the parent has children, expand or collapse them
            If objTargetDiv.children.length > 0 Then
                If objTargetDiv.style.display = "none" Then
                    objTargetDiv.style.display = ""
                Else
                    objTargetDiv.style.display = "none"
                End If
            End If
        End Sub

        Sub DoClick()
            If (window.event.srcElement.className = "parent") Or _
                (window.event.srcElement.className = "image") Then
                ExpandCollapse
```

(continued)

```
        End If
        window.event.cancelBubble = True
    End Sub
```

10. Save your changes to Sidebar.htm and then view the file using the Quick View tab.

    Notice that the parent items are displayed on the sidebar page.

11. Click on the Hotel Information, Reservations, and Site Services items to expand items.

    Notice that the child items are displayed below.

12. Click on the Hotel Information, Reservations, and Site Services items again to collapse items.

Exercise 2: Using DHTML Modify Item Appearance

In this exercise, you will write client script to change the appearance of the dynamic outline so that items can be expanded and collapsed when the user clicks them. You will write script to change the appearance of hyperlinks on the outline when the user moves the mouse cursor over them.

➤ **To change the appearance of text**

1. Create a VBScript procedure named DoMouseOver.

    This procedure will change the color of a link to red when the user moves the mouse cursor over it.

2. Add an If...Then statement to check the tagName property of the element that is the source of the event using the srcElement property.

    If tagName is equal to "A", meaning the source element is an anchor (hyperlink), then store the color style of the element in oldColor, and set its new value to "red".

3. Prevent the event from being bubbled up to parent elements by setting the cancelBubble property of the event object equal to True.

    Your code should look similar to the following:

```
Sub DoMouseOver()
    If window.event.srcElement.tagName = "A" Then
        oldColor = window.event.srcElement.style.color
        window.event.srcElement.style.color = "red"
    End If
    window.event.cancelBubble = True
End Sub
```

4. Create a VBScript procedure named DoMouseOut.

    This procedure will restore the old color of a link when the user moves the mouse cursor off it.

5. Add an If...Then statement to check the tagName property of the element that is the source of the event using the srcElement property of the event object.

   If tagName is equal to "A", meaning the source element is an anchor (link), then restore the color style of the element to oldColor.

6. Prevent the event from bubbling up to parent elements by setting the cancelBubble property of the event object equal to True.

   Your code should look similar to the following:

```
Sub DoMouseOut( )
    If window.event.srcElement.tagName = "A" Then
        window.event.srcElement.style.color = oldColor
    End If
    window.event.cancelBubble = True
End Sub
```

7. Add the following event items to the outlineDiv DIV tag that you created in Step 5 of Exercise 1.

```
onmouseover="domouseover" onmouseout="domouseout"
```

8. Save your changes, and view Sidebar.htm using the Quick View tab.

9. Click on the names for parent items in the outline to expand them. Then move the mouse cursor over links in the outline.

   Notice that their color changes to red when you move the mouse cursor over them, and see their old color restored when you move the mouse cursor off them.

Review

The following questions are intended to reinforce key information presented in this chapter. If you are unable to answer a question, review the appropriate lesson and then try the question again. Answers to the questions can be found in Appendix A, "Questions and Answers."

1. What are the advantages to using scriptlets?

2. What is event bubbling?

3. What is the Document Object Model (DOM) and how is it used?

C H A P T E R   4

Using Active Server Pages

About This Chapter

In this chapter, you will learn how to create a Web application that uses Microsoft Active Server Pages (ASP). You will also learn how to add server-side script that manipulates objects on a Web server.

ASP pages can call ActiveX components to perform tasks such as connecting to a database or performing a business calculation. With ASP, you can add interactive content to your Web pages or build entire Web applications that use HTML pages as a user interface. You will learn how ASP provides a server-side scripting environment that enables you to read information from a client and store information about a client.

Before You Begin

Before you completing this chapter, you must know how to write client-side script using either Microsoft Visual Basic Scripting Edition (VBScript) or JavaScript.

Lesson 1: Introduction to Active Server Pages

Much like Dynamic HTML (DHTML), ASP is a scripting environment that you can use to create and run dynamic, interactive Web server applications. With ASP, you can combine HTML pages, script commands, and ActiveX components to create interactive Web pages or powerful Web-based applications. However, ASP is different than HTML and DHTML in that the scripts run from different locations. DHTML, for example, is script that runs on the client's browser after the page has been sent from the server. An ASP page runs on the server before the page is sent to the client.

With ASP, you can develop many different types of Web-based applications, including extending sales and customer service to the Web. You can also provide access to corporate databases and applications that is browser independent.

After this lesson, you will be able to:

- Explain the purposes and functions of ASP.
- Describe the differences between ASP and CGI.
- Create an ASP page.
- Enable script debugging.

Estimated lesson time: 20 minutes

Overview of Active Server Pages

ASP is the server-side technology in Microsoft Internet Information Server (IIS) that enables you to run ActiveX scripts, such as VBScript and JScript, and ActiveX server components on a server. In order to run ASP, you must have Microsoft Windows NT Server 4.0 running IIS or Windows NT Workstation 4.0 running Peer Web Services. You can also install ASP on a Microsoft Windows 95 or Windows 98 computer running Personal Web Server (PWS). The PWS is a scaled-down version of IIS and can be downloaded from the Microsoft Web site at http://www.microsoft.com/NTServer/web/exec/feature/PWS.asp

With ASP scripting, you can use any scripting language for which an appropriate scripting engine is available. ASP includes scripting engines for VBScript and JScript. You can incorporate additional functionality using ActiveX components to process data and generate useful information. For example, a travel agency can extend their Web site beyond just publishing flight schedules using static HTML; it can use ASP scripting to enable customers to check available flights, compare fares, and reserve a seat on a flight.

How Active Server Pages Work

A common way to think about Internet development is in terms of client/server relationships. In this case, the client is the browser, and the server is the Web server. Most interactions on the Internet or an intranet can be thought of in terms of requests and responses. The browser makes a request to the Web server (usually to display a page the user wants to see), and the Web server returns a response (usually an HTML page, an element, or an image) to the browser.

Using ASP, you can generate a browser-independent page that can vary each time the page is requested (such as returning data from a database). The Web server processes the server script and then sends HTML to the browser for processing. An ASP script begins to run when a browser requests an .asp file from your Web server. The ASP engine then reads through the requested file from top to bottom, executes any script commands, and sends a Web page to the browser as illustrated in Figure 4.1.

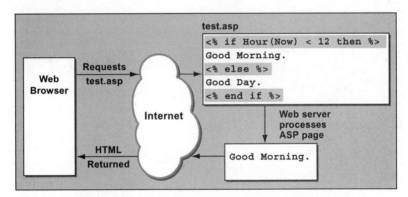

Figure 4.1 How Active Server Pages are processed

With ASP, Web pages can be customized for each user dynamically, based upon the user's actions or requests. For example, new visitors to your site can be shown a welcome page different from the one returning users see, or pages in an online catalog can be queries to a database so that customers always see the most current information and availability. Server-side scripts that are executed in response to (Hypertext Transfer Protocol) HTTP requests from a client-side Web browser can perform complex processing. However, more frequently, the scripts use server-side runtime ActiveX components to provide system services, data services, or implement business rules, as illustrated in Figure 4.2.

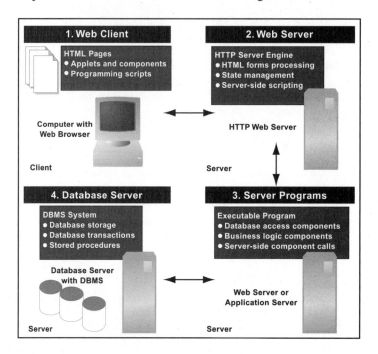

Figure 4.2 Web scripting architecture

Because your scripts run on the server rather than on the client, your Web server does all the work involved in generating the Web pages sent to client browsers. This means the resulting pages will be compatible with most browsers. Another benefit of this architecture is that your server-side scripts cannot be read or copied by users because only the results of the script (the HTML) can be seen in the browser. Users cannot view the script commands that created the page they are viewing.

ASP Compared with CGI

Common Gateway Interface (CGI) applications allow a Web server to run a program or script on the server and send the output to a Web browser. CGI is a widely used method for creating executable programs that run on your Web server. Remote users can start these executables by filling out an HTML form or by simply requesting a URL from your server.

ASP provides all the functionality of CGI applications in a more robust environment. ASP allows a server to access information in a form not readable by the client (such as a SQL database), and then act as a gateway between the two to produce information that the client can view and use.

With CGI, the server creates as many processes as the number of client requests received. The more concurrent requests there are, the more concurrent processes created by the server. However, creating a process for every request is time-consuming and requires large amounts of server RAM. In addition, this can restrict the resources available for sharing from the server application itself, slowing down performance and increasing wait times on the Web. ASP runs in the same process as the Web server, handling client requests faster and more efficiently. It is much easier to develop dynamic content and Web applications with ASP.

In addition, CGI languages such as Perl are not robust development tools by themselves. ASP provides a familiar framework and objects for building complex applications that require data from relational databases and legacy sources.

Features of Active Server Pages

Under IIS, an application is any collection of files in a directory whose properties can be set and that can run in a separate process space. An IIS application resides on a Web server, where it receives requests from a browser, runs code associated with the requests, and returns responses to the browser. This allows dynamic content to be displayed in a browser, and allows browsers to request information. The server, instead of returning a static page, runs a script or application and returns HTML that reflects up-to-date, accurate information.

ASP applications are just one type of application that can run under IIS to provide dynamic content. IIS supports ASP, Internet Server Application Programming Interface (ISAPI), CGI, Internet Database Connector (IDC), and Server Side Include (SSI) applications. Like ASP, gateway interfaces such as CGI and ISAPI allow users to add dynamic content to the Web. The ISAPI model was originally developed to be a higher-performing alternative to CGI. The ISAPI model provides a number of advantages over the CGI model, including low overhead, fast loading, and better scalability.

However, ISAPI applications require you to develop a DLL file written in C++, making them more difficult to create and maintain. With ASP files, an HTML author can write script to access an external component and then format the resulting output. In addition, ASP separates layout and design from business logic.

ASP applications are like conventional stand-alone applications. They can retain user information between sessions, or uses, of the application. These types of applications can also retain information while the user moves from one page to another. ASP applications have two important features:

- A starting-point directory
- Global data

A Starting-Point Directory

When you create an application, use Internet Service Manager to designate the application's starting-point directory for your Web site. All the files and directories under the starting-point directory in your Web site are considered part of the application until another starting-point directory is found. This means you use directory boundaries to define the scope of an application. Although you can have multiple applications in a Web site, each application has a different configuration. Microsoft Visual InterDev handles all these tasks for you when you create a new Web project.

Note Under IIS, Web applications are handled like Microsoft Visual Basic applications: You can unload them in the same way that you can unload Visual Basic applications. You can also set your application to run in a process space separate from IIS.

Global Data

ASP applications declare global data in a Global.asa file. The .asa extension stands for Active Server Application. This file is an optional file in which you can specify event scripts and declare objects that have session or application scope. It is not a content file displayed to the users, but instead stores event information and objects used globally by the application. In a Global.asa file, you can:

- Initialize application or session variables.
- Declare COM components with application or session scope.
- Declare a global data connection to a database.
- Perform other operations that pertain to the application as a whole.

The Global.asa file must be stored in the root directory of the application, and there can be only one Global.asa file in an application. The Global.asa file is processed by the Web server and can be used to make data available to all pages in the application. The server processes a Global.asa file automatically whenever the following processes occur:

■   The application starts or ends.

     An application does not start until a user requests an ASP file in the starting-point directory.

■   Individual users start and stop browser sessions that access the application's ASP pages.

Web Applications and HTTP

Web applications use HTTP to implement communication between browsers and servers. When a user requests a page, the browser creates an HTTP request message and sends it to the server. The server responds by creating an HTTP response message that is returned to the Web browser. The response message contains an HTML document.

The illustration in Figure 4.3 shows an HTTP session and the process that occurs when a user opens an HTML document on a Web server. The following steps describe this process:

1. The browser creates a TCP/IP connection to the server.

2. The browser packages a request for an HTML document from the server into an HTTP request message, and then sends the message to the server by using a TCP/IP connection. The first line of the message contains the HTTP request method. The Get method is used for a simple page request.

3. The server receives the HTTP request and processes it based on the request method contained in the request line.

4. The server then sends back an HTTP response message. Part of the response message is a status line that contains code indicating whether the attempt to satisfy the HTTP request was successful.

5. When the Web browser receives the HTTP response message, the TCP/IP connection is closed and the HTTP session terminates.

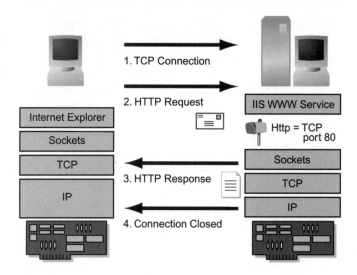

Figure 4.3 An HTTP session

If the requested HTML document contains embedded objects such as background sounds, the browser makes subsequent requests for each embedded object. For example, if a page contains three JPEG images, a background sound, and an ActiveX control, six separate HTTP sessions are required to retrieve the entire page—five for the embedded objects and one for the page itself.

Note Connections are maintained after a connection's initial request is completed only if both the Web browser and Web server support HTTP Keep-Alive packets and retransmissions. The connection still is active and available for subsequent requests. Keep-Alives avoid the substantial cost of establishing and terminating connections. Internet Information Server version 1.0 (and later), Microsoft Internet Explorer, and Netscape Navigator all support Keep-Alives.

Developing Active Server Pages

Server script and client script look very much alike because they use the same languages. The main difference is in how script blocks are specified. Server-side script is contained either in <% %> delimiters or in a <SCRIPT> tag. When server-side script is used in the <SCRIPT> tag, you must include a reference to the RUNAT attribute as shown in the following example.

```
<SCRIPT LANGUAGE=javascript RUNAT=Server>
```

The RUNAT attribute specifies whether this scripting code should be run on the server or on the client. By default, script found in a <SCRIPT> tag will be reserved for execution in the client Web browser. When a Web server processes an ASP page, it runs any script code between the <% and %> delimiters. These delimiters are used to separate the script code from the HTML in a Web page. This is because generally an ASP page contains HTML code mixed with server-side script. The server-side script programmatically determines what information will be returned to the user. The following example uses the Now and Hour procedures contained in the <% and %> delimiters to determine the current time, and then greet the user with either "Good Morning" or "Good Day," depending on the time.

```
<% if Hour(Now) < 12 then %>
Good Morning.
<% else %>
Good Day.
<% end if %>
```

If it is 8:00 A.M., the HTML returned to the user will be:

```
Good Morning.
```

The following example uses VBScript to test the value of a variable in an ASP file:

```
<%Dim MyVar
MyVar = 3
Select Case MyVar
    Case 1
        %><BOLD>The value is one.</BOLD><%
    Case 2
        %><BOLD>The value is two.</BOLD><%
End Select%>
```

You can also display HTML to the user with output from the script by using the <%= %> syntax. The following example displays the current time to the user:

```
The time here is now <%= Time %>.
```

If it is 8:34 A.M., the HTML returned to the user is:

```
The time here is now 8:34 A.M.
```

In addition, you can add server-side script to an HTML <SCRIPT> tag by setting the RUNAT attribute to Server. In a <SCRIPT> section, you can create server-side functions and sub procedures that can be invoked from other scripts on the page. In the <SCRIPT> section, any code that is not contained in a procedure runs when the Web server processes the .asp file. Code in a procedure will not run until the procedure is explicitly invoked by server-side script. The following example uses server-side script to determine whether it is morning or afternoon:

```
<SCRIPT LANGUAGE=VBScript RUNAT=SERVER>
Function ComputeAMPM()
    If Hour(Now) < 12 Then
        ComputeAMPM = "morning"
    Else
        ComputeAMPM = "afternoon"
    End If
End Function
</SCRIPT>
```

You can display the result directly from the HTML <SCRIPT> section by using the Response.Write method. The following example displays a message based on the time of day:

```
<SCRIPT LANGUAGE=VBScript RUNAT=SERVER>
Response.Write "Time for your " & ComputeAMPM() & " classes."
</SCRIPT>
```

If it is 6:00 A.M., the HTML returned to the user will be:

```
Time for your morning classes.
```

Creating an Active Server Page

In this practice, you will use Visual InterDev to create a Web project, and then create an .asp file that you will preview in a Web browser. You will use VBScript in your .asp file.

➤ **To create a new project**

1. Start Microsoft Visual InterDev.

2. Create a new Web Project named Ch4-Prac1.

3. Select <none> for a layout and a theme when the Web Project Wizard appears.

4. Click Finish to create the Ch4-Prac1 project.

➤ **To change the default scripting language**

1. In the Project Explorer, right-click on the <Web server name>/Ch4-Prac1 icon, and then click Properties from the context menu.

   The IDispWebProject dialog appears.

2. Click the Editor Defaults tab, select VBScript for the Server Default Script Language as illustrated in Figure 4.4, then click OK.

Figure 4.4 Using VBScript as the server default script language

➤ **To create a new Active Server Page**

1. From the Project menu, click Add Item.

2. In the Add Item box, click ASP Page.

3. In the Name box, enter MyPage, and then click Open.

   The MyPage.asp file appears in the editor window.

   The first line of script sets the server-side language for the page. For example, if you set the language to VBScript, the following line of script will be added to the Active Server Page:

```
<%@ LANGUAGE="VBSCRIPT" %>
```

4. Replace <P> </P> with the following VBScript:

```
<% If Hour(Now) < 12 Then %>
Good Morning!
<% Else %>
Good Afternoon!
<% End If %>
```

5. In the Project Explorer window, right click mypage.asp and select View In Browser.

   When Visual InterDev prompts you to save the file, click Yes.

   Depending on what time your computer is set to, the appropriate greeting will be displayed.

ASP Built-In Objects

Because script in ASP pages runs on the server, the script has access to a number of objects that are available on the server. These objects are features built into the ASP architecture, and you can use six objects that are intrinsic to ASP to add more functionality to a Web application. With these objects, you can:

- Share information among all users of your application
- Store information for a specific user
- Retrieve information passed from the user to the server
- Send output to the user
- Work with the properties and methods of components on the server

The following table lists the objects and their use.

Object	Description
Request	Retrieves the values that the user passes to the Web server during an HTTP request.
Response	Controls what information is sent to a user in the HTTP response message.
Session	Stores information about a particular user session.
Application	Shares information among all users of a Web application.
Server	Provides access to resources that reside on a Web server.
ObjectContext	Commits or aborts a transaction managed by Microsoft Transaction Server (MTS) for ASP pages that run in a transaction. You will learn about MTS in Chapter 8.

Using the Script Outline for Server Script

You use Script Outline to develop server script just as you would use it to develop client script.

The initial tree view state of Script Outline displays the nodes described in the following list:

Node	Description
Client objects and events	The elements that support client script or have client script attached to them with a list of events for the elements.
Client scripts	The client script for the page with each function or subroutine defined within the script block.
Server objects and events	The elements that support server script or have server script attached to them with a list of events for the elements.
Server scripts	The server script for the page with each function or subroutine defined within the script block.

Adding Objects and Writing Script for Them

When you add design-time and server components to a page in your project, the HTML editor adds the ID for the object and all the events associated with the object to Script Outline.

➤ **To add a Textbox design-time control to a project**

1. Click the Design-Time Controls tab in the Toolbox.

2. Move the Textbox control to an appropriate location on the page. The HTML editor will add the ID for the textbox to Script Outline under Server Objects and Events.

3. The editor will also add header and footer information to the page for handling data from the control.

Note Design-time controls can be targeted for client or server script, which determines the node in which they will appear. For more information, see the section, "How Data-Bound Controls Work" in Chapter 5.

Creating Dynamic Channels

Internet Explorer 4.0 introduced a feature that allows Web designers to group Web pages with common themes such as entertainment, sports, and news into *channels*. The Active Desktop feature of Internet Explorer 4.0 includes a special desktop item called the *channel bar*. In a browser, channels are presented on a channel bar, and users access them by clicking a channel icon. Channels are automatically updated transparently to users; they do not need to visit your site again to get the latest pages downloaded to their browsers.

Using ASP, you can write scripts to gather user preferences and then dynamically create channels. A channel definition file (CDF) establishes the organization and scheduling of the channel contents. Commands in the CDF file use syntax similar to HTML tags, which makes them easy to generate from a script. When you write an ASP script to create a channel definition file, give the script a .cdx extension. When ASP reads a file with a .cdx extension, it automatically sends the application/x-cdf content type, which tells the browser to interpret the bytes as channel definitions.

The following is an example of how you can use channels. The HTML form asks the user to select channels. When submitted, the form calls a script in a .cdx file to create the channel definitions.

```
<P> Choose the channels you want. </P>
<FORM METHOD="POST" ACTION="chan.cdx">
<P><INPUT TYPE=CHECKBOX NAME=Movies> Movies
<P><INPUT TYPE=CHECKBOX NAME=Sports> Sports
<P><INPUT TYPE="SUBMIT" VALUE="SUBMIT">
</FORM>
```

The script in Chan.cdx builds the channel definitions based on the form values submitted with the request.

```
<% If Request.Form("Movies") <> "" Then %>
    <CHANNEL>
    ' Channel definition statements for the movie pages
    </CHANNEL>
<% End If %>

<% If Request.Form("Sports") <> "" Then %>
    <CHANNEL>
    ' Channel definition statements for the sports pages
    </CHANNEL>
<% End If %>
```

Debugging Server Script

You can debug server script that executes on IIS from Visual InterDev if IIS is running on your computer. You can debug server script in much the same way that you debug client script. Typically you use Local mode to build, test, and debug portions of the application in isolation from the rest of your development team. In this case, you run a local copy of IIS on your Windows NT development computer to debug Web pages before checking them into a master Web project.

Before you can debug script in ASP pages, you must first enable debugging. You must be running IIS 4.0 or later.

➤ To enable script debugging in ASP pages

1. In the Project Explorer window, right-click the project and then click Properties to display the Property Pages dialog.

2. Click the Launch tab.

3. Under Server script, make sure Automatically Enable ASP Server-Side Debugging On Launch and Automatically Enable ASP Client-Side Debugging On Launch are checked.

When these options are set, Visual InterDev checks to see that the server is correctly configured for debugging. This includes:

- Setting the IIS application to run in its own memory space
- Enabling the IIS application's debugging options
- Setting up a Microsoft Transaction Server package to allow you to attach the debugger to the Web application

You can set breakpoints in server script, client script, or both. If you set breakpoints in both, the debugger will stop at the server script breakpoints first. When you continue running and the page is sent to the browser, the debugger will then stop at breakpoints in the client script. When you quit your debugging session, Visual InterDev restores the server debugging settings and out-of-process settings to their previous values.

Remote Debugging

In addition to debugging scripts and processes that are running on your computer, you can debug errors in server script running on a remote Web server . This is referred to as *remote debugging*. With remote debugging, you can attach the debugger running on your computer to a script running on the server and issue debugging commands across the network.

Note This process is limited in that only one user can use remote debugging on one server at a time.

To use remote debugging, you must perform several setup steps. The first step is to ensure that the proper debugging components have been installed on the server. A full server installation of the Visual InterDev will load the proper components. However, if you did not perform a full server installation, you can follow the procedures below to install these components.

➤ **To install debugging components on the server**

1. On the server computer, start the Visual Studio Enterprise Edition setup program.

2. Under Add/Remove Options, choose Server Applications And Tools.

3. On the next page, select Launch BackOffice Installation Wizard, and then choose Install.

4. When the BackOffice Business Solutions wizard is displayed, click Custom and then click Next.

5. Proceed until you see the page offering you a list of components to install. Uncheck all components except the following:

   • Remote Machine Debugging

   • Visual InterDev Server

6. Complete the installation.

You must be able to provide the name and password of a Windows NT user who has administration privileges for the server in order to debug remotely. All developers who will be using remote debugging should be established as administration-level users on the server computer. You can use Windows NT facilities on the server to specify administration privileges for all users who will be debugging remotely.

Handling Run-Time Errors

When you handle run-time errors in server script, you use many of the same tools that are used for client script. The most important of these tools are the On Error Resume Next statement and the Err object, as you learned in Chapter 3.

Lesson Summary

Active Server Pages (ASP) is the server-side technology that allows you to generate Web pages that change each time the page is requested (such as returning data from a database). To do this, the Web server processes the server script included in the page and sends the resulting HTML to the browser for processing.

In addition to supporting ASP applications, IIS also supports Internet Server Application Programming Interface (ISAPI), CGI, Internet Database Connector (IDC), and Server Side Include (SSI) applications.

Because script in an ASP page runs on the server, the script has access to a number of objects that are available on the server. These objects are features built into the ASP architecture. Some common ASP objects include:

- Request
- Response
- Session
- Application
- Server
- ObjectContext

In addition, because ASP returns standard HTML, most Web browsers can view ASP pages.

Lesson 2: Reading Requests and Sending Responses

A Web application can use information from an HTTP request when a user requests an HTML document. For example, when a user submits a form by using the Get method, the values of the controls on the form are passed in the body of the HTTP request. A Web application can then read these values and use them to return a customized HTML document to the user. In this lesson, you will learn how to read and use the information provided by a user.

After this lesson, you will be able to:

- Explain the purpose of the Request object.
- Describe how an ASP page uses a Request object.
- Explain the purpose of the Response object.

Estimated lesson time: 20 minutes

HTTP Request and Response Messages

Two actions take place when a Web browser, or client, communicates with a server via HTTP.

1. A browser requests a page.
2. A server responds with the requested page.

The request from the browser comes in one of two forms: either a request is made to simply retrieve a page, or a request is made for information that will be used on the page before the page is returned to the browser. To handle this exchange of data, HTTP request and response messages have two parts: a header and a body, as illustrated in Figure 4.5. The header contains one or more header fields. The body contains information sent by the browser or the server. For example, when a browser requests a page from a server, only the header information is necessary. When a browser requests a page and form data is included in the request, both the header and the body are used. Responses from servers typically use both header and body information.

Message

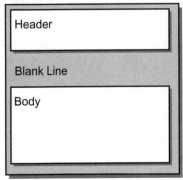

Figure 4.5 HTTP response format

The following table lists the types of header fields and describes the types of messages they use.

Header Field	Message Type	Description
Content-Type	Request and Response	The media type contained in the body.
Date	Request and Response	The date and time the message was generated.
Expires	Response	The date and time the content should be considered obsolete.
From	Request	The Internet e-mail address of the user running the browser.
If-Modified-Since	Request	Used with the Get request method to return a page only if it has been modified after the specified date.
Location	Response	The absolute URL of the page.
Refer	Request	The URL initiating the request.
User-Agent	Request	Information about the client software initiating the request.

For more information about header fields, go to the HTTP Specification Web site at http://www.w3.org/Protocols/Specs.html

HTTP Request Messages

When a user requests a Web page, the request is submitted as an HTTP request. An ASP application uses the Request object to interrogate the HTTP request and extract the incoming values. For example, when a user submits a form, the values of the controls on the form are passed in the body of the HTTP request. A Web application can then read these values and use them to return a customized Web page to the user. Each HTTP request message contains a unique identifying element called the method line (also referred to as the method field). A request method line has the following basic syntax:

```
HTTP-method   resource-identifier   HTTP/version
```

The method will be either Get or Post. The resource identifier is the requested file. The HTTP/version is the version number of the HTTP protocol being used in the request.

For example, a request to view the URL http://www.company.com/default.htm will use this Get method line:

```
GET default.htm HTTP/1.0
```

Note The domain name for the resource identifier is unnecessary because the HTTP request message created a TCP/IP communication session prior to establishing a connection with the server.

The following list describes two important types of HTTP methods.

- Get

  Retrieves a specified page. With the Get method, any information will be appended to the HTTP request for a page and sent in the message header. The size of the information sent with the Get method is limited to 1024 characters. This is the default of a request.

- Post

  Sends data to a page. With the Post method, any data is sent in the body of the HTTP request message.

HTTP Response Messages

When an HTTP server receives a request, it responds with a status message that includes the message's protocol version and a success or error code, followed by a Multipurpose Internet Mail Extensions (MIME) message containing server information, entity meta-information, and sometimes body content. The header of a response message is composed of a status line and any additional response header fields. If the body section is present, a blank line precedes it.

The Request Object

HTTP requests contain information about the current user, any data they entered prior to making the request, and arguments that tell the Web server how to process and respond to the request. You can use the Request object to retrieve information from or about the current user, and to access to all of the information passed in any HTTP request.

Most frequently, you use the Request object to retrieve information from an HTML form. For example, you might retrieve all the form elements passed back in a Submit event. The following example shows how you might use the Request object to gather information from the browser:

```
Private Sub Webitem1_Submit
    ' Define variables to hold information retrieved from the request
    Dim first as String
    Dim last as String
    ' Retrieve form information and assign it to the variables, using
    ' The Request object and its Form collection.
    First = Request.Form("Firstname")
    Last = Request.Form("Lastname")
End Sub
```

Request Object Collections

The Request object contains five collections, described in the following table. You can use the Request object's associated collections to access information.

Collection	Description
ClientCertificate	The values of the certification fields in the HTTP request.
Cookies	The values of cookies sent in the HTTP request.
Form	The values of form elements posted to the body of the HTTP request message by the form's Post method.
QueryString	The values of variables in the HTTP query string, specifically the values following the question mark (?) in an HTTP request.
ServerVariables	The values of predetermined Web server environment variables.

Each collection of the Request object contains variables you use to retrieve information from an HTTP request. You can use the values of these variables to return information to the user. In the following example code, the SERVER_NAME variable of the ServerVariables collection retrieves the type of Web browser the client is using, and then displays different HTML based on that information.

```
<%@ Language=VBScript %>
<HTML>
<TITLE>Welcome to My Search Page</TITLE>
<%
Dim cBrowserType
cBrowserType = Request.ServerVariables("HTTP_USER_AGENT")
If InStr(cBrowserType, "MSIE") Then
%>
    <!--Browser type is Internet Explorer -->
    <CENTER><FONT SIZE=6 COLOR='RED'>
    Thanks for choosing Internet Explorer!<BR>
    Where do you want to go today?
    </FONT></CENTER>
<%Else%>
    <!-- The Browser is not Internet Explorer-->
    <CENTER><FONT SIZE=6 COLOR='RED'>
    Wouldn't you rather be running Internet Explorer?
    </FONT></CENTER>
<%End If%>
<CENTER><INPUT TYPE=Textbox Name=txtSearch>
<INPUT TYPE=Button Value=Go!></CENTER>
</HTML>
```

Using the QueryString Collection

You can also use the QueryString collection of the Request object to extract information from the header of an HTTP request message. For example, when a user submits a form with the Get method, or appends parameters to a URL request, you use the QueryString collection to read the submitted information. The values you read from the request are the parameters that appear after the question mark (?). For example, if a user clicks the Submit button on the form illustrated in Figure 4.6, the following HTTP request is made:

```
http://name_age.asp?name=Paul&age=24&sport=Hockey
```

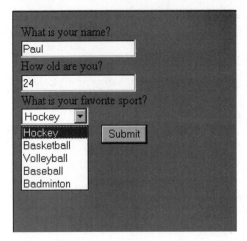

Figure 4.6 A form containing a Submit button that creates an HTTP request

You can loop through all of the values in a query string to extract information passed by the user. The following example code loops through all of the values in an HTTP request:

```
<%For Each Item In Request.QueryString
    ' Display the Item
Next %>
```

If more than one value is submitted with the same value name (which can occur with a multi-select list box on a form), you can use the index of the QueryString collection variable to access the individual values. The following example code shows how to access the first and second values of a variable called "sport" in the QueryString collection:

```
Request.QueryString("sport")(0)
Request.QueryString("sport")(1)
```

Using the Form Collection

The Form collection contains the values of each standard HTML control that has a NAME attribute. You use the Form collection of the Request object to extract information from the body of an HTTP request message. When a user submits a form with the Post method, you can read the values of the controls by using the Form collection. For example, a user completes and submits a form with the following HTML:

```
<FORM ACTION="submit.asp" METHOD=POST>
Name: <INPUT TYPE=TEXT NAME="name"><P>
Favorite Color: <SELECT MULTIPLE NAME="color">
       <OPTION>Red
       <OPTION>Green
       <OPTION>Blue
       </SELECT><P>
<INPUT TYPE=SUBMIT NAME="cmdSubmit" VALUE="Submit">
</FORM>
```

You can read the submitted information by using the following script in the Submit.asp file:

```
Request.Form("name")
Request.Form("color")
```

You can also loop through all of the values on a form to extract information passed by the user. The following example code loops through all of the standard HTML controls in an HTTP request:

```
<% For Each Item in Request.Form
     ' Display Item
Next %>
```

If more than one value is submitted for a control on a form with the same value (which can occur with a multi-select list box), you can use the index of the Form collection variable to access the individual values. The following example code shows how to access the first and second color values selected in the color list box:

```
Request.Form("color")(0)
Request.Form("color")(1)
```

Posting Values to a Form

With ASP, you can define a form that posts its input values back to the .asp file that contains the form. To do this, you break the .asp file into two parts—one part that displays the form and a second part that responds to the submitted form.

To determine whether a request for an ASP page has resulted from the form being submitted, you test to see if the HTML controls contain values. If the controls do not contain values, the user has not yet submitted the form; therefore you need to display a blank form that the user can complete and submit.

The following example code displays a blank form:

```
<% If IsEmpty (Request.Form("txtName")) Then
    ' Display form
Else
    ' Form was submitted
End If %>
```

The Response Object

After you determine what the user requested in an HTTP request, you can return the appropriate information to the user by using the properties and methods of the Response object. The Response object allows you to respond to an HTTP request and control the information sent to a user by the HTTP response message. This means that the Response object can be used to return information to the client browser.

The Response object provides properties and methods you can use when sending information to the user. The following table describes some properties of the Response object.

Property	Description
Buffer	Indicates whether a response is buffered.
Expires	Specifies the length of time before a page cached on a browser expires. If the user returns to the same page before it expires, the cached version is displayed.
ExpiresAbsolute	Specifies the date and time on which a page cached on a browser will expire.
IsClientConnected	Indicates whether the client has disconnected from the server since the last Response.Write.
Status	Specifies the value of the status line returned by the server. Status values are defined in the HTTP specification.

The following table describes some methods of the Response object.

Method	Description
Clear	Clears any buffered response.
End	Stops the processing of a Web page and returns whatever information has been processed thus far.
Flush	Sends buffered output immediately.
Redirect	Sends a redirect message to the user, causing the response message to try to connect to a different URL.
Write	Writes a variable to the current HTTP output as a string.

Using the Write Method

You use the Write method of the Response object to send information to a user from within the server-side script delimiters. The Write method adds text to the HTTP response message, as shown in the following example code:

```
Response.Write variant
```

The variant can be any data type (including characters, strings, and integers) that is supported by your default scripting language. The variant cannot contain the character combination %>, which is used to denote the end of a script statement. Instead, you can use the escape sequence %\>, which the Web server will translate when it processes the script. The following code sends a different greeting to the user depending on whether the user has visited the page before.

```
<%@ Language=VBScript %>
<HTML>
<%
Dim FirstTime
If FirstTime = True Then
    Response.Write "<H3 ALIGN=CENTER>Welcome to the Overview Page</H3>"
Else
    Response.Write "<H3 ALIGN=CENTER>Welcome Back to the Overview" & _
        "Page</H3>"
End If
%>
</HTML>
```

You can also use the Write method within a loop to display the values of each standard HTML control on a form that is sent in an HTTP request, as shown in the following code.

```
<%For Each Item In Request.Form
    Response.Write Item
Next %>
```

In the following example code, an HTML tag is added to a Web page. The string returned by the Write method cannot contain the characters %> in an HTML tag, so the escape sequence %\> is used instead.

```
<% Response.Write "<TABLE WIDTH = 100%\>" %>
```

Setting the Buffer Property

A Web server processes all script commands on a page before any content is sent to the user by default. This process is known as buffering. You can use the Buffer property of the Response object to disable buffering so that the Web server returns HTML and the results of scripts as it processes a page. The advantage of buffering your .asp files is that you can abort sending a Web page if, for example, the script processing does not proceed correctly or if a user does not have appropriate security credentials. You can also use Response.Buffer to prevent the Web server from returning the HTTP header before a script can modify the header. Some properties and methods, such as Response.Expires and Response.Redirect, modify the HTTP header.

Although buffering is enabled by default for ASP applications, you can use the IIS snap-in to disable buffering for an entire ASP application. To enable buffering, you set the Buffer property to *True*, as shown in the following example code:

```
Response.Buffer = True
```

You cannot set the Buffer property after the server has sent output to the user. For this reason, you should set the Buffer property in the first line of the .asp file as shown in the following example.

```
<%
' Turn on buffering. This statement must appear before the <HTML> tag.
Response.Buffer = True %>
<html>
<body>
<%
If Request("FName") = "" Then
    Response.Clear
    Response.Redirect "/samples/test.html"
Else
    Response.Write Request("FName")
End If
%>
</body>
</html>
```

The Redirect Method

Instead of sending content from the response message to the user, you can use the Redirect method to redirect the user to another URL, as shown in the previous example. When you use the Redirect method of the Response object, you provide the URL as an argument to the method.

```
Response.Redirect URL
```

The URL specifies the absolute or relative location to which the browser is redirected. In addition to doing redirects programmatically with ASP, an IIS administrator can also change settings through Internet Service Manager to redirect requests for files in a directory to other files or programs.

The following example code uses the Redirect method to display a page in high or low resolution, depending on the user's screen resolution:

```
<%
If Request.ServerVariables("HTTP_UA_PIXELS") = "640x480" Then
    Response.Redirect "lo_res.htm"
Else
    Response.Redirect "hi_res.htm"
End If
%>
```

If an error occurs during processing, you can use the Redirect method of the Response object with buffering enabled. First you clear the buffer with the Clear method, and then you use the Redirect method. When an error occurs, the following example code will clear the buffer and redirect the user to an error page:

```
Response.Buffer = True
On Error Resume Next
' Code that may cause an unrecoverable error,
' Such as failing to open a data connection
If Err.number <> 0 Then
    Response.Clear
    Response.Redirect "error.htm"
End If
```

Note If you use the Redirect method after information has already been sent to the user, an error message will be generated.

Lesson Summary

When a Web browser, or client, communicates with a server via HTTP, two actions take place:

1. A browser requests a page.
2. A server responds with the requested page.

When a user requests a Web page, that request is submitted as an HTTP request. An ASP application uses the Request object to interrogate the HTTP request and extract the incoming values. For instance, when a user submits a form, the values of the controls on the form are passed in the body of the HTTP request. A Web application can then read these values. It then uses the values to return a customized Web page to the user.

When an HTTP server receives a request, it responds with a status message . This message includes protocol version and a success or error code, followed by a Multipurpose Internet Mail Extensions (MIME) message. MIME typically contains server information, entity metainformation, and sometimes body content.

After the server determines what the user requested in an HTTP request, it can return the appropriate information to the user by using the properties and methods of the Response object. The Response object enables you to respond to an HTTP request. You can control the information sent to a user by the HTTP response message, because the Response object can be used to return information to the client browser.

Lesson 3: Saving State Data

So far in this chapter, you have learned that most of the functionality you can build into ASP comes from objects on the server. You have learned that IIS comes with built-in objects: for example, the Request object gets information from the user, and the Response object sends information to the user. In this lesson, you will learn how the Session object enables you to manage information about the current session, and how the Application object stores information for all sessions. These objects allow you to maintain state, which is the ability to retain user information in a Web application. The HTTP protocol alone does not provide this ability.

HTTP is a stateless protocol, meaning that your Web server treats each HTTP request for a page as an independent request—the server retains no knowledge of previous requests. This is true even if previous requests occurred only seconds prior to a current request. This inability to remember previous requests means that it is difficult to write applications, such as an online catalog, where the application might need to track the catalog items a user has selected while jumping between the various pages of the catalog.

ASP provides a unique solution for the problem of managing session information. Using the ASP Session object and a special user ID generated by your server, you can create clever applications that identify each visiting user and collect information that your application can use to track user preferences or selections. In this lesson, you will learn how ASP enables you to maintain state in a Web application. You can maintain two types of state data for a Web application:

- Application state

  Information is available to all users of a Web application.

- Session state

  Information is available only to a user of a specific session.

After this lesson, you will be able to:

- Describe the purposes of the Application object.
- Describe the purpose of the Session object.
- Explain the role of a cookie in a Web site.

Estimated lesson time: 30 minutes

The Application Object

The Application object can store information that persists for the entire lifetime of an application. This feature makes the Application object a good place to store information that has to exist for more than one user, such as a page counter. You can also use the Application object to share information among all users of a Web application. For example, you can store the total number of visitors to a Web site in an application-level variable.

An Application object is created when the user of the application requests an .asp file from the starting-point directory of the ASP application. It is destroyed when the application is unloaded. The two most significant events of the Application object are the Application_OnStart and Application_OnEnd events. These events are automatically fired when the Web server is first contacted and when the application ends. For example, whenever the first ASP file of a Web application is called, or when a user who doesn't yet have a session requests an ASP file, ASP reads the Global.asa file and fires the Application_onstart and Session_onstart events. However, the OnStart and OnEnd procedures reside in a file called Global.asa instead of in an ASP file. Every application can have only one Global.asa file, and it must be in the Web server's root directory. The following example shows how you create an application-level variable called anVisitors in Global.asa.

```
<SCRIPT LANGUAGE=VBScript RUNAT=Server>
Application("anVisitors") = 0
Sub Application_OnStart
    ' Your code goes here
End Sub
</SCRIPT>
```

In the following example code, MyVar is a variable that contains a string. MyObj is a component instance. To assign a component instance to an application variable, you use the VBScript Set statement.

```
<% Application("MyVar") = "Hello"
Set Application("MyObj") = Server.CreateObject("MyComponent") %>
```

Locking and Unlocking the Application Object

All users share the same Application object, so it is possible that two users might attempt to modify the object simultaneously. The Lock and Unlock methods of the Application object prevent this possibility. To reduce the inconvenience of a user not being able to access the Application object when he or she needs it, try to minimize the amount of time you use the Lock method. The following sample code shows how to use the Lock and Unlock methods when changing the value of a hit counter used in a Web application:

```
<%
Application.Lock
Application("NumVisits") = Application("NumVisits") + 1
Application.Unlock
%>
This application has been visited <%= Application("NumVisits") %> times.
```

Notice that the Application object needs to be locked only while it is being modified. If you don't call the Unlock method explicitly, the Web server unlocks the Application object when the script ends or times out.

The Session Object

The Session object is a built-in object for IIS that provides you with an easy way to manage session state data. You use the Session object to store information that is needed for a particular user session. When a user first requests an ASP page within an application, IIS automatically creates a new Session object for that user in the Web server. You can use the Session object to store and retrieve user properties. For example, if a user indicates that he or she prefers not to view graphics, you can store that information in the Session object. You do not have to create the Session object, assign a session cookie to the user, or retrieve the Session object for the current user—this is handled automatically by IIS.

Session Object Syntax

The Session object has two properties and one method that use the following syntax:

```
Session.property|method
```

The following table describes the uses for these features.

Feature	Description
SessionID property	Determines the session identification of a user.
Timeout property	Sets the amount of time that needs to elapse before the server can shutdown an unused session.
Abandon method	Destroys a Session object and releases its resources.

To store a variable in the Session object, you simply assign it to a named entry as shown in the following example.

```
<% Session("nickname") = "Nancy"
Session("hometown") = "Redmond" %>
```

To retrieve a session variable, you access the entry where it is stored as shown in the following example.

```
Hello <%= Session("nickname") %>.<BR>
How is the weather in <%= Session("hometown") %>?<BR>
```

Variables stored in the Session object will not be discarded when the user goes between pages in the Web application. Instead, these variables will persist for the entire user session.

Beginning a Session

The Web server automatically creates a Session object when a session starts. When the session expires or is abandoned, the Web server will destroy the Session object.

A session can begin in three ways:

- A new user requests a URL that identifies an .asp file in an application, and the Global.asa file for that application includes a Session_OnStart procedure.
- A user stores a value in the Session object.
- A user requests an .asp file in an application, and the application's Global.asa file uses the <OBJECT> tag to instantiate an object with session scope. See "Using COM Components" in this chapter for more information about using the <OBJECT> tag to instantiate an object.

A session automatically ends if a user has not requested or refreshed a page in an application for a specified period of time, which is 20 minutes by default. You can change the default for an application by setting the Session Timeout property on the Application Options tab of the Application Configuration property sheet in Internet Service Manager. Set this value according to the requirements of your Web application and the memory capacity of your server. For example, if you expect that users browsing your Web application will linger on each page for only a few minutes, then you might want to significantly reduce the session time-out value from the default. A long session time-out period can result in too many open sessions, which can strain your server's memory resources.

If, for a specific session, you want to set a time-out interval that is shorter than the default application time-out interval, you can set the Timeout property of the Session object. For example, the following script sets a time-out interval of 5 minutes:

```
<%  Session.Timeout = 5   %>
```

You can set the time-out interval to be greater than the default value, which is the value determined by the Session Timeout property.

You can also explicitly end a session with the Abandon method of the Session object. For example, you can provide a Quit button on a form with the *ACTION* parameter set to the URL of an .asp file that contains the following command:

```
<% Session.Abandon %>
```

A session starts the first time a user requests an .asp file. When the session starts, the Web application generates a session ID. The session ID is stored as a cookie that is sent back to the browser.

Using Cookies

Cookies are a mechanism by which state can be maintained in a file on the user's computer. For example, cookies store user preferences or other personalization information that should be saved between sessions. A cookie file is typically stored in a folder named Cookies.

The first time a user requests an .asp file within a given application, ASP generates a SessionID, a number produced by a complex algorithm, which uniquely identifies each user's session. At the beginning of a new session, the server stores the Session ID in the user's Web browser as a cookie. Then ASP reuses the cookie to track the session, even if the user requests another .asp file, or requests an .asp file running in other applications. Likewise, if the user deliberately abandons the session or lets the session time out and then requests another .asp file, ASP begins a new session using the same cookie.

Note   ASP assigns the user ID by means of an HTTP cookie, which is a small file stored on the user's browser. So if you are creating an application for browsers that do not support cookies, or if your customers might set their browsers to refuse cookies, you should not use ASP's session management features.

A cookie is like a token for a specific page that a Web server sends to a user. The user sends the cookie back to the server during each subsequent visit to that page or to a number of pages. Cookies enable information to be associated with a user. You can set and get the values of cookies by using the Cookies collection.

When the Web server returns an HTTP response to a user, the response message might also include a cookie. The cookie includes a description of the saved range of URLs for which that cookie is valid. A cookie is introduced to the user by including a Set-Cookie header as part of an HTTP response. Any HTTP requests made by the user included in that range will provide a transmittal of the current value of the cookie from the user back to the server.

Creating Cookies

To set the value of cookies that your Web server sends to a user, you use the Cookies collection of the Response object. If the cookie does not already exist, Response.Cookies collection will create a new cookie on the user's computer.

The following example code creates a cookie with the city set to Redmond:

```
<% Response.Cookies("city") = "Redmond" %>
```

If you want the cookie to apply to all of the pages in your Web application, you set the Path attribute of the cookie to "/". For example:

```
Response.Cookies("city").Path = "/"
```

The browser will then send the cookie during each request for a page in your Web application.

You can set other attributes for cookies, such as a cookie's expiration date:

```
Response.Cookies("Type").Expires = "July 31, 1998"
```

The browser will send cookies to the appropriate pages in your Web application. To read the value of a cookie, you use the Cookies collection of the Request object. For example, if the HTTP request sends a cookie with the city set to Redmond, then the following example code will retrieve the value of Redmond:

```
<%= Request.Cookies("city") %>
```

Disabling Cookies

If a user selects Disable All Cookie Use on the Advanced tab of the Internet Options dialog of Internet Explorer, the session ID cookies cannot be created for that user. Session state can be disabled through the Internet Service Manager and through the following ASP processing directive:

```
<%@ ENABLESESSIONSSTATE=True|False %>
```

Personalization and Membership

Personalization and membership services can be a powerful tool when tied to Commerce Server. When users enter information about themselves, such as placing an order or registering on your site, the information is stored in a database. Using ASP, this information can be compiled into pages that specifically meet a user's needs. For instance, each time a specific user returns to your site, a page could be generated that displays his or her current order status, offers upgrades, or updated documentation for products already purchased. These pages can also tell about new products that may interest the user or lets the user know about an online chat event just for special members. The Site Server Personalization system can be integrated with e-mail, Web sites, or Active Channels. This provides the Web developer with several options to deliver information to users.

The personalization and membership features of Site Server are based on a membership directory—a centralized repository for storing member records and personal profiles. ASP pages on the site access that directory. For smaller sites the information can be stored in a Microsoft Access database. For larger sites Microsoft SQL Server is used to manage the information. Several types of user authentication are also a part of the Membership Services in Site Server. Microsoft Site Server comes with a sample site, a tutorial, and documentation to help you learn more about the personalization and membership services.

Lesson Summary

ASP allows you to easily manage session information by using objects. Using the ASP Session object and a special user ID generated by your server, you can create applications that identify each visiting user and collect information that your application can use to track user preferences or selections.

One way to do this is by using the Application object, which can store information that persists for the entire lifetime of an application. This feature makes the Application object a good place to store information that has to exist for more than one user, such as a page counter.

Another way to manage session information is by using the built-in Session object. You use the Session object to store information that is needed for a particular user session. When a user first requests an ASP page within an application, IIS automatically creates a new Session object for that user in the Web server. You can use the Session object to store and retrieve user properties.

Cookies are a mechanism by which state can be maintained in a file on the user's computer. A cookie is like a token for a specific page that a Web server sends to a user. The user sends the cookie back to the server during each subsequent visit to that page or to a number of pages. Cookies enable information to be associated with a user. You can set and get the values of cookies by using the Cookies collection. A cookie file is typically stored in a folder named Cookies.

Lesson 4: Using COM Components

The Component Object Model (COM) is a technology that allows applications and objects to communicate. COM components have methods and properties.

You can run COM components (formerly known as Automation servers) on a Web server in response to a user request. These components allow you to extend the functionality of an ASP page with any resource, such as a database, located on the Web server. In this lesson, you will learn how to use COM components in your Web application.

After this lesson, you will be able to:

- Explain how to create a Component instance.
- Define the Browser Capabilities component.
- Describe the function of the File Access Component.

Estimated lesson time: 20 minutes

Creating Component Instances

To use a server component, you first need to understand how to create an instance of the component, called an object. There are two ways to create an object: you can use either the <OBJECT> tag or the Server.CreateObject syntax.

To use the <OBJECT> tag, you set the RUNAT attribute to Server. You can set the scope of the component by setting the SCOPE attribute to Application or Session. If you do not set the SCOPE attribute, the component will have page scope, meaning it can be referenced only on the current page. To specify the type of component to be created, you can use either its registered name, PROGID, or its registered number, CLASSID. In the following example code, the registered name (PROGID) is used to create a session-scope instance of the fictitious component:

```
<OBJECT RUNAT=Server SCOPE=Session ID=MyComp PROGID="MS.MyComponent">
</OBJECT>
```

In the following example code, the registered number (CLASSID) method is used to create an application-scope instance of MyComponent:

```
<OBJECT RUNAT=Server SCOPE=Application ID=MyComp
CLASSID="Clsid:00000293-0000-0010-8000-00AA006D2EA4">
</OBJECT>
```

When you use the <OBJECT> tag to declare a session-scope or application-scope instance of a component, the variable you assign to the component is stored in the session or application namespace. You do not need to use the Session or Application objects to access the instance of the component.

The following example code opens the instance of MyComponent that has been declared in the previous example code:

```
<%= MyComp.GetSomething("some.txt") %>
```

Note When you drag a component from the Server Objects tab of the Toolbox, Visual InterDev adds an <OBJECT> tag for the component to your ASP page. It does not set the SCOPE attribute in the tag, so components created this way will have page scope.

Using the CreateObject Method

You can also use the CreateObject method of the Server object to create an instance of a component.

The following example code creates a reference to the Browser Capabilities component using its PROGID.

```
<% Set bc = Server.CreateObject("MSWC.BrowserType") %>
```

Using Installable Components Provided for ASP

To help you create Web applications, IIS provides a large number of COM components that are available on the Server Objects tab of the Toolbox. The following table describes several of these server objects.

Server Objects	Description
Ad Rotator	Automatically rotates advertisements displayed on a Web page, according to a specified schedule.
ADO Command, ADO Connection, and ADO Recordset	ActiveX Data Objects (ADO) that access information stored in a database or other tabular data structures.
Browser Capabilities	Determines the capabilities, type, and version of a user's browser.
CDONTS NewMail and CDONTS Session	Collaboration Data Objects for NTS.
Content Linking	Creates a table of contents for Web pages, and links them sequentially, like pages in a book.
File Access	Uses the FileSystemObject object to retrieve and modify information stored in a text file on the server.

COM components enable you to package and reuse common functions, such as accessing a database and writing information to text files in an ASP application.

You can access the components installed on a Web server by using an .asp file with the CreateObject method of the Server object.

The Browser Capabilities Component

The Browser Capabilities component enables you to determine the capabilities of the user's browser. The Browser Capabilities component compares the browser type and version number provided in the header of the HTTP request to entries contained in the Browscap.ini file stored on the Web server. If a match is found, the component uses the capabilities for that particular browser. If a match is not found, the component uses default capabilities in the Browscap.ini file. By default the Browscap.ini file is found in the Windows\Winnt\System32\inetsrv folder.

You can declare property definitions for multiple browsers in the Browscap.ini file. You can also set default values that will be used when a browser that is not listed in the Browscap.ini file makes an HTTP request. For each browser definition, you provide an HTTP User Agent header, along with the properties and values you want to associate with that header.

You check values of properties of the Browser Capabilities component to present Web content in a format that is appropriate for a specific browser. The following table describes some possible properties of the Browser Capabilities component.

Property	Description
ActiveXControls	Specifies whether the browser supports ActiveX controls.
Backgroundsounds	Specifies whether the browser supports background sounds.
Beta	Specifies whether the browser is beta software.
Browser	Specifies the name of the browser.
Cdf	Specifies whether the browser supports the Channel Definition Format for Webcasting.
Cookies	Specifies whether the browser supports cookies.
Frames	Specifies whether the browser supports frames.
Javaapplets	Specifies whether the browser supports Java applets.
Javascript	Specifies whether the browser supports JScript.
Platform	Specifies the platform on which the browser runs.
Tables	Specifies whether the browser supports tables.
Vbscript	Specifies whether the browser supports VBScript.
Version	Specifies the version number of the browser.

In the following example code, the Browser Capabilities component is used to determine whether a browser supports ActiveX controls. If it does, an HTTP response that contains ActiveX controls will be sent.

```
<% Set objBrowser = Server.CreateObject("MSWC.BrowserType")
If objBrowser.ActiveXControls = "True" Then
    ' Insert ActiveX Control here
Else
    ' Handle Without Control
End If %>
```

The File Access Component

You can use the File Access component in your Web application to create and read from any text file stored on the Web server. With text files, you can store the state of your Web application when the Web server shuts down.

Creating and Opening Text Files

The File Access component contains the FileSystemObject object, which you use to open or create a text file. To open a text file, create a TextStream object by using the OpenTextFile method of the FileSystemObject object. To create a text file, create a TextStream object by using the CreateTextFile method of the FileSystemObject object. The following example code creates a TextStream object and opens a text file:

```
' Creates a FileSystem Object
Set fsVisitors = Server.CreateObject("Scripting.FileSystemObject")
' Creates a TextStream Object and opens a text file
Set fileVisitors = fsVisitors.CreateTextFile("c:\visitors.txt", True)
```

If a text file already exists, the CreateTextFile method will overwrite the existing file if the overwrite argument is equal to True.

Reading and Writing Text

After you have created a TextStream object with either the CreateTextFile or OpenTextFile method, you can use the methods of the TextStream object to read and write text. You can also use the ReadLine and WriteLine methods of the TextStream object to read from and write to a text file. The following example code sets an Application object value equal to the value read from a text file with the ReadLine method:

```
Application("visitors") = fileVisitors.ReadLine
```

The following example ensures that the number of visitors to the Web site is retained even when the Web server shuts down and the Web application ends. The code also uses the events of the Session and Application objects to count the number of visitors to the Web site and stores that number in a text file.

```
' When application starts, read hit counter information from a text file
Sub Application_OnStart
    ' FileSystemObject object
    Dim fsVisitors
    ' TextStream object
    Dim fileVisitors

    Set fsVisitors = Server.CreateObject("Scripting.FileSystemObject")
    Set fileVisitors = fsVisitors.OpenTextFile("c:\visitors.txt")
    ' Read counter value from text file
    Application("visitors") = fileVisitors.ReadLine
    fileVisitors.Close
End Sub

' When application ends, save hit counter in a text file
Sub Application_OnEnd
    ' FileSystemObject object
    Dim fsVisitors
    ' TextStream object
    Dim fileVisitors

    Set fsVisitors = Server.CreateObject("Scripting.FileSystemObject")
    Set fileVisitors = _
        fsVisitors.CreateTextFile("c:\visitors.txt", True)
    ' Write counter value to text file
    fileVisitors.Writeline(Application("visitors"))
    fileVisitors.Close
End Sub

' When session starts, increment the hit counter
Sub Session_OnStart
    Application.Lock
    ' Increment counter
    Application("visitors") = Application("visitors") + 1
    Application.Unlock
End Sub
```

Lesson Summary

COM allows applications to communicate with objects. You can run COM components on a Web server in response to a user request. COM components allow you to extend the functionality of an ASP page with any resource located on the Web server.

Instances of a component are called objects. There are two ways to create an object: you can use either the <OBJECT> tag or the Server.CreateObject syntax.

A specific COM component is the Browser Capabilities component. This enables you to determine the capabilities of the user's browser. The Browser Capabilities component compares the browser type and version number provided in the header of the HTTP request to entries stored on the Web server. Once a match is found, the component uses the capabilities for that particular browser. If a match is not found, the component uses default capabilities in the Browscap.ini file.

Use the File Access component in your Web application to create and read from any text file stored on the Web server. With text files, you can store the state of your Web application even when the Web server shuts down.

Lesson 5: Using Page Objects

A page object is an ASP page that contains server script that you use in your application. The functions or subroutines on the page can become methods for the page object. For example, you can have an ASP page in your application that you call from a form to display a list of employees. Procedures on the target page construct different queries for displaying the list in different order, using different fields, or with different selection criteria. When you convert the page to a page object, you can specify each of these procedures as a method. You can then invoke the methods from other pages in your application.

Page objects also allow you to create properties, which maintain state over multiple round trips to the server. Page objects provide you with the following abilities:

- Simplified navigation

  You can navigate to other pages in your application using standard object references, without having to track the URL of the page.

- An easy way to execute specific script on another page

  By exporting procedures as methods, you can jump directly to a specific procedure on another page without writing script to parse hidden form elements or query strings.

- A way to maintain state information

  You can define properties on a page object that maintain their value for the duration that you specify. The duration could be the page lifetime, session, or application.

- A way to execute server script from a page displayed in the browser.

After this lesson, you will be able to:

- Create a Page object and specify its method and property.
- Describe how to call Page Object Methods.

Estimated lesson time: 30 minutes

Creating Page Objects

Using design-time controls and the scripting object model in Visual InterDev allows you to create and script a Web page using standard object-oriented techniques. You can specify any ASP page as a page object. To do this, you use the PageObject design-time control. A page object is an ASP page that contains server script that you use in your application. The functions or subroutines on the page can become methods for the page object. Page objects also allow you to create properties, which maintain state over multiple round trips to the server.

Page objects enable the following capabilities:

- Simplified navigation
- An easy way to execute specific script on another page
- A means of maintaining state information
- A way to execute server script from a page displayed in the browser

➤ **To specify a page as an object**

1. Create or open an .asp file in the HTML editor.

2. Enable the scripting object model for the page.

   a. Right-click anywhere in the page away from an object or control, choose Properties, and then choose the General tab.

   b. Under ASP settings, choose Enable Scripting Object Model. The HTML editor adds the scripting object model framework to the page in <META> tags. You should not alter the content of these tags.

   c. Make sure that you have set options to view controls graphically. From the View menu, choose View Controls Graphically. To set this option as the default, use the HTML node of the Options dialog.

3. From the Design-Time Controls tab of the Toolbox, drag a PageObject control onto your page. You can drag the control anywhere on the page, although it must be inside the framework of the scripting object model blocks.

4. In the Name box on the PageObject control, type a name for the page object. This will be the name that you can use to reference the object in script.

The name you give your page object is registered in your Web project so that it is available to any other page. Even if you move the page to another location, its page object name remains the same.

Defining Methods and Properties of a PageObject

Once you have added a PageObject control to an ASP page, you can define methods and properties for the page. Page objects can define two types of methods. A client page calls the Navigate method to load the ASP page and run a procedure on the page. A common use for navigate methods is to process a form. A client page can also call the Execute method to run a procedure on the ASP page, without leaving the current page. A common use for execute methods is to validate a user-entered value by looking it up in a database. All page objects have a default navigate method called Show, which displays the contents of the page.

➤ **To define a method for a page object**

1. If the page does not already have one, add a PageObject control to the page and give the control a name.

2. Write the procedures in a script block that has the attribute RUNAT=SERVER. Procedures can take any number of parameters, but all are passed by value.

Note Parameters are converted to strings when you call a page object method so that they can be successfully passed across the Web. In your page object scripts, you should convert parameter values to the appropriate data type as required.

---

3. Right-click the PageObject control, and then choose Properties to display the Property Pages dialog.

4. Determine whether the method will be available via navigation or execution. Then in the list under either Navigate methods or Execute methods, find the first blank line. From the drop-down list box, select the procedure that you want to define as a method for the page object.

Page object properties have lifetime and visibility features, as described in the following table.

Feature	Settings	Description
Lifetime	Application	Available to any page of your application. Application values use application variables to store values.
	Page	Available to scripts anywhere on the page until you navigate to another page.
	Session	Available to any page in your application for the current session. Session values use session variables to store values.
Visibility	Client	None, Read, Read/Write
	Server	None, Read/Write

➤ **To define a property for a page object**

1. If the page does not already have one, add a PageObject control to the page and give the control a name.

2. Right-click the PageObject control, choose Properties to display the Property Pages dialog, and then click the Properties tab.

3. In the Name column, find the first blank line, and then enter the name of the property you want to create.

4. Select the characteristics for the new property from the Lifetime, Client, and Server columns.

To make properties accessible to your scripts, page objects implement Get and Set methods. For example, if you define a property named Color, you can read its value using the getColor method and set it using the setColor method.

Using Methods and Properties

To access the methods or properties of another page object, you must first create a reference to that page on the current page.

➤ **To reference another page object**

1. If the page does not already have one, add a PageObject control to the page and give the control a name. If your scripting target is Server, the scripting object model must be enabled for the page.

2. Right-click the PageObject control, choose Properties to display the Property Pages dialog, and then choose the References tab.

3. In the Name column, click the three-dot button to display the Create URL dialog.

4. Select the .asp file that you want to reference as a page object. Enter options for how to call the page object, and then click OK.

Calling Page Object Methods

Page objects support two types of methods—Navigate methods and Execute methods. Each method is called according to the following general syntax:

pageObject.navigate.*methodName*(*parameters*)

pageObject.execute.*methodName*(*parameters*)

However, there are additional considerations for calling Execute methods, which can be called in two ways:

- Synchronously

  Your script calls the remote procedure and waits for it to return. This is useful if you need the results of the remote procedure before you proceed.

- Asynchronously

  Your script makes the call to a remote script, and then continues processing. The page remains available to users. Asynchronous calls are useful in Web applications because a remote procedure can take a long time while the request goes to the server and back.

When you call an Execute method either synchronously or asynchronously, it will not return a single value as you might expect. Instead, it returns a call object, which is an object that contains return and status information about the method that you called.

The most commonly used property of the call object is return_value. It contains the single value calculated or looked up by the method. Other call object properties allow you to retrieve more information about the state of the method call.

Accessing Page Object Properties

When you define a property for a page object, the scripting object model creates a Get method and a Set method that you use to access the property. For example, if you have defined a property called UserName, you can read the value of the property using the method getUserName, and set it using setUserName, as shown in the following example:

```
newUser = PageObj1.Navigate.getUserName()
PageObj1.Navigate.setUserName(txtUserName.Value)
```

When working with properties, you need to be aware of their lifetimes. For example, if you have defined the property's lifetime as "page," you can get and set its value only until you leave the page and display another one. (Calling the same page again to execute a method retains property values scoped to the page.) However, after you navigate to another page, the property is reset.

Note You can call methods and use properties on the current page using the default page object name of thisPage.

Lesson Summary

Using design-time controls and the scripting object model in Visual InterDev allows you to create and script a Web page using standard object-oriented techniques. You can specify any ASP page as a page object. To do so, you use the PageObject design-time control. A page object is defined as an ASP page that contains server script that you use in your application. The functions or subroutines on the page can become methods for the page object. Procedures on the target page construct different queries for displaying the list in different order, using different fields, or with different selection criteria. When you convert the page to a page object, you can specify each of these procedures as a method. You can then invoke the methods from other pages in your application.

Once you have added a PageObject control to an ASP page, you can then define methods and properties for the page. Page objects support two types of methods—Navigate methods and Execute methods.

Lab 4: Working with Active Server Pages

In this lab, you will use the Request object to validate entries into fields on a reservation form. Then you will write code that will display selected fields in a reservation request form when a guest checks in. You will also save selected form variables into a cookie for later retrieval during checkout.

To see a demonstration of this lab, run the Lab04.exe animation located in the Animations folder on the companion CD-ROM that accompanies this book.

Before You Begin

You should have already completed Labs 2 and 3. If you have not, follow the steps in Lab 2 to create the Chateau Web project and use the files in the Labs\Lab03\Partial folder to obtain the necessary files to complete this lab.

Estimated lab time: 45 minutes

Exercise 1: Validating Request Object values

In this exercise, you will validate form variables using the ASP Request object. First you will add code to the Reservation form so that the forms' data can be submitted to an ASP. Then you will write the validation code to direct the user back to the form if a field is left blank.

➤ **Add existing files to the project**

1. In Visual InterDev, highlight the <server-name>/Chateau node in the Project Explorer window.

2. From the Project menu, click Add Item.

   The Add Item dialog box appears.

3. Click on the Existing tab and then navigate to the \Labs\Labs04\Partial folder. Change the file mask to All Files (*.*). Select the Reservation.htm, reservation.asp, checkin.asp, checkout.asp, and invoice.asp files and then click Open.

   The files are added to the list of project files in the Project Explorer window. (Expand the Chateau project node if necessary.)

4. Add the Reservation.gif file from the Labs\Lab04\Partial folder to the Images folder of your project.

5. In the Project Explorer window, right-click the node Default.htm, and from the context menu, choose View In Browser.

6. You should now be able to open the Reservation form from both the main page and the menus to the right.

➤ **To add the form tags to the reservation form**

1. Open the Reservation.htm file for editing.

2. Click the Source tab on the HTML editor window.

3. Locate the following HTML code:

```
<!--Insert Lab04 Form tag here-->
```

4. Place the insertion point below the HTML shown in step 3 and insert the following form tag:

```
<FORM action="checkin.asp" id=FORM1 method=post name=FORM1>
```

5. Below the </TABLE> tag, end the form with the following tag entry.

```
</FORM>
```

6. Save and close the Reservation.htm file.

   The information you enter into the Reservation form will now be posted to the checkin.asp page.

➤ **To validate data posted from the reservation form**

1. Open the checkin.asp file for editing.

2. Click the Source tab on the HTML editor window.

3. Insert the following ASP code at the beginning of the document after the <%@ Language=VBScript %> ASP code.

   This code will validate the fields posted from the form. If none of the fields are blank, a confirmation of the reservation will be displayed. :

```
<%
' Stores the fullname of the guest
Dim GuestName
' Stores checkin date
Dim CheckInDate
' Stores checkout date
Dim CheckOutDate
' Stores the party size
Dim PartySize
' Stores the type of room
Dim RoomType
' Validation returncode to display blank fields
Dim ReturnCode
ReturnCode = ""
for each item in Request.Form
    ' Check for blank items
    if Request.Form(item) = "" then
```

(continued)

```
            Select Case Item
                Case "FirstName"
                    ReturnCode = ReturnCode & "First Name<br>"
                Case "NumberofPeople"
                    ReturnCode = ReturnCode & "Number in Party<br>"
                Case "NumberofDays"
                    ReturnCode = ReturnCode & "Number of Days<br>"
                Case "ExpDate"
                    ReturnCode = ReturnCode & "Expiration Date" & _
                        " on Credit Card<br>"
                Case "LastName"
                    ReturnCode = ReturnCode & "Last Name<br>"
                Case "CardNumber"
                    ReturnCode = ReturnCode & "Credit Card Number<br>"
                Case "InDate"
                    ReturnCode = ReturnCode & "Check in Date<br>"
                Case "cboRoomType"
                    ReturnCode = ReturnCode & "Room Type<br>"
                Case "NumberofPeople"
                    ReturnCode = ReturnCode & "Rate<br>"
            End Select
        end if
        ' Check for radiobutton status
        if Request.Form(item) = "on" then
            Select Case item
                Case "optSmoke"
                    Smoking = "Yes"
                Case "optNoSmoke"
                    Smoking = "No"
                Case "optVisa"
                    PaymentMethod = "Visa"
                Case "optMC"
                    PaymentMethod = "Mastercard"
                Case "optDiscover"
                    PaymentMethod = "Discover"
                Case "optAmEX"
                    PaymentMethod = "American Express"
            End Select
        end if
    next
    ' If blank items, display error
    if ReturnCode <> "" then
        Response.Write "<H2>The following fields on the Reservation" & _
            " form need to be filled in:</H2><br>"
        Response.Write ReturnCode
        Response.Write "<H2>Press the back button on your browser to" & _
            " make the appropriate changes.</H2>"
    else
        ' If no blank items, set variables
```

```
GuestName = Request.Form("LastName") & ", " & _
       Request.Form("FirstName")
    CheckInDate = Request.Form("InDate")
    CheckOutDate = dateadd("d", Request.Form("NumberofDays"), _
       Request.Form("outdate"))
    PartySize = Request.Form("NumberofPeople")
    RoomType = Request.Form("cboRoomType")
%>
```

4. Place the insertion point in front of the </BODY> tag at the bottom of the document and insert the following ASP code:

    ```
    <%end if%>
    ```

    This will end the conditional statement that determines if the confirmation is displayed.

5. Edit the Sidebar.htm file to create a link to the Reservation.htm page as shown in the following code:

    ```
    Call AddChild(intParentID, "Reserve a Room", "Reservation.htm")
    ```

6. Save your changes to Checkin.asp and Sidebar.htm, then test the code you have written by viewing Default.htm in the browser and selecting Reserve a Room from the menu.

7. Fill out the Reservation form, leaving one or more of the fields blank, and then click the Check In button to submit the form.

    A message will display the fields you left blank and ask you to return to the form to fill them in.

8. Click Back on your browser and fill in the remaining fields you left blank. This time when you submit the form, a confirmation appears.

Exercise 2: Using Cookies to Save State Data

In this exercise, you will write ASP code to save reservation requests to a file using the Cookies collection. Additional ASP code will be used to retrieve the cookie allowing guests with reserved rooms to check out at the end of their stay.

1. Open the checkin.asp file for editing.

2. Click the Source tab on the HTML editor window.

3. Review the code from the previous exercise and locate the point where the validation has succeeded and the values from the form are being set to variables.

    This code is located below the following comment:

    ```
    ' If no blank items, set variables
    ```

4. Use the credit card number as a usercode to uniquely identify each reservation. Save the first name, last name, subtotal, check-in date, party size, expiration date, and credit card type to the cookie.

Your code should look similar to the following:

```
usercode = Request.Form("CardNumber")
response.cookies(usercode)("LastName") = Request.Form("LastName")
response.cookies(usercode)("FirstName") = _
    Request.Form("FirstName")
response.cookies(usercode)("SubTotal") = Request.Form("Rate")* _
    Request.Form("NumberofDays")
response.cookies(usercode)("ExpDate") = Request.Form("ExpDate")
response.cookies(usercode)("InDate") = Request.Form("InDate")
response.cookies(usercode)("NumberofPeople") = PartySize
response.cookies(usercode)("optVisa") = Request.Form("optVisa")
response.cookies(usercode)("optMC") = Request.Form("optMC")
response.cookies(usercode)("optDiscover") = _
    Request.Form("optDiscover")
response.cookies(usercode)("optAmEX") = Request.Form("optAmEX")
response.cookies(usercode)("OutDate") = CheckOutDate
```

Notice that the Subtotal is obtained by multiplying the rate by the number of days.

5. You also need to set an expiration date for the cookie so that it will not be deleted at the end of the session:

```
response.cookies(usercode).expires = dateadd("y",1,now)
```

6. Save your work and close the checkin.asp file.

➤ **To display the saved cookies in a select list**

1. Open the checkout.asp file for editing.
2. Click the Source tab on the HTML editor window.
3. Locate the select tag with an id of cboCheckOut.
4. Write ASP code that will loop through each cookie looking for valid reservations. For each reservation that is found, set the guests name as a value in the select list. If no valid cookies are found, display "No records found".

Your code should look similar to the following:

```
<%
' Variable to hold the cookie
Dim strKey
' Variable to determine if any reservations exist
Dim blnGuestKey
' Assume that no reservations exist
blnGuestKey = false
For Each strKey In Request.Cookies
```

```
        If Request.Cookies(strKey).HasKeys and _
            Request.Cookies(strKey)("LastName") <> "" Then
            ' A valid cookie found representing a reservation
            blnGuestKey = true
    %>
        <optionvalue="<%=strKey%>"><%=Request.Cookies(strKey) _
("LastName") & ", " & Request.Cookies(strKey) _
("FirstName")%></option>
    <%
        End If
Next
' If no reservations found tell the user
if blnGuestKey = false then
    %>
    <option value="0">no records</option>
    <%
end if
%>
```

5. Save your changes and close checkout.asp

➤ **To display the saved cookies in a form**

1. Open the Reservation.asp file for editing.

2. Click the Source tab on the HTML editor window.

3. Write ASP code that will retrieve the usercode Querystring from the checkout.asp page. If the usercode is not empty, display the Reservation Checkout form.

   Your code should look similar to the following:

```
<%
Dim usercode
' Get the fields from the cookie
usercode = Request.QueryString("usercode")
if usercode <> "" then
    %>
    ' Get values from cookies
    <%
else
    Response.Write "<H3>There was an error" & _
    " retrieving the selected guest for checkout.</H3>"
end if
%>
```

Notice that the split in the code indicates the HTML code on the page. Thus, the first part of the code needs to be entered at the beginning of the page and the second part needs to be entered after the </BODY> tag on the page.

4. Now you need to retrieve the values from the cookie using the usercode and place them on the form. First you set the option buttons for the credit card as follows:

```
if Request.Cookies(usercode)("optVisa") = "on" then _
optVisa = "checked"
if Request.Cookies(usercode)("optMC") = "on" then optMC = "checked"
if Request.Cookies(usercode)("optDiscover") = "on" then _
optDiscover = "checked"
if Request.Cookies(usercode)("optAmEX") = "on" then _
optAmEX = "checked"
```

5. Now find each option button in the HTML code and insert the variable. For example:

```
<INPUT id=optVisa name=optVisa <%=optVisa%> readonly type=radio>
```

6. Next you need to insert each of the other values from the cookie into their respective fields on the form. For example:

```
value="<%=formatcurrency(Request.Cookies(usercode)("SubTotal"))%>"
```

Notice that the VBScript FormatCurrency function can be used to properly format SubTotal.

7. Finally, fill in the Card Number field using the usercode Querystring:

```
value="<%=Request.QueryString("usercode")%>"
```

8. Save your work and test the application by checking in a guest and then checking them out.

Review

The following questions are intended to reinforce key information presented in this chapter. If you are unable to answer a question, review the appropriate lesson and then try the question again. Answers to the questions can be found in the Appendix A, "Questions and Answers."

1. What is an ASP page used for?

2. How does an ASP page use a request object?

3. What is the Browser Capabilities component?

4. Explain the purpose of using a cookie.

CHAPTER 5

Accessing Databases

About This Chapter

In this chapter, you will learn how to display data from a database in an ASP page. You add a data environment to your Microsoft Visual InterDev project and learn how to view and use data from the database in the Data View window. You will also be introduced to Database Designer, a tool for creating and manipulating database tables, and Query Designer, a tool for creating SQL queries.

Before You Begin

To complete the lessons in this chapter you must be able to:

- Use objects from an object model.
- Write simple server-side and client-side scripts.

Lesson 1: Introduction to ActiveX Data Objects (ADO)

In this chapter, you will learn about OLE DB and its relationship to universal data access. You will learn about ActiveX Data Objects (ADO), including the ADO object model and how ADO relates to OLE DB. This chapter discusses how to use the Data Environment to quickly build applications using ADO and how ADO communicates with a database. In addition, you will learn about several data access models and the object hierarchy provided by ADO.

After this lesson, you will be able to:

- Describe the features of Universal Data Access.
- Explain the functions of the Connection, Command, and Recordset objects.

Estimated lesson time: 30 minutes

Universal Data Access

Universal Data Access (UDA) is the Microsoft strategy for providing access to all types of information from a variety of sources besides the traditional relational database. These data sources include mainframe ISAM/VSAM, hierarchical databases, e-mail, file systems, text, and graphical data. OLE DB is the underlying interface that enables UDA. The development interface for OLE DB is Microsoft ActiveX Data Objects (ADO). ADO replaces previous database programming interfaces, such as Data Access Objects (DAO) and Remote Data Objects (RDO). Because ADO is built on top of OLE DB, ADO benefits from the UDA infrastructure.

The strength of the Microsoft UDA strategy is that it is delivered through a common set of object-oriented interfaces. These interfaces are based on the Microsoft Component Object Model (COM), which allows software and components to communicate. Today's data-intensive applications require the integration of information stored not only in traditional database management systems but also in file systems, spreadsheets, e-mail, and more. OLE DB, which is based on COM, is used to provide access to all types of data across an organization, as illustrated in Figure 5.1.

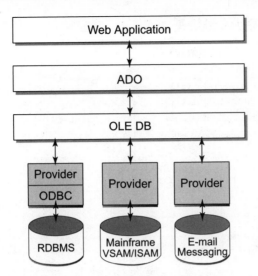

Figure 5.1 How a Web application uses ADO

OLE DB Components

OLE DB is an open specification that extends the capabilities of Open Database Connectivity (ODBC). It does this by providing an open standard for accessing all types of data. Whereas ODBC was created to access relational databases, OLE DB is designed for relational and non-relational information sources. OLE DB includes direct support for ODBC to enable backward compatibility for the broad range of ODBC relational database drivers available today.

OLE DB components consist of data providers, data consumers, and service components, as illustrated in Figure 5.2.

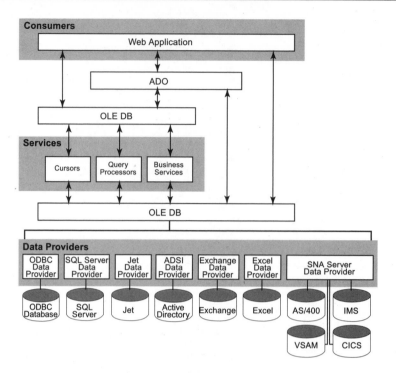

Figure 5.2 How OLE DB components work together

OLE DB Providers

An OLE DB provider is any software component that exposes an OLE DB interface. OLE DB interfaces can be directly exposed by a data store or by a separate code component that communicates at a lower level with an interface on the data store. In both cases, the code that exposes the OLE DB interfaces is referred to as the *data provider*. For example, the OLE DB provider for Microsoft Active Directory Service allows ADO to connect to heterogeneous directory services through the Active Directory Service Interfaces (ADSI).

OLE DB Services

An OLE DB service component is an OLE DB component that implements a common set of OLE DB functionality. Service components are automatically invoked when a consumer requests OLE DB functionality that is not supported by the data provider. An example of a service component is a cursor engine that can consume data from a sequential, forward-only data source to produce scrollable data.

OLE DB Consumers

An OLE DB consumer is a component that consumes OLE DB data. Examples of consumers include services such as query processors; high-level data access models such as ADO; business applications written in languages such as Microsoft Visual Basic, Microsoft Visual C++, or Java; and development tools.

Benefits of Using ActiveX Data Objects

The solution to the problem of accessing different kinds of data throughout the enterprise is to use OLE DB as a data provider and ADO as the data access technology. ADO provides an application-level interface to OLE DB, which gives developers access to the data. Data access based on OLE DB and ADO is suitable for a wide range of application design requirements, from small, single workstation processes to large-scale Web applications. ADO provides consistent, high-performance access to data and supports a variety of development needs, including the creation of front-end database clients and middle-tier business objects. ADO is designed to be the only data interface required regardless of the application type.

ADO Compared with Other Data Access Methods

ADO is the data access method Microsoft recommends for new applications. To fully understand its benefits, however, you should understand how it compares with other data access methods. All of the following data access methods can be used from a variety of tools, including Visual InterDev, Visual Basic, Microsoft Access, and Microsoft Office. However, there are some major differences between the methods:

- ADO is an object model for accessing all types of data through OLE DB.

    Languages such as VBScript and JScript can use ADO, which can then access data from any OLE DB source. You can use ADO to access relational data as well as e-mail or data contained in a spreadsheet.

- RDO is an object model for accessing relational data through ODBC.

    RDO was designed to give developers the ability to access ODBC data without having to code to the ODBC API. RDO is a interface to the ODBC API and provides the functionality of ODBC in a programmable object model. It is designed to take advantage of database servers that use sophisticated query engines, such as SQL Server and Oracle.

- DAO is an object model for accessing local or SQL data through Microsoft Jet databases.

    DAO is the oldest of the three data access methods. With DAO, you can access data in Microsoft Jet databases, Microsoft Jet–connected ODBC databases, and installable indexed sequential access method (ISAM) data sources, such as FoxPro, Paradox, or Lotus 1-2-3. Compared with the newer ADO and RDO technologies, DAO is a slower, less capable data access alternative. DAO, like its companion Microsoft Jet database engine, was originally designed to support ISAM data access.

After reviewing each data access method, you might be wondering why you need ADO if you already use RDO and DAO. The following list describes the benefits of ADO:

- ADO can access all types of data, whereas RDO and DAO can access only relational data.

- The ADO object model is not as complex as that of RDO or DAO and therefore is easier to use, with less coding required.

- ADO combines the best features of RDO and DAO.

- ADO is the standard data access object model across Microsoft tools, including Visual InterDev, Visual Basic, Access, Office, and Microsoft Internet Information Server (IIS).

- ADO can be used in Active Server Pages.

Remote Data Service

Another benefit that ADO provides is the ability to use Remote Data Service (RDS), which is a high-performance Web-based technology that provides database connectivity to your applications. RDS does this by extending ADO and allowing you to access data on a server and manipulate the data on the client. This reduces the number of round trips to the server. Both ADO and RDS are collections of COM objects. They are installed with the Windows NT Option Pack as part of Microsoft Data Access Components (MDAC).

MDAC is the key technology that enables Universal Data Access. MDAC includes the latest versions of the following components:

- ActiveX Data Objects (which includes Remote Data Service)
- OLE DB Provider for ODBC
- ODBC Driver Manager
- Updated ODBC drivers for Microsoft SQL Server, Microsoft Access and Oracle.

The client components of MDAC ship with Microsoft Internet Explorer. The server components ship with the Windows NT Option Pack. You can download the latest version of MDAC at http://www.microsoft.com/data/.

The ADO Object Model

You can use ADO with VBScript, JavaScript, Visual C++, Visual Basic, and any platform that supports both COM and automation. The ADO object model has fewer objects and is easier to use when compared with other data access objects such as RDO and DAO.

The ADO object model provides an easy-to-use set of objects, properties, and methods for creating applications that access and manipulate data. Although ADO objects are creatable outside the scope of a hierarchy, the objects exist within hierarchical relationships, as shown in Figure 5.3. For example, unlike with previous database programming interfaces, you do not have to create a Connection object before accessing the Recordset object. With ADO, you can directly create a Recordset object, which automatically creates an implied connection. This concept is sometimes called a "flat" object model.

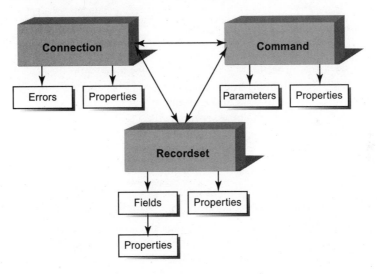

Figure 5.3 The ADO object model

The ADO object model has seven objects, described in the following table:

Object	Description
Command	Maintains information about a command, such as a stored procedure in a SQL Server database. You can execute a command string on a Connection object or a query string as part of opening a Recordset object without defining a Command object. The Command object is useful where you need to define query parameters or execute a stored provider.procedure that returns output parameters.
Connection	Maintains connection information with the data
Error	Contains extended error information about a condition raised by the provider. Since a single statement can generate two or more errors, the Errors collection can contain more than one Error object, all of which result from the same incident.
Field	Contains information about a single column of data within a recordset. The Recordset object supports the Fields collection.
Parameter	Contains a single parameter for a parameterized command. The Command object supports the Parameters collection.
Property	Contains a provider-defined characteristic of an ADO object. The Property object is used when a data provider needs to support specific information about its data source that ADO does not already support. The Property object makes ADO extensible.
Recordset	Contains a set of records returned from a query. You can open a recordset without explicitly opening a Connection object. However, if you first explicitly create a Connection object, you can open multiple Recordset objects on that same connection. This reduces application and server overhead.

Each ADO object features a set of properties and methods that allow you to manipulate the object and its contents. When you work with ADO programmatically, you typically use the following three ADO objects: Connection, Command, and Recordset objects.

The ADO Connection Object

The ADO Connection object establishes a connection to a data source. It allows your application to pass client information to create a connection. For example, before establishing a connection, an application can create a connection string that includes the user's logon name and password. The Connection object also allows you to configure the CommandTimeout property. This property specifies how long ADO should wait when establishing a connection before terminating the attempt and generating an error. In Chapter 6, you will learn how to use the Connection object through ADO code.

The ADO Command Object

Command objects define specific detailed information about what data is retrieved from a database connection. Command objects can be based on either a database object (such as a table, view, or stored procedure) or a SQL query.

A Command object opens a new connection or it uses an existing connection, depending on what you specify in the ActiveConnection property. If you set the ActiveConnection property with a reference to an existing Connection object, the Command object uses that connection. If you specify the ActiveConnection property with a connection string, a new connection is established for the Command object. However, since more than one Command object can use the same Connection object, to increase efficiency you might want to first manually establish a connection via the Connection object. You will learn how to use ADO Command objects in your applications in Chapter 6.

The ADO Recordset Object

An ADO Recordset object represents the entire set of records from a database table or the results of an executed command. You use Recordset objects to manipulate data from a provider. All Recordset objects are constructed using records (rows) and fields (columns).

When you use data in a Recordset object, you are working with a database *cursor*. A cursor is a database object used by applications to manipulate data by individual records rather than by the entire set of records. For example, when you create a recordset, only one record is active at a time. You can change or delete this active record without affecting the other records in the current set, then make the next, or previous, record active.

Setting the CursorType Property

The CursorType property determines how you can use the records in a recordset. You set the CursorType property prior to opening a recordset. If you do not do this, a forward-only cursor is used by default. Four different cursor types are available in ADO, as described in the following table:

Cursor	Description
Dynamic	Provides the most functionality of the cursor types, but uses the most overhead. Dynamic cursors allow you to view additions, changes, and deletions by other users as the modifications occur. In OLE DB, a bookmark is a value that identifies a record (or row) in a recordset. Bookmarks allow data consumers to move quickly to a record and access records randomly based on the bookmark value. A Dynamic cursor allows any type of movement through the recordset that does not rely on bookmarks. It also allows bookmarks if the provider supports them. The dynamic cursor is a good choice if your application must detect all concurrent updates made by other users.
Forward-only	Behaves identically to a static cursor except that it allows you to scroll only forward through records. This improves performance in situations where you need to make only a single pass through a recordset. If your application does not require scrolling through the recordset, the forward-only cursor is the best way for retrieving data quickly with the least amount of overhead.
Keyset	Behaves like a dynamic cursor, except that it prevents you from seeing records that other users add and prevents access to records that other users delete. Data changes by other users are still visible. It always supports bookmarks and therefore allows all types of movement through the recordset.
Static	Provides a static copy of a set of records for you to use to find data or generate reports. It always allows bookmarks and therefore allows all types of movement through the recordset. Additions, changes, or deletions by other users are not visible. If your application does not need to detect data changes, the static cursor is the best choice.

Lesson Summary

Universal Data Access (UDA) provides access to all types of information, from a variety of sources besides the traditional relational databases. UDA is enabled by an interface called OLE DB. The development interface for OLE DB is Microsoft ActiveX Data Objects (ADO).

The solution to the problem of accessing different kinds of data throughout the enterprise is to use OLE DB as a data provider and ADO as the data access technology. ADO provides an application-level interface to OLE DB, which gives developers access to the data.

You can use ADO with VBScript, JavaScript, Visual C++, Visual Basic, and any platform that supports both COM and automation. An advantage of the ADO object model is that it has fewer objects and is easier to use when compared with other data access objects such as RDO and DAO.

Lesson 2: Adding a Data Connection

The Data Environment designer is an object you can add to your project to provide an interactive, design-time environment that allows you to add data connections. At design time, you can set property values for Connection and Command objects associated with a Data Environment. You can write code to respond to ADO events, execute commands, and return records from a data source.

After this lesson, you will be able to:

- Explain the purpose of the Data Environment.
- Create an OLE DB data connection.
- Describe the two types of DSN.

Estimated lesson time: 45 minutes

Using the Data Environment

The data environment is the repository for storing and reusing data connections and data commands in a Visual InterDev project. A data environment contains the information required to access data in a database, and it contains one or more data connections. Each of these data connections can contain one or more data commands that represent a method for querying or modifying a database.

The first time you add a data connection to your project, Visual InterDev creates a DataEnvironment folder as a subfolder of the Global.asa file, because data connection information is stored in application level variables in Global.asa. Multiple ASP pages can use this information. The illustration in Figure 5.4 shows you the location of the data environment within a project.

Figure 5.4 A DataEnvironment folder in a Web project

Using Visual Data Tools

Visual InterDev offers a suite of database integration features. The following list describes these features and their capabilities.

- Database projects

  These are types of projects that you can add to your Visual InterDev solution. They include tools required to build and manage your database as a separate component from Web pages.

- Data View window

  This is a window that provides a live view of the data to which your database or Web project is currently connected.

- Visual Database tools

  This is a set of tools for managing and querying your database. It includes Database Designer and Query Designer.

- Data environment

  This is a repository in your Web project for information required to connect to and access data in a database.

- Data-bound controls

  These are controls such as textboxes and buttons that you can put on your Web page. They can be bound to specific fields in a database record.

Creating a Connection

In order to display or edit data on your Web pages with Visual InterDev, you must connect to a data source, such as a database. A data connection provides your Web project with access to a particular database in order to display its data on your Web page. Visual InterDev allows you to connect to databases using two protocols: OLE DB and ODBC.

The preferred protocol among developers is OLE DB because it is an efficient, full-featured protocol that allows access to a wide variety of data sources. When you install Visual InterDev, the OLE DB data provider for several commonly used databases, including Microsoft Jet (Access), Microsoft SQL Server, and Oracle, are installed on your computer.

If you have an OLE DB provider for the database, you should use that provider. A list of available OLE DB data providers is displayed when you start the process of creating a data connection, as illustrated in Figure 5.5.

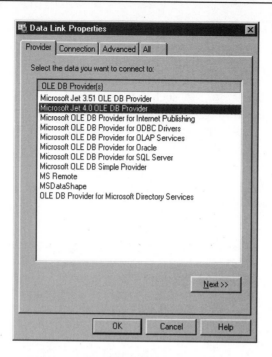

Figure 5.5 A list of OLE DB providers displayed in the Data Link Properties dialog

➤ **To create an OLE DB data connection**

1. Click your project icon in the Project Explorer.

2. From the Project menu, click Add Data Connection.

   The Data Link Properties dialog appears.

3. In the Provider tab, select the data provider for your database.

4. Click Next to open the Connection tab, and then fill in details for the data connection.

   In the Connection tab, you can fill out information such as the name of the database, user name, and password. Each OLE DB provider has different options in the Connection tab.

5. Click Test Connection to be sure that the information you entered is correct.

6. Click OK to create the data connection.

   The Data Connection is created, and Properties dialog for the new connection is dispalyed. You can enter a new name for the connection if desired, and then click OK.

After the data connection has been created, it is displayed under the DataEnvironment folder in your project, underneath the Global.asa folder. You can also browse and edit the data from this database in the Data View window.

Creating a Data Source Name

If you do not have an OLE DB provider for your database, you can use an ODBC driver to create a data connection. To do this, you provide a *connection string*. A connection string is a list of parameters used to connect to the database that typically includes information such as the server name, database type and name, and login information. This connection string can point to a data source name (DSN) that stores information about how to connect to a specific data provider.

A DSN specifies:

- The physical location of the database.
- The type of driver used for accessing the database.
- Any other parameters needed by a driver to access the database.

There are two ways to create a DSN for a Visual InterDev project.

1. Create a DSN while adding a data connection to your project.
2. Use the ODBC Data Source Administrator in the Control Panel before you begin a project.

There are two different types of DSNs: machine DSNs and file DSNs. A machine DSN stores information for a database in the system registry, making it more secure. A file DSN is a text file that contains connection information for a database. This file is saved on your computer. If the production version of the database doesn't reside on the local computer, the file DSN is used. If the production version of the database is on the local computer, the machine DSN is used.

You can add a DSN to a project when adding a data connection. You do this from the Select Data Source dialog. The following steps outline the process for creating a new DSN when adding a data connection.

1. Start the process of creating a new data source. You do this by clicking New in the Select Data Source dialog.
2. Set the driver for the data source. You do this by choosing Select The Database Driver Name in the Create a New Data Source dialog.
3. Locate the data source that you want to connect to your project. Do this by browsing available data source locations and selecting the appropriate name. This creates a file with the extension .dsn.

Setting Data Connection Properties

You need to add a data connection to your project if you want your ASP page to access data in a database.

A data connection tells the project how to access the database, and usually contains information about:

- The type of database to be accessed (for example, SQL Server) and the server name (if appropriate)
- The name of the database (for example, pubs)
- The user name
- The password

You can add as many data connections to a project as you need. For example, if your application requires access to three different databases, you would add three data connections. The illustration in Figure 5.6 shows you the location of the data connection within a project.

Figure 5.6 A data connection within a data environment

➤ **To add a data connection to your project**

1. On the Project menu, click Add Data Connection.

2. Add the name of a data source.

3. Set the Connection Name and Connection String properties for the connection.

Note You can also add a data connection or a data command to your project by right-clicking Data Environment and using the popup menu.

Lesson Summary

The data environment is where data connections and data commands are stored for a Visual InterDev project. A data environment contains the information required to access data in a database. It can have one or more data connections. Each of these data connections can contain one or more data commands that represent a method for querying or modifying a database.

The Visual InterDev tools you use to integrate databases include:

- Database projects
- Data View window
- Visual Database tools
- Data environment

In order to display or edit data on your ASP pages with Visual InterDev, you must connect to a data source, such as a database. A data connection provides your Web project with access to a particular database in order to display its data on your Web page. You can connect to databases using either the OLE DB or ODBC protocols.

Lesson 3: Adding a Data Command Object

After you have added a data connection, you can add a data command object. A data command contains specific information about accessing a particular database object. For instance, a data command can query the author's table of the pubs database so that you can display the contents of that table in a Web page. A data command can run a SQL statement or a stored procedure. In this lesson, you will learn how to add a data command to an ASP page that displays and uses data from a database.

After this lesson, you will be able to:

- Create a data command.
- Use the Query Designer to create a SQL command.

Estimated lesson time: 30 minutes

Creating a Data Command

Once you've created a connection to your database, you can use the Data Environment designer to create Command objects that give you access to data. For example, you can create a simple Command object that gives you access to the data in a table, or a more complex Command object based on a query. You can then use a data environment Command object as a data source in your application. To create a data command, right click on a Connection in the data environment, and click Add Data Command as illustrated in Figure 5.7.

Figure 5.7 Creating a new Data Command object

Note When you move a data command onto an HTML page or an Active Server Page, a Recordset control is added to the page.

A data command can run a SQL statement or a stored procedure depending on the options you select in the data command's property dialog. Figure 5.8 shows you the property dialog for a data command named comByRoyalty.

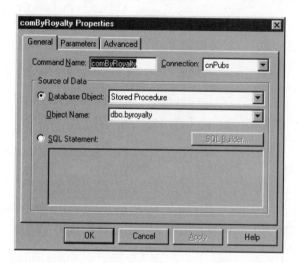

Figure 5.8 A data command that runs a stored procedure

As you can see in the previous figure, the comByRoyalty Command object will run a stored procedure in the Pubs database in SQL Server. You can also use Command objects to return records from tables or from queries based on SQL statements.

Using Query Designer

The Microsoft Query Designer is a graphical tool for creating SQL commands, or queries. By inserting tables, setting options, and entering values, you can create complex, multitable queries.

Query Designer can distinguish the differences between databases such as SQL Server and Oracle, so it can generate and recognize database-specific SQL commands. Queries created in Query Designer can both return data using SQL SELECT commands and create queries that update, add, or delete records in a database, using UPDATE, INSERT, and DELETE.

Query Designer consists of four panes, which are described in the following table:

Pane	Function
Diagram	Displays the input sources—the tables or views—that you are querying

Grid	Displays your specific query options:
	    Which data column to display
	    What rows to select
	    How to group rows

SQL	Displays the SQL statement for the current query
Results	Displays the results of the most recently executed query

➤ **To open and use Query Designer**

1. Right-click the Command object.

2. Click Properties.

3. Select SQL Statement.

4. Click SQL Builder.

5. From the Data View window, drop the table or tables that you want to include in the query into the Diagram pane.

Lesson Summary

After you have created a connection to your database, you can use the Data Environment designer to create Command objects that will give you access to data.

A data command object can run a SQL statement or a stored procedure depending on the options you select in the data command's property dialog.

To graphically create a SQL command, or query, you use the Microsoft Query Designer. By inserting tables, setting options, and entering values, you can create complex, multi-table queries.

An advantage of using Query Designer is that it can distinguish the differences between databases such as SQL Server and Oracle, so it can generate and recognize database-specific SQL commands.

Lesson 4: Adding Data-Bound Controls

In this lesson, you will learn about using the data-bound controls in your data connection that are available in Visual InterDev. Visual InterDev contains a wide selection of data-bound controls that make data access, display, and manipulation easy.

After this lesson, you will be able to:

■ Describe the two types of data-bound controls.

■ Distinguish between client and server-based access.

■ Use the RecordsetNavbar control.

Estimated lesson time: 45 minutes

Types of Controls

Data-bound controls are user interface elements, such as labels, text boxes, and option groups that can display the contents of a database. They are connected, or bound, to the database through a Recordset control. Data-bound controls are located on the Design-Time Controls tab on the Toolbox, and can be added to an ASP page by dragging the control onto the page.

Data-bound controls can be divided into two categories:

■ Data display controls

Data display controls include labels, text boxes, and list boxes. Windows developers should be familiar with these types of data-bound controls.

- Button
- Checkbox
- Grid
- Label
- List box
- OptionGroup
- Text box

■ Data manipulation controls.

Data manipulation controls include Recordset, RecordsetNavBar, and other controls.

- Recordset

    Connects controls on an ASP page with fields in the tables of a database. A Recordset control is a data source for data-bound design-time controls. Recordset controls do not appear on an ASP page.

- RecordsetNavBar

  Creates a set of forward and backward buttons that lets users navigate the data being displayed on an ASP page.

- FormManager

  Creates sets of event-driven forms, such as a data-entry form with Browse, Edit, and Insert modes. For more information, see the section "Using the FormManager Control" later in this chapter.

How Data-Bound Controls Work

Data-bound controls in Visual InterDev are a special form of a design-time control (DTC) that support data binding. You bind fields to the control in a database by setting the control's design-time properties.

A design-time control is a user interface element that creates application functionality. Setting properties of a design-time control generates script that executes at run time. For example, when you need to get text information from a user, you place a design-time text box control on the form to receive the data.

During design time, these controls act just like controls that you would put on a form in an environment such as Visual Basic. You set the controls' properties to specify their appearance and behavior. However, when you change a property, you also change the script that is executed when the page runs.

Advantage of Using Design-Time Controls

An advantage to using design-time controls is their flexibility in targeting—you do not need to write one script for client side processing and another for server-side processing. For example, if you want a Web application to run on many different browsers, you target the server as the platform .All of the generated code will run on the server. However, if you want your Web application to take advantage of Internet Explorer's client-side data binding capability you can generate script that will run on the client.

Connecting Controls to the Data

Once a connection to a data source has been established, you connect fields in a database to the data-bound controls on an ASP page. The key to data access in ASP pages is the Recordset control. The Recordset control does not appear as a part of the user interface. Instead the Recordset control connects items in a database to data-bound controls on an ASP page.

The Recordset control specifies:

- A Data Connection object.
- A database object within that connection or a SQL statement querying the database.
- Other properties that determine how data is read from and written to a database, such as cursor type and cursor location.

Adding a Recordset Control to a Page

There are a number of ways to add a Recordset control to an ASP page. The recommended method is to drag a Data Command object onto a page. Visual InterDev automatically creates the control and binds it to the Data Environment object. You can also manually add the Recordset control from the Toolbox. The illustration in Figure 5.9 contains an example of a Recordset control on an ASP page.

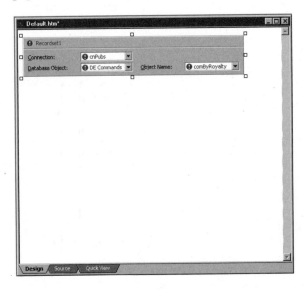

Figure 5.9 A Recordset control on a Web page

You can bind a Recordset control to:

- A Data Command object
- A stored procedure
- A table
- A view

Recordset Control Properties

Recordset controls have a number of properties that you can manipulate. The following table describes some of the important choices. All of them are found on the Advanced tab of the Recordset Property dialog.

Control	Description
Cache size	Sets the size of the cache that will be used for the recordset. Default setting is 100KB.
Command timeout duration	Sets the amount of time, in seconds, that is allotted for a command to execute before processing is stopped and the timeout message is returned from the database.
Cursor location	Sets the location for the cursor, either client-side or server-side. Default setting is client-side cursor.
Cursor type	Sets the types of cursor that will be used to view and manipulate the data. Default setting is 3 - Static.
Lock type	Sets the type of record locking that takes place when several users try to access records simultaneously. Default setting is 3 - Optimistic.
Maximum records to display	Sets the maximum number of records that will be displayed in the browser.

Client-Based vs. Server-Based Access

When setting the properties for a Recordset control, you can specify either the server-side (ASP) or client-side (DHTML) scripting platform. You can change the setting at any time and Visual InterDev will automatically generate the appropriate code to populate the recordset and its related data-bound controls. There are two types of targeting options you can use. One option is to target non-Microsoft browsers from a server using ADO. The other option is to target Microsoft browsers only and reduce the number of round trips to the server. This is done from the client RDS.

Note When you change the scripting platform for the Recordset control, all the controls that are bound to it automatically inherit the scripting platform.

Recordset Cache Properties

On the Implementation tab you can also set how much of the recordset is maintained in memory and which record appears when the recordset is opened. The illustration in Figure 5.10 contains the Implementation tab from the Recordset Property Pages dialog.

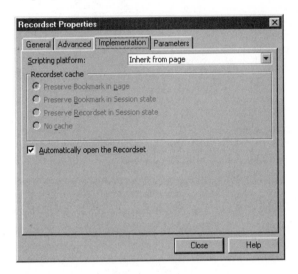

Figure 5.10 The Implementation tab of the Recordset control's Properties dialog

Adding Recordset Navigation

To make an ASP page user friendly, you will want to limit the number of records displayed on the page. You can do this in one of two ways:

- If you are displaying data from a database in individual data-bound controls, use the RecordNavBar control.

- If you are displaying data from a database in a grid control, use the settings on the Navigation tab of the Property Pages dialog for the grid.

The RecordsetNavbar control is located on the Design-Time Controls tab of the Toolbox, as illustrated in Figure 5.11.

Figure 5.11 The RecordsetNavbar control available in the Toolbox

Add it to your page as you would any other design-time control. However, you must add it after you have placed all the controls that it will be managing.

➤ **To use the RecordsetNavbar control on your ASP page**

1. Add the design-time controls that will contain data from the database to your ASP page.

2. Add the RecordsetNavBar control to the page below the controls that it will be using.

3. On the General tab of the RecordsetNavbar Property Pages dialog, set the Recordset data property to the name of the appropriate recordset.

4. Check to see that the Recordset data properties for each of the data-bound controls on the page are set to the appropriate values.

Lesson Summary

Data-bound controls are user interface elements that can display the contents of a database. They are connected, or bound, to the database through a Recordset control. The data-bound controls in Visual InterDev are a unique form of a design-time control (DTC) that supports data binding. You can bind fields to the control in a database by setting the control's design-time properties. There are two types of data controls: data display and data manipulation. Data display controls include:

- Button
- Checkbox
- Grid
- Label
- List box
- OptionGroup
- Text box

Data manipulation controls include:

- Recordset
- RecordsetNavBar
- FormManager

Once you establish a connection to a data source, you can connect fields in a database to the data-bound controls on an ASP page. The key to data access in ASP pages is the Recordset control. The Recordset control connects fields in the tables of a database with controls on an ASP page. Recordset controls do not appear on an ASP page. There are a number of ways to add a Recordset control to an ASP page, but the recommended method is to drag a Data Command object onto a page.

When setting the properties for a Recordset control, you can specify either the server-side (ASP) or client-side (DHTML) scripting platform.

Lesson 5: Customizing Database Access

In this lesson, you will learn how to customize database access by using FormManager to create data input forms. So far in this chapter, you have been adding design-time controls to a page and implicitly using Visual InterDev scripting objects. While designing your user interface, you can set properties for design-time controls in the Properties window or in custom property pages. Script object properties are not displayed in the Properties window because they are run-time properties. In this lesson, you will learn how to use a scripting object programmatically at run time.

After this lesson, you will be able to:

- Define a script object.
- Use FormManager to create an input form.
- List the advantages of using scripting objects.

Estimated lesson time: 30 minutes

Using the Scripting Object Model

When the generated code for a design-time control runs, it dynamically creates a *script object*. The script object is the object you write script against, setting its properties, calling its methods, and responding to its events. You can create the visual interface for your application using design-time controls, and then write script to control the application. Visual InterDev provides you with the script objects found in the following list:

- Button
- Checkbox
- Grid
- Label
- Listbox
- OptionGroup
- PageObject
- Recordset
- RecordsetNavbar
- Textbox

Script objects are part of the scripting object model, which allows you to create Web applications in much the same way you create applications in environments such as Visual Basic. When you add a design-time control to your Web application and set its properties, you are actually creating and manipulating script objects. Using these script objects simplifies Web application development by reducing the complexity and quantity of scripting required to write applications involving interaction between the client (browser) and the server.

Using Script Objects

Each of these script objects have specific properties, methods, and events. However, the onchange event is common to all of these objects. Each of these script objects also has a common method—the Advise method. With the Advise method, you can extend the set of events available to an object by registering the object to be notified when the event occurs. After you have registered, or advised for an event, you can write event handlers for that event as you would for any other event. The following example code shows how to use some methods and properties of the Listbox and Recordset script objects:

```
Sub Listbox1_onchange()
    ' Make the current record be the class the user selected
    Recordset1.moveAbsolute(Listbox1.selectedIndex+1)
End Sub
```

Advantages of Using Scripting Objects

Script objects provide certain advantages. These include:

- Browser and platform independence
- Support for data binding
- Simplified page navigation
- Support for remote scripting

Enabling the Scripting Object Model

You must enable the scripting object model before you can use it so that it can construct the scripting object model framework for the page.

Note Visual InterDev design-time controls require the scripting object model. If you add a design-time control to a page that does not already have the scripting object model enabled, Visual InterDev will prompt you to enable it.

➤ **To enable the scripting object model for a page**

1. Right-click anywhere in the page away from an object or control, click Properties, and then click the General tab.

2. Under ASP settings, click Enable Scripting Object Model. The HTML editor adds the scripting object model framework to the page in <META> tags. You should not alter the content of these tags.

Note   Script objects are available only in Visual InterDev.

Responding to Events

Script objects can generate a predetermined (or implicit) set of events. For example, the script object for a Button design-time control can generate a click event, and the script object for a Textbox design-time control can generate an onchange event. To write a handler for a script object, create a procedure using the object's name and the event to handle. You can write event handlers in any scripting language supported by the browsers used for your application. The following example contains an event handler for a button called btnDisplay. The event handler's code will run when the onclick event occurs.

```
<SCRIPT LANGUAGE="VBSCRIPT">
Sub btnDisplay_onclick()
    Textbox1.value = "Button has been clicked"
End Sub
</SCRIPT>
```

Extending Events for an Object

Although each scripting object has a predetermined, or implicit, set of events to which it can respond, you can also take advantage of other events that the browser generates and use them with your script objects. You can use design-time controls on a client platform and take advantage of the events available in the DHMTL document object model. For example, the Textbox script object supports an implicit onchange event for which you can write handlers. However, on the client you can also write events for the onkeypress, or other events.

You can extend the set of events available to an object by *advising* for an event, or registering the object to be notified when the event occurs. After you have advised the object for an event, you can write event handlers for that object's event as you would for any other event.

To allow for advising, each object supports an Advise method that allows you to register a specific event. When you advise, you specify the name of the event and the name of a function that will be called when the event occurs.

Note Advising for events is generally practical only when your scripting target platform is client. If your platform is server and you advise for an event such as onkeypress, you will cause a round trip to the server each time the event occurs.

You can advise and unadvise for an event at any time. A common time to do so is when a page is loaded. For client scripting targets, you create a handler for the window object's onload event and call the advise method there. The following example shows how you how to advise at page initialization time to have a DHTML onkeypress event sent to a text box named Textbox1.

```
<SCRIPT LANGUAGE="VBScript">
Function window_onload()
    objAdviseTextbox1 = Textbox1.advise("onkeypress", "checkkeys()")
End function
</SCRIPT>
```

In the previous example, when the onkeypress event fires for Textbox1, it will call the function checkkeys. The result of the advise method is an Advise object named objAdviseTextbox1 that you can use later if you need to unadvise for the event.

The function you specify in the advise method works like any event handler. If the event passes parameters, you can get those using the DHTML window object's event method. The following example shows the handler for the onkeypress event in the previous example. It examines each keystroke that occurs in the Textbox1 object and copies only the numbers to the object Textbox2.

```
Function checkkeys()
    character = Chr(window.event.keycode)
    If character >= "0" and character <= "9" Then
        Textbox2.value = Textbox2.value & character
    End If
End Function
```

You can also cancel event notifications when you no longer need the event. You do this by calling the object's Unadvise method. The Unadvise method requires the advise object returned by the Advise method as well as the name of the event. The following shows an example of calling the Unadvise method.

```
Textbox1.unadvise("onkeypress", objAdviseTextbox1)
```

Using the FormManager Control

FormManager is a design-time control that facilitates the creation of data input forms with modes such as Browse, Edit, and Insert. You add the controls that you need; FormManager generates the script that enables and disables the buttons, and updates or cancels changes to the recordset. All you need to do is set values for methods and properties for the controls on the form. FormManager handles most of the other operations.

This control does not have a corresponding script object, but you can specify modes that handle property settings. It can manipulate the script objects of other controls associated with the form, such as the Recordset and Button controls.

➤ **To create an input form using FormManager**

1. Create the data entry ASP form in a project.

2. Add a Data Connection object to the project, along with a data source name.

3. Create a Recordset control.

4. Leave the Lock Type on the default 3 - Optimistic or any setting other than read-only.

5. Add data-bound controls that will display the fields in the database and make sure that the Recordset property points to the recordset you added above.

6. If you use separate data-bound controls to display the contents of the database, add a RecordsetNavbar control, and then set the Recordset property to the recordset that you added above.

7. Add the command buttons—such as add, delete, or save—that will implement the different modes your page will have.

8. Add a FormManager control at the bottom of your page.

➤ **To specify the modes that your page will use**

1. Identify each mode and specify the property settings and methods for the control while the mode is active.

2. Specify the transition events between the modes that trigger specific actions.

3. Add the actions that occur after the transition event is triggered but before the transition is complete.

Note In order to validate user input, you will need to develop and call separate validation functions.

Writing Appropriate Script for the Target Platform

What your scripts do is based on the target platform where scripts run. If the target platform is server, you can use the scripting object model and the ASP programming model, including IIS objects. If your target platform is the client, the scripting object model extends the document object model provided by DHTML.

Knowing what the target platform is will keep you from attempting to write procedures that are not appropriate for the context. For example, if your target platform is the server, you should not display messages directly to the user with functions such as MsgBox or the Alert method. Although these functions might work properly at times, they generally result in an error because the message displays on the server rather than to the user.

Lesson Summary

You can customize your database access by using the scripting object model. When the generated code for a design-time control runs, it dynamically creates a script object. The script object is the object you write script against, setting its properties, calling its methods, and responding to its events. Each script object has specific properties, methods, and events. However, the onchange event and the Advise method are common to each script object.

Script objects can generate a predetermined set of events. For example, the script object for a Button design-time control can generate an onkeypress event, and the script object for a Textbox design-time control can generate an onchange event. To write a handler for a script object, you create a procedure using the object's name and the event to handle. Event handlers can be written in any scripting language supported by the browsers used for your application.

The FormManager is a design-time control that facilitates the creation of data input forms with modes such as Browse, Edit, and Insert. You simply add the controls you need; FormManager generates the script that enables and disables the buttons, and updates or cancels changes to the recordset. All you need to do is set values for methods and properties for the controls on the form and FormManager handles most of the other operations.

Although the FormManager control does not have a corresponding script object, you can specify modes that handle property settings.

Lesson 6: Managing Databases

In this lesson, you will learn about several of the database management tools that are available with Visual InterDev. These tools include the Data View window and Database Designer. The Data View window is a graphical environment for creating, viewing, and editing database objects. It is your starting point for managing database objects such as database diagrams, tables, stored procedures, and more in any ODBC-compliant database. The Database Designer is a visual tool allowing you to create, edit, or delete database objects for databases while you're directly connected to the database in which those database objects are stored.

After this lesson, you will be able to:

- Create a database project.
- Use the Database Designer.

Estimated lesson time: 30 minutes

Using the Data View Window

Visual InterDev includes the Data View feature, which provides a visual interface to all of the databases being used within a Web application. The Data View also provides a live connection to each database, which allows you to work directly with these databases within the Visual InterDev during development. For example, you can open any database to view tables, defined views, and stored procedures.

In addition, the Data View can provide detailed information on objects and properties within each database. This includes table definitions and field types, key structures, and stored procedures. The Data View also works with the Query Designer and Database Designer features, and provides a sophisticated database development, administration, and maintenance system tightly integrated with the Visual InterDev. Figure 5.12 shows the Data View window with a connection to the Pubs database.

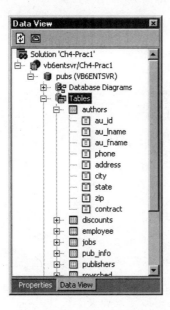

Figure 5.12 Viewing table properties with the Data View window

The Data View window is visible when a data connection has been established for your database or Web project. When you move a database object from the Data View window to the data environment, Visual InterDev automatically creates a data command that represents that database object.

Note Some databases have objects different from those listed here. For more information about the objects available from your databases, consult its documentation.

You can use Data View to open, design, edit, and delete views in your database. For each data connection, Data View displays any view in the database associated with the data connection. You can expand the Views folder to see the columns in the views. Furthermore, double-clicking a view icon in Data View opens the view and displays its data, which you can edit. You can also use the View Designer to modify a view's definition. The View Designer looks just like the Query Designer, but it creates a view rather than a query when you save your definition.

Using the Data View window you can:

- Identify the location of existing data.
- Identify the format of existing data.
- Identify migration considerations for a Web project.
- Identify data conversion requirements for a Web project.

Working with Stored Procedures in Data View

You can also use Data View to open, execute, debug, copy, delete, and rename stored procedures in your database. For each data connection, Data View displays any stored procedures in the database associated with the data connection. You can expand the Stored Procedures folder to see the parameters for the stored procedures.

Creating Database Projects

A database project is a collection of one or more data connections, which contain a database and the information needed to access it. When you create a database project, you can connect to one or more databases and view components through a graphical user interface.

➤ **To create a database project**

1. Start Visual InterDev.
2. Under Visual Studio, click Database Projects.
3. Give your project a name and click Open.
4. In the Select Data Source dialog, you will be queried to select or create a new data source. Click OK.

Note You can also create a database project by clicking New Project from the File menu.

The illustration in Figure 5.13 shows the location of a database project in Project Explorer.

Figure 5.13 A database project shown in the Project Explorer

By creating a database project, you can:

- Create, edit, or delete database objects in the Database Designer for SQL Server and Oracle databases while you are directly connected.
- Interact with SQL Server and Oracle server databases using database diagrams.

  Database diagrams graphically represent tables, the columns they contain, and the relationships between them. You can use database diagrams to view the tables in your database and their relationships, or perform complex operations to alter the structure of your database, such as changing table definitions, column names, and data types.

- Create, modify, execute, and save queries with the Query Designer.

  The Query Designer includes a visual query tool, an interactive SQL window, and an output window for viewing and updating records.

- Create and execute stored procedures.

Using the Database Designer

Database Designer is a visual tool that allows you to create, edit, and delete database objects while you are connected to a database. You interact with the server database using database diagrams, which graphically represent the tables in your database. These tables display the columns they contain and the relationships between the tables as illustrated in Figure 5.14.

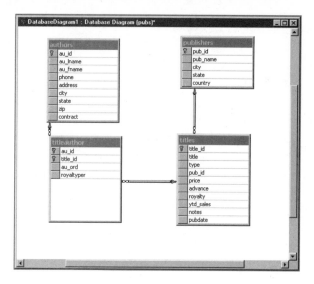

Figure 5.14 A database diagram showing relationships in the Pubs database

You use database diagrams to:

- View the tables and their relationships in your database.
- Alter the physical structure of your database.

Changing the structure of a database diagram does not automatically change the structure of the underlying database. Changes to the database are not saved until you save the table or database diagram that you have created.

Saving Changes to Database Diagrams

You have two choices for saving changes:

- Save the changes to the selected tables or the database diagram and have the changes modify the server database.
- Save a change script that contains the SQL code generated by your changes to the diagram. With a change script, you can edit the change script in a text editor and then apply the modified script to the server database.

Other Database Tools

Stored procedures can make managing your database and displaying information about that database and its users very easy. Stored procedures are a precompiled collection of SQL statements and optional control-of-flow statements stored under a name and processed as a unit.

Stored Procedures

Stored procedures are stored within a database and can be executed with one call from an application. They allow user-declared variables, conditional execution, and other powerful programming features. Stored procedures can contain program flow, logic, and queries against the database. They can accept parameters, output parameters, return single or multiple result sets, and return values.

A stored procedure executes faster than individual SQL statements because it is compiled on the server when it is created. When you create a stored procedure in Microsoft Visual Database Tools, the stored procedure appears in the Stored Procedures folder in Data View. You can expand a stored procedure in Data View to see a list of the parameters it contains, as illustrated in Figure 5.15.

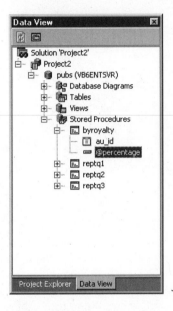

Figure 5.15 Parameter of the byroyalty stored procedure in the Data View window

Database Views

A view is a virtual table whose contents are defined by a precompiled query that is stored and maintained on the database server. For SQL Server databases, views are created, edited, and deleted in Microsoft SQL Enterprise Manager. A view looks like an actual database table made up of a set of named columns and rows of data.

However, a view does not exist as a stored set of data values in a database. Instead, it is a query result set that is maintained on the server and updated each time you open the view. You can use a view in the View Designer in Visual InterDev to extract and combine information you need from one or more existing tables, as illustrated in Figure 5.16.

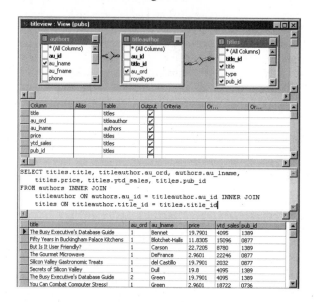

Figure 5.16 A view object from the Pubs database shown in the View Designer

In addition, you can modify data in a view—when you do this, you are actually changing data in the underlying database tables. Changes to data in those tables are automatically reflected in the views derived from them. You can use Data View to open, design, edit, and delete views in your database. For each data connection, the Data View displays any views in the database associated with the data connection. You can expand the Views folder to see the columns in the views.

Lesson Summary

Two database management tools that are available with Visual InterDev include the Data View window and Database Designer.

The Data View window provides a visual interface to all of the databases being used within a Web application. The Data View also provides a live connection to each database. This enables you to work directly with these databases within the Visual InterDev during development.

The Database Designer is a visual tool that allows you to create, edit, and delete database objects while you are connected to a database. You can interact with a server database using database diagrams, which are graphic representations of the tables in your database

Other tools include stored procedures and Microsoft SQL Enterprise Manager, the latter of which allows you to create and edit views. Stored procedures are a collection of SQL statements and optional control-of-flow statements stored under a name and processed as a unit.

Lab 5: Working with ActiveX Data Objects

In this lab, you will work with the Data Environment in Visual InterDev to create an ActiveX Data Objects (ADO) connection to a SQL server database. Then you will modify the Reservation form to use Data Bound controls to display data.

To see a demonstration of this lab, run the Lab05.exe animation located in the Animations folder on the companion CD-ROM that accompanies this book.

Estimated lab time: 30 minutes

Before you begin

You should have already completed Labs 2, 3, and 4. If you have not, follow the steps in Lab 2 to create the Chateau Web project and use the files in the Labs\Lab04\Partial folder to obtain the necessary files to complete this lab.

Exercise 1: Adding a Data Connection

In this exercise, you will install the Chateau database on your SQL 7 server. Then you will use the Data Environment to create an interface between the Chateau Web site and database.

➤ **To install the Chateau database**

1. Open Visual InterDev or select New Project from the file menu if it is already open.

2. In the New Project dialog, expand the Visual Studio folder in the left pane.

3. Expand the Database Projects folder and select the New Database Project icon in the right pane.

4. Name the project Data and select Open. You can put the project in the same local folder as Chateau.

5. You will now be presented with the Select Data Source dialog. Make sure that you have chosen the File Data Source tab and click New.

6. Select SQL Server from the list of drivers and click Next.

7. Type Data as the name of the DSN, and then click Save.

8. In the Create New Data Source dialog box, click Next, and then click Finish.

9. In the Description field type Install Chateau Database. In the Server field, type the name of your server or select (Local) if you are running on the same PC. Click Next.

10. Select an Authentication option that gives you full administrative rights to your SQL server. If you are not sure if your Windows NT access has administrative rights, select the With SQL Server Authentication option and type in sa for the login ID and the password for your sa account. Click Next.

11. Check the Change The Default Database To box and make sure that Master appears in the drop-down list. Click Next, and then click Finish.

12. Click Test Data Source… to make sure it is working correctly, and then click OK.

13. Click OK to close the dialog box.

14. In the Select Data Source dialog box, choose Data.dsn from the list of data sources and click OK.

15. Enter the password for sa and click OK.

16. Right-click the project icon in the Project Explorer window and select Add Data Connection from the menu.

17. Select Data.dsn from the list of data sources and click OK.

18. Type in a password if required and click OK.

19. Right-click the newly created connection and select Add SQL Script from the menu.

20. Choose the Existing tab and browse for the Chateau.sql file in the Labs\Lab05\Partial folder, and then click OK.

21. Double-click the Chateau.sql file that appears under the connection to open it in the design window.

22. Right-click in the design window and select Execute from the menu.

    You can also run the SQL script in the SQL Server 7.0 Query Analyzer.

23. After a few minutes, the Chateau database will be created.

24. Check the results window to make sure there were no critical errors.

➤ **To add a data environment to your project**

1. Open the Chateau project in Visual InterDev.

2. Right-click the project in Visual InterDev and select Add Data Connection from the menu.

   The Select Data Source dialog box appears.

3. Click the File Data Source tab and then click New.

4. Select SQL Server from the list of drivers and click Next.

5. Type Chateau as the name of the DSN, click Next, and then click Finish.

6. In the Description field, type Chateau Data Source. In the Server field, type the name of your server or select (Local) if you are running on the same PC. Click Next.

7. Select the With SQL Server Authentication option, type Chateau for the login ID and leave the password blank, and then click Next.

8. Select the Change The Default Database To box, select Chateau inform the drop-down list, and then click Next.

9. Click Next, and then click Finish to close the dialog box.

10. Test the data source to make sure it is working correctly, and then click OK.

11. Choose Chateau.dsn from the list of datasources and click OK.

12. When the SQL Server Login dialog box appears,type your login ID and password, and then click OK to log in.

13. Change the name of Connection1 cnChateau, and then click OK.

➤ **To create a Data Command**

1. Right click the cnChateau connection that you created and select the Add Data Command.

2. Change the name of the command to cmdChateau.

3. Select the SQL Statement option, and then click the SQL Builder button.

4. In the Data View window, expand the Chateau icon and the Tables icon below it.

5. Locate the Rooms table and drag it into the upper pane of the SQL Builder.

6. Select the Type and Rate checkboxes to include these columns in the query.

7. After the word SELECT in the query pane type the word DISTINCT.

   Your Select statement should resemble this:

   ```
   SELECT DISTINCT Type, Rate
   FROM dbo.Rooms
   ```

8. Save your work and close the SQL Builder.

Exercise 2: Using Design-Time Controls

In this exercise, you will modify the Reservation form to lookup room types and automatically fill in the rate for that room using Design Time controls.

1. Open the Reservation.htm file for editing.

2. Click the Design tab on the HTML editor window.

➤ **To add a Recordset control**

1. Select the Design-Time Controls tab in the toolbox and drag a Recordset control onto the reservation page.

2. Right-click the Recordset control and select Properties. Change the General properties to reflect the following values:

Property	Value
Name	rsRoomType
Connection	cnChateau
Database Object	DE Commands
Object Name	cmdChateau

3. Close the Properties dialog.

➤ **To bind a Design-Time control to the Recordset**

1. Select the Room Type field on the form and delete it.

2. Drag and drop a Listbox Design Time control in place of the Room Type field.

3. Right-click the Listbox control and select Properties. Set the following properties for the control:

Property	Value
Name	cboRoomType
Style	Dropdown
Recordset	rsRoomType
Field	Type

4. Proceed to the Lookup tab and set the following properties:

Property	Value
Row source	rsRoomType
Bound Column	Rate
List field	Type

Note You will use Rate as the bound column so you can set the Rate when the Type changes.

5. Close the Properties dialog.

6. Drag and drop an HTML textbox to the right of the cboRoomType Listbox.

7. Click the Source tab on the HTML editor window and locate the new textbox you added. Change the HTML tag to resemble the following:

```
<INPUT id=Type name=Type style="display:none">
```

Note that this field will store the hidden Room Type text from the Listbox.

➤ **To set HTML controls when the recordset changes**

1. In the Script Outline window, locate the onchange event for cboRoomType and then double-click it to insert this event onto the page.

2. Add code to the onchange event to set the Rate and Type fields on the form to the selected index of the Listbox control.

   Your code should look similar to the following:

```
Sub cboRoomType_onchange()
    FORM1.Rate.value = _
        cboRoomType.getValue(cboRoomType.selectedIndex)
    FORM1.Rate.value = FormatCurrency(FORM1.Rate.value)
    FORM1.Type.value = cboRoomType.getText(cboRoomType.selectedIndex)
End Sub
```

3. Save your work and close Reservation.htm.

4. Open the checkin.asp file for editing.

5. Click the Source tab on the HTML editor window.

6. Change the display value in checkin.asp from cboRoomType to Type, as follows:

```
RoomType = Request.Form("Type")
```

7. Save your work and test the application by checking in a guest.

   Notice that the Rate automatically appears when you change the room type. When you check in a guest, the form should display the room type that you selected.

Review

The following questions are intended to reinforce key information presented in this chapter. If you are unable to answer a question, review the appropriate lesson and then try the question again. Answers to the questions can be found in Appendix A, "Questions and Answers."

1. What is Universal Data Access?

2. What is the purpose of the Data Environment?

3. What are some advantages of using scripting objects?

4. Define a script object.

CHAPTER 6

Understanding Data Access Technologies

About This Chapter

In this chapter, you will learn how to create Web pages that retrieve and update information in a database by using ActiveX Data Objects and the Remote Data Service.

Before You Begin

To complete the lessons in this chapter you must be able to

- Write client-side script.
- Write server-side script.
- Use methods and properties exposed by an object.

Lesson 1: Overview of Structured Query Language

Structured Query Language (SQL) is a language used for querying, updating, and managing relational databases. SQL can be used to retrieve, sort, and filter specific data from the database. In addition, you can add, change, and delete data in a database using SQL statements.

A fundamental understanding of the SQL language will help you to create applications that communicate effectively with the database. An application using SQL can ask the database to perform tasks rather than requiring application code and processing cycles to achieve the same result. More important, effective use of SQL can minimize the amount of data that must be read from and written to a remote database server. Finally, effective use of SQL can minimize the amount of data sent across the network. Minimizing disk I/O and network I/O are the most important factors for improving application performance.

After this lesson, you will be able to:

- Describe the purpose of SQL.
- Define the syntax of a simple SQL statement.
- Filter records in a query using a simple SQL statement.

Estimated lesson time: 25 minutes

Relational Database Concepts

In this chapter, you will learn how to use ADO to work with relational databases, for which you must have a basic understanding of a relational database model. The relational model is the standard for database design. In this model, the database stores and presents data as a collection of tables. A structure is defined by establishing relationships between tables; the relationship between tables links data in the database instead of modeling the relationships of the data according to the way the structure is physically stored. The relational database model offers the following benefits:

- Organizes data in a collection of tables making the design easy to understand.
- Provides a relationally complete language for data definition, retrieval, and update. It is nonprocedural and criteria-based.
- Provides data integrity rules that define consistent states of the database to improve data reliability.

A relational database management system (RDBMS) is software that allows you to represent your data according to the relational model. Relational databases support a standard language called Structured Query Language (SQL). SQL is a comprehensive language for controlling and interacting with a database management system (DBMS), and is a standard approved by the American

National Standards Institute (ANSI). The Northwind database is a sample relational database that is included with Microsoft SQL Server 7.0.

Note Structured Query Language is discussed in detail later in this lesson.

Tables

The relational database model presents data as a collection of tables. A table is a logical grouping of related information. For example, the Northwind database has a table that lists all the employees and another table that lists all the customer orders. Tables are made up of rows and columns—rows are often referred to as records and columns are referred to as fields. Figure 6.1 shows the Employees table from the Northwind database.

EmployeeID	LastName	FirstName	Title	TitleOfCourtesy	BirthDate	HireDate
1	Davolio	Nancy	Sales Representative	Ms.	12/8/48	5/1/92
2	Fuller	Andrew	Vice President, Sales	Dr.	2/19/52	8/14/92
3	Leverling	Janet	Sales Representative	Ms.	8/30/63	4/1/92
4	Peacock	Margaret	Sales Representative	Mrs.	9/19/37	5/3/93
5	Buchanan	Steven	Sales Manager	Mr.	3/4/55	10/17/93
6	Suyama	Michael	Sales Representative	Mr.	7/2/63	10/17/93
7	King	Robert	Sales Representative	Mr.	5/29/60	1/2/94
8	Callahan	Laura	Inside Sales Coordinato	Ms.	1/9/58	3/5/94
9	Dodsworth	Anne	Sales Representative	Ms.	1/27/66	11/15/94

Figure 6.1 The Employees table from the Northwind database

Records

A record contains information about a single entry in a table. For example, a record in an Employees table would contain information on a particular employee.

Fields

A record is composed of multiple fields. Each field in a record contains a single piece of information about the record. For example, an Employee record has fields for Employee ID, Last Name, First Name, and so forth.

Keys

To uniquely identify a row, each table should have a primary key. The primary key is a field, or combination of fields, whose value is unique for each row, or record, in the table. For example, the Employee ID field is the primary key for the Employees table. No two employees can have the same ID.

A table can also contain fields that are foreign keys. A foreign key "points to" a primary key field in a related table. For example, in the Northwind database, the

234 Web Applications with Microsoft Visual InterDev 6.0 MCSD Training Kit

Orders table contains a Customer ID field. Each Customer ID in the Orders table identifies which customer made the order.

The relationship between the Orders and Customers table is a one-to-many relationship—that is, each customer might have more than one order. Figure 6.2 illustrates how one customer can have many orders.

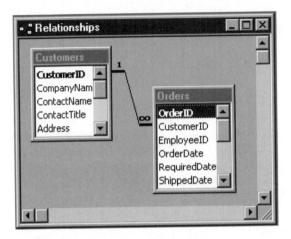

Figure 6.2 Relationship between an Orders table and a Customers table

The SQL Select Statement

The SQL Select statement returns information from the database as a set of records. The Select statement is divided into three major sections:

- SELECT

    The SELECT section allows you to specify which fields will be returned from the query.

- FROM

    The FROM section allows you to specify which tables will be used to get the fields specified in the SELECT section of the SQL statement.

- WHERE (Optional)

    The WHERE section allows you to specify a criteria used to limit the selection of records. You can filter queries based on multiple fields.

The minimum syntax for a Select statement is:

SELECT *fields* FROM *tables*;

To perform this operation, the database engine searches the specified table or tables, extracts the chosen fields, selects rows that meet the criterion, and sorts or groups the resulting rows into the order specified. You can select all fields in a table by using the asterisk (*). For example, the following SQL statement will return all the fields of all the records from an Employees table:

```
SELECT *
FROM Employees;
```

However, it is not very efficient to always return all the data from a table. By adding a WHERE clause to the end of the statement, you can specify that only certain records be returned. The following example retrieves all fields from all records in the Employees table that have a last name equal to Davolio:

```
SELECT *
FROM Employees
WHERE LastName = 'Davolio';
```

Note the use of the apostrophes surrounding the word Davolio in the previous example. Apostrophes are used when the value in a WHERE clause is a string. In this case, LastName is a string value in the database. When a numeric value is specified in a WHERE clause, apostrophes are not used, as shown in the following example.

```
SELECT *
FROM Employees
WHERE EmployeeID = 1;
```

The WHERE IN Clause

Using the WHERE clause with the In operator, you can determine whether the value of an expression is equal to any of several values in a specified list. For example, you can use the WHERE IN clause to return the last names and residing countries of all employees, as illustrated in the following example code and in Figure 6.3.

```
SELECT LastName, Country
FROM Employees
WHERE Country IN ('UK', 'USA');
```

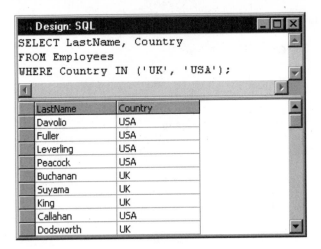

Figure 6.3 Using the In operator with a WHERE clause to filter records

The WHERE BETWEEN Clause

A selection of records between two criteria can also be returned. Note that you must include number signs (#) around the dates as shown in the following example:

```
SELECT OrderID
FROM Orders
WHERE OrderDate
BETWEEN #01/01/93# AND #01/31/93#;
```

Using the Like Operator

You can use the Like operator to find values in a field that match a pattern that you specify. You can specify the complete value, as in Like 'Smith', or you can use wildcard characters to find a range of values, as in Like 'Sm%'. If you enter Like 'C%' in an SQL query, the query returns all field values beginning with the letter C. In the following example, all records where the last name starts with the letter D are returned.

This is also illustrated in Figure 6.4.

```
SELECT LastName
FROM Employees
WHERE LastName Like 'D%';
```

Figure 6.4 Syntax and results of a SQL statement using the Like operator

The ORDER BY Clause

By default, records are returned in the order they were entered in the database. The optional ORDER BY clause can be used to sort a query's resulting records on a specified field, or fields, in ascending or descending order. The ASC option indicates ascending order, DESC indicates descending order. The default sort order is ascending (A to Z, 0 to 9). The following example selects all fields from the Employees table sorted descending by last name:

```
SELECT *
FROM Employees
ORDER BY LastName DESC;
```

Lesson Summary

The relational database model presents data as a collection of tables. A table is a logical grouping of related information.

- Each record in a table contains information about a single entry in the table. A record is composed of multiple fields.
- Each field in a record contains a single piece of information about the record.
- Each table should have a primary key to uniquely identify a row. The primary key is a field or combination of fields whose value is unique for each record in the table.

A table can also contain fields that are foreign keys. A foreign key "points to" a primary key field in a related table.

Structured Query Language (SQL) is a language used in querying, updating, and managing relational databases. SQL can be used to retrieve, sort, and filter specific data to be extracted from the database. The SQL Select statement returns information from the database as a set of records. The Select statement is divided into three major sections: SELECT, FROM, and WHERE. In different environments, databases have different implementations of the same SQL functionality, both syntactically and semantically. You must be aware that each implementation of SQL has its own support for different data types, referential integrity, and compiled queries.

Lesson 2: Using ADO in VBScript

In this lesson, you will learn how to connect to a data source using an ADO Connection object. You will also learn how to use ADO objects to create a connection from a Web page to a data source, retrieve and modify data, run stored procedures, and handle errors. In addition, you will learn how to use the Connection object to establish a connection to a data source and pass client information, such as user name and password, to the database for validation.

After this lesson, you will be able to:

- Establish a connection with a data source.
- Explain the purposes of the Recordset object.
- Define a Connection object.
- Describe error handling strategies for database access.

Estimated lesson time: 25 minutes

Establishing a Database Connection

As discussed in Chapter 5, a Connection object represents an open connection to a data source or OLE DB provider. You can use the Connection object to run commands or queries on the data source. When a recordset is retrieved from the database, it is stored in a Recordset object.

To create a Connection object, you supply the name of either an ODBC data source or an OLE DB provider.

Note To support as many data sources as possible, you can use ADO and ODBC to access a database. However, when using a data source that has an associated OLE DB provider—such as Microsoft Access, SQL Server, or Oracle—it is recommended that you use this provider instead of the older ODBC driver.

When you open the Connection object, you attempt to connect to the data source. A typical ADO-based application uses the following operations to access a data source:

1. Create the Connection object.

    Specify the connection string with information such as data source name, user identification, and password.

2. Open the connection.

    Open the ADO connection to the data source.

3. Execute a SQL statement.

   Once the connection is open, you can run a query. You can run this query asynchronously, if you choose, which means that ADO will populate the recordset in the background; this lets your application perform other processes without waiting.

4. Use the records returned from the query.

   The records are now available to your application to browse or update. A cursor is a temporary table in memory that contains the results of a query. Whether you can add, update, or delete data in the recordset depends on the cursor type, which you learned about in Chapter 5.

5. Terminate the connection.

   The connection to the data source is dropped.

Opening a Connection

To define the connection, you simply set properties for the Connection object. Using the collections, methods, and properties of a Connection object, you can do the following:

- Configure the connection using the ConnectionString, ConnectionTimeout, and Mode properties.
- Specify an OLE DB provider with the Provider property.
- Establish, and later close, the physical connection to the data source with the Open and Close methods.
- Execute a command, such as calling a stored procedure, with the Execute method.
- Manage transactions on open connections. You can also use nested transactions if the provider supports them. You manage transactions using the BeginTrans, CommitTrans, and RollbackTrans methods, as well as the Attributes property.

Note A transaction delimits the beginning and end of a series of data access operations that transpire across a connection. ADO ensures that changes to a data source using a transaction all occur successfully or not at all.

- Examine errors returned from the data source with the Errors collection.

➤ **To establish a connection with a data source**

1. Create a Connection object by calling CreateObject and passing it the ADODB.Connection parameter.

2. Set the ConnectionTimeout property of the Connection object. ConnectionTimeout determines, in seconds, how long the object will wait before timing out when connecting to a data source.

3. Set, in seconds, the CommandTimeout property of the Command object. CommandTimeout determines, in seconds, how long the object will wait for the results of a command or query.

4. Use the Open method to connect to the data source.

Using the Connection Object's Open Method

You use the Open method of the Connection object to establish a connection, and then, when the connection is active, issue commands against it and process the results. The syntax of the Open method is as follows:

*connection.*Open *ConnectionString, UserID, Password, Options*

The arguments for the Open method contain the following information:

- ConnectionString

  An optional String value containing connection information. This information is used to specify:

  - The name of a provider to use for the connection.

  - The name of a provider-specific file.

- UserID

  An optional String value containing a user name to employ when establishing the connection.

- Password

  An optional String value containing a password to use when establishing the connection.

- Options

  An optional ConnectOptionEnum value that determines whether the Open method should return after (synchronously) or before (asynchronously) the connection is established. You can set the value to either adConnectUnspecified or adAsyncConnect.

After the Open method succeeds in connecting to the data source, you can run queries. All the arguments for the Open method are optional because you can specify the connection information using the Connection object's ConnectionString property, as shown in the following code:

```
Sub MakeConnection()
    ' Declare the object variable
    Dim cnPubs

    ' This variable will contain the connection information
    Dim strConnect

    ' Instantiate the object variable
    Set cnPubs = CreateObject("ADODB.Connection")

    ' Define the OLE DB connection string
    strConnect = "Provider=SQLOLEDB;" & _
            "Data Source=VB6ENTSVR;" & _
            "Initial Catalog=Pubs"

    ' Open the database connection
    cnPubs.Open strConnect, "sa", ""
End Sub
```

Note The "Data Source=" value in the connection string is the name of the remote server. The "Initial Catalog=" value is the database name in the external data source.

Using Connection Information

Instead of using literal values for the Connection object properties, you can use application variables. When you use Microsoft Visual InterDev to add a data connection to a Web project, Visual InterDev automatically adds script to the Global.asa file that stores information about the connection in application variables. You can access these application variables from code in an .asp file.

The advantage to using application variables when creating a connection is that you can change the value of the variables in the Global.asa file. The new values will then be used by any of your .asp files that refer to the variables. Visual InterDev modifies the script in the Global.asa file to set the variables to the new values when you change the properties of a data connection.

The following example code shows how you can use application variables to create a connection:

```
Set conn = Server.CreateObject("ADODB.Connection")
conn.ConnectionTimeout = Application("Chateau_ConnectionTimeout")
conn.CommandTimeout = Application("Chateau_CommandTimeout")
conn.Open Application("Chateau_ConnectionString"), _
    Application("Chateau_RuntimeUserName"), _
    Application("Chateau_RuntimePassword")
```

Closing a Connection

Once you have finished working with the database, use the Close method of the Connection object to free any associated system resources. Using the Close method does not remove the object from memory. To do this, you must set the object variable to Nothing. The following example code closes a data connection and sets the object variable to Nothing:

```
conn.Close
Set conn = Nothing
```

Connecting to a OLE DB Data Source

Once you have created a Connection object, you can specify an OLE DB data source provider. You do this by setting the Provider property. Depending on the type of data source you are connecting to, you need to either specify an OLE DB provider or use an ODBC driver. The following table displays the provider parameter values for different OLE DB providers.

OLE DB Provider	ConnectionString
Microsoft Jet	"Provider=Microsoft.Jet.OLEDB.3.51;"
Microsoft ODBC Driver provider	"Provider=MSDASQL.1;DSN=dsnName;UID=userName; PWD='password';"
Oracle	"Provider=MSDAORA;Data Source=mydatasource;User ID=SA;Password='password' "
SQL Server	"Provider=SQLOLEDB;Data Source=sql65server;User ID=sa;Password=' ';Initial Catalog=pubs"

The final step before establishing a connection to a data source is to specify the connection information. You do this by setting the Connection object's ConnectionString property. Connection string arguments that are provider specific are passed directly to the provider, and are not processed by ADO.

When you are finished with the connection, use the Close method to disconnect from a data source. If you are connected to a remote database, any server-side resources that were in use under this active connection are released.

> **Note** While not required, it is proper coding technique to explicitly close all open connections before the application is terminated.

Connection Pooling

Frequently, Web database applications that establish and terminate database connections can reduce database server performance. Microsoft Internet Information Server (IIS) supports efficient connection management by using the connection pooling feature of ODBC 3.5.

Connection pooling maintains open database connections and manages connection sharing across different user requests to maximize performance. On each connection request, the connection pool first determines if there is an idle connection in the pool. If so, the connection pool returns that connection instead of making a new connection to the database.

To allow your ODBC driver to participate in connection pooling, you must set the driver's CPTimeout property in the Windows registry. The CPTimeout property determines the length of time that a connection remains in the connection pool. If the connection remains in the pool longer than the duration set by CPTimeout, the connection is closed and removed from the pool.

You can selectively set the CPTimeout property to enable connection pooling for a specific ODBC database driver by creating a registry key with the following settings:

```
\HKEY_LOCAL_MACHINE\SOFTWARE\ODBC\ODBCINST.INI\driver-name\CPTimeout =
timeout (REG_SZ, units are in seconds)
```

> **Note** By default, IIS activates connection pooling for SQL Server by setting CPTimeout to 60 seconds.

Creating a Connection with Code

In this practice, you will write code to connect to a database using an OLE DB provider.

➤ **To connect to an OLE DB provider using code**

1. Start Visual InterDev and create a new Web project named Ch6-Prac1.

2. Add a new HTML page to the project and set it as the start page for the project.

3. Open the new HTML page in Design view, then click the HTML section on the Toolbox.

4. Drag and drop a button on the page.

   The following HTML is inserted into the BODY section of the Web page:

   ```
   <P><INPUT id=button1 name=button1 type=button value=Button></P>
   ```

5. Enter the following HTML and VBScript code to connect to the Northwind database in SQL Server 7.0.

   ```
   <script language="VBScript">
   Sub button1_onclick()
       Dim cnData

       ' Instantiate the connection
       Set cnData = CreateObject("ADODB.Connection")
       cnData.ConnectionString = "Provider=SQLOLEDB.1;User ID=sa;" & _
           "Initial Catalog=Northwind;Data Source=vb6entsvr"
       cnData.Open

       If cnData.State = 1 Then MsgBox "Connection successful."
       ' Close the connection and release the cnData object
       cnData.Close
       Set cnData = Nothing
   End Sub
   </script>
   ```

Note The Data Source parameter must point to your SQL Server. Because your SQL Server name will most likely be different, you have to adjust that parameter value.

---

6. On the Debug menu, click Start.

   The Web page is opened in Microsoft Internet Explorer.

7. Click Yes if you receive a message box that says, "This page accesses data on another domain. Do you want to allow this?"

8. Click the button on the Web page.

   If the connection was succesful, you will receive a message box notifying you.

9. On the Debug menu, click End.

Managing Database Connections

Proper management of connections from both the server and the client applications is critical to optimal performance. Depending on the way you implement connections in a client application, you might use more system resources than required. For each connection you create, both the client and the server allocate available memory. If you do not carefully manage these connections, performance can be degraded. Each time a connection is established, the database must be contacted and the user must be authenticated. This can lower the performance of a client application. However, since you can create multiple Command objects and Recordset objects from the same Connection object, you might not need more than one connection. You need to determine, based on the application requirements, whether one connection, opened when the application starts and closed when the application terminates, is enough. In addition, most client/server databases such as SQL Server are designed to limit the number of concurrent connections. If a poorly written application opens too many connections, the server might refuse other user requests.

Retrieving Records

ADO allows you to retrieve data from a data source and present the resulting records to the user. You can create a recordset by itself or by using a Command object. You typically return records from a Command object by calling a stored query or a stored procedure. Depending on the functionality you provide, these records can be updated by the user and saved back to the data source.

In addition to returning records, you can also use the Command object to run queries that modify or delete records. These queries are sometimes called action queries. An action query is different from a traditional query because it does not return records. An action query is usually saved in the database in the form of a stored procedure (SQL Server).

To retrieve records from a database, you create a Recordset object. You use properties and methods of the Recordset object to manipulate the data in the recordset.

Creating a Recordset Using CreateObject

The following steps explain how to create a Recordset object.

➤ **To create a Recordset object**

1. Define a Recordset object variable by passing ADODB.Recordset as an argument to CreateObject.

2. Call the Open method of the Recordset object. (See below for details about the parameters that you pass to the Open method.)

Use the following syntax to access records in a data source:

recordset.Open *Source, ActiveConnection, CursorType, LockType, Options*

Note You can include a file named adovbs.inc in your ASP page that uses ADO. The file enables you to use VBScript constants for ADO option parameters so that you do not need to remember the numeric value for the option. The file is installed in the \Program Files\Common Files\system\ado folder of the Web server by the Windows NT Option Pack Setup program.

The following table describes the arguments used by the Open method:

Argument	Description
ActiveConnection	*Optional*. Either a Variant that evaluates to a valid Connection object variable name, or a String containing ConnectionString parameters.
CursorType	*Optional*. A CursorTypeEnum value that determines the type of cursor the provider should use when opening the Recordset.
Options	*Optional*. A Long value that indicates how the provider should evaluate the Source argument if it represents something other than a Command object, or that the Recordset should be restored from a file where it was previously saved.
LockType	*Optional*. A LockTypeEnum value that determines what type of locking (concurrency) the provider should use when opening the Recordset.
Source	*Optional*. A Variant that evaluates to an SQL statement or table name.

Types of Locking Modes

The following table describes your choices for types of locking modes.

Locking Mode	Scenario
Optimistic locking	Locks a record in a data source at the last possible moment during a call to the Update function.
Pessimistic locking	Locks a record at the earliest possible moment during a call to the Edit function and does not unlock it until after the call to the Update function.

The following example creates a dynamic recordset using optimistic locking:

```
rsTitles.Open "Select * from Titles", cnPubs, adOpenDynamic,
adLockOptimistic
```

Using an Explicit Connection Object

You can navigate through the records, or present them to the user, using the Recordset object. Depending on the options used when opening the recordset, you can also give the user the ability to edit, delete, or add new records. By default, a read-only recordset is created. In addition, the recordset supports only the MoveNext navigation method by default. This is called a *forward-only* recordset.

The following example opens a new recordset from an existing connection:

```
<SCRIPT language="VBScript">
Sub button1_onclick()
    Dim cnData
    Dim rsEmployees

    ' Instantiate the connection
    Set cnData = CreateObject("ADODB.Connection")
    cnData.ConnectionString = "Provider=SQLOLEDB.1;User ID=sa;" & _
        "Initial Catalog=Northwind;Data Source=vb6entsvr"
    cnData.Open

    ' Instantiate the recordset
    Set rsEmployees = CreateObject("ADODB.Recordset")

    ' Open the recordset from the existing connection
    rsStudents.Open "Select * from Employees", cnData
    Set rsEmployees = Nothing
    Set cnData = Nothing
End Sub
</SCRIPT>
```

Note Unless you use a Command object, you can pass only an SQL statement or a table name to the Open method.

Using an Implicit Connection Object

An alternative to using an existing Connection object is to open a new recordset using an implicit connection. One of the features of the ADO object model is the ability to call objects directly. When calling a recordset object directly, ADO automatically creates an implicit Connection object in the background.

The following example uses an implicit connection to return records from the Employees table:

```
' Declare the object variable
Dim rsEmployees

' Instantiate the object
Set rsCustomer = CreateObject("ADODB.Recordset")

' Open a new connection and return the appropriate records
rsCustomer.Open "Select * from Customers", _
    "Provider=SQLOLEDB.1;User ID=sa;" & _
    "Initial Catalog=Northwind;Data Source=vb6entsvr"
```

As you can see, using this technique reduces the amount of code you have to write. However, for each recordset that uses an implicit connection, a new connection will be created on the data source. In most cases, these additional connections use valuable resources. It might be more efficient to create a single Connection object and open the required recordsets from that connection. You can create multiple recordsets from one connection without using additional connection resources.

Note Using implicit connections can cause scalability problems. Therefore, you should consider using explicit Connection objects when accessing a data source.

Creating a Recordset Using the Execute Method

There are two other ways to create a recordset:

- Execute method on a Connection object
- Execute method on a Command object

In the previous example, records were returned based on an SQL string. Records in a Recordset are often returned as results from a stored procedure in a SQL Server database. You must use a Command object to call a stored query. As with the Connection and Recordset objects, you must declare and then instantiate a Command object variable before using it in code.

Using the Command object's CommandText and CommandType properties, you can associate a stored query with the object variable. The CommandText property must be set to the name of the stored query. If the name contains spaces, you must enclose the entire name in square brackets.

You can also issue SQL queries with the Connection object's Execute method. The following script uses the Connection object's Execute method to issue a query and returns all records from the Authors table in the Pubs database.

```
Sub ExecuteOnConnection()
    Dim cnPubs
    Dim rsAuthorIDs
    Dim strConnect
    Set cnPubs = CreateObject("ADODB.Connection")

    strConnect = "Provider=SQLOLEDB;" & _
        "Data Source=VB6ENTSVR;" & _
        "Initial Catalog=Pubs"

    cnPubs.Open strConnect, "sa", ""
    Set rsAuthorIDs = cnPubs.Execute("SELECT * From Authors")
End Sub
```

The following example uses the Execute method to issue an SQL statement to modify multiple records in a single database:

```
Sub UpdateTitles()
    Dim cnPubs
    Dim strConnect

    Set cnPubs = CreateObject("ADODB.Connection")
    ' Define the OLE DB connection string
    strConnect = "Provider=SQLOLEDB;" & _
        "Data Source=VB6ENTSVR;" & _
        "Initial Catalog=Pubs"
    ' Open the database connection
    cnPubs.Open strConnect, "sa", ""
    ' Execute the SQL statement
    cnPubs.Execute "UPDATE Titles Set Price = Price * 1.1"
    cnPubs.Close
    Set cnPubs = Nothing
End Sub
```

Navigating Records

Once you create the recordset and present the data to the user, you need to programmatically control how the user navigates the records. The following table describes the four primary methods for moving from one record to the next.

Method	Description
MoveFirst	Moves the user to the first record in the recordset.
MoveLast	Moves the user to the last record in the recordset.
MoveNext	Moves the user to the next record in the recordset. If they have moved to the end of the recordset, the EOF property is set to True. If the user attempts to move to the next record, past EOF, a run-time error will occur.
MovePrevious	Moves the user to the previous record in the recordset. If they have moved to the beginning of the recordset, the BOF property is set to True. If the user attempts to move to the previous record, past BOF, a run-time error will occur.

The Recordset EOF and BOF properties monitor whether the current record has moved outside the range of the recordset. If EOF or BOF are True, no record will be presented to the user. However, if the user attempts to navigate past this empty record, a run-time error will occur.

A Recordset object uses a cursor type to determine how records can be navigated and updated. You set the CursorType property prior to opening the recordset, or pass a CursorType argument with the Open method. If you don't specify a cursor type, ADO opens a forward-only cursor by default. Forward-only Recordset objects support only the MoveNext method. The following example uses the MoveNext method to navigate to the next record:

```
Sub btnMoveNext_onclick()
    rsEmployees.MoveNext

    ' Check if they moved past the last record
    If rsEmployees.EOF Then
        ' The last record was passed
        rsEmployees.MoveLast
    End If
End Sub
```

To retrieve data from a field in the current record, use the Fields collection and specify the name of the field, as in the following example code:

```
Employee = rsEmployees.Fields("First_Name")
```

You can also use the Fields collection to loop through all fields in the current record. The following example code displays all fields from the current record:

```
For i = 0 to rs.Fields.Count -1
    Response.Write rsEmployees.fields(i)
Next
```

Using the Resync and Requery Methods

Because static and forward-only cursors do not present updated record information to the user once the recordset has been built, you should consider using the Recordset object's Resync method to update the values of the records in the current recordset. Resync does not return new records based on the original query. To do this you must use the Requery method. Requery uses additional resources because the query is re-executed.

Additional Navigation Methods and Properties

You can also use any of the methods and properties shown in the following table to navigate a recordset object that supports moving forward and backward:

Method/Property	Description
AbsolutePage Property	Specifies in which page the current record resides.
AbsolutePosition Property	Specifies the ordinal position of a Recordset object's current record.
Move Method	Moves the position of the current record in a Recordset object.
NextRecordset Method	Clears the current Recordset object and returns the next Recordset by advancing through a series of commands.

Note The NextRecordset method is issued when returning multiple recordsets. Multiple recordsets are outside the scope of this class.

Finding a Record in a Recordset

In addition to navigating a recordset, you might want to allow the user to search for a specific record. There are two general ways to provide this functionality: requery the database using a specific WHERE clause, or use the Find method. Depending on the size of the recordset, network bandwidth, and server load, you might decide it is more efficient to locate the record in an existing recordset. To do this, call the Find method by using the following syntax:

```
RecordsetObject.Find (criteria, SkipRows, searchDirection, start)
```

The following table describes the arguments used by the Find method:

Argument	Description
Criteria	A string containing a statement that specifies the column name, comparison operator, and value to use in the search.
searchDirection	An optional value that specifies whether the search should begin on the current row or the next available row in the direction of the search. Its value can be adSearchForward or adSearchBackward. The search stops at the start or end of the recordset, depending on the value of *searchDirection*.
SkipRows	An optional Long value, whose default value is zero, that specifies the offset from the current row or *start* bookmark to begin the search.
Start	An optional Variant bookmark to use as the starting position for the search.

When specifying a criteria, you can use the following comparison operators: > (greater than), < (less than), = (equal), or *like* (pattern matching).

The following example locates a customer record using the Find method:

```
rsCustomer.Find "LastName = 'Smith'"
```

Note When using a string value in a Find, you must surround the value with single quotes.

Once the first record has been located, you can use the FindNext method to locate additional records. When the last record in the search has been found, EOF will be set to True. If the search direction was set to adSearchForward, BOF will be True.

Note You cannot use the Find method with a forward-only recordset. The recordset you create must be scrollable.

Using the Filter Property

ADO also supports the ability to filter the current recordset. Unlike Find, which searches for the first specific record based on a criteria, the Filter property will allow you to reduce the recordset to just records based on the criteria. Once you have finished using the filter, you must turn it off, which returns the recordset to its original state. The greatest benefit to using the Filter property is that you do not have to return to the database to rebuild the recordset; all the processing occurs on the client computer. Like the Find method, the recordset you create must support a scrollable cursor type (dynamic, keyset, or static). The recordset cannot be forward-only.

The following example uses the Filter property to limit the available records:

```
' This turns the Filter on
rsCustomer.Filter = "LastName Like 'S*'"
```

The following example returns the recordset to its original state:

```
' This turns the Filter off
Const adFilterNone = 0
rsCustomer.Filter = adFilterNone
```

The Filter property will accept the same operators as the Find method. In addition, you can build compound filters that provide a higher level of control over the available records without needing to return to the data source.

Modifying Data

When developing solutions that access a database, you usually need to include functionality to modify the records as well as present them to the user. When using ADO, you can programmatically control the Recordset object to edit, add, and delete records. However, to include this functionality in a multi-user environment, you will need to implement a locking scheme. Locking allows your Recordset to control how edits and deletions are applied when there is a possibility that more than one user may be working with the same record. ADO supports various locking options depending on the Recordset type being used. However, pessimistic and optimistic locking are the most common forms of locking. In the following example, a recordset is opened using pessimistic locking:

```
rsCustomer.Open "Select * from Customers", cnNorthwind, adOpenDynamic, _
    adLockPessimistic
```

Editing a Record

If the recordset has been opened for editing, you can allow the user to make changes and save the results back to the data source. To edit and post changes to a record, follow these steps:

1. Navigate to the appropriate record.
2. Change the field values (either programmatically or using bound controls).
3. Use the Update method to post the changes.

Records in a recordset are always in an edit state. You do not need to call a method to start the edit process. The following example changes the current record and then saves it to the data source:

```
rsCustomer!State = "CA"
rsCustomer.Update
```

Canceling an Edit

If you want to allow the user to cancel changes before they are posted, use the CancelUpdate method. When you call the CancelUpdate method, all the fields of the current record are restored to their initial values (the values they had when the recordset was first opened).

If your application has already opened a recordset, you can modify data using the recordset's methods. Modifying records with a Recordset object is limited to a single addition, deletion, or update at a time. The following example cancels an AddNew using CancelUpdate:

```
rsAuthors.AddNew
rsAuthors!au_fname = "Nancy"
rsAuthors!au_lname = "Davolio"
rsAuthors.CancelUpdate
```

Adding a New Record

If you open a recordset and use a locking scheme that allows records to be edited, you can also add new records to that recordset. In order to add a new record, you must first call the AddNew method. Unlike an edit, you must tell the Recordset object to start the add process. Once the appropriate data has been entered in each field, use the Update method to save the new record to the data source. Any new records that have been added to the current recordset will appear at the end of the recordset. Use the Refresh method to rebuild the recordset to include the new records in the appropriate order. The following example uses the AddNew method to add a new Author record:

```
rsAuthors.AddNew
rsAuthors!au_fname = "Nancy"
rsAuthors!au_lname = "Davolio"
rsAuthors.Update
```

Note To cancel the creation of a new record, use the CancelUpdate method.

Deleting Records

To delete the current record, use the Delete method of the Recordset object. After you delete a record, invoke a Move method to move to the next record; otherwise the current record pointer points to an empty record. The following example deletes the current record in the rsCustomer recordset:

```
rsCustomer.Delete
rsCustomer.MoveNext
```

When using a recordset to delete records, only one record can be deleted at a time, and unlike editing or adding a new record, you do not have to use the Update method to save the results to the data source. Therefore, be sure to verify with the user before calling the Delete method. In addition, only the current record is affected when the Delete method is called. Consider using the SQL DELETE command to delete multiple records in a data source.

Using the ADO Command Object

A Command object is a definition of a specific command that you intend to execute against a data source. It can be based on either a database object (such as a table, view, or stored procedure) or a SQL command.

A Command object either opens a new connection or uses an existing connection to perform queries, depending on what you specify in the ActiveConnection property. If you set the ActiveConnection property with a reference to a Connection object, the Command object uses the existing connection from the Connection object. If you specify the ActiveConnection property with a connection string, a new connection is established for the Command object. However, since more than one Command object can use the same Connection object, it is generally more efficient to use a single, existing connection. Once the Command object is created, you can use it to execute the specified command or build a recordset.

Query strings return records as a recordset, or they can simply change records in a database. For example, using a Select statement returns records, whereas the SQL Update or Delete statements only change records. In addition, if you submit more than one Select statement, you can return multiple recordsets with a single statement. Use the CommandText property to specify the SQL statement, or stored procedure, to run on the data source.

Due to the variety of possible commands you can place in the CommandText property, you must also use the CommandType property to specify the type of command used.

The following table lists the supported CommandType values:

Value	Description
adCmdFile	Use if the query string is the name of a file used to save the records in a previously created Recordset object.
adCmdStoredProc	Use if the query string is the name of a stored procedure.
adCmdTable	Use if the query string is the name of a table name.
adCmdText	Use if the query string is a SQL command.
adCmdTableDirect	Use specifically for OLE DB providers that support both SQL statements and the ability to directly open tables by their name. This is a variation on adCmdTable.
adCmdUnknown	Use when the command type is not explicitly known and the provider attempts to execute the command text first as an SQL statement, then as a stored procedure, and finally as a base table name. An error occurs only if all three of these attempts fail. Because the Command object must perform these extra steps to determine the type of query string, performance is degraded. This is the default value.

Executing a Command

You do not need to create a Recordset object to open a database and query on it. Instead, you can use a Command object and execute an SQL Insert, Update, or Delete statement to add or modify records. Using SQL statements is more efficient than creating recordsets and using recordset methods. The collections, methods, and properties of the Command object vary depending on the database provider. To create a Command object, you pass *ADODB.Command* as an argument to the CreateObject function.

➤ **To create a Command object**

1. Create a Command object by calling CreateObject and passing it the ADODB.Command parameter.

2. Set the CommandText property equal to the text you want to have executed.

3. Set, in seconds, the CommandTimeOut property of the Command object. The CommandTimeOut property determines how long the object will wait for the results of a command.

4. Make the Command object the active connection for the data source.

5. Call the Execute method to run the command.

The following example code retrieves a value from the Request object in an .asp file, creates a Command object, sets properties for the command, and then runs it:

```
frmPercent = Request("Percent")
Set cmdPubs = Server.CreateObject("ADODB.Command")
cmdPubs.CommandText = "exec Byroyalty " & frmPercent
cmdPubs.CommandTimeOut = 30
' Use existing Connection object
cmdPubs.ActiveConnection = cnPubs
cmdPubs.Execute
```

The syntax for the Execute method is as follows.

```
command.Execute RecordsAffected, Parameters, Options
Set recordset = command.Execute(RecordsAffected, Parameters, Options)
```

The Execute method can return a Recordset object containing the results of the query. However, if the Command is not a record-returning query, you do not need to specify a Recordset. In addition, you to ignore this return value if you do not want to specify a Recordset.

Note If Options is not explicitly stated, it will default to 8 - adCmdUnknown. It will try each option type one at a time against the command until it finds one that will run. This will slow execution time. Specify the option if you know it so that the command will execute immediately.

The following code uses a Command object to increase the discount percentage for all records in the Discounts table by 10 percent:

```
Dim comDiscountUpdate
Set comDiscountUpdate = Server.CreateObject("ADODB.Command")
With comDiscountUpdate
    .CommandType = adCmdText
    .ActiveConnection = "Provider=SQLOLEDB;" & _
        "User ID=sa;" & _
        "Data Source=VB6ENTSVR;" & _
        "Initial Catalog=Pubs"
    .CommandText = "UPDATE Discounts SET Discount = Discount * 1.1"
    ' Call the Execute method to update the Discounts
    .Execute
End With
```

Note A query string can also be the name of a stored procedure or table.

The following example code runs an SQL command that changes an author's last name. The code then displays the number of records affected by the update.

```
sql= "UPDATE Authors SET LName= " & _
     "'" & frmNewName & "'" & _
     " WHERE AuthorID = " & frmAuthorId
cmd.CommandText = sql
cmd.Execute iRecordsAffected, , adCmdText

Response.Write "Number of Records updated = " & iRecordsAffected
```

To execute an SQL command that returns a recordset, save the return value from the Execute method in a Recordset object variable. This example code runs the stored procedure byroyalty, which returns a recordset.

```
cmd.CommandText = "Exec Byroyalty " & frmPercentage
Set rs = cmd.Execute
```

Note Recordsets created from the Cmd.Execute method will have a forward-only cursor and will be of type read-only. If you need a different cursor type or write access, create a Recordset object independently and specify the cursor type in the Open method.

Running Stored Procedures with Parameters

To run a stored procedure that accepts parameters, you can create a Parameter object for each parameter. You then append the Parameter object to the Parameters collection of the Command object.

To create a Parameter object, you invoke the CreateParameter method of the Command object. The syntax of the CreateParameter method is as follows.

```
command.CreateParameter Name, Type, Direction, Size, Value
```

The following code that runs a command with parameters:

```
cmd.CommandText = "Byroyalty"
cmd.CommandType = adCmdStoredProc
Set parm = cmd.CreateParameter("Percentage", adInteger, _
    adParamInput, 4, 100)
cmd.Parameters.Append parm
```

Note You can pass parameters by assigning values to the Parameters collection without using CreateParameter. However, the disadvantage to this method is that each assignment causes the Command object to query the data source for the type of the parameter.

Using CreateParameter to create parameters explicitly and appending the Parameter objects to the Command object requires a few more lines of code but will avoid extra network trips to the database.

If a stored procedure returns an output parameter and a recordset, you must read the output parameters before accessing the recordset. Once you access the recordset, the output parameters can no longer be read.

Handling Errors

When you create Web applications that access a database, you should anticipate possible database errors and include error-handling code in your script. The best strategy for handling errors is to provide code that attempts to correct the error so that the user doesn't know an error has occurred. For example, if a database connection fails to open, you can write code that connects to a back-up database.

You can also try to prevent errors. For example, if you have a form in which the user enters a date range, you can place validation code on the form to verify the dates before the form is submitted.

If an error cannot be corrected or prevented, you can return an informative error message to the user. One way to supply a message is to redirect the user to another Web page that will display the message.

To redirect the user to another Web page, you call the Redirect method of the Response object. However, Redirect will work only if it has been placed in the server script before the <HTML> tag is read. By placing all the server script before the <HTML> tag, you can trap errors and display a different Web page if necessary.

The Errors Collection

The Connection object provides an Errors collection that contains information on database errors. To determine if an error occurred, you can use the Err object provided by VBScript or the Errors collection.

The advantage of using the Errors collection is that if multiple errors occur during a single database operation, all the errors will be stored in the collection. The Err object contains information only on the last error returned.

Performance Considerations for ADO

When using ADO in your applications, there are some important issues to consider. The following sections describe some techniques for improving performance in your applications when you use ADO.

Use SQL Commands Instead of a Recordset

When you create an ADO Recordset object, the recordset is created on the server. This is referred to as a server-side cursor. This is a memory intensive operation because it consumes much of your server system resources.

You can use SQL commands to update a database instead of creating a recordset and using methods of the Recordset object. For example, to insert a record into a table, you can execute a SQL Insert command rather than creating a recordset. When you use the SQL Insert command, no recordset is created.

Manage Recordset Size for Efficiency

If the records returned from a query can be displayed on only one Web page, you can write server-side script that creates a recordset, scrolls through the recordset, returns all the data as HTML text, and then closes the recordset. In this case, you can set the cursor type for the recordset to forward-only, which is the fastest type of cursor.

If the records returned from a query do not fit on one Web page, you can provide command buttons on the Web page for the user to request another page of records. To do this, you have several options to choose from.

- When you create the initial recordset, you can store the Recordset object in a session variable. When the user requests a new page of records, you use the stored Recordset object to retrieve the next set of records. Storing a Recordset object consumes server resources. Therefore, this approach might not be practical if your Web site has many concurrent users.

- You can save only the number of the current record in a session variable. In this case, you create a recordset, return one page of records, save the number of the last record returned, and then close the recordset.

- When the user requests the next page of records, you query the database again, use the saved recordset number to return the next page of records, and then close the recordset again. This approach reduces data server resources because no recordsets are kept open during a session.

- You can use RDS instead of using ADO. RDS stores a recordset on the client workstation rather than on the server. For more information on using RDS, see the section "Using the Remote Data Service" later in this chapter.

Place Data Updates in Business Objects

The best approach to working with data updates is to place the update code in business objects rather than directly in .asp files. The .asp file can then create an instance of the business object and invoke methods to perform an update. You can use ADO in Microsoft Visual Basic to implement business objects.

There are several reasons to place code for data updates in business objects.

- You can create multiple business objects, each one responsible for a discrete task. Breaking an application into discrete components simplifies maintenance and testing.

- Business logic should be isolated from the user interface, which is accomplished by the .asp file. Business logic determines how a database can be modified based on rules of the business. For example, at a university, there might be a rule that a student who has a grade point average below 2.0 cannot enroll in any new classes. When you write code to add a record to an enrollment table, you must ensure the student meets the required grade point average. By placing this logic in a business object, you isolate the code. If the business rule changes, you modify the business object rather than redesign the .asp file.

- Many types of clients, such as .asp files and Visual Basic or Microsoft Visual C++ applications, can invoke a business object. If you have a general business object that updates a database, many applications can use the object. Code in .asp files works only with browser clients.

- If a business object fails, the error is isolated. It will not cause the failure of the entire Web server.

For more information about creating business objects, refer to Chapter 7 and Chapter 8.

Lesson Summary

You can connect to a data source by using an ADO connection object. A Connection object is an open connection to a data source or OLE DB provider. To define a connection, you set properties for the Connection object. With ADO, you can also retrieve data from a data source and return the results to the user by creating a recordset. After you create a recordset and present the data to the user, you should programmatically control how the user navigates through the records. The four methods that facilitate this include:

- MoveNext
- MovePrevious
- MoveFirst
- MoveLast

With ADO, you can control the Recordset object to add, delete, and edit records.

The ADO Command object is a definition of a specific command that you intend to execute against a data source. You can base it on either a database object or a SQL command. The Command object either opens a new connection or uses an existing connection to perform queries.

When you create applications that access a database, anticipate possible database errors and include error-handling code in your script. A good strategy for handling errors is to provide code that attempts to correct the error. Another solution would be to include an error message letting the user know exactly what error occurred by redirecting them to another Web page.

Lesson 3: Using the Remote Data Service

In this lesson, you will learn how to use the Remote Data Service (RDS) to create Web pages that retrieve and update information in a database. RDS is a set of components that you can use to build Web applications for accessing ODBC-compliant databases. RDS binds the data from a recordset to data-aware HTML elements or ActiveX controls on a Web page.

To use RDS, you work with COM components, HTML, and client-side script. You add the RDS.DataControl object to an HTML document, and set properties to indicate the data to retrieve. You then set attributes on HTML elements to bind them to the RDS.DataControl object. You can also write client-side script to request a new set of records or submit changes to the database at run time.

After this lesson, you will be able to:

- List the RDS client side components and explain their uses.
- Add an RDS.DataControl object to your Web page.
- Identify performance considerations for RDS.

Estimated lesson time: 35 minutes

RDS Component Overview

As introduced in Chapter 5, the components of RDS are divided into client-side components and server-side components.

Client-Side Components

RDS client-side components run in an HTML document to provide dynamic data to the user. These components are not visible in the HTML document. Instead, they provide data from a recordset in data-bound ActiveX controls that are visible. The following list describes the RDS client components.

- RDS.DataControl

  The RDS.DataControl object runs queries and makes the resulting recordsets available to the data-bound controls on an HTML document. You set properties for the object to identify the Web server, data source, and SQL statement to retrieve records.

- RDS.DataSpace

  The RDS.DataSpace object creates instances of business objects that reside on a Web server.

  You can write client-side script to use these objects to invoke instances of your own custom business objects on the Web server.

- ADOR.Recordset

  The RDS.DataSpace object creates an ADOR.Recordset object when it retrieves records. This type of recordset object is similar to the ADO Recordset object, but does not include all of the same features. Because it includes fewer features, it is smaller and can download quickly.

The RDSServer.DataFactory Server Side Component

One server-side component of RDS is the RDSServer.DataFactory object. The RDSServer.DataFactory object is a business object that has been implemented as a COM server component. This is the default object used by the RDS.DataControl object to run queries.

How RDS Displays a Recordset

The following list outlines the sequence of events that occurs when RDS displays a recordset.

1. The user submits a query on an HTML document.
2. The client-side script assigns the query to the RDS.DataControl object and calls the Refresh method.
3. The RDS.DataControl object submits the query by using HTTP to the Web server.
4. RDS routes the query to the RDSServer.DataFactory object, which runs the query against the data source.
5. The resulting recordset is sent back to the RDS.DataControl object by using HTTP.
6. The data-bound controls on the HTML document display records from the recordset.
7. The recordset is cached on the client side.
8. When a user moves through the recordset, the controls display the data without making another trip to the Web server.

Binding Data to an Element

Data binding is based on a component architecture that consists of four major pieces:

- Data source objects, which provide the data to a page
- Data consumers, which are data-consuming HTML elements that display data

- Binding agents, which ensure that both provider and consumer are synchronized
- The table repetition agent, which works with tabular data consumers to provide a data set

Internet Explorer supports data binding and the use of data source objects. RDS is simply one more data source object.

Data Source Objects

To bind data to the elements of an HTML page in Internet Explorer, a data source object (DSO) must be present on that page. A DSO implements an open specification that allows the DSO developer to determine the following:

- How the data is transmitted to the page. A DSO can use any transport protocol it chooses. This might be a standard Internet protocol such as HTTP or simple file I/O.
- Whether the transmission occurs synchronously or asynchronously. Asynchronous transmission is preferred, as it provides the most immediate interactivity to the user.
- How the data set is specified. A DSO might require an ODBC connection string and an SQL statement, or it might accept a simple URL.
- How the data is manipulated through scripts. Since a DSO maintains data on the client, it also manages how the data is sorted and filtered.
- Whether updates are allowed.

Data Consumers

Data consumers are elements on the HTML page capable of rendering data supplied by a DSO. Elements include many of those intrinsic to HTML, as well as custom objects implemented as Java applets or ActiveX Controls. Internet Explorer supports HTML extensions to allow authors to bind an element to a specific column of data in a data set exposed by a DSO. Applets and ActiveX Controls support additional binding semantics.

Binding Agents

Binding agents perform the following two functions:

- When a page is first loaded, the binding agent finds the DSOs and the data consumers among those elements on the page.

- The binding agent also maintains the synchronization of the data that flows between all DSOs and data consumers. For example, when the DSO receives more data from its source, the binding agent transmits the new data to the consumers. Conversely, when a user updates a data bound element on the page, the binding agent notifies the DSO.

Table Repetition Agents

The repetition agents work with tabular data consumers (such as the HTML TABLE element) to repeat the entire data set supplied by a DSO.

Note   Individual elements in the table are synchronized through interaction with the binding agent.

Using a Data Source Object

To use a data source object on a page:

1. Insert the data source object onto a page using the <OBJECT> tag.

2. Set the DATASRC attribute/property of the HTML element to which you want to bind data equal to the ID of the data source object you inserted.

3. Set the DATAFLD attribute/property equal to the column of the data source from which you want data.

Inserting the RDS.DataControl Object

The RDS.DataControl functions like a recordset in ADO. It provides data to data-bound elements, like a text box control, on an HTML page in a Web application.

The RDS.DataControl object runs queries and makes the resulting recordset available to data-bound elements on an HTML page. You bind data from the RDS.DataControl to data-aware controls by setting attributes of the elements.

In order to use the RDS.DataControl in your Web application, you add the ActiveX control to your Web page.

➤ **To add the RDS.DataControl to your page**

1. Add the following object tag anywhere on the page:

```
<OBJECT classid="clsid:BD96C556-65A3-11D0-983A-00C04FC29E33"
    ID=myDataSource Width=1 Height=1>
    <PARAM NAME="SERVER" VALUE="http://example.microsoft.com">
    <PARAM NAME="CONNECT" VALUE="dsn=sample">
</OBJECT>
```

2. Set the ID attribute, for example myDataSource.

Setting Attributes

The following table describes the attributes you set for the RDS.DataControl object.

Attribute	Description
CONNECT	Specifies the data source name, user ID, and password.
SERVER	If you are using HTTP, ServerName is the name of the Web server computer.
SQL	Specifies the SQL statement to retrieve records.

➤ **To use the RDS.DataControl object**

1. Add the appropriate HTML controls to your HTML document.

2. Set the DATASRC attribute to the ID of the RDS.DataControl and place a # in front of it. For example:

```
<TABLE DATASRC=#myDataSource>
```

3. Set the DATAFLD attribute of the HTML control to a field in the DATASRC.

```
<TD DATAFLD=Name>
```

Scripting the Control

You can add client-side script to your HTML document to change properties of the RDS.DataControl object and submit a new query to the Web server at run time.

To send a new query to RDS, you modify the SQL property of the RDS.DataControl object and use the Refresh method to run the query. A new set of records will be retrieved and the data-bound controls will be updated automatically with the new data.

The following example code sets the SQL property of the RDS.DataControl object based on input from a user, and then queries the database again:

```
Sub cmdFind_onclick
    ADC.SQL = "exec byroyalty " & "'" & txtPercentage.value & "'"
    ADC.Refresh
End Sub
```

Changing the Current Record

The RDS.DataControl object uses a recordset that always specifies a current record. The current record is displayed in the data-bound controls.

To change the current record, you run script that uses one of the move methods of the RDS.DataControl object. The data-bound controls will display the new current record. Because the recordset is cached on the client workstation, a user can browse a large recordset without sending additional requests to the Web server for new data. The following example code moves the current record forward one record:

```
Sub cmdMoveNext_onclick
    ADC.MoveNext
End Sub
```

Data-bound controls enable the user to visually edit, add, or delete records. All changes made by the user are stored locally until the user explicitly submits or cancels the update.

Note To enable the user to change data on data-bound controls, you add the For Browse statement to the end of the query. Currently only SQL Server supports this statement.

To submit changes, invoke the SubmitChanges method of the RDS.DataControl object. To cancel changes, invoke the CancelUpdate method. The following example code shows how an Update button and a Cancel button can be used to submit or cancel changes to a recordset:

```
Sub Update_onclick
    ADC.SubmitChanges
End Sub

Sub Cancel_onclick
    ADC.CancelUpdate
End Sub
```

Using the RDSServer.DataFactory

In most cases, you will not need to use the RDSServer.DataFactory object directly. When you use the RDS.DataControl object, it invokes the RDSServer.DataFactory object for you.

However, when you use the RDS.DataControl object to create a recordset, you cannot write script that reads the data in the recordset programmatically. If you need to read the data in a recordset programmatically, you can use RDS.DataSpace and RDSServer.DataFactory objects to create the recordset.

You will need to programmatically read data in a recordset if you want to display the data from the recordset in controls that are not data-aware. In this case, you must write script to read the recordset and then set the value of the controls.

➤ **To create a recordset using the RDSServer.DataFactory object**

1. Insert the RDS.DataSpace control on your HTML document.
2. Create an instance of the RDSServer.DataFactory object by invoking the CreateRecordset method of the RDS.DataSpace object.
3. Create a recordset by invoking the Query method of the RDSServer.DataFactory object.
4. Assign data from the current record to HTML text box controls.

The following example code creates an RDSServer.DataFactory object, queries the Chateau St. Mark database for a list of all customers, and then assigns the first and last names from the current record to HTML controls.

```
set ADF = ADS1.CreateObject("AdvancedDataFactory","http://myserver")
set myRS = ADF.Query("DSN=Hotel;UID=sa;PWD=;","select * from customers")
txtFirstName.value = myRS.fields("First_Name")
txtLastName.value = myRS.fields("Last_Name")
```

If you also want to display the data from the recordset in data-aware controls, you can insert the RDS.DataControl object in your HTML document and add the data-aware controls. Then you set the Recordset property of the RDS.DataControl object to the recordset object returned by RDSServer.DataFactory. The following example code sets the Recordset property of the RDS.DataControl to the recordset variable myRs.

```
ADC.Recordset = myRS
```

Using the Bookmark Property

Some data-bound controls enable users to scroll through records. Depending on the purpose of your HTML document, you might want to update other controls in response to a user moving through the recordset. You can set the Bookmark property of a Recordset object to reposition the current record.

The following example code shows a data-bound list box that displays a list of customer IDs. When a user selects a customer ID in the list box, the script sets the Bookmark property of the recordset to the selected item from the list box and updates the HTML text boxes.

```
Sub DBList_click()
    myRS.BookMark = DBList.selecteditem
    txtFirstName.value = myRS.fields("First_Name")
    txtLastName.value = myRS.fields("Last_Name")
End Sub
```

Performance Considerations for RDS

With RDS, you can create efficient Web applications. This topic summarizes some of the advantages of using RDS to design and build applications that enable data retrieval and updates on your Web site.

RDS is ideal for retrieving and displaying records from both small and large recordsets. RDS caches records on the user's computer, which enables the user to browse all the records in a recordset without having to retrieve additional HTML documents from the Web server. In addition, your Web site will be easier to maintain and will serve a larger number of users if you isolate the data updates in business objects instead of placing the data update code directly in HTML documents. You use a tool such as Visual Basic or Visual C++ to create business objects. In the business object, you define methods that update the database. From an HTML document, you can use the RDS.DataSpace object to create an instance of your custom business objects and then invoke methods of the object.

Currently, RDS works only in Microsoft Internet Explorer 4.0 or later running on an Intel platform in Microsoft Windows 9x or Windows NT 4.0 or later.

Lesson Summary

The Remote Data Service (RDS) is a component that you can use to build Web applications for accessing ODBC-compliant databases. RDS binds the data from a recordset to ActiveX controls or to data-aware HTML elements on a Web page. RDS components are either client side or server side components. The client components include:

- RDS.DataControl
- RDS.DataSpace
- ADOR.Recordset

The server side components include the RDS.Server.DataFactory object.

RDS is very useful in retrieving and displaying records from both small and large recordsets. RDS caches records on the user's computer, which enables the user to browse all of the records in a recordset without having to retrieve additional HTML documents from the Web server.

Lab 6: Using ADO and Remote Data Services

In this lab, you will work with the Chateau database created in Lab 5. Using an ADO Connection and Recordset you will save guest and checkin information to the database. Then you will retrieve the guest information into the checkout form and complete the checkout process using Remote Data Services.

To see a demonstration of this lab, run the Lab06.exe animation located in the Animations folder on the companion CD-ROM that accompanies this book.

Before you begin

You should have already completed Labs 2, 3, 4, and 5. If you have not, follow the steps in Lab 2 to create the Chateau Web project and use the files in the Labs\Lab05\Partial folder to obtain the necessary files to complete this lab.

Estimated lab time: 60 minutes

Exercise 1: Using ADO to Save Guest Information

In this exercise, you will modify the checkin.asp file to save guest information to the Guests table of the Chateau database. Then you will insert a new record into the Reservations table to check the guest in.

1. Open the checkin.asp file for editing.

2. Click the Source tab on the HTML editor window.

3. Add the following code to the first line of ASP code on the page. This will expire the page immediately if the user leaves the page:

```
Response.Expires = 0
```

4. Dimension the new variables listed below. Put them below the existing variables:

```
' ADO connection
Dim cn
' ADO Recordset
Dim rs
' String for SQL statements
Dim SQL
' Boolean variable for smoking preference
Dim SmokingPref
' Smallint credit card type
Dim CreditType
' Unique ID for guests
Dim GuestID
' Display error messages with creating reservation
Dim ReservationCode
```

5. Below the variable declarations set the error trapping to on error resume next and set the ReservationCode equal to 0.

6. In the case statement for checking radiobutton status add the SmokingPref
    variable. Set the variable to 0 for optSmoke and –1 for optNoSmoke.

➤ **Create an ADO connection and recordset**

1. Above the code where you created a cookie in Lab 4, create an ADO
    connection using the cn variable. Use the cnChateau connection string from
    the global.asa file to open the connection:

```
Set cn = Server.CreateObject("ADODB.Connection")
cn.Open Application("cnChateau_ConnectionString")
```

2. Create an ADO recordset using the rs variable:

```
Set rs = Server.CreateObject("ADODB.Recordset")
```

➤ **To insert or update the Guests table**

1. Open the ADO recordset and look up the credit card number and last name of
    the guest to see if they are already in the database.

    Your select statement should resemble this:

```
rs.Open "Select GuestID from Guests where" & _
    CardNumber Like '" & Trim(Request.Form("CardNumber")) & _
    "' and LastName Like '" & Trim(Request.Form("LastName")) & _
    "'", Application("cnChateau_ConnectionString")
```

2. If the select statement does not return any records, insert a new record in the
    Guests table. If records are returned, update the existing record using the
    GuestID.

    Your code should resemble the following:

```
If rs.EOF And rs.BOF Then
    ' Insert the new record into the database.
    SQL = "Insert Into Guests(FirstName, LastName, SmokingPref, " & _
        "CreditType, CardNumber, ExpDate)" & _
        "Values('" & Trim(Request.Form("FirstName")) & "', '" & _
        Trim(Request.Form("LastName")) & "', " & SmokingPref & _
        ", " & CInt(CreditType) & ", '" & _
        Trim(Request.Form("CardNumber")) & _
        "', " & CDate(Request.Form("ExpDate")) & ")"

    ' Execute the SQL
    cn.Execute SQL

    ' Get the new GuestID
    rs.Requery
    GuestID = rs.Fields("GuestID")

    ' Close the recordset
```

```
            rs.Close
    Else
        ' Get the GuestID
        GuestID = rs.Fields("GuestID")

        ' Close the recordset
        rs.Close

        ' Update fields
        SQL = "Update Guests Set FirstName = '" & _
            Trim(Request.Form("FirstName")) & _
            "', " & "SmokingPref = " & SmokingPref & ", " & _
            "ExpDate = " & CDate(Request.Form("ExpDate")) & _
            " Where GuestID = " & GuestID

        ' Execute the SQL
        cn.Execute SQL
    End If
```

➤ **To insert the new reservation in the Reservations table**

1. Use the ADO recordset to retrieve the RoomID from the Rooms table:

```
rs.Open "Select RoomID from Rooms where " & _
    "Type Like '" & Trim(RoomType) & _
    "' and Smoking = " & SmokingPref, _
    Application("cnChateau_ConnectionString")
```

2. If there are no rooms available, notify the user. If there are rooms, insert a new record into the Reservations table:

```
If rs.EOF And rs.BOF Then
    ' Room not available
    Response.Write "<H2>No rooms are available meeting your" & _
        " reservation request</H2>"
    ReservationCode = 1
Else
    ' Save RoomID
    RoomID = rs.Fields("RoomID")
    ' Make the reservation
    SQL = "Insert into Reservations(RoomID, GuestID, " & _
        NumberOfPeople, " & _
        "CheckinDate, CheckOutDate, Charges) " & _
        "Values(" & RoomID & ", " & GuestID & ", " & _
        PartySize & ", " & CDate(CheckInDate) & ", " & _
        CDate(CheckOutDate) & ", " & _
```

(continued)

```
                CCur(Request.Form("Rate") * Request.Form("NumberofDays")) & _
                ")"
            cn.Execute SQL
    End If
```

Notice that the ReservationCode is set to 1 if no rooms are available. This will be used later to bypass the form that displays the Reservation Request results.

3. Update the code so that a cookie stores the first name and last name of the guest under the GuestID. The cookie should be created only if the reservation was successful.

   Hint: The GuestID must be explicitly converted into a string to use it as a cookie.

4. Write in-line error code to check for both VBScript and ADO errors. Use the err object to check for script errors and the Errors collection of the ADO connection to check for ADO errors. When an error occurs, display the description to the user.

   Your code should resemble the following:

```
If Err.Number <> 0 Then
    Response.Write "<h2>The following errors occurred" & _
        " while making your reservation:</h2>"
    Response.Write "<h3>" & Err.Description & "</h3>"
    For Each Error In cn.Errors
        Response.Write "<h3>" & Error.Description & "</h3>"
    Next
    ReservationCode = 2
    Err.Clear
End If
```

5. Write code to close the ADO objects and set them to Nothing.

6. If there was an error creating the new reservation, do not display the Reservation Request form. Use the ReservationCode variable to check for a valid reservation:

```
If ReservationCode = 0 Then
    ' Show the form
    %>
    .

    .
    <%
Else
    ' ReservationCode Errors
    Response.Write "<H2>Press the back button on your" & _
        " browser to make the appropriate changes.</H2>"
End If
```

7. Add a new row to the Reservation Request table to show the Room Number the guest is checked into below the Room Type.

Your code should resemble this:

```
<TR>
    <TD>Room Number:</TD>
    <TD><% =RoomID%></TD>
</TR>
```

8. Save your work and test the application by reserving a room for a guest.

Exercise 2: Using Remote Data Services

In this exercise, you will modify the checkout.asp and Reservation.asp files so that they use RDS to allow guests to be checked out of the hotel.

➤ **To select the guest to be checked out**

1. Open the checkout.asp file for editing.

2. Click the Source tab on the HTML editor window.

3. Remove the code from Lab 4 that retrieves the saved cookies into the cboCheckout combo box.

4. Insert a RDS DataControl object directly above the </BODY> tag at the bottom of the page. Name the control dcGuests:

```
<OBJECT CLASSID="clsid:BD96C556-65A3-11D0-983A-00C04FC29E33"
ID="dcGuests" width="14" height="14">
        <param name="Server"
        value="http://<%= Request.ServerVariables("SERVER_NAME") %>">
</OBJECT>
```

5. Use the Script Outline to insert the window_onload event into the VBScript block on the page.

6. Add code to the onload event to connect to the database using the DataControl object:

```
dcGuests.Connect = "<%= Application("cnChateau_ConnectionString")%>"
dcGuests.ExecuteOptions = 1
dcGuests.Fetchoptions = 1
```

7. Load the GuestID, FirstName, and LastName fields for each guest in the database that is currently checked in (Status = 0). Order the recordset by LastName:

```
dcGuests.SQL = "Select Guests.GuestID, FirstName, LastName" & _
    " from Guests Inner Join Reservations on Guests.GuestID" & _
    " = Reservations.GuestID Where Status = 0 Order by LastName"
dcGuests.Refresh
```

8. If there are any checked in guests, display them in the combo box. If not, display 'No Records' in the combo box.. Use LastName, FirstName for the Option text and GuestID for the option value:

```
If dcGuests.Recordset.EOF And dcGuests.Recordset.EOF Then
    ' All guests are checked out
    Set el = Document.CreateElement("OPTION")
    el.Value = "0"
    el.Text = "No Records"
    cboCheckOut.Add (el)
Else
    ' Show guests who are checked in
    Do Until dcGuests.Recordset.EOF
        Set el = Document.CreateElement("OPTION")
        el.Value = dcGuests.Recordset.Fields("GuestID")
        el.Text = Trim(dcGuests.Recordset.Fields("LastName")) & _
            ", " & Trim(dcGuests.Recordset.Fields("FirstName"))
        cboCheckOut.Add (el)
        dcGuests.Recordset.MoveNext
    Loop
End If
```

➤ **To display a guest for checkout**

1. Open the Reservation.asp file for editing.

2. Click the Source tab on the HTML editor window.

3. Remove the ASP code that retrieves the QueryString and sets the credit options. This is located at the top of the page.

4. Remove the ASP code at the bottom of the page that displays an error message.

5. Locate the beginning of the client code and retrieve the usercode **QueryString**. Set the value to a global variable called GuestID:

```
Dim GuestID

' Get the GuestID from the querystring
GuestID = <% =Request.QueryString("usercode")%>
```

6. Insert a RDS DataControl object directly above the </BODY> tag at the bottom of the page. Name the control dcGuests:

```
<object CLASSID="clsid:BD96C556-65A3-11D0-983A-00C04FC29E33"
ID="dcGuests" width="14" height="14">
    <param name="Server"
    value="http://<%= Request.ServerVariables("SERVER_NAME") %>">
</object>
```

7. Add code to the window_onload event to connect to the database using the DataControl object:

```
dcGuests.Connect = "<%= Application("cnChateau_ConnectionString")%>"
dcGuests.ExecuteOptions = 1
dcGuests.Fetchoptions = 1
```

8. Open a recordset containing information for the guest you are checking out. This should include all of the fields for the Reservation Checkout form and the Status field.

Your code should look similar to the following:

```
dcGuests.SQL = "Select Guests.GuestID, FirstName, LastName, " & _
        "CheckinDate, NumberofPeople, CheckOutDate, Charges, " & _
        "CreditType, CardNumber, ExpDate, Status from Guests " & _
        "Inner Join Reservations on Guests.GuestID = " & _
        "Reservations.GuestID Where Guests.GuestID = " & GuestID
dcGuests.Refresh
```

9. Find the FirstName field in the HTML for the form and remove the value setting. Bind the FirstName field to the dcGuests DataControl by setting the datasrc and datafld properties:

```
datasrc="#dcGuests" datafld="FirstName"
```

10. Repeat the above process for the LastName, NumberofPeople, and CardNumber fields. The remaining fields will be set in code so that they can be formatted.

11. Remove the value setting for the CheckinDate, CheckOutDate, ExpDate, and Subtotal fields. Find the ASP variables for setting the CreditType options to checked or not checked and remove them.

12. Below the code that opens the recordset in the window_onload event add code that checks to see if any records were returned. If no records are returned, display an error message and send the user back to the previous page. If a reservation record is returned then set the values for the remaining fields on the form.

Your code should resemble the following:

```
If dcGuests.Recordset.EOF And dcGuests.Recordset.BOF Then
    ' Display an error message and send them back to checkout page
    MsgBox "There was an error retrieving the selected guest. " & _
        "Please try again.", , "Reservations"
    History.Back
    Exit Sub
Else
    ' Format the Checkin and Checkout dates
    FORM1.InDate.Value = _
```

(continued)

```
            FormatDateTime(dcGuests.Recordset.Fields("CheckInDate"), 2)
    FORM1.OutDate.Value = _
            FormatDateTime(dcGuests.Recordset.Fields("CheckOutDate"), 2)
    ' Set Credit Type
    FORM1.optVisa.Checked = False
    FORM1.optMC.Checked = False
    FORM1.optDiscover.Checked = False
    FORM1.optAmEX.Checked = False
    Select Case dcGuests.Recordset.Fields("CreditType")
        Case 1
            ' Visa
            FORM1.optVisa.Checked = True
        Case 2
            ' Mastercard
            FORM1.optMC.Checked = True
        Case 3
            ' Discover
            FORM1.optDiscover.Checked = True
        Case 4
            ' American Express
            FORM1.optAmEX.Checked = True
    End Select
    ' Format Subtotal, other charges, and Total Due
    FORM1.SubTotal.Value = _
            FormatCurrency(dcGuests.Recordset.Fields("Charges"))
    If FORM1.OtherCharges.Value = "" Then
        FORM1.OtherCharges.Value = 0
    End If
    FORM1.TotalDue.Value = _
            FormatCurrency(CCur(FORM1.SubTotal.Value) + _
            CCur(FORM1.OtherCharges.Value))
    ' Format Expiration Date
    FORM1.ExpDate.Value = FormatDateTime( _
            dcGuests.Recordset.Fields("ExpDate"), 2)
End If
```

Notice that the existing code for setting and formatting the OtherCharges and TotalDue fields is included in the else statement.

➤ To complete the guest checkout process

1. Now you need to enter code that will save any changes to the form and complete the Reservation when the form is submitted:

```
Sub FORM1_onsubmit()
    ' Set the values
    dcGuests.Recordset.Fields("CheckOutDate") = FORM1.OutDate.Value
    If FORM1.optVisa.Checked Then _
        dcGuests.Recordset.Fields("CreditType") = 1
    If FORM1.optMC.Checked Then _
        dcGuests.Recordset.Fields("CreditType") = 2
```

```
          If FORM1.optDiscover.Checked Then _
              dcGuests.Recordset.Fields("CreditType") = 3
          If FORM1.optAmEX.Checked Then _
              dcGuests.Recordset.Fields("CreditType") = 4
          dcGuests.Recordset.Fields("ExpDate") = FORM1.ExpDate.Value
          dcGuests.Recordset.Fields("Charges") = FORM1.TotalDue.Value
          ' Complete the checkout
          dcGuests.Recordset.Fields("Status") = -1
          dcGuests.SubmitChanges
End Sub
```

2. Save your changes to Reservation.asp. You may also want to remove the code that deletes the cookie in invoice.asp since it is no longer being used.

3. Test the application by checking a guest in and then checking them out. Once checked out the guest should no longer appear on the checkout page.

Review

The following questions are intended to reinforce key information presented in this chapter. If you are unable to answer a question, review the appropriate lesson and then try the question again. Answers to the questions can be found in Appendix A, "Questions and Answers."

1. What is the purpose of SQL?

2. Explain how a Recordset object is used.

3. Explain how a Connection object is used.

4. What are some performance considerations you should remember when implementing remote data service (RDS)?

C H A P T E R 7

Creating COM Components

About This Chapter

In Chapter 1, you learned the importance of designing a Web site to accommodate the requirements of three different logical entities: user services, business services, and data services. In this chapter, you will learn how to create business services that can run on a Web server. You will also learn how to use Microsoft Visual Basic 6.0 to build Component Object Model (COM) components that contain business rules and how to call these COM components from a Web page.

Before You Begin

To complete the lessons in this chapter you must have installed Microsoft Visual Basic 6.0 Professional edition.

Lesson 1: Overview of Business Services

Business rules are self-imposed constraints that companies use to help them operate in their particular business environments. These business rules are used as goals for developers when developing applications.

Business components are objects that contain business rules that describe, in detail, specific areas of corporate policy. An example of a business rule is: "The hotel account managers may authorize discounts of up to 20 percent for regular customers." A business component can be created to implement this business rule. Because business rules can change, there is an advantage to implementing them as components—you can simply modify the business component, which has little or no impact on the rest of the application.

This lesson discusses the role of business components in distributed applications. You will study important factors to consider when encapsulating business logic into components. You will also learn how business rules in server components can increase your Web site's efficiency and learn about the attributes used to create business objects.

After this lesson, you will be able to:

- List the advantages of using object-oriented models.
- Explain the role of business rules.
- Describe the purpose of business processes.

Estimated lesson time: 30 minutes

Business Rules and Business Processes

There are two basic concepts of business services: business rules and business processes. A business rule is an algorithm that determines how information is processed. For example, if a credit card number is entered into a form, one business rule might check the credit card number for the limit available in that account. If the available credit limit exceeds the transaction, credit will be granted and the transaction will proceed. You can process a number of business rules together as part of a business service. Figure 7.1 illustrates how business rules can be used together to complete a business process.

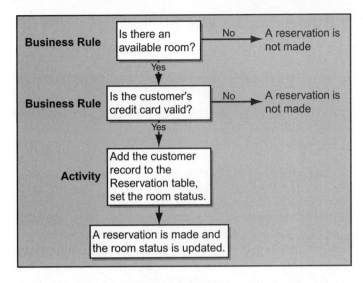

Figure 7.1 Business rules used in the Chateau St. Mark Hotel reservation system

A business process is a sequence of related tasks that produces a specific response to a user's request. For example, when a user submits an order form to purchase a product from an online catalog, a transaction is executed. This is a business process. Other examples of business processes include activities such as opening a new bank account, retrieving customer information, or retrieving benefit options for a specific employee. For each of these examples, a business process acts on a business rule. Figure 7.2 highlights the business processes for the Chateau St. Mark Hotel Web site.

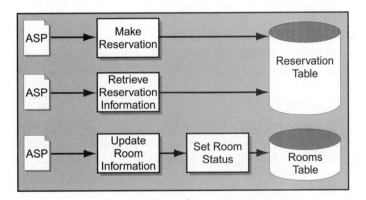

Figure 7.2 Business processes for the Chateau St. Mark Hotel

Business Objects and COM

Component software development is currently one of the most prominent trends in the software industry. Most of the software development tools that you can use today support component software development, including:

- Microsoft Visual Basic
- Microsoft Visual C++
- Delphi
- Microsoft Visual J++

Microsoft's effort to define an open, extensible standard for software component development and interoperability resulted in the Component Object Model (COM). COM is a specification that describes how software components can be built. COM enables software components you create to work with software components that are available commercially. COM components are units of code that provide specific functionality. Because COM components created by different software developers can be combined into a variety of applications, you can reuse code.

Business processes are commonly represented as middle-tier objects. Middle-tier objects typically contain the business logic that is shared by client applications. Using this approach, you can represent and implement business processes in an object-oriented environment as you plan your Web site. Furthermore, you can implement business services as COM components that encapsulate specific business functionalities. There are several advantages to using an object-oriented model to create business processes:

- Simplification of complex processes

   You can simplify a complex business process by separating its individual parts into smaller pieces, or objects. Conceptually you can think of each part of the process as a specific object, where an object performs a specific function of the process.

- Natural modeling techniques

   Because object-oriented methodology reflects a natural way of looking at real-world objects and processes, components are often easier to analyze, design, and develop with object-oriented techniques. Furthermore, it's easier to maintain and reuse such objects once they are developed.

- Encapsulation

   Each business object encapsulates the data and functionality needed to accomplish its task. A business object exposes only those methods needed by other business objects. By encapsulating only specific data and functionality in each object, business objects are self-contained and isolated from changes made to other objects.

Implementing Business Objects as COM Components

A business objects is a component that can be created with Visual Basic, Visual C++, or Visual J++. The purpose of a business object is to separate a business rule from application logic. This separation helps protect both the client and data tier from having to be constantly updated. For example, a business rule might be a formula for calculating the price of a hotel room. Hotel management doesn't want customers to know how the room price is calculated, and they also need to change the rule for calculating the price at a later time. Ideally, this kind of business rule should be contained in a COM object where clients can access its logic but not have direct access to the logic. In addition, the rule can be changed without affecting client applications. For example, if a business rule changes, only a single component might need to be recompiled. The client application that is providing the presentation services remains unchanged. This helps to lower support costs since each individual client computer does not need to be updated.

Business objects can exist on remote servers and can be invoked by client computers. By dividing your code into components, you can later decide the best way to distribute your application. For example, you can limit the workload of client computers by storing application logic on the client computer while the business rules and data services reside on remote computers, as illustrated in Figure 7.3.

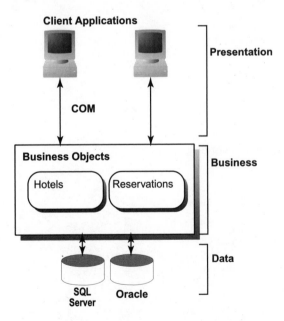

Figure 7.3 Division of business objects from presentation logic

COM components also offer several other benefits:

- They provide a standard method of creating reusable, higher-level components.
- They can be created with and used from a variety of programming languages such as Visual Basic, Visual J++, and C++. COM guarantees interoperability regardless of the language used to implement the components.
- They work with Microsoft Transaction Server (MTS). For information about MTS, see Chapter 8.
- They can be installed and used on both the server and the client.

Because COM components execute machine-dependent code, however, a fairly homogenous client environment is required, though this is not the case in a Web environment. Nonetheless, COM components can be used effectively on servers running Win32 operating systems, as well as on Macintosh systems and on certain types of UNIX systems.

Lesson Summary

Business rules are guidelines used by companies to help them operate effectively in their particular business environments. For Web applications, business rules define how information is processed. Business rules make up business components are designed to implement those rules by going through a sequence of tasks to produce a response to users' requests.

You can implement business processes in an object-oriented environment that has some definite advantages, including the following:

- You can simplify complex business processes by breaking them up into smaller discrete pieces
- You can reuse and maintain objects much easier once you develop them
- You can encapsulate business objects, thus isolating them from changes made to other objects.

Business objects and components can be created using a variety of software development tools including Visual Basic, Visual C++, Visual J++, and Delphi.

Lesson 2: Creating COM Components with Visual Basic

Now that you are familiar with business objects and COM, you will learn how to add class modules to business objects to create objects that encapsulate the internal functionality of a COM component. You will learn how to create a new ActiveX DLL project in Visual Basic 6.0. You will also learn how to expose methods from objects to make the COM components interoperable with other components and applications.

After this lesson, you will be able to:

- Explain the differences between in-process and out-of-process components.
- Explain the purpose of class modules.
- Create and use methods.
- Set properties for class modules.

Estimated lesson time: 45 minutes

Choosing the Type of Component

COM components can be either internal components, which are compiled into a project and are available only to that project, or external components, which are compiled into an executable (.exe) or dynamic-link library (.dll). Although COM components are typically libraries of classes, entire applications such as Microsoft Excel or Microsoft Internet Explorer are also COM components. Client applications use a technique called *automation* to take advantage of the services that such application-based components (called servers) provide. Any client application can use an external component. Client applications use components in the same way, whether the component was compiled in a .dll or an .exe.

To understand the significance of the two types of servers, you must understand processes. A process is a Windows application residing in an address space that the operating system has assigned to the application. A process has resources assigned to it, and one or more threads run in the context of the process. A process alone does not do anything; instead, threads are used to run an application.

A thread is the basic unit to which the operating system allocates processor time and is the smallest piece of code that can be scheduled for execution. It is the actual component of a process that is executing at one instant in time. A thread runs in the address space of the process and uses resources allocated to the process.

In-Process vs. Out-of-Process Components

COM components interact with your application and with each other through a client/server relationship. The client is an application that uses the features of a component. The server is a COM component that contains one or more class from which objects can be created. Components can be run in any one of three places:

- In the same address space as the client (in-process)
- On the same computer (out-of-process)
- On a remote computer (out-of-process)

Generally, if you create a COM component from an ActiveX EXE project, it is an out-of-process server and runs in its own process. However, if you create a COM component from an ActiveX DLL project, the component is an in-process server and runs in the same process as the client application.

In-Process Components

An in-process component is implemented as a dynamic-link library.dll and runs in the same process space as its client application. This enables the most efficient communication between client and component, because you need to call only the component function to obtain the required functionality. Each client application that uses the component starts a new instance of the component.

Out-of-Process Components

An out-of-process component is implemented as an executable file and runs in its own process space. Communication between the client and an out-of-process component is slower than with an in-process component because parameters and return values must be *marshaled* across process boundaries from the client to the component, and back again. However, a single instance of an out-of-process component can service many clients, share global data, and insulate other client applications from problems that one client might encounter.

Out-of-process components can also be stored on remote computers. Remote components are out-of-process components, but they are located on a separate computer from the client application. While communication time between a client and a remote component is much slower than with a local component, remote components allow processing to be done on a separate, and possibly more powerful, computer. The component can also be located closer to the work it is doing. For example, a component can be located close to a remote database with which it interacts.

When you use out-of-process components that reside on a remote computer, you should ensure that the client minimizes the number of calls to the object. This will help to improve application performance. For example, a well-designed component should have a way to pass data in bulk with as few calls as possible.

Advantages and Disadvantages

There are some advantages and disadvantages of using in-process and out-of-process components. For instance, applications that use in-process servers almost always run faster than those that use out-of-process servers because the application doesn't have to cross process boundaries to use an object's properties, methods, and events. However, an in-process component is less fault-tolerant so that if the DLL fails, the entire executable fails. An out-of-process EXE, however, is fault-tolerant. If the EXE fails, the other processes in the system will not fail. It can also be retained in memory as independent process. However, an out-of-process EXE is slower because of marshaling.

Each ActiveX component provides specific functionality:

- If you need a component that can run in the same process with your application, you'll want an ActiveX DLL. An example of this would be a component that performs complex calculations.

- If you need a component that can serve multiple applications and can run on a remote computer, you'll want an ActiveX EXE. For example, a business rules server that enforces tax rules would best be implemented as an ActiveX EXE.

Note Starting with version 4.0, Microsoft Internet Information Server (IIS) allows you to run server applications in a process separate from the Web server. For more information, see "Isolating Applications" in the Windows NT Option Pack Help.

Microsoft Transaction Server

Microsoft Transaction Server (MTS) is a tool that simplifies the development and deployment of n-tier applications that are built using COM technology. An MTS component is a type of COM component that executes in the MTS run-time environment. In MTS, components run under the control of MTS and are invoked by presentation services running on various types of clients. Clients can be Web browsers or Active Server Page (ASP) scripts running within IIS.

MTS places certain restraints and requirements on COM components that run under it. Under MTS, components:

- Must be compiled as an ActiveX DLL (in-process COM component).
- Must provide a type library that describes their interfaces.
- Must be self-registering.

Fortunately, Visual Basic satisfies the last two options automatically when building COM components. However, MTS requires that a component be a DLL. Components that are implemented as executable files (.exe files) cannot execute in the MTS run-time environment. For example, if you build an ActiveX DLL file with Visual Basic, you must rebuild it as a DLL to use it in MTS.

> **Note**   Although ActiveX DLLs are typically in-process components, they run out-of-process when used with MTS. This chapter focuses on using ActiveX DLL projects in Visual Basic to build components, and not ActiveX EXE projects. For more information about MTS components, see Chapter 8.

Project Templates

When you create a new project in Visual Basic, you first choose a template. To create a COM component, you choose either the ActiveX EXE or the ActiveX DLL template in the New Project dialog. Selecting either type of template sets a number of default values that are important for creating code components. Figure 7.4 shows the standard Visual Basic templates.

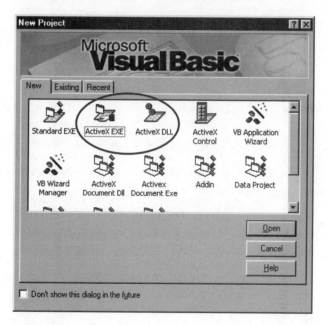

Figure 7.4 Standard project templates for Visual Basic

Setting Properties for Projects

When you create a new ActiveX DLL or ActiveX EXE project, you also set properties that affect how your component runs. You set project properties by clicking *<projectname>* Properties on the Project menu. Then, you click the General tab of the Project Properties sheet to select the options you want.

The following table describes the options you typically set for a new ActiveX DLL or ActiveX EXE project.

Option	Description
Project type	Provides the four template options: Standard EXE, ActiveX EXE, ActiveX DLL, and ActiveX Control. When you create a new ActiveX DLL or ActiveX EXE project, Visual Basic automatically sets the Project Type property. The project type determines how other project options can be set. For example, options on the Component tab are not available when the project type is set to Standard EXE. Specifies the SQL statement to retrieve records.
Startup object	Sets which form or Sub Main procedure in the current project runs first. For most ActiveX EXEs and ActiveX DLLs, you set the Startup Object field to (None). If you want initialization code to run when the component is loaded, set the Startup Object property to Sub Main. If you want initialization code to run when an instance of a class is created, use the Class_Initialize event.
Project name	Specifies the component name to which the client application refers.
Project description	Enables you to enter a brief description of the COM component, along with the objects it provides. The contents of this field will appear in the References dialog when you select references for other Visual Basic projects. The text also appears in the Description pane at the bottom of the Object Browser.
Unattended execution	Specifies whether the component will run without user interaction. Unattended components do not have a user interface. Any run-time functions, such as messages that normally result in user interaction, are written to an event log. If this box is checked, the project will be built to use the threading apartment model. Using this model will make your objects run more efficiently.
Threading model	The threading model list box is activated only for ActiveX DLL and ActiveX Control projects. The only options are single-threaded and apartment-threaded.

Note The business service objects created in this chapter will be built as ActiveX DLLs.

Using Class Modules

To create a COM component in Visual Basic, you first define a class module within an ActiveX DLL or ActiveX EXE project. Each class module defines one type of object in your component. In component projects, you can have several class modules.

At run time, you create an object by creating an instance of a class. A class is a template for an object, and an object is an instance of a class. Visual Basic objects can have

- Properties

  Data that describe an object
- Methods

  Actions that you tell the object to perform
- Events

  Actions the object performs; you can write code that is executed when events occur

You can think of an object as an item, properties as attributes of the item, methods as actions you can tell the item to do, and events as notifications that the item can express. For example, you can create an Employee class that has properties such as LastName and FirstName, and a method such as Hire.

Adding a Class Module to a Project

When you create a new ActiveX DLL project, by choosing the ActiveX DLL template in the New Project dialog, Visual Basic creates a project with one class module. You can add more class modules by clicking Add Class Module on the Visual Basic Project menu. You can then add methods, properties, and events to the class.

Creating an Instance of a Class

To create an instance of a class in the project that defines the class, you use the Dim and Set statements. This example code creates an instance of the Customer class:

```
Dim objCustomer As Customer
Set ObjCustomer = New Customer
```

You can also use the more compact syntax such as Dim ObjCustomer As New Customer instead of using the Set statement. Once you have created an object, you can use methods and properties of the object. This example code invokes the Add method of the Customer object.

```
ObjCustomer.Add "Joe", "Programmer", 31
```

Setting Properties for Class Modules

To determine the behavior of a component, you set properties for each class module in the component. The Name and the Instancing properties provide classes with information about components, which client applications use to instantiate objects.

Name Property

To create a name for the class, set the Name property in the Properties window. This name will be used by the client application to create an instance of an object.

For example, the following example code creates an instance of a class named MyClass, which is defined in the project named Project1.

```
Dim myObject
Set myObject = CreateObject ("Project1.MyClass")
```

The class name is combined with the name of the component to produce a fully qualified class name, also referred to as a *programmatic ID* or *ProgID*. In the previous example code, the fully qualified class name of the MyClass class is Project1.MyClass.

Instancing Property

The Instancing property determines whether applications outside of the Visual Basic project that defines the class can create new instances of the class, and if so, how those instances are created.

The available Instancing property settings are different for ActiveX EXE and ActiveX DLL projects in Visual Basic. Figure 7.5 shows the Instancing property settings for an ActiveX DLL project.

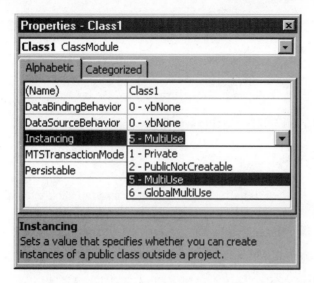

Figure 7.5 Setting the Instancing property for a class module

When you create a business object, set the Instancing property to MultiUse. Visual Basic also allows you to use other instancing property settings, including:

- Private

    With a Private property setting, other applications are not allowed access to type library information about the class and cannot create instances of it. Private objects are used only within the project that defines the class.

- PublicNotCreatable

    A PublicNotCreatable property setting allows other applications to use objects of this class only if the component creates the objects first. Other applications cannot use the CreateObject method or the New operator to create objects of this class. Set the Instancing property to this value when you want to create dependent objects.

- MultiUse

    With the MultiUse property setting, multiple clients can use the same instance of the component. If multiple clients create objects from the component, the same instance of the component is used for all clients.

- GlobalMultiUse

  The GlobalMultiUse property setting is similar to MultiUse except that properties and methods of the class can be invoked as though they were global functions. It is not necessary to create an explicit instance of a class because one will automatically be created.

Creating and Using Methods

For classes to be useful, they must contain methods that implement the functionality required of your component, such as business services. For every class module you create, Visual Basic automatically supplies two built-in event handlers called Initialize and Terminate (also known as event procedures) for which you can supply handler methods. You must add other general methods manually.

Initialize and Terminate Event Handlers

To add code to a class module event, you open a Visual Basic code window for the class, and then click Class in the Object drop-down list box. The Initialize event occurs when an instance of a class is created, but before any properties have been set. You use the Initialize event handler to initialize any data used by the class, as shown in the following example code:

```
Private Sub Class_Initialize()
    ' All methods in this class use a global Log object
    ' to record each method call
    Set objLog = New Log
    objLog.Write "Object Initialized"
End Sub
```

The Terminate event occurs when an object variable goes out of scope or is set to Nothing. You use the Terminate event handler to save information, unload forms, and perform tasks that you want to occur only when the class terminates, as shown in the following example code:

```
Private Sub Class_Terminate()
    objLog.Write "Object Terminated"
    Set objLog = Nothing
End Sub
```

General Methods

Methods represent the functionality your class provides. For example, SetFocus is a method supported by most controls, such as a text box. To create a method for your own object, you must create a Public Sub or Function procedure within a class module.

Note   You must add the Public keyword before Sub or Function to make the procedure available to other objects and applications. Otherwise, the procedure is private and can be accessed only from the object.

The following example code creates a method that accepts a number and then returns the number squared:

```
Public Function SquareIt (Num As Integer) As Integer
    SquareIt = Num * Num
End Function
```

The following example contains code for a Save method for a File class.

```
Private m_Filename As String
Private m_textFileContents As String

Public Sub Save(Optional strFileName As String)
    Dim FileLocation As String
    Dim FileNumber As Integer

    ' If a file name is not specified
    ' as an argument, use the private variable
    ' m_FileName. Otherwise, use the argument
    FileLocation = IIf(IsMissing(strFileName), m_Filename, strFileName)
    ' Get a file handle
    FileNumber = FreeFile()
    ' Open the file for output
    Open FileLocation For Output As #FileNumber
    ' Write text to the file
    Write #FileNumber, m_textFileContents
End Sub
```

Note   Remember that these methods will be the interfaces of the COM components running as part of the IIS server process. As a general rule, server processes should not have a user interface (UI). Therefore you must not call Windows graphic user interface (GUI) methods, such as MsgBox, in the methods you create.

Using the Object Browser

The Object Browser allows you to view *type libraries*. Type libraries are resources that contain detailed descriptions of classes, such as properties, methods, events, and named constants. Visual Basic creates type library information for the classes you create, provides type libraries for the objects intrinsic to Visual Basic, and lets you access the type libraries provided by other applications.

You can use the Object Browser to display the classes available in projects and components, including the classes you defined. The objects you create from those classes will have the same members (properties, methods, events, and so on) that you see in the Object Browser.

Lesson Summary

COM components are units of code that provide specific functionality. They can be either internal components, which are compiled into a project and used exclusively by that project, or external components, which are compiled into an executable (.exe) or dynamic-link library (.dll).

COM components can be run on the same address space as the client, on the same computer, or on a remote computer. In-process components are implemented as DLLs. They run on the same process space as their client application. Out-of-process components, however, are implemented as EXEs and run on their own process space.

MTS components are types of COM components that run in the MTS run-time environment. Under MTS, various types of clients including Web browsers and Active Server Pages (ASP) can invoke components.

To create a COM component in Visual Basic, you must define a class module within an ActiveX DLL or ActiveX EXE project. Each class module defines one type of object in your component. By setting the properties for a class module you can determine the behavior of the component.

Visual Basic automatically supplies two event handlers for each of your class modules: the Initialize event handler, and the Terminate event handler. You must add other event handlers by yourself.

Lesson 3: Working with COM Components

Having created a business component, you can now work with it in a variety of scenarios to enhance a Web site's functionality. In this lesson, you will learn how to call COM components from a Web page and how to include them directly in a Visual InterDev project. In addition, you will learn how to register a component and how to set version compatibility options from within Visual Basic.

After this lesson, you will be able to:

- Register a DLL component.
- Create a COM DLL in Visual Basic.
- Call a component from an ASP.

Estimated lesson time: 60 minutes

Registering and Unregistering Components

Before you can use a COM component, you must ensure that it is available on your computer. There are several ways to register a COM DLL:

- Run the Setup program.

    When you run the Setup program, the component is registered.

- Compile the DLL in Visual Basic.

    When you compile the DLL, it is automatically registered on the computer where you compiled it.

- Run Regsvr32.exe.

    When you run the Regsvr32 utility, it registers the DLL.

When you run the installation program for a component, the program adds any required files and, typically, also registers the component. If you are using a component that does not have an installation program, use the Regsvr32 (Regsvr32.exe) utility to register the component yourself.

Note When you create your own ActiveX EXE program and run it from the Visual Basic Integrated Development Environment (IDE), the program is automatically registered on your computer.

Using the Regsvr32 Utility

The Regsvr32 utility is located in the system directory (for example, C:\Windows\System). You can run Regsvr32 either from an MS-DOS prompt or from the Run command on the Windows Start menu. Because you cannot run a DLL by itself, you must use the Regsvr32 utility to register a DLL component.

Regsvr32 has several options. For example, use the /u (unregister) option to unregister a COM server, and use the /s (silent) option to register a server without displaying subsequent dialogs. You can see a list of all Regsvr32 options by running Regsvr32.exe without specifying a DLL name, as shown in Figures 7.6 and 7.7.

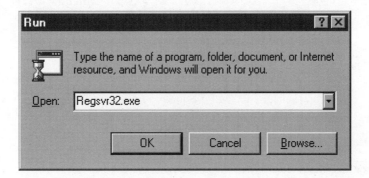

Figure 7.6 Running Regsvr32 without specifying a DLL name

Figure 7.7 The RegSvr32 options dialog

➤ **To register a DLL component**

1. Click the Windows Start button.

2. On the Start menu, click Run.

3. In the Run dialog, type the following command:

```
Regsvr32.exe <DLL Path>\<DLL name>.dll
```

   A dialog similar to that shown in Figure 7.8 appears.

4. Click OK.

Figure 7.8 RegSvr32 confirmation dialog

You can register a COM EXE simply by running it or by double-clicking the file in Windows Explorer. In addition, if you use the command-line options /regserver and /unregserver, you can register or unregister any COM EXE without invoking the program's user interface.

Note You unregister a component to manually remove component references from the system registry. You can then delete the component's EXE or DLL file.

➤ **To register or unregister an EXE component**

Type the filename of the component (including the path) followed by /regserver or /unregserver.

```
C:\MyProject\MyComponent.exe /regserver
```

Component Information Stored in the Registry

When you register a COM DLL, entries are placed in the registry to allow clients to locate, create, and use classes in the COM DLL. The registry entries for COM classes are located in HKEY_CLASSES_ROOT in the system registry. Visual Basic generates three registry keys when you compile a COM DLL:

- ProgID key

  The ProgID key is a string value representing the component name followed by the class name. For example, the ProgID key for a class identified as Employees.Manager is \HKEY_CLASSES_ROOT\Employees.Manager. The ProgID has a subkey named CLSID that contains the class ID (CLSID) for the class, and this is how you can map a ProgID to the CLSID that is then used to instantiate a COM class.

- CLSID key

  The CLSID key is used to identify a class. Visual Basic automatically generates a globally unique identifier (GUID) for each public class and interface in your component. These GUIDs are usually referred to as CLSIDs and interface IDs (IID). Class IDs and interface IDs are the keys to version compatibility for components authored using Visual Basic.

- TypeLib key

  The TypeLib key locates a type library for a component. The TypeLib keys are located at HKEY_CLASSES_ROOT\TypeLib\<libid>. You can find the LIBID from the TypeLib subkey in the CLSID key.

Testing and Debugging Components

Once you create a COM component, you will want to test and debug the component from within Visual Basic using a compiled version. Visual Basic provides two different component debugging options. For in-process components, you can load a Standard EXE test project and one or more component projects into the development environment as a *project group*. You can run all the projects in the group together and step directly from test project code into in-process component code.

For out-of-process components, you can debug using two instances of the development environment. One instance of Visual Basic runs the test project, while the second instance runs the component project. You can step directly from test project code into component code and each instance of Visual Basic will have its own set of breakpoints and watches.

Using a Project Group to Test a COM DLL

In this practice, you will create an ActiveX DLL project that has a property and a method that a client application can use. You will add a Standard EXE project to your ActiveX DLL project, which will create a project group you can use to test your COM DLL.

➤ **To create a COM DLL in Visual Basic**

1. Create a new ActiveX DLL project in Visual Basic.

2. Name the project SampleDLL.

3. In the General Declarations section of the Class1 module, type the following code:

```
Private UserName As String
Private strMessage As String
Public Sub SayHello()
    MsgBox "Hello " & UserName & "!"
End Sub
Public Property Let Name(Name As String)
    UserName = Name
End Property
Public Property Get Message()
    strMessage = "Hello from DLL."
    Message = strMessage
End Property
```

> **Note** Normally you would need to register the DLL before calling it. Leaving it running in Visual Basic allows us to test the DLL because it is currently loaded in memory.

➤ **To create a test project**

1. On the File menu, click Add Project.

2. In the Add Project dialog, double-click Standard EXE.

3. Click the Standard EXE project in the Project Explorer.

4. On the Project menu, click References.

5. Select the checkbox next to SampleDLL, and then click OK.

6. Add a CommandButton control to Form1.

7. In the Click event procedure for the CommandButton control, type the following code:

```
Dim obj As SampleDLL.Class1
Dim strMessage As String

Set obj = New Class1
obj.Name = "John"
obj.SayHello

strMessage = obj.Message
MsgBox strMessage, , "Message from DLL"
```

8. Right-click the Standard EXE project in the Project Explorer, and then click Set As Start Up on the drop-down menu.

9. On the File menu, click Save Project Group.

   Save the files to the \Practice\Ch03 folder on your hard drive.

10. On the Run menu, click Start.

    You will see two message boxes. The first message box is displayed from the SayHello method of your ActiveX DLL. The second message box displays the value of the Message property of the object you declared in the Command1_Click event procedure.

11. Click OK to close each message box that appears.

12. On the Run menu, click End.

Registering a Server Component from Visual InterDev

If a component in your Web application is designed to run on the server, you must make sure it is registered on the production server. In a Visual InterDev Web project, you can designate a component to be registered as a server component.

When you use the Copy Web Application feature in Visual InterDev, your component will be automatically registered on the server.

➤ **To mark a server component for registration**

1. In the Project Explorer, add the component to your Web project.

2. Select the component you want to register on the server.

3. In the Properties grid, select Custom.

4. In the Component Installation tab of the Custom property page, select Register on server, and then choose OK.

Note The deployment of a Web application with components requires the presence of Microsoft FrontPage Server Extensions on the production server. For more information about this deployment method, search for "Deploying an Integrated Web Solution" in Visual InterDev Help.

You can deploy COM components as part of your Web project directly from the Project Explorer in Visual InterDev. This enables you to distribute an integrated solution that includes files created using other Microsoft Visual Studio tools such as Visual Basic. For example, you can integrate a .dll file created with Visual Basic into your Visual InterDev project.

➤ **To deploy a Web application with components**

1. In the Project Explorer, select the project that points to the Web application you want to deploy.

2. On the Project menu, click Web Project, and then click Copy Web Application.

3. In the Copy Project dialog, choose the copy of the application you want to deploy.

Note If you work on a team, you typically deploy the master version because it includes the updated files from the team members.

---

4. In the Server Name box, enter the name of the Web server you want to use.

5. In the Web project box, enter the name you want the users to type for the URL.

6. Select Register server components and click OK.

Visual InterDev adds a new application to the destination Web server and copies the files in the Web application to that new folder. The name you specified in the Copy Web Application dialog becomes part of the application's URL. You can now test the application on the production server. Figure 7.9 shows the Copy Project dialog.

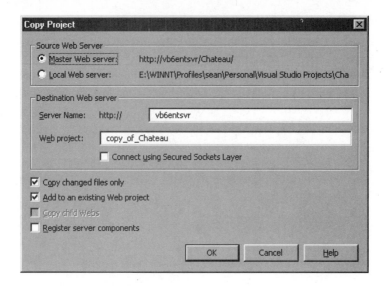

Figure 7.9 Copying a Web project

Calling a Component from an ASP

Using an ASP page, you can create an instance of a COM component by using the CreateObject method. Once you have created an instance of a component, you can access its properties and methods.

Using the CreateObject Method

The following example code shows how to use the CreateObject method, and then output the return value of a method to an HTML response:

```
<% Set bc = Server.CreateObject ("MyServer.MyObject") %>
<% Response.Write bc.method( ) %>
```

When you build your COM component, you should specify that all parameters be passed using the ByVal keyword. This is the most efficient way to pass a parameter to a COM component.

Note If you pass parameters using ByRef, you must convert each parameter into the data type that the method expects. This is because Microsoft Visual Basic Scripting Edition (VBScript) uses variants for all variable types. If you call a method of a COM component that does not accept parameters of type variant, then you must explicitly convert the arguments to the correct type.

The following example code shows how to call the SquareIt method on the Math object. It also shows how to convert the argument to an integer data type and print the result to an HTML response.

```
<% Set mathobj = Server.CreateObject ("Math.Object") %>
<%= mathobj.SquareIt (cint(5)) %>
```

Note Once you have created a COM component by using the CreateObject method, its corresponding DLL will remain loaded in memory by IIS until the Web service stops running. If you are testing the DLL, you will not be able to recompile until the DLL is freed from memory. To force IIS to free the DLL, stop and restart the Web service in the Internet Service Manager.

Using RDS to Create a Remote Business Object

In Chapter 6, you learned that the Remote Data Service (RDS) of ActiveX Data Objects (ADO) allows a client to create instances of remote business objects. To create an instance of a remote business object, you insert the RDS.DataSpace object into an HTML document and then call the CreateObject method of the RDS.DataSpace object.

CreateObject creates an instance of the business object on a Web server. In the case of an out-of-process component, it creates a proxy on the client to marshal method calls to the object. CreateObject returns an object reference, which you use to invoke methods of the business object. The syntax of the CreateObject method is as follows.

RDS.DataSpace.CreateObject ProgID, ServerName

The following example code uses the CreateObject function to create an instance of the Chateau.Reservation business object using DCOM. It then invokes the Activate method of the object to make a reservation active.

```
set objRsvn = ADS1.CreateObject("Chateau.Reservation","myserver")
objRsvn.Activate (ReservationID, RoomID)
```

Client vs. Server

There are several reasons for creating an instance of a business object by using the RDS.DataSpace object on the client rather than by using an ASP page on the server. RDS.DataSpace provides the following advantages:

- The ability to call multiple business objects from a single Web page without retrieving new pages.

    This permits more flexibility in the design of a Web page. An ASP can also call multiple business objects; however, it can get information only from a submitted HTML form, which is more limiting.

- The ability to use the RDS.DataSpace object to retrieve the data and cache it on the client.

  This improves performance by reducing the load on the server, and is especially useful if business objects return a large amount of data.

However, you should use an ASP page instead of RDS.DataSpace in the following situations:

- Business objects that must perform secure transactions.

  Using the RDS.DataSpace object would expose the code of the business objects by creating them on a Web page, where the code could be misused. When the code is placed in server-side script in an ASP page, it will never be returned to a client.

- The client cannot run ActiveX controls.

Controlling Version Compatibility

When you compile a project, Visual Basic creates a unique CLSID, a unique IID, and a unique type library ID. Applications using your component employ these identifiers to create and use objects. If these identifiers change in a new version of a component, existing applications will not be able to use the new version.

Type Library IDs

A COM component stores its data type information and object characteristics, including descriptions of methods and properties, in a type library. When a COM component is registered with Microsoft Windows, an entry is created under HKEY_CLASSES_ROOT\TypeLib in the registry, associating a GUID with its type library data. By providing access to an object's type library through a unique type library ID, a client can manipulate the methods and properties of the object.

Version Compatibility

Version compatibility is important when you are building components for use in a distributed environment. When you compile an ActiveX EXE or ActiveX DLL project, its classes expose methods that clients will use. If at some point you change a class in a component by deleting or changing the signature of a property or method, that component will no longer work with old clients. When you next compile the component, a new type library ID will be created, which will be incompatible with existing versions of the component used by clients.

Setting Version Compatibility Options

Visual Basic provides three options to help control version compatibility, shown in the following table.

Option	Description
No compatibility	Each time you compile the component, the type library ID, CLSIDs, and IIDs are recreated. Because none of these identifiers match the ones existing clients are using, backward compatibility is not possible.
Project compatibility	Each time you compile the component, the CLSIDs and IIDs are recreated, but the type library remains constant. This is useful for test projects so that you can maintain references to the component project. However, each compilation is not backward compatible with existing clients. This is the default setting for a component.
Binary compatibility	Each time you compile the component, Visual Basic keeps the type library ID, CLSIDs, and IIDs the same. This maintains backward compatibility with existing clients. However, if you attempt to delete a method from a class, or change a method's name or parameter types, Visual Basic will warn you that your changes will make the new version incompatible with previously compiled applications. If you ignore the warning, Visual Basic will create new CLSIDs and IIDs for the component, breaking its backward compatibility.

➤ **To set the version compatibility**

1. From the Project menu, click Project Properties.

2. On the Project Properties dialog, select the Component tab.

3. Select the appropriate Version Compatibility option.

If you make any change to the component (for example, if you delete a property) that is incompatible with the version on your Web server specified in the Project

Compatibility field, Visual Basic displays a warning message and generates a new type library ID. Figure 7.10 shows the Component tab of the Project Properties sheet.

Figure 7.10 Setting version compatibility for a component

Lesson Summary

Before you use a COM component, you must register it on your computer. You do this by running the setup program, by compiling the DLL in Visual Basic, or by running Regsvr.exe.

After you create a COM component, you need to test and debug it in the Visual Basic IDE. To debug an in-process component, you load a Standard EXE test project and one or more component projects into the development environment. To debug an out-of-process component, you use one instance of Visual Basic to run the test project, and a second instance of Visual Basic to run the component project.

In an Active Server Page, you can create an instance of a COM component by using the CreateObject method. After you have created an instance of a component, you can access its properties.

Once you compile a project, Visual Basic creates a unique CLSID, a unique IID, and a unique type library ID. All applications that use your component will use these identifiers to create and use objects.

Lab 7: Enforcing Business Rules with a COM Component

In this lab, you will create a COM component in Visual Basic that will handle guest reservations for the Chateau St. Mark Hotel. The COM component will enforce two business rules that are not being handled by the current ASP-based process. First the component will check for available rooms of the type requested by the guest. Then it will make sure the number of people in the party does not exceed the room capacity. If both of these requirements are met, the reservation will be made.

To see a demonstration of this lab, run the Lab07.exe animation located in the Animations folder on the companion CD-ROM that accompanies this book.

Before you begin

You should have already completed Labs 2, 3, 4, 5, and 6. If you have not, follow the steps in Lab 2 to create the Chateau Web project and use the files in the Labs\Lab06\Partial folder to obtain the necessary files to complete this lab.

Estimated lab time: 30 minutes

Exercise 1: Creating the COM Component

In this exercise, you will create an ActiveX DLL component in Visual Basic. This component will query the Chateau database using stored procedures to get an available room and check the room's capacity. Then it will insert the reservation using an ADO connection if a room is available and the capacity is not exceeded.

1. Open Visual Basic and create a new ActiveX DLL project named Chateau.vbp. This project is also located in the \Labs07\Partial folder.

2. Change the name of the Class Module to Reservation.

3. Add a reference to the Microsoft ActiveX Data Objects 2.1 Library.

4. Create a new public function in the Reservation class. Name the function Checkin and have it return an Integer. Set the following arguments for the function:

```
GuestID As Integer
NumberofPeople As Integer
CheckinDate As Date
CheckoutDate As Date
Charges As Currency
RoomType As String
SmokingPref As Boolean
ServerName As String
```

5. Declare the variables listed below:

```
Dim RoomID As Integer
Dim Capacity As Integer
Dim NumberofDays As Integer
```

6. Create an error trapping routine that writes an event to the event log if an error occurs in the function.

➤ **Create an ADO Connection and Command object**

Declare an ADO connection and Command object. Open the connection to the SQLOLEDB provider. Use the Chateau login created in Lab 5 and the following ServerName argument:

```
Dim TheADOCommand As ADODB.Command
Dim TheADOConnection As ADODB.Connection

Set TheADOCommand = New ADODB.Command
Set TheADOConnection = New ADODB.Connection

' Create the ADO connection.
TheADOConnection.Provider = "SQLOLEDB"
TheADOConnection.Open "Server=" & ServerName & _
    ";Database=Chateau;UID=Chateau;PWD=;"
TheADOCommand.ActiveConnection = TheADOConnection
```

➤ **Execute the GetAvailableRoom and GetCapacity stored procedures**

1. Compute the length of stay in days and assign it to the NumberofDays variable:

```
NumberofDays = DateDiff("d", CheckOutDate, CheckinDate)
```

2. Create two input parameters and a return value parameter for the GetAvailableRoom stored procedure. Then execute the stored procedure assigning the return value to the RoomID variable. Delete the parameters when finished.

Your code should resemble the following:

```
' Create Parameters for Checking if Rooms are available
TheADOCommand.Parameters.Append _
    TheADOCommand.CreateParameter("TheReturnRoomID", _
    adInteger, adParamReturnValue)
TheADOCommand.Parameters.Append _
    TheADOCommand.CreateParameter("TheRoomType", _
    adVarChar, , Len(RoomType), RoomType)
TheADOCommand.Parameters.Append _
    TheADOCommand.CreateParameter("TheSmokingPref", _
```

(continued)

```
            adInteger, , , CInt(SmokingPref))

        ' Tell ADO that the command text is a SP.
        TheADOCommand.CommandType = adCmdStoredProc

        ' Tell ADO which SP to call.
        TheADOCommand.CommandText = "GetAvailableRoom"

        ' Execute the SP.
        TheADOCommand.Execute

        ' Set the ReturnValue.
        RoomID = TheADOCommand.Parameters("TheReturnRoomID").Value

        ' Delete the parameters
        TheADOCommand.Parameters.Delete "TheReturnRoomID"
        TheADOCommand.Parameters.Delete "TheRoomType"
        TheADOCommand.Parameters.Delete "TheSmokingPref"
```

3. If the RoomID returned is valid (not 0), execute the GetCapacity stored procedure. Otherwise, set the function to return 0 The GetCapacity stored procedure takes RoomID as an input parameter and returns the capacity.

    Your code should resemble the following:

```
If RoomID > 0 Then
    ' Create Parameters for Checking capacity
    TheADOCommand.Parameters.Append _
        TheADOCommand.CreateParameter("TheReturnCapacity", _
        adInteger, adParamReturnValue)
    TheADOCommand.Parameters.Append _
        TheADOCommand.CreateParameter("TheRoomID", adInteger, , , _
        RoomID)

    ' Tell ADO that the command text is a SP.
    TheADOCommand.CommandType = adCmdStoredProc

    ' Tell ADO which SP to call.
    TheADOCommand.CommandText = "GetCapacity"

    ' Execute the SP.
    TheADOCommand.Execute
```

```
' Set the ReturnValue.
   Capacity = _
       TheADOCommand.Parameters("TheReturnCapacity").Value

   ' Delete the parameters
   TheADOCommand.Parameters.Delete "TheReturnCapacity"

   TheADOCommand.Parameters.Delete "TheRoomID"
Else

   ' Room not available
   Checkin = 0
End If
```

➤ To insert the new reservation in the Reservations table

1. If the capacity is less than or equal to the NumberofPeople, use the ADO command to insert the reservation. If the NumberOfPeople exceeds the capacity, the function should return –1. Use the NumberOfDays variable to calculate the full charges for the stay.

    Your code should resemble the following:

```
If Capacity >= NumberofPeople Then
    ' Tell ADO that the command type is text
    TheADOCommand.CommandType = adCmdText

    ' Create the Insert text
    TheADOCommand.CommandText = "Insert into Reservations" & _
        " (RoomID, GuestID, NumberOfPeople, CheckinDate," & _
        " CheckOutDate, Charges)" & _
        " Values(" & RoomID & ", " & GuestID & ", " & _
        NumberofPeople & ", " & CheckinDate & ", " & _
        CheckOutDate & ", " & Charges * NumberofDays & ")"

    ' Execute the Insert Statement
    TheADOCommand.Execute

    ' Return the RoomID
    Checkin = RoomID
Else
    ' Not enough room for the Party size
    Checkin = -1
End If
```

Remember that the reservation should be made only if a room is available and the NumberOfPeople does not exceed the room capacity. Nest your If...Then statements appropriately.

2. Close the ADO connection and Command before leaving the function and the error code, as follows:

```
TheADOCommand.ActiveConnection = Nothing
Set TheADOCommand = Nothing
Set TheADOConnection = Nothing
```

3. Save your code and compile the Chateau.dll. If you are working from a separate client PC, you will need to compile the component on the server.

Exercise 2: Using a COM Component in ASP

In this exercise, you will modify the checkin.asp page to use the Chateau.dll component for reservations.

1. Open the checkin.asp file for editing.

2. Click the Source tab on the HTML editor window.

3. In the ASP code, declare a variable for the COM object named Chateau.

4. Remove the ASP code that selects a RoomID and makes the reservation.

5. Create an instance of the Chateau.dll, as follows:

```
Set Chateau = Server.CreateObject("Chateau.Reservation")
```

6. Execute the Checkin function and assign the return value to the RoomID variable:

```
RoomID = Chateau.Checkin(CInt(GuestID), _
            CInt(PartySize), _
            CDate(CheckinDate), _
            CDate(CheckOutDate), _
            CCur(charges), _
            Trim(RoomType), _
            CBool(SmokingPref), _
            Request.ServerVariables("SERVER_NAME"))
```

Notice that the Server Name is retrieved from the ASP request object. This allows for the creation of a non-DSN connection.

7. If a valid RoomID is not returned, display the following appropriate message to the user indicating that the reservation was not made:

```
If RoomID = 0 Then
    ' Room not available
    Response.Write "<H2>No rooms are available meeting your" & _
        " reservation request</H2>"
        ReservationCode = 1
ElseIf RoomID = -1 Then
    ' NumberofPeople exceeds Room capacity
    Response.Write "<H2>There are too many people in your" & _
    " party to reserve this room." & _
```

```
            "<BR>You need to either select a larger room size or" & _
            " make additional reservations.</H2>"
            ReservationCode = 1
        Else
            ' Use the GuestID instead of the CardNumber to store cookie
            usercode = CStr(GuestID)

            Response.Cookies(usercode)("LastName") = _
                Trim(Request.Form("LastName"))
            Response.Cookies(usercode)("FirstName") = _
                Trim(Request.Form("FirstName"))

            ' Expire the cookie after 1 year
            Response.Cookies(usercode).Expires = DateAdd("y", 1, Now)
        End If
```

8. Set the Chateau variable to Nothing and save your changes to checkin.asp.

9. Test the application by checking in a guest. Try putting in a party size of 10 to see what happens. There is only one non-smoking penthouse in the Chateau. Try reserving it twice to see what happens.

Review

The following questions are intended to reinforce key information presented in this chapter. If you are unable to answer a question, review the appropriate lesson and then try the question again. Answers to the questions can be found in Appendix A, "Questions and Answers."

1. What are business rules?

2. What are some advantages and disadvantages of using in-process components?

3. Give an example of a business process.

C H A P T E R   8

Using Microsoft Transaction Server

About This Chapter

In Chapter 7, you learned how to build COM components that implement business rules for business processes. In this chapter, you will learn how Microsoft Transaction Server (MTS) provides advanced transaction and resource management for server-based COM components. You will also learn how to create MTS components, which are COM components that work within the MTS architecture.

Before You Begin

To complete the lessons in this chapter you must have done the following:

- Installed Microsoft Transaction Server.
- Read Chapter 7.

Lesson 1: Overview of Microsoft Transaction Server

Historically, the transition from simple, single-user desktop applications to distributed applications has been a difficult and time-consuming process. A significant amount of development time must be spent to create the application architecture on which distributed applications can run. Microsoft Transaction Server (MTS) eases the transition from single-user to multi-user development by providing the application infrastructure and administrative support for building scalable, robust enterprise applications.

In this lesson, you will learn about the benefits, architecture, and overall operation of MTS. You will also learn about the basic concepts of transactions and see how they are supported by MTS.

After this lesson, you will be able to:

- List the benefits of using MTS.
- Describe the MTS services.
- Explain the ACID test.

Estimated lesson time: 30 minutes

How MTS Supports Distributed Applications

As you learned in Chapter 1, the n-tier (or distributed) architecture enables application components to run on middle-tier servers independent of both the presentation and database services. When you develop these solutions, you are not required to run each tier on a different physical computer. However, to deliver maximum benefit, n-tier systems must run with presentation components on desktop clients (or Web browsers), application logic on middle-tier servers, and data on dedicated database servers. The independence of application logic from presentation and data in a distributed application offers many benefits:

- You can develop reusable application components.

  In Chapter 7, you learned that you can encapusulate business rules in stored procedures. While this provides an optimal solution for two-tier applications, the ability to create COM DLLs to encapsulate business rules in an n-tier application provides you with more flexibility than using a limited stored procedure language such as Transact-SQL.

- Application components can run on multiple computers simultaneously.

  This spreads client workloads across multiple computers to enable higher availability, scalability, and performance.

- Application components can share database connections.

   By sharing database connections, resources required by the database server are lowered, thereby improving performance. With two-tier systems, the database must allocate a connection for every user.

- Middle-tiered application components can be secured centrally.

   You can grant or deny access on a component-by-component basis to simplify administration.

As you learned in Chapter 7, MTS provides an application-programming model used for developing distributed component-based applications. MTS also includes a run-time infrastructure for deploying and managing these applications. When combined with Microsoft SQL Server, MTS provides the easiest way to run scalable, robust applications on the Microsoft Windows NT Server operating system. It is much easier to develop a distributed application with MTS since many of the advanced requirements of developing a scalable application have been provided for you. This means that as a Microsoft Visual Basic developer, you can build and test COM components in a single-user environment, and using MTS, deploy those same components into a large multi-user environment.

MTS focuses on managing the way applications use components, not just on managing transactions. Although transaction management is an integral part of many applications, MTS also provides useful services for applications that do not use transactions at all.

MTS simplifies the development and deployment of scalable n-tier applications that are built using COM technology. Components that encapsulate application logic run under the control of MTS and are invoked by presentation services from a variety of clients. These clients include:

- Traditional applications (developed using Visual Basic or other languages that support COM).
- Web browsers.
- Active Server Page (ASP) scripts running within Microsoft Internet Information Server (IIS).

Many services, such as database connection pooling, are provided automatically. MTS also supports automatic transactions so that access to data and resources are protected.

Benefits of Microsoft Transaction Server

MTS provides the required infrastructure that enables applications to operate efficiently as well as be shared by a large number of users. This lowers the complexity and cost of building applications, enabling you to focus on building business logic without having to build infrastructure. With MTS, you can use your existing skills with languages such as Visual Basic to build sophisticated n-tier applications. To do this, you develop components as COM DLLs that run on middle-tiered servers under the control of MTS. Then, when clients call your COM DLLs, Windows NT Server routes the requests to MTS automatically. Other benefits of using MTS include:

- The ability to access databases and other resources, such as mainframe applications with full transaction protection.
- Simplified component deployment via drag-and-drop interfaces (built into the administration utility, MTS Explorer) and automated client installation utilities.
- Automatic use of scalability features such as thread pooling, database connection pooling, and just-in-time (JIT) object instantiation.
- Easy component management via the MTS Explorer.
- The ability to call the same objects from IIS and ASP.
- Full support for the Microsoft Windows NT operating system with a subset of functionality when running on Microsoft Windows 98.

Note MTS will form a core piece of the COM+ run-time service initiative. For more information, visit the Microsoft COM home page at http://www.microsoft.com/com/. This Web site contains many resources on COM, COM+, and MTS.

MTS Services

The application infrastructure in a multi-user environment is composed of the services that enable many users to access an application and underlying data at the same time. Furthermore, these services maintain the integrity of the data and processes that keep the business in working order. The application infrastructure includes services that manage resources, such as threads and database connections, security, and transactions.

While the n-tier model has been available for some time, developers in the past were required to spend a large portion of development time creating the application infrastructure under which these applications could run. MTS eases the transition from single-user to multi-user development by providing the application infrastructure for building scalable, robust enterprise applications. This is possible because MTS provides specific services that are transparent to the user during the execution of an application.

Component Transactions

Component transactions are similar to database transactions. However, rather than encompassing SQL statements, a component transaction consists of methods running on one or more components. MTS monitors components as they interact with transactional resources, such as databases, and coordinates changes. Access to resources can be from a single component or from multiple components that are called together to form a single business operation. After all the work in a transaction completes, MTS initiates a two-phase commit protocol. Each resource will transparently ensure that all databases and other resources included in a request will commit or abort as a unit. If an MTS component aborts a transaction, MTS facilitates the rollback of any changes made by that component as well as any changes made by other components running under the same transaction context.

Object Brokering

One advantage of using MTS is that it acts as an object broker by servicing requests made from various clients for instances of a component. MTS acknowledges requests for object creation from remote clients. MTS then coordinates the creation, maintenance, and destruction of COM component instances and the threads that execute inside them. Another advantage is location independence of the component from the client. This feature supports dynamic reconfiguration, changing the execution location of an object without having to change the client application code after the development phase.

Resource Pooling

MTS provides pooling and automatic management of two critical server resources: threads and database connections. A pool of connections to a database, managed by the ODBC or OLE DB driver, provides high-performance access without forcing the developer to manage complex database synchronization issues. MTS employs a pool of threads to make the components respond to client requests quickly. MTS also provides a mechanism that makes it easy to share data among multiple parallel executing objects without forcing you to program complex state sharing and synchronization logic.

Just-in-Time Activation

In most distributed object environments, instances of server-based objects remain active, and consume server resources, as long as one or more clients hold a reference to the object. In multi-user environments, this can result in tremendous server resource requirements. To address this issue, MTS extends the COM object model with JIT activation, where components consume server resources only while they are actually executing.

After an MTS-based component indicates that it has completed its work, MTS deactivates the component and recycles its resources. So long as the component is deactivated, only limited server resources remain allocated to it. When the component is called again, MTS reactivates it by reacquiring any resources that the component needs. Most important, from the client's perspective, only a single instance of the component exists from the time the client creates it to the time it is finally released. No special programming is required.

JIT activation gives you additional control over object lifetime and allows you to use server resources more efficiently. From the client's perspective, only a single instance of the object exists from the time the client creates it to the time it is finally released. In actuality, however, the object might be deactivated and reactivated many times. Object instance management and JIT activation enables MTS applications to scale better than most component applications built with traditional object-oriented infrastructures.

Administration

MTS includes an administration utility called the MTS Explorer. The MTS Explorer is a GUI-based systems management interface that makes it easy for administrators to create and manage packages, configure component properties such as security and transaction behavior, and monitor/manage operating servers. Other MTS Explorer features include:

- Advanced ease-of-use features, such as drag-and-drop support for installing components into the MTS environment and multiple item selection to make the same changes to more than one object at a time.

- Operational features, such as the ability to lock packages to prevent changes while in deployment, view execution status, and rename packages and security roles.

- The ability to manage IIS applications running under MTS and packages created by Microsoft SNA Server 4.0.

- A Software Development Kit (SDK) for developing applications that installs and configures MTS applications automatically.

You can use the MTS Explorer in both the development and deployment stages of a client/server system.

MTS Explorer is a part of the new Microsoft Management Console (MMC), a graphical application that looks like Microsoft Windows Explorer, as illustrated in Figure 8.1.

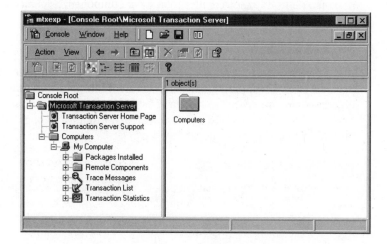

Figure 8.1 MTS Explorer within Microsoft Management Console

Several items can be administered with the MTS Explorer including:

- Installed components
- Component locations
- Transaction monitoring
- Diagnostic output
- Security role definitions

Support for Component Packages

Assembling different software components into a single solution can present configuration and deployment issues. To address these issues, MTS provides *packages* to make it easy for developers to combine different COM components into a single manageable unit. A package contains a group of related component classes and their associated type libraries. You create a package and add components to it by using the MTS Explorer. You can then deploy and administer the components in the package as a group. Each component that runs under MTS must belong to a package.

Components in a package execute in the same process space, share common security, and can be deployed as a single unit. Packages also increase application deployment flexibility. An entire application can be distributed as a single package and then partitioned into multiple packages to optimize performance, load balancing, and fault isolation.

Process Isolation

MTS enables multiple components to be grouped together into packages, with each package operating in its own protected address space in memory. This is critical when you are integrating a software component purchased from a third party into an existing solution because data corruption in one component cannot propagate to components in another package.

Automatic Thread Pooling

One way that developers can gain more scalability from their applications is to use Windows NT threads instead of processes for application execution. To make it easy for developers to use threads, MTS provides an automatic thread pooling mechanism. When a request for component execution comes in to MTS from a client, MTS automatically locates an available thread from a pool, executes the component on the thread, and returns the thread to the pool. This simplifies programming and reduces the overhead of thread creation and deletion to improve performance.

Automatic Transactions

MTS supports both objects that need transactions and objects that do not. If an object requires a transaction, MTS creates it when the object is called. When the object returns to the client, the transaction either commits or aborts. When you place components in MTS, the entire infrastructure for processing and managing a transaction is provided for you.

Security

MTS provides a distributed security implementation for component-based applications. MTS uses Windows NT security to authenticate users, but provides its own options for authorization. MTS provides two complementary models called *declarative security* and *programmatic security*. Declarative security, which is used by default, is specified when components are added into a package, and does not require developers to do any programming. Administrators declare which users and groups of users have access to a package using the MTS Explorer. This enables deployment-specific security, which can be used with prebuilt components purchased from third parties.

In contrast, programmatic security lets you build custom access controls directly into components by explicitly using *roles*. Roles define logical groups of users and are central to the MTS security model. At development time, you use roles to define declarative authorization and programmatic security logic. At deployment time, you bind these roles to specific groups and users. For example, roles in a banking application could be called "Teller" and "Manager", and components could check to make sure that the current user has been given manager privileges before performing certain operations. Administrators associate users with roles using the MTS Explorer. More important, components themselves have no embedded knowledge of specific users and don't have to make explicit calls to the Windows NT Security environment. This dramatically improves the ability of a component to be both secure and reusable.

Transaction Processing Concepts

From a business point of view, a transaction is an action that changes the state of an enterprise. For example, a customer transferring funds from his or her savings account to a checking account constitutes a banking transaction.

Consider a simple bank funds transfer application assembled from three components: Transfer, Credit, and Debit, each built by a different developer.

- Credit adds an amount to a specified account.

- Debit subtracts an amount from a specified account.

- Transfer moves money from one account to another by calling Credit and Debit.

Assume that Transfer begins by calling Debit and then subsequently calls Credit. First, Debit succeeds and subtracts $100 from the user's savings account. Next, assume Credit fails because the database was temporarily locked by another process. Unless the developer of Transfer has included code that executes in the event one of the components has failed, the application will withdraw $100 from the savings account without adding it to the user's checking account. Wrapping the call to Debit and Credit in a single transaction allows an application to better manage the possibility of failure. Although this scenario may be easy to manage in an application using only a few components, typical business applications involve hundreds of components running across multiple servers. In this environment, management becomes very difficult without the use of transactions. With component-based development, an automatic distributed transaction infrastructure is the only way to address these issues in a cost-effective manner. Figure 8.2 illustrates the difference between performing a transfer within a transaction and performing a transfer without using a transaction.

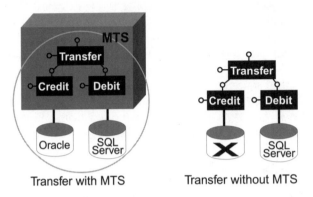

Transfer with MTS   Transfer without MTS

Figure 8.2 Comparison of performing a transfer within and without a transaction

MTS makes transaction management transparent to the component developer so that they do not have to write begin or end transaction statements into their application code. Developers can even use different tools and languages to build their components. They simply declare components to be transactional using the MTS Explorer. Then, when a component begins execution, MTS starts a transaction automatically if one is required.

When the component accesses a resource such as a database or mainframe application, MTS automatically enlists the resource in the transaction. If the component calls another component, the called component is automatically included in the transaction. When all components in a transaction complete their work, MTS initiates a full two-phase commit to either commit or abort the work.

Two-Phase Commit Process

When one or more servers process a transaction, a two-phase commit process ensures that the transaction is processed and completed either on all of the servers or on none of the servers. There are two phases to this process: prepare and commit.

An analogy of a business contract will help illustrate the two-phase commit process. In the prepare phase, each party involved in the contract commits by reading and agreeing to sign the contract. In the commit phase, each party signs the contract. The contract is not official until both parties have made a commitment. If one party does not commit, the contract is invalid.

MTS coordinates and supports the two-phase commit process, ensuring that all objects of the transaction can commit and that the transaction commits correctly.

Commit or Abort

Transactions provide an all-or-nothing simple model for managing work—either all of the objects succeed and all of the work is committed, or one or more of the objects fail and all of the work is aborted. For example, in the bank funds transfer example application used earlier in this section, both databases must be changed successfully or the entire transaction will fail and the objects will be rolled back to their previous states. In either scenario, any database tables or files affected by the work will either all be changed, or none will be changed. They will not be left in an inconsistent state.

The ACID Test

A transaction changes a set of data from one state to another. For a transaction to succeed, it must have the following properties, commonly known as the ACID (Atomicity, Consistency, Isolation, and Durability) test:

- Atomicity

   A transaction is an indivisible unit of work: all its actions succeed or they all fail.

- Consistency

   After a transaction executes, it must leave the system in a correct state or it must abort. If the transaction cannot achieve a stable end state, it must return the system to its initial state.

   In the transaction described earlier, money can be debited from one account and not yet credited to the other account during the transfer process. When the transaction is finished and able to commit, either both the debit and credit occur, or neither occurs.

- Isolation

   Concurrent transactions are not aware of each other's partial and uncommitted results. Otherwise, they might create inconsistencies in the application state.

   For example, in the transaction of transferring money, if two transfers occur at the same time, neither will know of the partial debit or credit from an incomplete transfer.

- Durability

   Committed updates to managed resources (such as database records) survive communication, process, and server system failures. Transactional logging enables you to recover the durable state after failures.

Together these properties ensure that a transaction does not create problematic changes to data between the time that the transaction begins and the time that it must commit.

MTS Architecture

MTS introduces a new programming and run-time environment model that is an extension of the COM. The basic structure of the MTS run-time environment involves several parts working together to handle transaction-based components.

MTS and the Supporting Environment

The MTS architecture comprises one or more clients, application components, and a set of system services. The application components model the activity of a business by implementing business rules and providing the objects that clients request at run-time. Components that share resources can be packaged to enable efficient use of server resources. The illustration in Figure 8.3 shows the structure of the MTS run-time environment (including the MTS components) and the system services that support transactions.

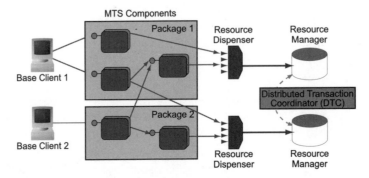

Figure 8.3 The MTS run-time environment structure

Base Client

The base client is the application that invokes a COM component running under the MTS environment. The base client could be a Visual Basic executable file running on the same Windows NT server computer, or running on a client computer that communicates through a network. In this course, the base client is an ASP page running under IIS on behalf of an Internet user.

Note A base client never runs under the MTS environment.

MTS Components

MTS components are COM components that are registered to run in the MTS environment. These COM components must be created as in-process dynamic-link libraries (DLL). However, more than one COM component can be placed in a single DLL. COM components created specifically for the MTS environment commonly contain special code that takes advantage of transactions, security, and other MTS capabilities.

System Services

The diagram shown in Figure 8.3 illustrates several important parts of MTS:

1. Resource managers are system services that manage durable data. Resource managers work in cooperation with Microsoft Distributed Transaction Coordinator (MSDTC) to guarantee atomicity and isolation of an application.

2. Resource dispensers are part of the MTS programming model and run-time environment. Application components use resource dispensers to access shared information. Resource dispensers are similar to resource managers, but without the guarantee of durability. Resource dispensers are responsible for database connection pooling.

   MTS provides two resource dispensers: the ODBC resource dispenser (for ODBC databases) and the Shared Property Manager for synchronized access to application-defined, process-wide properties (variables).

3. Microsoft Distributed Transaction Coordinator is a system service that coordinates transactions among resource managers. Work can be committed as an atomic transaction even if it spans multiple resource managers on separate computers.

4. MTS Executive (MTX), which was not shown in Figure 8.3, provides run-time services for MTS components.

MTS Packages

An MTS package is a container for a set of components that perform related application functions. All components in a package run together in the same MTS server process. Benefits of using packages include shared security setting and deployment information among all the components in the package.

MTS Explorer is typically used to register COM components as MTS components through a two-step process. First an MTS package is created. Then the COM components are added to the package. For more information on this topic, see "Using MTS Explorer" later in this chapter.

Package Location

Components in a package can be located on the same computer as MTS on which they are being registered, or they can be distributed across multiple computers. Components in the same DLL can be registered in different MTS packages. Note the following limitations and recommendations:

- A COM component can be added only to one package per computer.
- Because COM components in the same DLL can share programmatic and operating system resources, place related COM components in the same DLL.
- Because MTS components in the same package share the same MTS security level and resources, place related MTS components in the same package.

Package Guidelines

Note the following relationships between the MTS parts:

- Packages typically define separate process boundaries. Whenever a method call in an activity crosses such a boundary, security checking and fault isolation occur.

- Components can call across package boundaries to components in other packages. Such calls can access existing components or create new components.

- On a single computer, an MTS component can be installed only once. The same component cannot exist in multiple packages in the same machine. However, multiple copies (objects) of the same component can be created and can exist at any time.

MTS Concepts and Processes

A programmer or Web developer can use popular tools such as Visual Basic, Microsoft Visual C++, or Microsoft Visual J++ to easily build server applications that run within the MTS environment. The MTS architecture uses several important concepts and processes to implement the complexity behind transaction processing in a distributed enterprise system.

Activities

All MTS objects run in activities. An activity is a set of objects that run on behalf of a base client application to completely fulfill its request. When an object runs in an activity, it can create additional objects to perform work. All of these objects will run within the same activity and can be viewed as running on a single logical thread. The objects in an activity can be distributed across one or more processes, and can execute on one or more computers.

Every MTS object belongs to one activity. This is an intrinsic property of the object and is recorded in the object's context. The association between an object and an activity cannot be changed. MTS tracks the flow of execution through each activity, preventing inadvertent parallelism from corrupting the application state. This simplifies writing components for MTS.

Contexts

A context is an object associated with another object. It is a programmatic and run-time entity that is used to keep track of the state and support processing of its associated object. The MTS run-time environment manages a context for each object.

MTS Context Objects

MTS creates a context object for each MTS server component. As the component runs within the activity, the context object tracks properties of that component, including the activation state, its security information, and transaction state (if any). This frees the object from tracking its own state.

Transaction Context Objects

When multiple objects participate in a single transaction, the associated context objects work together to track the transaction. MTS uses a transaction context object to ensure that the transaction is consistent for all objects. The transaction context object, in conjunction with each of the individual context objects, guarantees that the whole transaction either commits or aborts.

MTS maintains the relationship between transaction server components and their associated context objects.

Server Process

A server process is a system process that hosts the execution of one or more MTS components. A server process can service potentially up to thousands of clients. Each package has an associated activation property that determines whether the components in the package run (as a group) in a separate, new server process (a server package) or run in their caller's process (a library package).

Note Some MTS capabilities, such as security checking and fault tolerance, are enabled only for server package activation.

Lesson Summary

Microsoft Transaction Server (MTS) facilitates the transition from single-user to multi-user development. MTS accomplishes this by providing the application infrastructure that enables applications to scale based on large enterprise requirements, such as multiple user environments like the Internet. This decreases the cost and complexity of building applications, allowing you to focus on building business logic without having to build infrastructure.

The application infrastructure in a multi-user environment is made up of the services that allow many users to access an application at the same time. These services maintain the integrity of the data and processes that keep the business in working order. The application infrastructure includes services that manage resources, such as threads and database connections, security, and transactions.

MTS has a new programming and run-time environment model that is an extension of COM. The basic structure of the MTS run-time environment involves several parts working together to handle transaction-based components, including:

- Resource managers
- Resource dispensers
- Microsoft Distributed Transaction Coordinator
- MTS Executive (MTX)

Lesson 2: Installing and Configuring Microsoft Transaction Server

The Distributed Component Object Model (DCOM) is the standard transport for calling MTS components. When a client calls an MTS component, DCOM provides the communications infrastructure that allows clients to communicate with the MTS component located on a different computer. DCOM is installed with Windows NT version 4.0 Service Pack 3 or higher and Windows 98 with TCP/IP installed. If you want to use Microsoft Windows 95–based clients with MTS, you must install DCOM for Windows 95 on the client. This lesson describes the requirements for installing MTS and describes various configuration options. The specific procedures in this lesson are particular to the use of MTS within Microsoft Management Console in Windows NT. Some tasks might be performed differently when using MTS Explorer in Windows 95 or Windows 98.

After this lesson, you will be able to:

- Install MTS on Windows 95, Windows 98, or Windows NT.
- Identify the MTS installation options.
- Use the MTS add-in for Visual Basic.

Estimated lesson time: 20 minutes

MTS System Requirements

Before you install MTS, you must install Windows NT 4.0, Windows 98, or Windows 95 with DCOM support on your computer. You can install MTS on your computer by using the Windows NT 4.0 Option Pack with Internet Information Server (IIS) or other Option Pack components. The Windows NT Option Pack requires that you install Microsoft Internet Explorer 4.0 or later, which automatically installs DCOM.

Note DCOM support for Windows 95 is automatically installed with Internet Explorer 4.0 or later. If you are running Windows 98, DCOM is already supported by the operating system. When using Windows NT Server, you must install Windows NT Service Pack 3 or later. You can download Windows NT Service Pack 4 from http://www.microsoft.com/ntserver/.

➤ **To install MTS using the Windows NT 4.0 Option Pack**

1. Start the Windows NT 4.0 Option Pack Setup program.

   If you are not currently running Internet Explorer 4.0 or higher, you will be prompted to install Internet Explorer 4.01 before setup will continue.

   If you are running Windows NT 4.0 SP4 or higher, you may receive warnings that the Option Pack has not been tested on SP4. It is OK to continue if you receive these warnings.

2. Choose Custom install.

3. Uncheck all Option Pack components.

4. Select the Transaction Server checkbox.

   Checking Transaction Server will also check Microsoft Data Access components and common files. For Windows NT 4.0, it also checks Microsoft Management Console.

5. Click the Show Subcomponents button.

6. Verify that the Transaction Server Core Components option is checked, as illustrated in Figure 8.4.

7. Click OK and finish the setup program.

   This will install MTS with only the required Option Pack components.

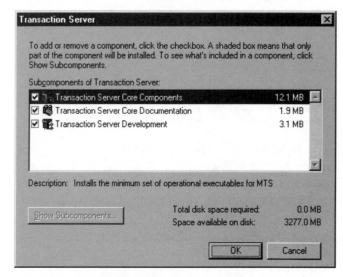

Figure 8.4 Transaction Server installation options

Configuring Your MTS Server

By default, the computer on which you install MTS is managed in the MTS Explorer as My Computer, as illustrated in Figure 8.5.

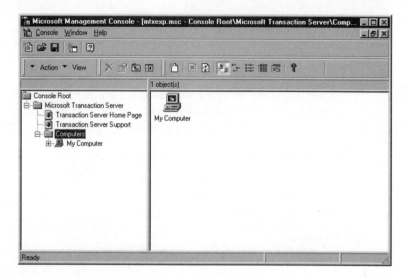

Figure 8.5 My Computer managed by MTS Explorer

You can also use the MTS Explorer to manage other computers. You can add any new computers that you need to administer to the Computers folder in the MTS Explorer by doing one of the following:

- Select the My Computer icon in the right pane, choose New, and then choose Computer from the Action menu.

- Select the My Computer icon in the right pane, and then click the Create A New Object toolbar button.

- Right-click the Computer folder in the left pane, choose New, and then choose Computer.

In the displayed Add Computer dialog, enter a computer name in your Windows NT domain to add the remote computer as a top-level folder. In order to access and display the MTS Explorer on a remote server, your logon account must be assigned to the Reader role. If you want full read and write privileges with the MTS Explorer on a remote server, your logon account must be mapped to the Administrator role.

Configuring Your Development Computer

In most cases, your MTS components will run on a remote Windows NT Server computer. In addition, most of your component development will be performed on a workstation such as Windows 95, Windows 98, or Windows NT Workstation instead of on a server running MTS. In order to configure your development computer to use the MTS type libraries, choose the Transaction Server Development option when you set up MTS, as illustrated in Figure 8.6.

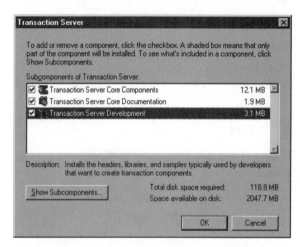

Figure 8.6 Installing the MTS development files on your computer

Configuring Visual Basic to Use MTS

Although you can create COM components for use in MTS with other development tools, in this course you will use Visual Basic. Therefore, it is important to know how to configure Visual Basic to develop MTS components.

Whenever you recompile a COM DLL (or ActiveX DLL) project in Visual Basic, Visual Basic rewrites all of the registry entries for all of the components (Visual Basic classes) that are contained within that DLL. Additionally, Visual Basic may generate new GUIDs (depending on your project's compatibility configuration) to identify the components in that DLL. This means that your MTS components are no longer properly registered in the *MTS catalog*—the MTS data store that maintains configuration information for components, packages, and roles.

To eliminate this problem, load the add-in named Transaction Server AddIn for VB. The Transaction Server add-in enables a feature that will automatically refresh your components after recompiling them, as illustrated in Figure 8.7.

Figure 8.7 Using the MTS add-in to refresh components after recompiling

The next time you run Visual Basic, the Transaction Server add-in will automatically install in your Visual Basic Integrated Development Environment (IDE). If you decide you want to refresh all of your MTS components at any given time, you can use the Refresh All Components Now command on the Add-Ins\MS Transaction Server menu.

Using the Transaction Server add-in will properly refresh the MTS catalog, even after Visual Basic compilations that generate new component GUIDs. Refreshing the MTS catalog depends on you not changing the ProgIDs of your components. In Visual Basic, a component's ProgID is formed by the following concatenation: project name.class name. If you change either of these items, you will have to reinstall your component(s) in the MTS Explorer. The following is an example of a ProgID.

```
Chateau.Hotel
```

When developing MTS components, you should set the project's Version Compatibility option to binary compatibility, as illustrated in Figure 8.8.

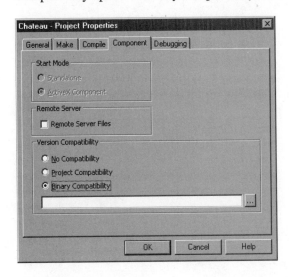

Figure 8.8 Setting the version compatibility option to Binary Compatibility

Building your component in Visual Basic without selecting the Binary Compatibility option replaces its class identifier (CLSID) and interface identifier (IID) on each compile. This has the following disadvantages when developing an MTS component, even with the Transaction Server add-in enabled:

- Roles you assigned to the interface using the MTS Explorer are lost since the interface IID is obsolete.
- Proxies and registry configurations you distributed to remote machines no longer refer to your component and must all be updated.
- Packages you exported that contain your component require re-exporting since the package definition file GUIDs are now out of sync.

Lesson Summary

An MTS component is a COM DLL that executes in the MTS run-time environment. Because MTS uses DCOM for communication between components, DCOM support for Windows 95 must be installed on Windows 95 clients. DCOM is already supported by the Windows 98 operating system. When using Windows NT, you must install Windows NT Service Pack 3 or later to ensure DCOM support. In MTS, packages are used to store components. In most cases, your MTS components will run on a remote Windows NT Server computer. In addition, most of your component development will be done on a workstation such as Windows 95, Windows 98, or Windows NT Workstation instead of on a server computer running MTS. In order to configure your development computer to use the MTS type libraries, you should choose the Transaction Server Development option when you set up MTS. In addition to installing the MTS libraries, you should also make sure that you load the Transaction Server add-in. This will ensure that components are properly registered in the MTS catalog, which is a data store that maintains configuration information for components, packages, and roles. When developing MTS components with Visual Basic, you should also make sure that the Binary Compatibility option is set for the project. This will ensure that the CLSIDs and IIDs for the component will maintain compatibility on each compile.

Lesson 3: Creating Microsoft Transaction Server Components

When designing components for MTS, you focus on organizing components based on business functionality, reuse, and possible upgrading. MTS utilizes COM technology to allow you to run components on remote servers. In this lesson, you will learn the differences between how DCOM instantiates objects and how MTS instantiates objects. You will also learn how to design components to run in MTS, move your components into MTS, and deploy your MTS components to clients.

After this lesson, you will be able to:

- Create an MTS component using Visual Basic.
- Deploy an MTS component.
- Develop a transactional ASP page.

Estimated lesson time: 45 minutes

Designing MTS Components

In addition to separating components based on business functionality, you might want to separate your business rule components from your data components, both of which are part of the middle tier. Business components encompass business rules and data components encapsulate data manipulation and access functions. Business components should focus more on the front-end aspects dealing with client requests and issues, whereas the data components should act as intermediaries between business components and the data tier.

For example, suppose Chateau St. Mark Hotel provided special pricing for guests who frequently visit the hotel. You could create the two following separate components to provide this discount:

1. The business component could determine if the guest is eligible to receive special pricing.

2. The data component could actually do the work of retrieving the price from the data source.

By carefully designing your components this way, you greatly improve your ability to update the application. If the business rules for one part of the application change, you have to recompile only one component. A well thought-out design also determines how an application can be optimized. If many people will be reserving standard suites in a hotel, but few will be reserving presidential suites, having two separate components that handle the two different business activities allows you to focus on the particular performance requirements of each component. After your component is designed, you can focus on utilizing MTS as a way to incorporate it into an n-tier solution.

Creating MTS Components in Visual Basic

You create MTS components in Visual Basic by adding MultiUse classes to an ActiveX DLL project. After you compile your DLL, you move the DLL into MTS by dragging and dropping its file into an existing package in the MTS Explorer. You can also create a new package and add components to it by using the MTS Explorer.

➤ **To create a new package**

1. In the left pane of the MTS Explorer, double-click the computer in which you want to create a new package.

2. Click the Packages Installed folder.

3. Right-click the Packages Installed folder, point to New, and then click Package.

4. In the Package Wizard, click Create An Empty Package.

   You can click Install Pre-Built Packages to add an existing package that is created with the package export function. For more information, see "Deploying MTS Components" later in this chapter.

5. Enter a name for the new package, and then click Next.

6. In the Set Package Identity dialog box, select the appropriate Account option.

   This setting specifies which Windows NT user account the package will use when it runs as a server process.

7. Click Finish, and the new package will appear in the Packages Installed folder.

Setting Package Properties

Once you have created a package, you can set package properties, such as how the package is accessed, how it participates in the security system, and how it ends when the system is shut down.

➤ **To set properties for a package**

1. Right-click the package in Microsoft Transaction Server Explorer, and then click Properties.

   The Package Properties dialog boxes will be displayed.

2. Select the appropriate tab.

The following table describes the basic package properties and lists under which tab they can be set:

Property	Description	Tab
Activation Type	Specifies either Library or Server activation for the package activation.	Activation
Authorization	Enables MTS to check the security credentials of any client that calls the package.	Security
Description	Displays a description of the package.	General
Name	Friendly name of the package (ID number is also listed).	General
Process Shutdown	Determines whether the server process associated with a package always runs, or whether it shuts down after a specified period of idle time.	Advanced

Activation Property

You use an activation property of a transaction server package to specify the process where the package's components will run when activated. The activation property determines whether the components in a package will run (as a group) in a separate, new server process (a server package) or will run in their caller's process (a library package). MTS security and fault tolerance are available only for server packages. The following table describes the activation property settings for a transaction server component.

Setting	Description	Advantage
Library Package	Will run in the same process as the client that creates it.	Minimum overhead
Server Package	Will run in its separate process; shared by all the components in the current package.	Fault tolerance, package security enabled

During development, a component should generally be activated as a server package to prevent any faults that might occur from crashing other processes.

Once you have created a new package, you can add components that implement related business services. A component can be included only in one package on a single computer. You should keep this in mind when organizing your components into packages. For example, if you have a general-purpose component that will be used by many MTS applications, you should put this component and others like it into a single package. You can then install this package as a unit where needed.

➤ **To add a component to a package**

1. Double-click the Packages Installed folder, and then double-click the package in which you want to install a component.

2. Click the Components folder.

3. Right-click the Components folder, click New, and then select Component, as illustrated in Figure 8.9.

4. Click Install New Component(s).

5. In the Install Components dialog, click Add Files to select the component.

6. In the Select Files to Install dialog, select the files you want to add, and then click Open.

7. In the Install Components dialog, click Finish.

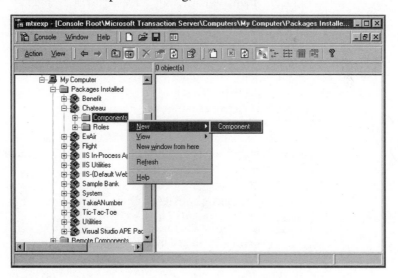

Figure 8.9 Adding a component to an MTS package

After you add your component to a package, MTS modifies the component's registry entries on the server so that it will run in the MTS run-time environment. This ensures that the package's server process can load the component.

How Remote Objects are Created

In order to create a remote object, COM needs to know the network name of the server computer. In the DCOM architecture, once the server name and the CLSID for a component are known, an element of the COM library called the service control manager (SCM) on the client machine connects to the SCM on the server machine and requests creation of this object. The SCM is a remote procedure call (RPC) server that allows service configuration and service control programs to manipulate services on remote computers.

Clients can instantiate an object in the MTS environment using the New operator or the CreateObject function; however, you should use the CreateObject function when creating an object from within the same COM DLL. When a client application requests an instance of a new object, it sends a request to the SCM on the client computer. The client-side SCM forwards the request to the SCM of the computer containing the MTS component. The server-side SCM responds by making a local activation request on the package containing the component.

The component in the MTS package appears to be a typical COM component to the client. However, MTS performs some additional tasks to modify a component's functionality. When a COM DLL is added to MTS, the CLSIDs for its components are modified to reroute the activation requests made by clients. The LocalServer32 key for the CLSID in the registry is given a new path pointing to the Mtx.exe file followed by the GUID for the MTS package, as shown in the following example.

```
C:\WINNT\SYSTEM32\Mtx.exe /p:{7CC3DBE3-EC38-11D2-8ED1-00105AA66B27}
```

The Mtx.exe file runs the MTS Executive (MTX), which provides run-time services for MTS components. These services include thread and *context* management. Context is a state that is implicitly associated with an MTS object. Context contains information about the object's execution environment, such as the identity of the object's creator and any transaction encompassing the work of the object. An object's context is similar in concept to a process that the Windows operating system maintains for an executing program.

When a client creates an MTS object, MTX intercepts the activation request and connects the client to a context object. The actual MTS object inside of the context object is then activated by the MTX. The context object will forward all method calls made to the MTS object. This entire process is transparent to the client. The client cannot tell the difference between communicating with an MTS object or any other COM object through DCOM.

Using Transactions in MTS Components

Much like implementing transactions in SQL Server, you can implement transactions in your MTS components to perform a series of tasks as a single unit of execution. To use MTS transaction services, you must set a reference to Microsoft Transaction Server Type Library (mtxas.dll).

After setting a reference to the MTS library, the first thing you do when working with a transactional MTS component is to get a reference to an ObjectContext object. This allows you to control how MTS processes a transaction. To obtain a reference to a context object, you call the GetObjectContext function. This function returns a reference to the ObjectContext instance for your object. The following example calls GetObjectContext to return an ObjectContext object:

```
Dim ctxObject As ObjectContext
Set ctxObject = GetObjectContext()
```

You can use the ObjectContext object in your code to:

- Declare that the object's work is complete.
- Prevent a transaction from being committed, either temporarily or permanently.
- Instantiate other MTS objects and include their work within the scope of your object's transaction.

MTS objects can use other MTS objects to complete a series of tasks. If an object created by another MTS object is to participate within the same transaction, it must inherit its context from the creating object. For example, a component named Transfer could create a Debit and Credit object to perform transfer services. In this situation, the Transfer object must have its MTSTransactionMode property set to RequiresNewTransaction, as illustrated in Figure 8.10.

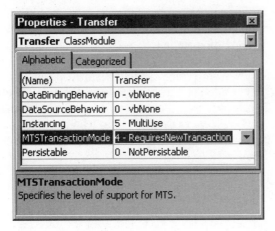

Figure 8.10 Setting the MTSTransactionMode property for the Transfer class

Calling the CreateInstance Method

You can use methods in the Debit and Credit objects within the same transaction. Simply create the objects using the CreateInstance method on the ObjectContext object, as shown in the following example code.

```
' Get the object's ObjectContext and create an instance
Set ctxObject = MTxAS.GetObjectContext
Set objRsvn = ctxObject.CreateInstance("Chateau.CRsvn")
```

Instead of setting the MTSTransactionMode property to RequiresNewTransaction, the object that is being created must have its MTSTransactionMode property set to RequiresTransaction or UsesTransaction. Any other MTSTransactionMode setting will not associate the object in the existing transaction. For example, to include the Debit and Credit objects in a transaction along with the Transfer object, the Debit and Credit object's MTSTransactionMode property should be set to UsesTransaction.

When CreateInstance is called to create a Debit and Credit object, a new context is created for them because all MTS objects always have an associated context object. Then the context object inherits information such as the current activity, security information, and current transaction. At this point, the new object participates in the same transaction as the calling object. The following example code creates an instance of a Debit object.

```
' Get the object's ObjectContext and create an instance
Set ctxObject = GetObjectContext()
Set objDebit = ctxObject.CreateInstance("Account.Debit")
```

Note If CreateInstance is used to create a non-MTS object, the object does not have a context object and does not participate in the existing transaction.

Although you use the CreateInstance function to create objects that will participate in a transaction, you use the CreateObject function and New keyword to create objects that will not participate in a transaction. If you are creating an instance of an object from the same Visual Basic project, use the CreateObject function. Although the New keyword offers a slight performance increase over CreateObject, you should not use the New keyword to create objects from the same project. This is because the object must be created internally in Visual Basic, instead of using COM services to create it. MTS hosts objects by intercepting creation calls through COM. If COM is not used to create an object, MTS is not able to host the object.

Committing or Aborting a Transaction

Once you have a reference to the context object for your object, use the SetComplete and SetAbort methods to notify MTS of the completion status of the work performed by your object. Each method that runs for an MTS object should indicate whether it has completed work successfully or unsuccessfully. If the method has completed successfully, it calls the SetComplete method on the ObjectContext object before returning from the method call.

The SetComplete method informs the context object that it can commit transaction updates and can release the state of the object along with any resources that are being held. If all other objects involved in the transaction also call SetComplete, MTS commits the transaction updates of all objects.

However, if an MTS object's method that completes a transaction is unsuccessful, it must call the SetAbort method of the ObjectContext object before returning. SetAbort informs the context object that the transaction updates of this object and all other objects in the transaction must be rolled back to their original state. If an object involved in a transaction calls SetAbort, the updates roll back even if other objects have called the SetComplete method. The following example code calls the SetComplete method when an operation completes successfully, or calls the SetAbort method if an error occurs.

```
' Operations were successful - commit the transaction
ctxObject.SetComplete
Exit Function
HandleError:
    ' One or more operations failed - rollback changes
    ctxObject.SetAbort
    MsgBox Err.Description
End Function
```

Using the Activate and Deactivate Events

Components built with Visual Basic have Initialize and Terminate events that you can use to implement startup and shutdown code for each class. However, the context object is not available in the Initialize and Terminate events. For example, if you need to read security credentials in the Initialize event, you cannot get that information because the Visual Basic run-time environment calls Class_Initialize before the object and its context are activated, so any operations that Class_Initialize attempts to perform on the object or its object context will fail. Similarly, the object and its context are deactivated before Class_Terminate is called, so operations that this method attempts on the object and its context will also fail.

To utilize the context object during initialization or shutdown, implement the ObjectControl interface in your class. The ObjectControl interface exposes the following methods:

- Activate

  The Activate method allows an object to perform context-specific initialization whenever it's activated. This method is called by the MTS run-time environment before any other methods are called on the object.

■ CanBePooled

The CanBePooled event allows an object to notify the MTS run-time environment of whether it can be pooled for reuse. Return *True* if you want instances of this component to be pooled, or *False* if not.

■ Deactivate

The Deactivate event allows an object to perform whatever cleanup is necessary before it's recycled or destroyed. This method is called by the MTS run-time environment whenever an object is deactivated.

You can add startup and shutdown code to these methods to handle activation and deactivation more appropriately, plus you have access to the context object within these methods, as shown in the following code:

```
Implements ObjectControl

Private Sub ObjectControl_Activate()
    Set ctxObject = GetObjectContext()
    ' Connect to database
End Sub

Private Function ObjectControl_CanBePooled() As Boolean
    ObjectControl_CanBePooled = True
End Function

Private Sub ObjectControl_Deactivate()
    cn.Close
    Set cn = Nothing
End Sub
```

Note If you implement the ObjectControl interface, you must also implement the CanBePooled method. Since object pooling is not currently supported in MTS, the easiest way to implement this method is to return *True*.

Deploying MTS Components

After you have developed and tested your MTS application in a development environment, you will deploy the application to production servers and clients. To do this, you create an MTS package, add your components to the package, and then export it. Exporting packages allows you to copy a package from one MTS computer to another. For example, you can use the MTS Explorer to export a package from a server on which the package was developed to another MTS server for testing.

➤ **To export a package from a server**

1. Double-click the computer that contains the package you want to export, and then double-click the Packages Installed folder.

2. Select the package you want to export.

3. Right-click the package and select Export.

4. In the Export Package dialog, enter the path or browse for the folder where you want to create the package file. Type a name for the file. The component files will be copied to the same folder as the package file.

   If you want to include any Windows NT user IDs that have been mapped to roles for the package, select the Save Windows NT User IDs Associated With Roles checkbox.

5. Click Export.

When you export a package, MTS creates a package file (.pak) in the folder you specified. The component files that are copied include the COM DLLs, associated type libraries, and necessary proxy stub DLLs. A Clients folder is also created within the Package folder, which contains an executable file that you can use to configure a client computer to access the package components.

When you export a package, MTS creates a client application executable in the Clients folder where the package file is exported. You can run this executable from a client machine to configure it to access the components in the package remotely. In addition, you can use the MTS Explorer to generate a client application executable that configures a client computer to access a remote package. The client computer must have DCOM support, but does not require any MTS server files other than the client application executable to access a remote MTS server application.

➤ **To install a client application executable on a client system**

1. Export the package that is to be used by client computers.

2. Locate the folder into which you exported your package.

3. Run the executable on the client computer.

   For example, you can copy the executable and run it on client computers, provide a shared folder for users to copy and run on their computers, or incorporate an executable into an HTML document using the <OBJECT> tag.

When you run the executable, the client application executable performs the following tasks:

- Copies the client application executable to a temporary folder named Clients and extracts the necessary client-side files, including type libraries and custom proxy-stub DLLs.

- Transfers type libraries and proxy-stub DLLs for the server package to the Remote Applications folder in the Program Files folder.

- Updates the system registry with the required entries for clients to use the server package remotely through DCOM, including information related to application, class, programmatic, interface, and library identifiers.

- Registers the application in the Add/Remove Programs option in the Control Panel so that the application can be uninstalled at a later date. All remote applications are prefaced with "Remote Application" so that you can easily find your application in the Add/Remove Programs list of installed components.

- Removes the Clients subfolder and files generated during installation.

After the client computer is completely configured, components can be created from a remote server running MTS. In addition, the components run remotely on the MTS server when the client uses them.

Handling Errors

MTS performs extensive internal integrity and consistency checks. In this way, MTS automatically provides fault isolation to maximize the stability of an application. However, as a component developer, you may want to design your components to take a more active role in error handling.

Unhandled Errors in MTS Components

MTS does not allow unhandled errors to propagate outside of an MTS component. If an error occurs while executing within an MTS context and the component doesn't catch the error before returning from the context, MTS detects the error and terminates the process. This error detection and process termination action is called a *failfast policy*. The failfast policy in this case is based on the assumption that the exceptional condition has put the process into an indeterminate state—it is not safe to continue processing.

MTS interprets all aborted processes as exceptional conditions. If the transaction aborts and you do not raise an error to the client, MTS will force an error to be raised. It will set the HRESULT return value to CONTEXT_E_ABORTED informing the client that the call aborted. However, if an MTS object has set an HRESULT error code, MTS never changes this returned value.

Types of Errors

There are three types of errors that can occur in an MTS application: business rule errors, internal errors, and Windows exceptions.

Business Rule Errors

When an activity performs an operation that violates business rules, the activity causes a business rule error. This error would occur, for example, when a client attempts to withdraw money from an empty account. The MTS objects that you write must detect these types of errors. They enforce the business rules by checking client actions against existing business rules. For example, a Debit object should check an account balance before withdrawing money.

Business rules can also be enforced in the database itself. For example, if a client attempts to withdraw money from an empty account, it might be the database that detects and raises the error (back to the Debit object).

In either case, you might want to take the following two actions:

1. Abort the current transaction by calling SetAbort.
2. Report the error to the MTS client. To report the error back to the client, raise the error using the Err.Raise method, typically with a custom error you have defined.

The client application, whether an ASP page, Visual Basic, or other client, must be able to interpret the error that you raise to display the proper message to the user. In the debit example, this might mean transferring money from other funds into the account.

Internal Errors

Internal errors are unexpected errors that occur while objects are working on behalf of a client. For example, a file could be missing, network problems could prevent connecting to a database, or creation of a dependent COM component could fail.

In Visual Basic, these errors will be detected and raised by Visual Basic itself. Like business rules errors, you can write code to trap these errors, and then attempt to correct them or abort the transaction.

Optionally, you may want to raise the error to the client using the Err.Raise method to pass the same error back. This will inform the client that an error occurred, and that it must display an appropriate error message. The client should take appropriate action, perhaps by displaying a friendly error message to the user, or by recording the error in an event log.

Windows Exceptions

If for some reason your MTS object causes a Windows exception (a crash), MTS will shut down the process that hosts the object and log an error event in the Windows NT event log. When this failfast policy occurs, the process hosting the object is terminated. An HRESULT indicating the type of error will be returned to the client. The MTS run time can also raise exceptions that cause your object to fail. In this case, your object automatically aborts.

Creating Efficient Objects

Transaction components place a heavy demand on server resources, but certain programming techniques enable you to gain the maximum efficiency from transaction components. You need to consider the network, database, and processing resources used by the component in the transaction, and how long an object will be active.

Stateless Objects

While an object is active, it maintains data. An object is referred to as stateful if data is maintained across multiple client calls. An object is stateless if the data is reset with each client call. In general, MTS objects should be stateless. Using stateless objects provides the following benefits:

- Helps ensure transaction isolation and database consistency by not introducing data from one transaction to another.
- Reduces the server load by not storing data indefinitely.
- Improves scalability because of the reduced server load and because there are fewer internal data dependencies in the stateless object.

Persistent states shared between objects can be implemented in a database or through the shared property manager. For information on the latter, see the topic "Sharing State" in the Windows NT Option Pack Help.

Maximizing Performance

Following is a list of ways in which you can improve the efficiency of the objects you manage using MTS:

- Pass arguments by value (ByVal) whenever possible. The ByVal keyword minimizes trips across networks.
- Use methods that accept all of the property values as arguments. Avoid exposing object properties. Each time a client accesses an object property, it makes at least one round-trip call across the network.
- Avoid passing or returning objects. Passing object references across process and network boundaries wastes time.

- Avoid creating database cursors. Cursors create a large amount of overhead. Whenever you create a Recordset object, ActiveX Data Objects (ADO) creates a cursor. Instead of creating Recordset objects, run SQL commands whenever possible.

- When making updates keep resources locked for as short a time as possible. This will maximize the availability of resources to other objects.

- Enable MTS to run simultaneous client requests through objects by making them apartment-threaded. In Visual Basic 6.0, you make objects apartment threaded by selecting the Apartment Threaded option in the Project Properties dialog. (Since these are typically server-based objects, you'll also want to select the Unattended Execution option.)

MTS and ASP

Web-based business applications often need to run both scripts and components within the same transaction. Starting with IIS 4.0 and MTS 2.0, support has been added for including ASP pages within MTS transactions. In Chapter 4, you learned how to invoke COM components from an ASP page using the following two techniques:

- Use the CreateObject method of the built-in ASP Server object.

- Use the HTML <OBJECT> tag and supply the RUNAT, ID, and PROGID (or CLSID) attributes.

MTS components should be created only from ASP clients using the first technique, Server.CreateObject. Using the <OBJECT> tag will cause the created object to run outside of the MTS environment.

To code a transactional ASP page, follow these steps:

1. Declare the page to be transactional with the @TRANSACTION directive. The following example code creates a new MTS transaction.

   ```
   <%@ TRANSACTION = value %>
   ```

   The value argument can be one of the following:

   - Requires_New—Starts a new transaction.
   - Required—Starts a new transaction.
   - Supported—Does not start a transaction.
   - Not_Supported—Does not start a transaction.

   The @TRANSACTION directive must be the very first line on the page, otherwise an error is generated. You must add the directive to each page that should be run under a transaction. The current transaction ends when the script finishes processing.

2. Optionally, add code to interact with the transaction, either completing or aborting it, or handling transaction events. You can use the ontransactioncommit and ontransactionabort events to write different responses to the user as shown in the following example code:

```
<%@ TRANSACTION = Required %>
<%
' Buffer output so that different pages can be displayed.
Response.Buffer = True
%>
<HTML>
<BODY>
<H1>Welcome to the online banking service</H1>
<%
Set BankAction = Server.CreateObject("MyExample.BankComponent")
BankAction.Deposit(Request("AcctNum"))
%>
<P>Thank you. Your transaction is being processed.</P>
</BODY>
</HTML>
<%
' Display this page if the transaction succeeds.
Sub ontransactioncommit()
    Response.Write "<HTML>"
    Response.Write "<BODY>"
    Response.Write "Thank you. Your account has been credited."
    Response.Write "</BODY>"
    Response.Write "</HTML>"
    Response.Flush()
End Sub
%>
<%
' Display this page if the transaction fails.
Sub ontransactionabort()
    Response.Clear()
    Response.Write "<HTML>"
    Response.Write "<BODY>"
    Response.Write "We are unable to complete your transaction."
    Response.Write "</BODY>"
    Response.Write "</HTML>"
    Response.Flush()
End sub
%>
```

A transaction can involve only one ASP page. The page creates and uses MTS components that are automatically enlisted in the page's transaction. Because a single ASP page can create multiple components, you can use transactional ASP pages to associate unrelated MTS components programmatically into the same transaction.

Determining Transactional Status of an ASP Page

A transaction associated with an ASP page completes when all the script on the page executes. If any transactional MTS components are created, the transaction completes successfully only if *all* the components call SetComplete. The transaction aborts if there is a script processing error (such as syntax error) on the page; if the page times out; or if ObjectContext.SetAbort is invoked.

Using the MTS Explorer

As you learned earlier in this chapter, the MTS Explorer is the administration utility included with MTS. It is a snap-in component of Microsoft Management Console (MMC) and is the graphical interface you use to create, distribute, install, export, import, maintain, and manage MTS packages and their components.

The MTS Explorer helps the following computer professionals to work with transactions:

- Programmer (MTS component developer)—creates packages; adds MTS components to packages; creates roles; and helps monitor and debug MTS components.
- Web developer—installs, imports, and exports packages; assigns identities to packages; maps roles to NT users; troubleshoots and profiles MTS activities.
- Web administrator—updates and maintains packages; manages Windows NT users mapped to roles; monitors MTS transactions; and manually resolves transactions under failure conditions.

Component Location and Versioning Issues

Adding a component to a package does not physically copy or move the implementation file (usually a DLL) from its original folder location; adding a component simply registers it with MTS. You can force package processes to shut down, which is common when replacing one or more MTS components with a newer version. Shutting down the server processes forces the MTS run time to unload DLLs from memory.

➤ **To shut down a package process**

Right-click My Computer in the left pane of the MTS Explorer window and click Shutdown Server Processes.

Note If later you change the name or physical location of the component implementation file, or you replace it with a newer component implementation with a different type library, you must reregister the component in MTS. MTS does not track file changes automatically.

Setting Component Properties

When you set the properties of a component at design time, you:

- Determine the process in which the component will run.
- Define the component's role with respect to the current transaction.

➤ **To set the properties of a component**

Right-click the component in the MTS Explorer window, and then click Properties.

Transaction Property

Each transaction server component has a transaction property. Whenever an instance of a component is created, MTS checks the transaction property of the component to determine whether it needs a transaction to do its work. Most MTS components are marked either Supports Transactions or Requires A Transaction. The illustration in Figure 8.11 shows the different options for setting transaction options on the Transaction tab.

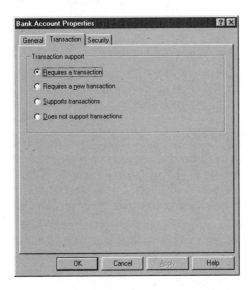

Figure 8.11 Transaction property setting for a Bank.Account component

Lesson Summary

You create MTS components in Visual Basic by adding MultiUse classes to an ActiveX DLL project. When a COM DLL is added to MTS, the CLSIDs for its components are modified to reroute the activation requests made by clients to MTS. After setting a reference to the MTS library in a COM DLL, the first thing you do when working with a transactional MTS component is to get a reference to an ObjectContext object. To obtain a reference to a context object, you call the GetObjectContext function. You can then create instances of other MTS objects to complete a series of tasks as a single unit of execution.

To utilize the context object during initialization or shutdown, implement the ObjectControl interface in your class. In addition, you should use the objectcontrol_activate and objectcontrol_deactivate event procedures instead of Initialize and Terminate because the context object is not available in these events. Use the SetComplete and SetAbort methods to notify MTS of the completion status of the work performed by your object.

After you have developed and tested your MTS application in a development environment, you will deploy the application to production servers and clients by creating an MTS package. You can then add your components to the package and export it. A Clients folder is created with the package, and contains an executable file that you can use to configure a client computer to access the package components.

Lab 8: Deploying a COM Component in MTS

In this lab, you will add the Chateau.dll COM Component you created in Lab 7 to Microsoft Transaction Server (MTS). Then you will change the code of the Checkin.asp page to support MTS transactions.

To see a demonstration of this lab, run the Lab08.exe animation located in the Animations folder on the companion CD-ROM that accompanies this book.

Before You Begin

You should have already completed Labs 2, 3, 4, 5, 6, and 7. If you have not, follow the steps in Lab 2 to create the Chateau Web project and use the files in the Labs\Lab07\Partial folder to obtain the necessary files to complete this lab.

Estimated lab time: 45 minutes

Exercise 1: Creating an MTS Package

In this exercise, you will create an MTS package for the Chateau.dll Component. Before doing this, you will need to set the Component up for MTS in Visual Basic.

1. Using Visual Basic, open the Chateau.vbp project you created in Lab 7. This project is also located in the \Labs08\Partial folder.

2. In the Project Properties dialog, make sure the component is set to Binary Compatibility under the Component tab.

3. Save the project and recompile the DLL.

➤ **To create an MTS Package with the Component**

1. Open the MTS Explorer.

2. Expand the Console Root in the left pane to \Microsoft Transaction Server\Computers\My Computer. If you are doing this from a remote location, use the name of your server in place of My Computer.

3. Right-click the Packages Installed folder and select New Package. This will execute the Package Wizard.

4. Select the Create An Empty Package icon and enter Chateau as the name of the package. Click Next.

5. For the identity of the package, select Interactive User, and then click Finish.

6. Expand the Packages Installed folder and locate the Chateau package. Expand this folder. You will see two folders: Components and Roles.

7. Right-click the Components folder and select New Component. This will open the Component Wizard.

8. Select the Install New Components icon.

9. Click the Add Files button and browse to Chateau.dll. Click Finish to close the Component Wizard.

10. Right-click My Computer and select Refresh All Components.

11. Test the application by checking in a guest. Notice that the Chateau.Reservation Component spins briefly while the component is being accessed.

Exercise 2: Coding a Transactional MTS Page

In this exercise, you will add code to the Checkin.asp page to support an MTS transaction for the Chateau MTS package. If the transaction fails, an error message will be displayed.

1. Open the Checkin.asp file for editing.

2. Click the Source tab on the HTML editor window.

3. Modify the first line of the page so that a MTS transaction is required. ASP allows only one '@' line in a page. Modify this line as follows:

```
<%@ Language=VBScript Transaction=Required %>
```

4. Create event handlers for the ontransactioncommit and ontransactionabort events that MTS provides. If the transaction was successful, you want to display the Reservation Request form. If not, you want to display an error message.

5. First you will move the If…Then…Else statement that returns an error if invalid information is entered into the form. To do this, move the End If for this statement from the bottom of the page and place it above the code that checks the Reservation code.

6. The ReservationCode needs to determine if the Reservation Request form is displayed. Copy the ReservationCode = 0 line at the top of the page to the code block that executes when a reservation is made. This is where the cookie is created.

7. Change the ReservationCode line at the top of the page so that it equals −1 instead of 0. Now the Reservation Request form will not display unless the reservation completes successfully.

8. Enclose the Reservation Request form and the code for checking the Reservation code in an ontransactioncommit event.

   Your code should look similar to the following:

```
Sub ontransactioncommit()
    If ReservationCode = 0 Then
        'Show the form
%>
.

.

<%
    Else
    ' ReservationCode Errors
    Response.Write "<H2>Press the back button on your browser" & _
        " to make the appropriate changes.</H2>"
    End If
End Sub
```

Form is here

9. Below the ontransactioncommit event, insert an ontransactionabort event that displays an error message. Use the following code:

```
Sub ontransactionabort
    Response.Write "<H2>There was an error making the" & _
        " reservation.</H2>"
End Sub
```

10. Save your changes and test the application.

Exercise 3: Supporting MTS in the COM Component

In this exercise, you will add code to the Chateau.vbp project so that an MTS transaction is required for the component. The SetComplete and SetAbort methods of the context object that MTS provides will be used.

1. Using Visual Basic, open the Chateau.vbp project you created in Lab 7. This project is also located in the \Labs08\Partial folder.

2. In the Project References dialog, add a reference to the Microsoft Transaction Server Type Library.

3. Display the Properties page for the Reservation ClassModule and change the MTSTransactionMode for the module to 2–RequiresTransaction.

4. Set a reference to the context object. Put this at the top of the code below the variable declarations and the On Error GoTo statement as follows:

```
Dim objOContext As ObjectContext
Set objOContext = GetObjectContext()
```

5. Call SetComplete if the code runs correctly. Call SetAbort in the error trapping code to rollback the transaction if an error occurs. Save your changes.

➤ **To modify the MTS Package for the new Component**

1. Open the MTS Explorer.

2. Expand the Console Root in the left pane to \Microsoft Transaction Server\Computers\My Computer. If you are doing this from a remote location, use the name of your server in place of My Computer.

3. Right-click My Computer and select Shut Down Server Processes. This will verify that no server processes are running that would interfere with updating the component.

4. Locate the Chateau.Reservation component in the Chateau package and delete it.

5. Switch back to the Chateau project in Visual Basic and recompile the DLL.

6. After the DLL has been recompiled successfully, switch to the MTS Explorer and right-click the Components folder in the Chateau Package. Select New Component.

7. Add the Chateau.dll component following the steps listed in Exercise 1.

8. Right-click the newly created Chateau.Reservation component and select Properties. Click the Transaction tab and select the Requires A Transaction option. Click OK to save your changes.

9. Right-click My Computer and select Refresh All Components to complete the process.

10. Save your work and test the application. The Chateau MTS package will now run in a transaction.

Review

The following questions are intended to reinforce key information presented in this chapter. If you are unable to answer a question, review the appropriate lesson and then try the question again. Answers to the questions can be found in Appendix A, "Questions and Answers."

1. Explain the benefits of using MTS in your Web project.

2. List and describe three services provided by MTS.

3. What is the ACID test?

Implementing Security

About This Chapter

In this chapter, you will learn about implementing security in a Web site application. There will be a general security discussion, followed by in-depth information about specific security requirements. These requirements will be grouped by product, such as Microsoft SQL Server security and Microsoft Transaction Server security. By the end of this chapter, you will be able to describe general security issues you need to consider when developing a Web site and how to implement security using various Microsoft technologies.

Before You Begin

To complete the lessons in this chapter you must have

- A basic understanding of Microsoft Windows NT Server security implementation, including:
  - Plain text user validation
  - Windows NT Challenge/Response user validation
- The ability to use the Internet Service Manager to configure Web site security.

Lesson 1: Security Issues

Developing single-tier stand-alone applications for the individual user typically does not require advanced security considerations. Because the user is physically sitting at their computer and using an application that does not connect to other computers, you can generally assume that their ability to log in to their computer is adequate security for simple applications. However, when you begin developing multitier applications, especially those that run over the Internet, implementing security becomes a greater consideration. Securing both the application (in terms of which features can be accessed by the user) and securing the underlying database (and general access to the server) present developers with a complex array of security options. For example, implementing security in SQL Server does not necessarily prohibit users from initially accessing a Web site application. Security must be implemented on the client, in the application (on the server), and in the database. To do this, you must become familiar with the security features of Microsoft Internet Explorer, Microsoft Windows NT Server, Microsoft SQL Server, and Microsoft Transaction Server (MTS).

After this lesson, you will be able to:

- Describe why security is important in a networked environment.
- List potential security threats.
- Describe various security considerations when developing a Web site.
- Compare and contrast security considerations on the client and on the server.
- Describe how Microsoft technologies help developers implement security.

Estimated lesson time: 45 minutes

Overview

One of your main objectives when creating a Web site is having data that is reliably secured. Security issues on the Web are not much different than security issues that have always been in your organization. At the most basic level, you need to keep both malicious hackers and careless users from causing problems with your Web servers. The first step and most important part of the process is to evaluate your security needs. Ask questions, such as the following:

- How sensitive is data accessed through the Web site?
- How many ways are there to access the data?
- Who would want this data and why?
- How many people need to access each set of data?

Security is a combination of technology and policy. Good security policy includes physically securing access to sensitive resources, and ensuring that local logon rights to sensitive resources are given only to trusted individuals. You can do this by enforcing a strong password policy (there are tools in Windows NT to enforce this), and by using the extensive auditing facilities in Windows NT to track the state of security on your networks.

Because Microsoft Internet Information Server (IIS) is a service that runs on Windows NT, it relies heavily on Windows NT's user accounts and the file system type (NTFS or FAT) that has been implemented.

In this chapter, you will learn how to utilize Windows NT to establish security on your Web sites.

In addition, business rules are often complex and can contain sensitive or secure information. Therefore, it is not always wise to send these rules back with HTML to a Web browser. Your goal should be to limit the amount of information sent back to the client, while minimizing the number of round trips between client and server. Because bandwidth is also an important consideration (more so with the Internet versus an intranet), you can implement some of the business rules on the client, thus reducing round trips to the server. For example, you may want simple data validation rules for your client, such as one to ensure that a value is not greater than 999. It is efficient to perform these types of checks on the client with most of the sensitive business rules existing on the server in the middle-tier. MTS provides a good environment for hosting your middle-tier objects because it can handle security as well as transactions. This feature allows you to focus primarily on providing the business logic specific to your application.

Security in Networked Systems

Ever since the first computers were connected to one another through a network, security has been a major concern of network operating system vendors, developers, and administrators. Designing and implementing a security plan can help protect a computer system from loss, corruption, and unauthorized use.

In addition, the Internet has made the need to address security concerns even more critical. All computers connected directly to the Internet, or indirectly though a proxy server, are potential victims of security attacks.

Access Control

The most fundamental security concept is access control: determining who has or does not have access to your site or to specific areas on your site. For example, if you have implemented a membership with content restricted to those members, you need to understand each method of access control and decide which works best in your situation.

The following table describes various access control methods.

Access Control Method	Description
Anonymous	Allows anyone to view the content on your site.
Basic	Requires a user ID and password. This access method is not very secure because data is sent as clear text or base64-encoded. However, it is appropriate for some applications, and is the most widely used authentication method.
Digest Authentication	Conceptually similar to Basic; however, the password is not sent over the network. Instead, a hashed version of the password is used. The hashing algorithm forms a hexadecimal representation of a combination of user name, password, the requested resource, the HTTP method, and a given randomly generated value sent with the return challenge from the server. Digest Authentication is not as secure as Kerberos or a client-side key implementation, but it does represent a stronger form of security than Basic Authentication.
Content Rating	This is a self-selecting type of access control that you cannot manage as an administrator. Users must configure a response to this access in their browsers.
NTFS security	Allows you to specify permissions at the file level, based on user or group.
Windows NT LAN Manager (NTLM)	Also known as Windows NT Challenge/Response, this is the most secure of the three basic authentication methods supported by IIS. However, you must be using Internet Explorer clients to support NTLM.
Site Server membership	Part of the Site Server product, which sits on top of NTS and IIS. Use when you need Windows NT authentication, but want higher scalability or are on the World Wide Web, where your users may not participate in a Windows NT domain model. This is ideal for a large subscription service.
TCP/IP addresses	Allows you to restrict access based on a user's IP address or domain. You can programmatically restrict access according to a domain as well.

Note The Anonymous, Basic, and NTLM access control methods can all be set through the same IIS dialog using the Microsoft Management Console (MMC).

Auditing

You can use auditing when it is important to determine which files or pages have been accessed, and what may have been compromised or tested on your site. For example, if you want to know who is accessing a file, you can set up logging that will record any access, failed or successful. You can use the following logging options to do this.

- Windows NT Event Logs

  These are basic Windows NT logs used to store system events, such as access violations, low disk space, and so on.

- IIS Logs

  IIS logs are more comprehensive than the Windows NT Event log because they can determine who is accessing your site and specifically what content they viewed.

- Custom Logs

  If you need to generate log files in a format that differs considerably from the manner in which IIS generates log files, you can create your own custom logging module. To do this, you create a COM component that can be called by IIS to log requests, just as if it were a built-in logging module.

Authentication

Use authentication when it is necessary to prove the identity of the user. For example, if you were creating a private financial transaction, such as a bank-balance transfer, you would secure the channel. You would also ensure that whomever executed the transaction was the true owner.

To do this, you can use client certificates, which are values available to ASP through the Request object. You must have a server certificate and secure connection to use client certificates. In addition, you can use Microsoft Visual C++ to create ISAPI filters that can implement your own authentication scheme.

Privacy and Data Integrity

Privacy techniques ensure that unauthorized users do not have access to your secure communication. Data integrity means that the data you send is the data your user receives, and vice versa. For example, financial transactions need to be protected from the possibility of having their data corrupted or being maliciously altered, which requires that both privacy and data integrity measures be taken.

Privacy and data integrity are interrelated; if your communication is secure, the data should not be susceptible to alteration.

The following list describes some tools and protocols you can use to ensure privacy and data integrity.

- Client Certificates

  A client certificate is a piece of digital ID for the users accessing your site, and it can be mapped directly to Windows NT accounts.

- Encryption

  Encryption is the general term used for setting up a secure channel. To establish a secure channel, you generally need a valid server certificate. You can either make your own through Certificate Server, or request one through a third-party certificate authority.

- Microsoft Transaction Server (MTS)

  MTS is now part of Windows NT and integrated with IIS. MTS allows you to easily use ASP to set up transactions around database access to create a robust transaction processing system. You can even mark an entire ASP page as transactional.

- Private Communication Technology (PCT)

  PCT is another protocol used to create a secure Internet or intranet channel. Like Secure Sockets Layer (SSL), PCT is intended to prevent eavesdropping on communications in client/server applications, with servers always being authenticated and clients being authenticated at the server's option. While PCT is an enhancement over SSL, secure PCT channels are often referred to as SSL. PCT is compatible with SSL, but it differs from SSL in that it has an improved "handshake" phase that eliminates a number of problems currently found in the original SSL.

- Secure Sockets Layer (SSL)

  SSL is a specific protocol used to provide a secure channel by providing a security handshake that is used to initiate the TCP/IP connection. This handshake results in the client and server agreeing on the level of security they will use, and fulfills any authentication requirements for the connection. In addition, SSL is used to encrypt all the information in both the HTTP request and HTTP response, including the URL the client is requesting, any submitted form contents (such as credit card numbers), any HTTP access authorization information (user names and passwords), and all the data returned from the server to the client.

- Transport Layer Security (TLS)

  TLS is a new secure channel protocol under development by the Internet Engineering Task Force. TLS builds on existing protocols to create an improved Internet secure channel protocol, and is a protocol used primarily in messaging applications using SMTP.

Categories of Security Threats

Security threats can be divided into four categories based on the consequences of the attack. The following table describes each type of security threat (listed in decreasing order of seriousness).

Security Threat	Description
System modification attacks	Unauthorized or malicious actions that alter computer files or settings. For example, a program that surreptitiously deletes important operating system files.
Invasion of privacy attacks	Unauthorized access to private computer data or monitoring of the computer user's actions. For example, a program that surreptitiously reads the contents of the user's file-system and reports this information back to a software vendor.
Denial of service attacks	Overuse of a computer's resources, which effectively blocks the user from using that aspect of the computer. For example, Java applets can be created that lock up browsers, forcing the user to close the browser.
Misdirection attacks	Any purposely misleading information presented to the user. For example, a program can mimic system dialogs to try to mislead the user into performing unnecessary actions.
Antagonistic attacks	Any purposefully annoying, but essentially harmless, action. For example, changing the user's desktop color settings in an unauthorized manner.

A security violation will often consist of a combination of the categories described above. A complete security strategy will include deterrence, protection, detection, and response measures. This course will focus on protection measures implemented programmatically or through administrative tools.

Web Security

Because of the ubiquitous nature of the Web, security issues can be much more complex than those of a typical file server environment. When planning a Web site, you must consider various aspects of Web technology and develop a security plan based on specific scenarios. The illustration in Figure 9.1 shows the architecture of a Web site and highlights important security issues.

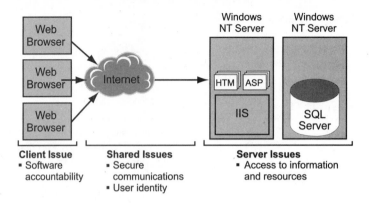

Figure 9.1 Web site architecture and security

Client and Server Issues

Security issues can typically be categorized as being related to either the client or the server. However, certain issues can be shared between the two.

Generally, the client's main concern is that the browser or the downloaded dynamic content does not endanger the user. Client compatibility with server-based user validation is an important security concern, especially in a heterogeneous client environment such as the Web. For example, although basic (plain text) authentication is not as secure as the Windows NT Server Challenge/Response (NT/CR) mechanism, all commercial Internet browsers support basic authentication. Only Internet Explorer currently supports NT/CR.

The most important security concerns for the server are to determine who can access your Web site, what files a user can access, and what type of access rights—read, write, or execute—the user has.

Secure communications and user identity are critically important for both the client and the server. Certain security issues and technologies apply differently to internal (trusted) users versus external (inherently non-trusted) users. A whole class of products—such as Internet proxies and firewalls—has been created to contend with the different concerns of these two types of access.

Microsoft Security Solutions

When designing a Web-based solution using Microsoft tools, you can implement security by using existing security features of both server and client products. Microsoft client and server security technologies make up an extensible security model on which you can build your solution.

Client Solutions

Internet Explorer relies on a number of security technologies to protect the client from malicious attacks, including the following:

- The Internet Options dialog allows the user to configure the security level for Java applets, ActiveX controls, cookies, scripts, Certificate Authorities (CAs), and other options. You can set these options during installation with the Microsoft Internet Explorer Administrator's Kit (IEAK).

  Using Internet Security Zones, security restrictions can be specified for the following Internet zones: Local, Trusted, Internet, Restricted.

- Microsoft Java Virtual Machine (JVM) protects the user against non-trusted applets by running them in a secure process space called a sandbox.

- The ActiveX Scripting architecture of Internet Explorer allows only safe embedded scripts to be executed from within a Web page.

- Authenticode allows trusted code to be downloaded, optionally installed, and run on the client's computer. Authenticode uses digital signatures and certificate authorities to identify the author and assure the authenticity of a component.

Server Solutions

Every Microsoft server product has access-related security features that are integrated with Windows NT Server's Access Control Security. This security model uses Access Control Lists (ACLs) to determine which users have which rights to access files, printers, and other server resources.

Note Fore more information about Windows NT Server's Access Control Security, see "Access Control" in Windows NT Server Online Help.

Having Access Control Security integrated into all server products satisfies two requirements:

- Verification of user identity (authentication)

  All users must have a Windows NT account to log on to the network. An account consists of a unique account name and password. This is called the Windows NT Challenge/Response logon protocol. The User Manager tool is used to set users, groups, and rights.

- Controlled access to resources (authorization)

  Each user or group of users is given access rights to the computer's resources. Windows NT Explorer is used to set access rights to files and folders.

Shared Solutions

Both the client and server can utilize Windows NT Server's Access Control Security to provide secure communications and user authentication.

In addition, Microsoft Internet products support the Windows NT security model and extend it in the following ways:

- IIS also allows anonymous and basic text log on of Internet users. The Internet Service Manager tool can be used to set security options for this Web server and each Web site it supports.

- Microsoft Certificate Server enables the creation of certificates that can be used for identifying Internet users, establishing private communications, and signing code components.

- IIS and Internet Explorer support SSL 3.0, PCT 1.0, and Secure Electronic Transaction (SET) protocols for private point-to-point communication.

Lesson Summary

Security is becoming increasingly important when developing solutions. There are different security threats to be taken into account, such as system modification attacks and denial of service attacks. Security considerations can generally be categorized as affecting the client or the server. However, in some cases, such as a proxy support, the security implementation may be shared between client and server.

In order to help developers resolve these concerns, Microsoft has implemented a number of features in both its client technology (such as Internet Explorer) and in its server technology (such as Internet Information Server and Certificate Server). Although many of these features require Microsoft technologies on the client (such as support for Windows NT Challenge/Response) developers can still create secure Web applications that are client independent.

Lesson 2: Implementing Security in a Web Application

One advantage of using IIS is that it can utilize the high level of security built into the core of the Windows NT operating system. In order to implement Windows NT security to access HTML, ASP, and other files, every user accessing your Web site must be associated with a Windows NT user account for authentication. In this lesson, you will learn about security issues as they relate to Web applications.

The four levels of security related to Web applications that will be discussed in this lesson are as follows:

- ASP application security supported through Microsoft Visual InterDev
- IIS-level security
- Operating system file-level security
- SQL database-level security

After this lesson, you will be able to:

- Create and customize permissions.
- List the five levels of security provided by Internet Service Manager.

Estimated lesson time: 45 minutes

Overview of Web Application Security

When you create a Web application, you should consider security issues such as using dynamic ASP pages and cookies to implement controlled user access and protection for your application's resources. Fortunately, you can use Windows NT security features to protect your Web applications. Moreover, elements of a Web application that cannot be directly secured by Windows NT are securable though IIS configuration options.

Security for Web applications is a complicated subject because security can be set at several levels in several different ways. The choices depend on the system and servers used and the needs of the Web application. The main Web security issues are:

- Authenticating user identify.
- Controlling user access to files and resources.

The following table identifies these security issues, the location for their control, their purpose, and the options available for managing them.

Issue	Location	Purpose	Security Option
User authentication	Web server	Identify the user requesting files in a Web application	Basic Authentication; Anonymous Logon; Windows NT Challenge/Response
File permissions	Web server	Control access to files in the application	Read, write, script, and execute permissions for files and folders
File permissions	Web application	Control access to files in the application	FrontPage Server Extensions
File permissions	Operating system	Control access to files in the application	Access Control Lists in NTFS
Database permissions	Database	Control access to objects in the database	Standard Security; Integrated Security

Visual InterDev uses the Microsoft FrontPage server extensions to interact with your Web server. FrontPage server extensions can use the existing security features in your operating system and Web server. For example, the extensions are integrated with Windows NT and IIS to manage Web application security. You interact with the FrontPage extensions through the Visual InterDev user interface as illustrated in Figure 9.2.

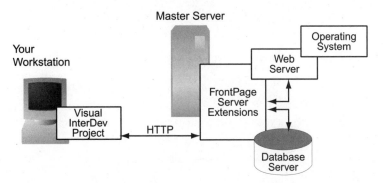

Figure 9.2 Visual InterDev and security components

When setting security options for your Web application, you could:

- Allow anyone to execute ASP pages and read HTML pages.
- Restrict access to registered Web visitors.
- Allow Web developers and authors to write to files at design time.
- Restrict Web administration to only authorized users.

Every Web application on a Web server has permission settings that identify authorized users and specify their privileges. These settings are specified from the Settings tab of the Permissions dialog, as illustrated in Figure 9.3.

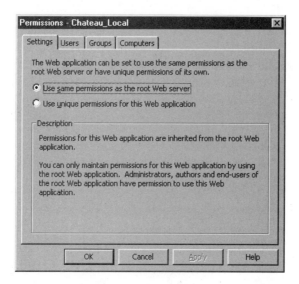

Figure 9.3 Setting Web application permissions

You can set the design-time permissions for your Web application using Visual InterDev. By default, a new Web application inherits the same permissions as the root Web server. You can customize these permissions and then control the permissions for individual users and groups.

Customizing Permissions

With Visual InterDev, you can set one of three levels of user permissions. The following table lists these choices and specifies which of these are design-time or run-time permissions.

User Permission Level	Type of Permission
Administer	Design-time and run-time
Author	Design-time only
Browse	Design-time and run-time

Note In order to set Web application security in Windows NT, the Web application files must be stored on a disk using the NTFS file system, not File Allocation Table (FAT).

➤ **To set unique permissions for a Web application**

1. In the Project Explorer window, select the project for which you want to set permissions.

2. From the Project menu, click Web Project and then Web Permissions.

3. On the Settings tab, select Use Unique Permissions For This Web Application.

    This specifies that the current Web application does not inherit its permissions setting from the root Web application.

4. Click Apply.

After you have set custom permissions for your Web application, you can add individual users and control their permissions.

➤ **To add users to a Web application**

1. From the Projects menu, click Web Project and then Web Permissions.

2. On the Settings tab, click Use Unique Permissions For This Web Application, and then click Apply.

3. On the Users tab, click Add.

4. In the Add Names box, type the domain and user name for the new user in this format: *domain\username*.

    You can also click the domain and add users from the Names field in the Obtain List From box.

5. In the New Users Can box, select the permission level of the new users.

   The selected permission level applies to all new users in the Add Names field.

6. Click Apply.

You can limit browse access to the Web application from this dialog by clicking the Only Registered Users Have Browse Access option on the bottom of the Users tab in the Permissions dialog, as illustrated in Figure 9.4.

Figure 9.4 Setting browse access for Web application users

➤ **To change permissions for a user**

1. From the Projects menu, click Web Project, and then click Web Permissions.

2. On the Users tab, select the user to edit and choose Edit.

3. In the Edit Users box, select the new level of permission for the user.

4. Click Apply.

Setting IIS Permissions

You use the Internet Service Manager to set the access permission on the virtual directories of your Web site. The Internet Service Manager is a snap-in component of the Microsoft Management Console (MMC). Figure 9.5 illustrates the five possible levels of permission that you can grant for a virtual directory.

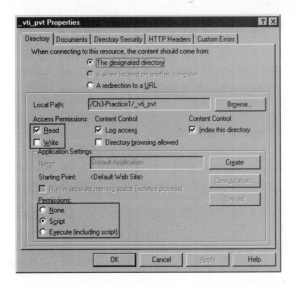

Figure 9.5 Setting directory permissions with the MMC

The following table describes the differences among these settings.

Setting	Description
Execute	Enables any application to run in this directory, including applications mapped to script engines as well as .dll and .exe files.
None	Does not allow any programs or scripts to run in this directory.
Read	Enables Web clients to read or download files stored in a home directory or a virtual directory. Gives Read access permission only to directories containing information to publish (HTML files, for example). Disables Read permission for directories containing Common Gateway Interface (CGI) applications and Internet Server Application Program Interface (ISAPI) DLLs to prevent clients from downloading the application files.
Script	Enables applications mapped to a script engine to run in this directory without having Execute permission set. Uses Script application permission for directories that contain ASP scripts, Internet Database Connector (IDC) scripts, or other scripts. Script permission is safer than Execute permission because you can limit the applications that can be run in the directory.
Write	Enables Web clients to upload files to the enabled directory, or to change the content in a write-enabled file.

If the directory is on an NTFS drive, the NTFS settings for the directory must match these settings. If the settings do not match, the most restrictive settings take effect. For example, if you give a directory Write permission in this property sheet but give a particular user group only Read access permissions in NTFS, those users cannot write files to the directory because the Read permission is more restrictive

Allowing Anonymous Access

Windows NT requires assigned user accounts and passwords. If you want to allow everybody to access your Web server, you must either provide a valid Windows NT account for every user or allow anonymous logon.

Anonymous logon allows users to access your Web server without providing a user ID and password. When an IIS Web server receives an anonymous request, it maps the user to a special anonymous logon account, referred to as the Internet Guest account. The user receives the access rights that have been granted to this account.

➤ **To enable anonymous logon**

1. Start the Internet Service Manager, which opens the MMC.

2. Within the virtual root, right-click Default Web Site.

3. Click Properties.

4. Select the Directory Security tab.

5. Click Edit in the Anonymous Access And Authentication Control group box.

6. Click the Allow Anonymous Access check box.

Setting the Account Used for Anonymous Access

When you install IIS, it creates an account named IUSR_*computername*. For example, if the computer name is "marketing", the account name will be IUSR_marketing. By default, this account is used for anonymous Internet logons.

IIS adds the IUSR_*computername* account to the Guests group and receives any permissions assigned to that group. You should review the settings for the Guests group to ensure that they are appropriate for the IUSR_*computername* account.

➤ **To change the account name and/or password used for anonymous logon**

1. Start the Internet Service Manager, which opens the MMC.

2. Within the virtual root, right-click Default Web Site.

3. Click Properties.

4. Select the Directory Security tab.

5. Click Edit in the Anonymous Access And Authentication Control group box.

6. Click the Allow Anonymous Access check box and disable the Basic Authentication and Windows NT Challenge/Response options.

7. Click Edit.

8. Disable Enable Automatic Password Synchronization.

9. Set the Username and Password text boxes to the values that you want.

10. Click OK to close the Anonymous User Account dialog.

11. Click OK to close the Authentication Methods dialog.

12. Click OK to close the Default Web Site Properties dialog.

Preventing Anonymous Logon

With the Prevent Anonymous Logon option, each request made to your Web server must include a valid Windows NT logon ID and password. To obtain this information, the browser will prompt the user for an account name and password.

➤ **To prevent anonymous logon**

1. Start the Internet Service Manager, which opens the MMC.

2. From the MMC, under the virtual root, right-click Default Web Site.

3. Click Properties.

4. Select the Directory Security tab.

5. Click Edit in the Anonymous Access And Authentication Control group box.

6. Disable Allow Anonymous Access.

7. Enable Basic Authentication, Windows NT Challenge/Response, or both.

By setting the authentication method, you can specify how the logon information is sent from the Web browser to the Web server.

Basic Authentication

If you select Basic Authentication as illustrated in Figure 9.6, the user name and password is sent from the Web browser to the Web server as plain text. This method is useful because all Web browsers generally support it.

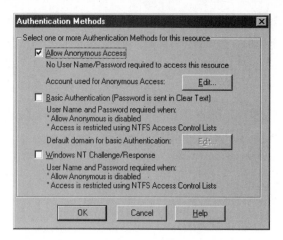

Figure 9.6 Selecting Basic Authentication

Windows NT Challenge/Response

The Windows NT Challenge/Response authentication option (NTLM authentication) illustrated in Figure 9.7 is the most secure form of authentication because the user name and password are not sent across the network. Instead, the Windows Security Provider interface is used to provide an encrypted challenge/response handshake mechanism that is functionally unbreakable. This method of authentication is supported by Internet Explorer 4.0 and later.

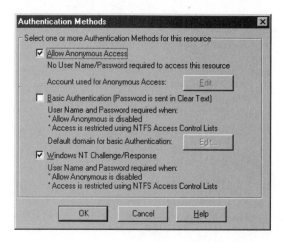

Figure 9.7 Selecting the NTLM authentication option

If you select both Basic Authentication and Windows NT Challenge/Response authentication, Windows NT Challenge/Response will be used if the browser supports it. Otherwise, Basic Authentication will be used. However, if you select all three methods of authentication (Anonymous, Basic, and Windows NT

Challenge/Response), every request to a Web page will attempt to access the page as anonymous. If the request fails, the user will be prompted for a login ID and the request will be attempted again.

Setting NTFS Permissions

You should place your Web pages and data files on an NTFS partition, because when you use an NTFS partition, you can set permissions for users or groups of users on individual files and folders.

➤ **To set permissions on files and folders**

1. Start Windows NT Explorer.
2. Right-click the file or directory for which you want to set permissions.
3. Click Properties.
4. Select the Sharing tab.
5. Enable Shared As and give the folder or directory a Share Name.
6. Click Permissions.
7. Add or remove users and specify the type of access allowed for each user.

You can use a combination of IIS settings, NTFS permissions, and server script to protect your Web pages.

For example, if you want to allow all users to access most of your Web site—but restrict a few pages to certain users—you can configure your Web site as follows:

- In Internet Service Manager, enable Allow Anonymous, Basic Authentication, and Windows NT Challenge/Response.
- For the pages you want to restrict, use Windows NT FS file permissions to remove the Anonymous account IUSR_*computername* from the access list, and then add the users for whom you want to allow access.

When a user requests a Web page, the user is logged on as anonymous and IIS attempts to access the Web page. If access is denied, the user will then be prompted for a login ID and password. Only users who provide a valid login ID and password will be able to access the restricted page.

Database Level Authentication

Visual InterDev allows you to connect to a wide variety of data sources. The security measures you set for your database depend on the database management system you are using. For file-based systems such as .mdb files in Microsoft Access, you can control security through the sharing permissions available on the folders and files for the operating system. If you are using SQL Server, you can use the features for granting and revoking privileges offered within the database management system. For example, SQL Server has a Security Manager that allows you to specify the privileges available to a single user or a group of users.

When using SQL Server security, the standard security option is recommended. Standard login security requires a login ID and a password to access the server. Your Web application provides this information through the data connection and your users do not need to provide any additional identification.

Using the Global.asa File

Visual InterDev supports Web applications that make full use of ASP. One of the features of an ASP is the automatic processing of a Web application's Global.asa file, if present, at the start of a new session with that Web application. You can use the Web application and session to control access and processing of your Web application. The user never actually sees the Global.asa file and the security provisions you add to it.

To fully secure an ASP application, be sure to set NTFS file permissions for the appropriate user or group on your application's Global.asa file. If your Global.asa includes commands that return information to the browser and you do not secure Global.asa, that information will be returned to the browser, even if the application's other files are secured.

Lesson Summary

Most Web applications are used by a large number of people, many of whom are unknown users. Web application security involves using Visual InterDev with other products, including Windows NT Server, IIS, MTS, and possibly FrontPage. Many security measures that you implement are not related to Visual InterDev specifically, but are implemented through NTFS, SQL Server, and the Internet Service Manager in IIS.

Lesson 3: Implementing SQL Server Security

Most Web-based applications require a back-end database for storing information. For example, in the Chateau St. Mark reservation system that you are creating as part of this course's lab exercise, reservation and guest information is stored in a SQL Server database. Implementing database security requires more than just writing code on the client. Advanced database systems, such as SQL Server, have their own security architecture that offer network administrators (and ultimately developers) a variety of security options. Once these options have been implemented, the developer can build the appropriate client interfaces to the data.

After this lesson, you will be able to:

■ Describe the user authentication options in SQL Server.

■ Describe how Visual InterDev integrates with SQL Server security when developing a Web application.

Estimated lesson time: 40 minutes

Setting SQL Server Login Authentication

SQL Server databases are most commonly used by a large number of users, which means that you must implement security controls to ensure that only individuals with the proper authority and expertise perform certain activities. For example, only human resources or accounting personnel should perform payroll disbursements and updates. In addition, company information must be protected, and cannot be shared with everyone in the company, or even with the general public. A person must have the proper credentials to access sensitive and confidential information stored in a SQL Server database.

Security must be set up correctly to ensure that only authorized users can access data and objects stored in SQL Server. Understanding how to set up security correctly can help simplify ongoing management. SQL Server can operate in one of two security models for verifying the authenticity of a user login ID.

■ Windows NT Authentication Mode

When a user connects through a Windows NT user account, SQL Server verifies that the account name and password were validated when the user logged on to Windows. When a network user tries to connect, SQL Server uses Windows NT to determine the validated network username. SQL Server then permits or denies login access based on that network username alone, without requiring a separate login name and password.

- Mixed Mode

    The Mixed Mode security model allows users to connect using Windows NT Authentication or SQL Server Authentication.

If a user attempts to connect to SQL Server by providing a blank login name, SQL Server automatically uses Windows NT Authentication. Additionally, if a user attempts to connect to a SQL Server configured for Windows NT Authentication Mode by using a specific login, the login is ignored and Windows NT Authentication is used.

The SQL Server Logon Process

Certain steps must occur during the logon process. For example, a Web user requests an ASP page that connects to a SQL Server database on a separate computer running Windows NT. The user is first logged on to the computer running Windows NT, and then on to the SQL Server. The illustration in Figure 9.8 shows the logon process from a Web browser to a SQL Server database.

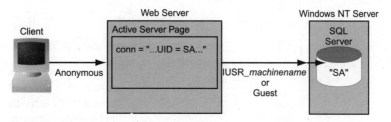

Figure 9.8 A client logging on to SQL Server

The following steps outline the logon process that occurs when a user requests an ASP page that connects to a SQL Server database.

1. If the Web server allows anonymous log on, the user is mapped to the anonymous account.
2. The .asp file runs script to connect to a SQL Server database.
3. For the .asp file to connect to the SQL Server database, the user is first logged on to the Windows NT –based computer where SQL Server is installed.
4. Finally, the user is logged on to the SQL Server itself.

Run-Time vs. Design-Time Authentication

Visual InterDev contains the data environment to let you easily test database access during development. You can quickly switch between design-time and run-time authentication from the Authentication tab on the Connection Properties dialog, as illustrated in Figure 9.9.

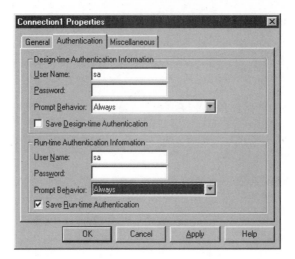

Figure 9.9 Two types of authentication that are available

Scenarios for Design-Time and Run-Time Authorization

When specifying design-time authorization, you choose the type of security for your authorization. For maximum security, you can choose to be prompted for a password each time you connect to the database. For less stringent security, you can choose not to be prompted. In this case, Visual InterDev encrypts your password and stores it in the project.

When you specify run-time authorization, you do not have this choice: You cannot prompt users for a password because the prompting would occur on the Web server. Therefore, you must include the password with the user name. The password is encrypted and stored in the project so that it can be passed to the database each time a user connects to the database when the application is running.

Replicating Rich Text and Graphical Content

SQL Server can replicate complex text and image data that is popular on Web sites. Replication allows an organization to avoid exposing sensitive database information on an intranet by selectively replicating data from production SQL Servers to a Web-connected SQL Server. SQL Server replication also solves the traditional client/server challenge of distributing and synchronizing information throughout an organization, while guaranteeing integrity and reliability. Replication solves a similar set of problems for Internet and intranet sites, allowing Webmasters to manage and synchronize multiple copies of published information.

Lesson Summary

SQL Server databases typically are used by a large number of users. You must implement security controls to ensure that only individuals with the proper authority and expertise are allowed to perform certain activities.

Understanding how to set up security correctly can help simplify ongoing management. SQL Server can operate in one of two security models for verifying the authenticity of a user login ID; the Windows NT Authentication Mode and the Mixed Mode.

Visual InterDev offers a new feature that allows you to easily test database access during development. You can switch quickly between design-time and run-time authentication from the Authentication tab.

Lesson 4: Security Issues with MTS

Like SQL Server, MTS utilizes the security capabilities of Windows NT. This lesson explains how *roles* are used in building secured COM components that execute in the MTS run-time environment.

After this lesson, you will be able to:

- Explain the difference between declarative security and programmatic security.
- Create MTS roles.
- Describe the purpose of using roles in MTS.

Estimated lesson time: 50 minutes

Distributed Application Security

Distributed applications separate business logic from user interface and data services. Instead of accessing a database from the front end (user interface service), the front end requests data services from components running in MTS. The MTS component can then retrieve data from a SQL Server or perform updates on behalf of the front-end user. In this scenario, you split security into two types:

- Application security

  Application security authorizes users' access to specific components and interfaces in MTS packages, limiting their capabilities. Therefore, you map users to the application functionality that applies to them. For example, you might map hotel clerks to a Reservation class that creates new reservations, whereas you map hotel managers to a Payroll class that performs pay increases based on employee performance. Application security is implemented in the middle tier by using MTS, as you will learn later in this lesson.

- Data security

  Data security assigns rights to MTS packages for access to the database. You implement data security in the data services tier by using SQL Server.

More planning is required when determining an application's security requirements in all three tiers. Figure 9.10 shows how security works in a distributed (n-tier) application.

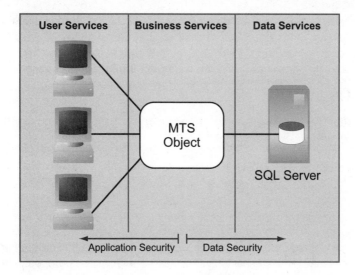

Figure 9.10 How security works in a distributed n-tier model

Advantages to implementing security in an n-tier model include the following:

- MTS components can totally encapsulate all database access because the user does not log on directly to the database. By performing data manipulation in middle-tier components, you preserve data integrity.

- Multiple MTS components can use the same database connection to reduce resources used on the server. In addition, multiple concurrent users connect to the database with the same package identity, improving scalability.

- You reduce Administration when setting up the application because each user does not need a login to the server.

- Instead of establishing end-user security based on databases and tables, you can use MTS to implement security based on roles that individuals play in an organization.

Declarative Security: Roles and Identities

The traditional approach to file security in the Windows NT operating system is to define users and user groups (typically with the User Manager for Domains administrative tool), and then set access permissions for a file (typically with Windows Explorer).

Because of security considerations at both the development and distribution phases of a project, MTS extends the traditional approach to security through *declarative security*. With this approach, security is configured directly with MTS Explorer. In declarative security, MTS introduces the concept of package roles.

MTS Roles

A *role* is a logical group of users that defines security access to the components of a package. The component programmer or Web developer creates roles at development time. Roles are subsequently mapped onto actual Windows NT users and user groups during package deployment by the Web developer or administrator. The following list describes two important consequences of the role architecture:

- Packages define security boundaries.

  MTS uses roles to determine who can use an MTS component any time a call is made into the package. Method calls from one component to another inside a package are not checked because components in the same package trust each other.

- Security is checked for each method call that crosses packages boundaries.

  MTS checks security on each method call because it is possible for one client (that is authorized) to pass an interface pointer to another client (that may not be authorized). MTS also checks security when a client creates an object from outside the package.

Note Because declarative security uses Windows NT accounts for authentication, you cannot use declarative security for a package running on a computer that uses the Microsoft Windows 95/98 operating system.

MTS Package Identity

By default, components take on (or impersonate) the process identity of the calling client. For example, if a process started by the Windows NT guest account calls a component, that component operates with the security privileges of the guest account. MTS introduces the new concept of package identities to give components a separate, independent security identification.

Rather than impersonate the client, MTS packages typically use declarative identity features of MTS to associate themselves with a Windows NT user account. Therefore, when any component in the package accesses resources such as files or databases, the component's access rights correspond to this identity. Package identities are set during deployment.

Setting Package Security

Using declarative security to set MTS package roles is a three-step process:

1. During package creation, associate one or more roles with the package.

   You can use existing roles or create new roles at this time.

2. During deployment time, map Windows NT users and groups to roles.

   Note that this gives the Web administrator great flexibility in determining access to MTS activities.

3. Enable security at the package and component level.

   If you do not enable security for the package, roles for the component or interface will not be checked by MTS. In addition, if you do not have security enabled for a component, MTS will not check roles for the component's interface.

Creating and Assigning Security Roles

After you have created a package and added components to it, you can create roles for that package. Roles are defined at the package level and, once created, are mapped to components or interfaces within the package.

Although you usually add new roles during package development, you may have to add a new role to an existing package. Roles represent a set of system-level privileges that are required for a particular business function. Roles are set at the package level. You can use the MTS Explorer to map Windows NT users or groups of users to the roles that you create.

➤ **To create a new role**

1. In the left pane of the MTS Explorer, select the package that will include the role.

2. Open the Roles folder.

   In the MTS explorer, the Roles folder contains the roles assigned for a selected package. MTS allows you to define roles that determine user access for a package, component, or interface.

3. Right-click the Roles folder, point to New, and then click Role, as illustrated in Figure 9.11.

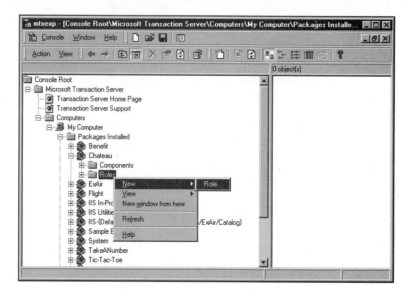

Figure 9.11 Adding a new role to an MTS package

4. In the New Role dialog box that appears, type the name of the new role, as illustrated in Figure 9.12.

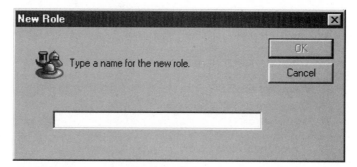

Figure 9.12 Assigning a name to the new role

5. Click OK.

Mapping Users to Roles

When you install and deploy your application, you must map Windows NT users and groups to any existing roles. The roles you map users to determine what components and interfaces those users can access.

➤ **To assign users to roles**

1. In the left pane of the MTS Explorer window, open the package in which you will assign users to roles.

2. Open the Roles folder and double-click the role to which you want to assign users.

3. Open the Users folder.

4. Right-click the Users folder, select New, and then click Users.

5. In the Add Users and Groups to Role dialog, add user names or groups to the role.

6. Use the Show Users and Search buttons to locate a user account and then click OK.

Enabling Security

There are two levels at which security is enabled: package-level security and component-level security. Package-level security is set once at the package level. Component-level security is set at the component level for each component in the package. The following table shows the implications of enabling or disabling authorization checking for packages and components.

Package Security	Component Security	Result
Enabled	Enabled	Security is enabled for the component.
Enabled	Disabled	Security is disabled for the component, but will be enabled for other components that have security enabled.
Disabled	Enabled or Disabled	Security is disabled for all components.

➤ **To enable or disable authorization checking for packages or components**

1. In the left pane of the MTS Explorer window, click the package or component.

2. Right-click the package or component, and then click Properties.

3. Click the Security property sheet.

4. Select or clear Enable Authorization Checking.

Setting Package Identity

There are two general identity types a package can assume:

- The interactive user (the default)

  This setting allows the package to assume the identity of the user that is currently logged on. However, if no user is logged on to the server when a client accesses the package, the package will fail to create a server process. This identity is often used for development testing purposes.

- A specific Windows NT user account

  This setting assigns a specific Windows NT user account to the package. When a client accesses the package, the package creates a server process using this account as its identity. All components running in the package share this identity.

➤ **To set package identity**

1. Select the package whose identity you want to change.

2. Right-click the package and click Properties. Then select the Identity tab.

3. To set the identity to a user account, select This User and enter the user domain followed by a backslash (\), user name, and password for the Windows NT user account. Or, to set the identity to Interactive User, select the Interactive User option.

The illustration in Figure 9.13 shows the Identity tab of the Properties sheet.

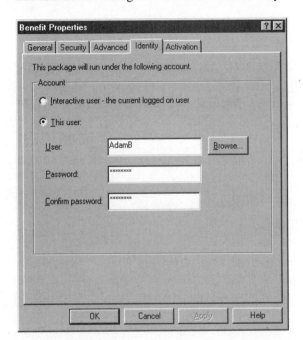

Figure 9.13 Running a package under a specific user account

Package Identity and Database Access

Package identity is important when your MTS components access databases, because database connections can be pooled if a process has many connections using the same user ID and password. If components impersonate clients, each user ID is different and the connections cannot be pooled. By using package identity, each component can use the same user ID and each connection therefore can be pooled.

Note If you want to use package identity to restrict access to a database, you must set database access privileges for the user account of that package.

Using Programmatic Security

In addition to the default declarative security that MTS offers, you can also use another type of security called *programmatic security*. Programmatic security is provided by code that you write in your component to determine if a client is authorized to perform an operation. You can use MTS security methods after you set a reference to the Microsoft Transaction Server Type Library in Visual Basic to declare an ObjectContext object variable.

The ObjectContext object provides two methods for basic programmatic security:

- IsCallerInRole
- IsSecurityEnabled

The IsCallerInRole method determines whether a client that invokes a method of an object (caller) is assigned to a role. You can use roles to determine whether the caller has access to objects in the server process. The following example checks to see if the caller is in the Managers role if over $500 is to be spent.

```
' Check for security in the Payment object
If (lngAmount > 500 Or lngAmount < -500) Then
    If Not ctxObject.IsCallerInRole("Managers") Then
        Err.Raise Number:=ERROR_NUMBER, _
            Description:= "Need 'Managers' role" + _
            " for amounts over $500"
    End If
End If
```

The IsSecurityEnabled method determines whether security checking is enabled on the component's package. IsSecurityEnabled can be a useful check to make before using IsCallerInRole to verify that the package supports authorization checking. The following example checks to see if security is enabled, and then checks to see if the caller is in the Managers role.

```
Dim objContext As ObjectContext
Set objContext = GetObjectContext()

If Not objContext Is Nothing Then
    ' Find out if Security is enabled
    If objContext.IsSecurityEnabled Then
        ' Find out if the caller is in the right role
        If Not objContext.IsCallerInRole("Managers") Then
            ' Error - must be a manager
        Else
            ' Process expenditure
        End If
    Else
        ' Security is not enabled
    End If
End If
```

However, MTS security is enabled only if an object is running in a separate server process. If the object is running in the client's process, there is no security checking and IsSecurityEnabled will always return False. This could be either because the object's component was configured to run in a client's process, or because the component and the client are in the same package.

Lesson Summary

A distributed application separates business logic from user interface and data services. Instead of accessing a database from the front end, the front end requests data services from components running in MTS. The MTS component then retrieves data from a SQL Server or performs updates on behalf of the front-end user. Using this method, you split security into two types:

- Application security
- Data security

Because of security considerations in the development and distribution phases of a project, MTS extends the traditional approach to security through *declarative security*. With this approach, security is configured directly with MTS Explorer.

You can also use another type of security called *programmatic security*. Programmatic security is provided by code that you write in your component to determine whether a client is authorized to perform an operation.

Lab 9: Securing the Chateau St. Mark Web Site

In this lab, you will secure the checkout process for the Chateau St. Mark Hotel so that only users with Windows NT security can check out a guest.

To see a demonstration of this lab, run the Lab09.exe animation located in the Animations folder on the companion CD-ROM that accompanies this book.

Before You Begin

You should have already completed Labs 2, 3, 4, 5, 6, 7, and 8. If you have not, follow the steps in Lab 2 to create the Chateau Web project and use the files in the Labs\Lab08\Partial folder to obtain the necessary files to complete this lab.

Estimated lab time: 45 minutes

Exercise 1: Setting File Permissions in IIS

In this exercise, you will modify the file permissions for Checkout.asp, Reservations.asp, and Invoice.asp so that anonymous Internet users can no longer access these pages. Each request made to these files will not require a Windows NT login.

1. Open the Internet Service Manager

    On the Start menu, choose Programs, and then Windows NT 4.0 Option Pack. Click Microsoft Index Server and Index Server Manager.

2. In the left pane, expand the Console root to display the Default Web Site icon. Then locate and expand the Chateau folder.

3. Right-click the Checkout.asp file and select Properties from the menu.

4. Select the File Security tab on the properties dialog and edit the Anonymous Access And Authentication Control for the file.

5. Clear the box allowing anonymous access and make sure the Windows NT Challenge/Respond box is checked.

6. Click OK on each dialog to close it.

7. Repeat steps 3 through 6 for the Reservation.asp and Invoice.asp.

8. Test your work by accessing the Web application from an account that does not have permissions to the server.

Exercise 2: Securing the Chateau Database

In this exercise, you will modify the current database security from standard SQL security to Windows NT integrated security. You will then modify the Web security so that anonymous access will be granted through Windows NT integrated security.

➤ **To create a Windows NT group and user for Chateau**

1. Open the User Manager for Domains on your server.

2. Select New Local Group from the User menu.

3. Create a group called Chateau with a description of Chateau Users.

4. Select New User from the User menu.

5. Name the user ChateauUser with a full name of Chateau User.

6. Set a password and uncheck User Must Change Password At Next Logon.

7. Click the Groups button and add the Chateau User to the Chateau group.

8. Save your changes and close the User Manager for Domains.

➤ **To add the Windows NT group and user to SQL Server**

1. Open the SQL Server 7 Enterprise Manager.

2. Expand the server group to your Server in the left pane of the Enterprise Manager. You might need to register your server if it is not listed.

3. Locate and expand the security folder under your server.

4. Right-click Logins to display the current logins in the right pane of the Enterprise Manager.

5. Locate and delete the current Chateau login with standard security type.

6. Right-click Logins in the left pane and select New Login.

7. Enter Chateau in the name field and select Windows NT authentication. Select your domain from the drop-down list.

8. Click OK to create the new login. Verify that the login was created as type NT Group.

9. Verify that there is also a standard login of guest.

10. Locate and expand the Chateau database in the tree for your server on the left pane.

11. Click Roles and verify that there is a public role in the list. If not, create a public role.

12. Double-click Public Role to bring up its properties. Click Permissions in the Properties dialog.

13. Verify that the Public Role is assigned all rights for each of the tables and stored procedures in the database. Some of the system databases and stored procedures will not allow you to set certain rights under the Public Role.

14. Right-click Roles in the left pane and select New Database Role.

15. Enter Chateau as the name for the role. Save your changes.

16. Click Users, which appears above the Roles. Verify that there is a Guest user in the list of users.

17. To create a guest user for the database, right-click Users in the left pane and select New Database User.

18. Select guest from the list of users in the in the Login name drop-down menu.

19. Verify that the Public Role is checked in the Permit In Database role, and then click OK to save the user.

➤ To use the ChateauUser for anonymous Web access

1. Open the Internet Service Manager.

   On the Start menu, choose Programs, and then Windows NT 4.0 Option Pack. Click Microsoft Index Server and Index Server Manager.

2. Expand the Console Root in the left pane to \Internet Information Server\<server name>\Default Web Site.

3. Right-click the Chateau Web application and select Properties.

4. Select the Directory Security tab and edit Anonymous Access And Authentication Control.

5. Edit the account used for Anonymous Access and browse for the ChateauUser login. Click OK to close each of the dialogs and save your changes.

➤ To change the data connection to use Integrated Security

1. Open the Chateau project in Visual InterDev.

2. Expand the Data Environment under Global.asa and right-click cnChateau connection.

3. On the Authentication tab, delete the user information for run-time authentication.

4. On the General tab, click Build located to the right of the existing connection string.

5. Go to the Provider tab and change the provider to Microsoft OLE DB Provider For SQL Server. Click Next.

6. Follow the directions on the Connection tab to enter a Server Name and use Windows NT Integrated Security.

7. Select the Chateau database and test the connection before closing the dialog.

8. Save your changes and test the Chateau Web application.

Review

The following questions are intended to reinforce key information presented in this chapter. If you are unable to answer a question, review the appropriate lesson and then try the question again. Answers to the questions can be found in Appendix A, "Questions and Answers".

1. Describe various security considerations when developing a Web site.

2. Describe the user authentication options in Microsoft SQL Server.

3. Explain the difference between declarative security and programmatic security.

C H A P T E R   1 0

Integrating Server Side Technologies

About This Chapter

As Web applications become more mission-critical to corporations, it becomes imperative that a complete Web solution integrates with other services. Web developers can use various server-side technologies to enhance their Web sites and provide users with richer functionality. In this chapter, you will learn how to use the Simple Mail Transport Protocol (SMTP) service of Microsoft Internet Information Server (IIS) 4.0 to send e-mail from a Web site. You will also learn how to enable custom search capabilities for a Web site.

Before You Begin

There are no prerequisites for this chapter.

Lesson 1: Integrating Mail Services

By supporting standard interfaces and protocols such as Messaging API (MAPI), Simple Mail Transfer Protocol (SMTP), and Collaboration Data Objects (CDO), Microsoft Windows NT provides an extensive messaging infrastructure that can benefit both developers and users.

The ability to use a simpler, non-API-based object library with an SMTP service is particularly useful for the Web developer, whose primary concern is to generate and deliver simple e-mail messages (notifications) from a Web site. If required, you can combine the CDO 1.2 library and Microsoft Exchange Server 5.5 to provide more sophisticated messaging functionality.

You can enhance your Web sites by integrating messaging capabilities that enable users to send and receive e-mail, participate in threaded news discussions, and perform other messaging tasks. Windows NT provides an ideal platform to accomplish this because of its broad range of messaging support, particularly through the SMTP service of IIS and the Exchange Server platform. In this lesson, you will learn how to use Active Server Pages (ASP) script with an SMTP server to create and send e-mail from a Web site.

After this lesson, you will be able to:

- List and describe four mail access technologies.
- Describe how SMTP service works.
- Describe CDO for Windows NT Server.

Estimated lesson time: 45 minutes

Mail Services for Windows NT

Windows NT provides a robust and flexible messaging platform with mail service support that includes programmability options. Web developers can use the mail services offered through Windows NT to enable messaging from their Web sites.

Mail Servers

Mail servers are a primary element of an electronic messaging system's infrastructure. Windows NT supports different server options for implementing a messaging system, depending on the functionality required by users of the system.

Standard Internet Mail Services

Internet users who want only to send and receive e-mail should use the following two server programs:

- SMTP server

  Used in a TCP/IP network to transport mail between mail nodes on the Internet. SMTP is often referred to as a delivery service because it only moves e-mail from one location to another. SMTP does not support such user services as log in and mailbox creation.

- Post Office Protocol (POP or POP3) server

  Provides user services and administrative functions of a mail server. Users interact directly with POP3 services to log in, access mail, create new messages and mail folders, and perform other messaging tasks. Internet Message Access Protocol (IMAP) is a specification for newer, more powerful Internet post office services.

Note For more information about POP3, see "Standards Track" for the POP3 specification at http://src.doc.ic.ac.uk/computing/internet/rfc/rfc1939.txt. For information about IMAP services, see "Standards Track" for the IMAP specification at http://src.doc.ic.ac.uk/computing/internet/rfc/rfc2060.txt.

The Microsoft Windows NT Option Pack contains the Microsoft SMTP Service. SMTP Service is a commercial-grade implementation of SMTP designed to meet the needs of high-traffic loads required by mission-critical applications. It is implemented as an extension to IIS 4.0.

Microsoft Exchange Server

Microsoft Exchange Server 5.5, a component of the Microsoft BackOffice suite, provides a messaging platform that extends rich messaging and collaboration capabilities to businesses of all sizes. In addition to providing high performance and high availability, Exchange Server is fully compatible with existing Internet standards, including POP3, IMAP, LDAP, NNTP, and MAPI. It also provides tools for developers to create ASP pages.

Mail Access Technologies

In addition to providing support for different messaging server options, Windows NT supports options for creating programmable messaging objects in the form of a messaging API and various libraries. Clients such as Microsoft Visual Basic, C and C++, Microsoft Visual C++, and Microsoft Visual Basic Scripting Edition (VBScript) applications can use these libraries. The following list describes some types of mail access technologies.

- Collaborative Data Objects (CDO)

   A COM-based set of technologies that enables any MAPI-based application to act as the Exchange data store. The CDO library, included with Exchange Server 5.5, defines a set of objects that supports calendaring, collaboration, and workflow capabilities. (CDO supercedes the Microsoft Active Messaging 1.1 library for Exchange Server.)

- CDO for Windows NT Server (CDONTS)

   This subset of the CDO library is used for building simple, scalable applications, based on the SMTP mail protocol. This library runs in both IIS (with the SMTP mail service) and Exchange Server environments.

- CDO Rendering Objects

   A component of CDO that can be used to display Exchange data in HTML format. This library increases the efficiency and manageability of similar approaches using ASP scripting.

- MAPI

   An industry-standard C-level mail and messaging interface. MAPI enables multiple applications to interact with multiple messaging systems across a variety of hardware platforms.

How SMTP Service Works

An SMTP server functions as a gateway that enables all disparate clients to interact with the same messaging backbone. The SMTP protocol is layered on top of the standard TCP protocol. SMTP defines a simple process for transporting messages. An e-mail message is created, typically by a user of a mail package, and then delivered to the SMTP server of the user's domain. The SMTP server relays the messages to another SMTP node—either another SMTP server or the final mail recipient. Through a process called *hopping*, a message might pass through several SMTP servers before it is delivered.

SMTP Service uses a designated TCP port (port 25 by default) for delivering and sending messages. You can use the Internet Service Manager snap-in program to configure delivery, security, domain, and other administrative options.

Delivering Messages (Inbound)

SMTP Service uses the following process to deliver inbound messages:

1. A message arrives via the designated inbound TCP port.

2. The message is placed in the Queue directory \INetPub\mailroot\Queue.

    - If the message recipients are local to that domain, the message is placed in the Drop directory designated for the default domain.

    - If the recipients are not local, the message is processed for remote delivery. These messages are placed in the Queue directory for delivery. At this stage they are equivalent to queued outbound messages.

    - If a message can neither be delivered nor returned to the sender, it is placed in the BadMail directory.

Sending Messages (Outbound)

SMTP Service uses the following process to deliver outbound messages, as illustrated in Figure 10.1:

1. An outbound message that is created as a text file is placed in the Pickup directory \INetPub\mailroot\Pickup.

2. Microsoft SMTP Service collects the message and initiates delivery.

    - If the message recipients are local (to the current domain), the message is placed in the Drop directory designated for the current domain.

    - All other outbound messages are sent directly to the Queue directory for delivery.

    - If a message can neither be delivered nor returned to the sender, it is placed in the BadMail directory.

3. Queued messages are transmitted through the designated outbound TCP port to a receiving mail server for the designated remote domain.

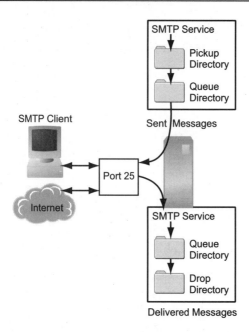

Figure 10.1 Sending and delivering messages through the SMTP Service

SMTP Service is compliant with the open Internet specifications in Request for Comments (RFC) 821 and RFC 822.

Note The SMTP protocol specification is referred to as an Internet Draft. Internet Drafts are working documents of the Internet Engineering Task Force (IETF).

Collaboration Data Objects for Windows NT Server

Collaboration Data Objects for Windows NT Server (CDONTS) is a smaller and faster subset of CDO 1.2, available only on IIS for Windows NT Server. CDONTS contains an object model and exposes messaging objects for use by Visual Basic, Visual C and C++, and ActiveX Scripting (such as VBScript and JScript) applications.

CDONTS has no underlying MAPI infrastructure. Instead it works by itself on IIS or on a combination of IIS and Exchange. CDONTS supports the sending of anonymous e-mail through a system-wide inbox drop directory under IIS. CDO 1.2 provides support for anonymous messaging, but only at the public folder level.

Like CDO 1.2, CDONTS supports the following types of message content:

- Plain text
- HTML and MHTML
- UUEncoded or Base64 content
- File-attachment encoding
- The creation of large bodies of text from files
- URLs

CDONTS also supports the standard COM interface, Istream, which enables developers to create Web-based applications that read message content directly from a hard drive or from in-memory objects.

CDONTS Object Model

The CDONTS object model, illustrated in Figure 10.2, is organized as a log-on session with a top-level Session object. Creating a Session object is necessary when using other objects in CDONTS. The Session object includes other objects, collections of objects, properties, and methods.

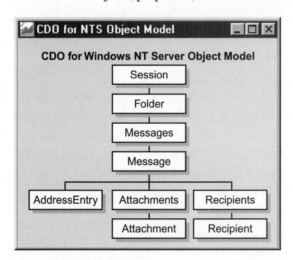

Figure 10.2 CDONTS object model

Sending E-Mail from an ASP Script

CDO 1.2 provides programmatic access to a broad range of standard mail server functionality such as scheduling and folder administration. Most Web developers require that their Web sites be able to create and send e-mail messages. CDONTS, with its SMTP-based messaging support, enables quick and easy e-mail notification from an ASP script.

Using the NewMail Object

The NewMail object can generate and send an automatic e-mail notification to a variety of independent messaging systems. The NewMail object is self-contained and independent of the CDONTS object hierarchy. So there is no need to log on to a session or deal with a folder or a Messages collection.

Note The CDO component is available only with Windows NT Server and is installed with the SMTP Service for IIS.

➤ **To use the CDONTS component to send e-mail**

1. Create an instance of a NewMail object.

2. Set properties, such as To, From, Cc, and Subject.

3. Use the Send method to send the message.

4. Remove the NewMail object from memory by setting it to Nothing.

The following example code shows how to use the CDONTS component to send a simple e-mail message:

```
Set objNewMail = Server.CreateObject("CDONTS.NewMail")
objNewMail.Send "me@company.com", _
    "you@companya.com; someone@companyb.com", _
    "Testing 1,2,3", 1
```

When the Send method completes successfully, the NewMail object is invalidated. Because it is not removed from memory, however, you should do one of the following:

- If you do not intend to send another message with this object, set it to Nothing to remove it from memory, as shown in the following example code:

  ```
  Set objNewMail = Nothing
  ```

- If you want to send another message with this object, reassign it to another NewMail object, as shown in the following example code:

  ```
  Set MyMail = CreateObject("CDONTS.NewMail")
  ```

The Send method has the following parameters:

- Body

  The Body parameter is an optional value that contains the text of the message.

- From

  The From parameter is an optional string value that contains the full messaging address to be identified as the sender.

- Importance

  The Importance parameter is an optional Long value that dictates the significance of the message.

- objNewMail

  The objNewMail is a required parameter that contains a reference to this NewMail object.

- Subject

  The Subject parameter is an optional string value that contains the subject line for the message.

- To

  The To parameter is an optional string value that contains a list of full messaging addresses of recipients. The individual recipient addresses are separated by semicolons.

Limitations of the NewMail Object

Because the NewMail object is designed to send notification mail from a Windows NT service, there is no user interface and no user interaction during the creation and sending of the mail. It is not possible to remove attachments or recipients that have been added to the NewMail object, nor can the NewMail object itself be deleted. The following example code shows how to use the objects provided by the CDONTS component from within an ASP script. It first uses the Server.CreateObject method to create an instance of the NewMail object. Next, the most important NewMail properties are set, including the From, To, Subject, and Body properties. Finally, the Send method of the NewMail object is invoked to send the message to the specified destination.

```
<% @Language=VBScript %>
<% Option Explicit %>

<HTML>
<HEAD>
<TITLE>CDO Component</TITLE>
</HEAD>
<BODY bgcolor="white" topmargin="10" leftmargin="10">
<!-- Display Header -->
<font size="4" face="Arial, Helvetica">
<b>CDO Component</b></font><p>
This sample demonstrates how to use the Collaboration
Data Objects for NTS Component to send a simple
e-mail message.

<p>To actually send the message, you must
have the SMTP Server that comes with the
```

(continued)

```
Windows NT Option Pack installed.
<%
Dim myMail
Set myMail = Server.CreateObject("CDONTS.NewMail")

' For demonstration purposes, both From and To
' properties are set to the same address.

myMail.From = "someone@Microsoft.com"
myMail.To = "someone@Microsoft.com"

myMail.Subject = "Sample"
myMail.Body = "I hope you like the sample"

myMail.Send
%>
</BODY>
</HTML>
```

Sending Mail Through Exchange Server

Using CDO 1.2 with Exchange Server to send e-mail differs from using CDONTSwith the SMTP server provided with the Windows NT Option Pack. Because the NewMail object is not available in CDO 1.2 for Exchange Server, you must first establish a MAPI session before any MAPI functionality is available to you.

Exchange Server includes several extensive examples on how to use scripting to create messaging solutions both inside a Web application and within the Exchange Server environment. For example, the "Full Send" example application demonstrates how to create a browser-based client capable of composing and sending messages.

Sending E-Mail via the Pickup Directory

CDONTS provides the best approach for generating e-mail messages for most ASP applications. However, SMTP Service provides a second, file-based technique for creating messages using the Pickup directory.

Using this technique, you create the text-based e-mail message and place it in a file in the SMTP server's Pickup directory. The server does not distinguish between this new message and any other message that has been queued in the Pickup directory by other mail processes. This simple mechanism forms the basis of how SMTP sends and relays e-mail messages.

➤ **To send a message using the Pickup directory**

1. Compose a plain text message using an editor or word-processing program, or programmatically through standard file and string library calls.

   The beginning of the message must have the appropriate mail headers such as the "x-sender", "x-receiver," and so on. After a carriage return/line feed (CRLF) pair, enter the body of the message. The following is an example of such as message:

   ```
   x-sender: johns@CompanyA.com
   x-receiver: mariab@CompanyB.com
   From: johns@CompanyA.com
   To: mariab@CompanyB.com
   Subject: Hello from John

   Hello, how have you been?
   ```

2. Save this message as a file in a temporary directory.

3. Move or copy this file to the SMTP service's Pickup directory. By default, this directory's location is \InetPub\MailRoot\PickUp.

SMTP Service periodically searches the \InetPub\MailRoot\PickUp directory for messages. When it finds a new message in the Pickup directory, SMTP Service moves it to the Queue subdirectory where it processes the message for immediate delivery.

Note The two methods of creating e-mail messages—using the NewMail object and creating a file in the Pickup folder—are equivalent because the NewMail object simply generates a file in the Pickup folder.

Lesson Summary

Windows NT provides messaging platform with mail service support that includes mail servers and programmability options. Mail servers are a primary element of an electronic messaging system's infrastructure. Windows NT supports different server options, such as SMTP and POP or POP3, for implementing a messaging system, depending on the functionality required by users of the system.

In addition to providing support for different messaging server options, Windows NT supports options for creating programmable messaging objects in the form of a messaging API and various libraries. Different types of mail access technologies include:

- CDO
- CDO for Windows NT Server (CDONTS)
- CDO Rendering Objects
- Messaging API (MAPI)

An SMTP server functions as a gateway that enables all disparate clients to interact with the one messaging backbone. The SMTP protocol is layered on top of the standard TCP protocol. First an e-mail message is created and delivered to the user's SMTP server. Then the SMTP server relays the messages to another SMTP node—either another SMTP server or the final mail recipient.

ASP script allows you to send mail to a variety of messaging systems by using the NewMail Object. The NewMail object is designed to send notification mail from a Windows NT service. There is no user interface and no user interaction during the creation and sending of the mail.

Lesson 2: Adding Search Services

Microsoft Index Server 2.0, a component of IIS, adds powerful searching and indexing capabilities to IIS Web sites. Organizations can create Web sites that contain a broad range of document formats, which can then be indexed and queried by users. Web developers can use Visual Basic, VBScript, C, C++, Java, and JavaScript to create dynamic, flexible, customized query and result forms. Because Index Server is integrated with the Windows NT file and security system, it provides automatic indexing of content that follows the security policies set by the Web and Windows NT Server administrators. Administrators do not need to manually update or manage indices.

Many organizations are now creating intranets to provide their employees with documents that have the same ease of use as the World Wide Web. Because organizations often produce large amounts of information, they need to utilize indexing and searching technology to help their users find the right documents quickly. In this lesson, you will learn how to use Index Server in conjunction with the Windows NT Server operating system to provide search capabilities for an intranet or Internet site.

After this lesson, you will be able to:

- Describe the functionality features of Search Bot.
- Process a search request with ASP.

Estimated lesson time: 60 minutes

The Microsoft FrontPage Search Bot And Index Server

Microsoft Visual InterDev uses a Microsoft FrontPage 98 WebBot component to provide a default search form that users can use to search a Web site. This functionality relies upon FrontPage Server Extensions, which can be obtained in one of the following ways:

- From the Visual InterDev Server Setup program
- As a part of the Minimum and Typical IIS setup
- As separate downloadable components

When a user submits a search form that contains words to locate, the Search Bot performs a full-text search over all pages in a Web site. It then returns hyperlinks to all pages that contain the words.

How the Search Bot Works

The FrontPage Search Bot is a convenient interface to the actual search engine located on the Web server. The FrontPage Search Bot can use either of two following search engines:

- Wide Area Information Server (WAIS)

  The WAIS search engine is an implementation of an older, Internet-standard search service. It is the default search engine included with the FrontPage Server Extensions, but is not installed as part of Visual InterDev or the Windows NT Option Pack.

- Index Server

  Index Server is a content-indexing and search component included with IIS. If Index Server has been installed as part of IIS, the Search Bot uses Index Server instead of the WAIS search engine.

Introduction to Microsoft Index Server

Microsoft Index Server is a standard extension component of IIS that indexes the content of a Web site and allows queries against that content. Index Server enables any client using an HTML browser to search a Web site by using a normal HTML form.

Index Server Features

Index Server combines flexible search techniques with support for multiple document formats. In addition, it is fully integrated with Windows NT and IIS security, logging, and administration facilities. By indexing the contents and properties of documents on a single Web site, you can enable clients to search the contents of that site.

Flexible Search Strategies

Clients can search an indexed Web site using several query types, as described in the following table.

Query type	Description
Basic query	Enables the user to search for multiple separate words and phrases.
Complex query	Boolean, UNIX-like regular expression matching, weighted, and fuzzy word capabilities enable the user to search with wild cards, regular expression matching, and linguistic stemming to find all tenses of a verb.
Free text query	Enables the user to express a search as a question. For example: "How do I sign up for a math course?"
Document property query	Enables the user to query against file size, time stamp, author's name, HTML meta parameters, and so on.

Filtering Proprietary Document Formats

Index Server is designed to work directly with text and HTML files. It also includes support (via filters) for Microsoft Office formats. Other companies may also provide filters for their file formats. For example, Adobe Systems has announced plans to create a filter for its popular Portable Document Format (PDF) files.

You can create custom filters for other document formats by implementing the IFilter COM interface. You can download the IFilter SDK from the Microsoft BackOffice Download and Trial Center page at http://www.microsoft.com/backoffice/promo/downtrial/default.htm.

Consistent and Integrated Security, Logging, and Administration

The following table describes how Index Server uses the security, logging, and administration features of Windows NT and IIS.

Feature	Index Server implementation
Administration	Administered through a snap-in component of Microsoft Management Console (MMC). This tool provides a simplified way to create, adjust, and monitor catalogs and directories.
Logging	Logs system errors to the application event log; these can be viewed with the Event Viewer administration tool. If logging is enabled in IIS, user search requests are recorded by the standard IIS logging mechanism.
Security	Uses Access Control List (ACL) security built into Windows NT Clients can find information about and access files or directories only for which they have proper permission.

How Index Server Works

With Index Server, you typically use the following process to add search capabilities to a Web site:

1. After you install Index Server, the Content Index service starts and will begin indexing all the documents in a computer's virtual directories. This process creates a master index, which along with some process information is written to a file named the default catalog.

2. To enable users to utilize Index Server's search capabilities, a query form is created and published on the Web site. Users fill out the fields on the form and submit their queries to the Web server.

3. IIS passes the query information to Index Server. Index Server reconciles most queries against the master index, returning the results as one or more HTML pages.

Figure 10.3 depicts the process of passing a query from a client browser to the Web server, and shows how Index Server returns the results of the query to the client.

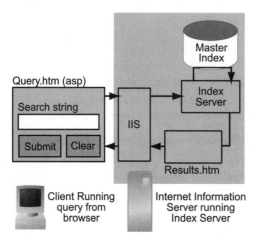

Figure 10.3 How a client communicates with Index Server

There are three techniques for integrating Index Server into a Web site:

- You can use ASP pages to create and process query forms, and to directly access the search capabilities of Index Server through its built-in query and utility objects.

- You can use Index Server extension files to create and publish three types of related files: an HTML search form, an Internet data query (.idq) file that defines query parameters, and an HTML extension (.htx) file that acts as a template for the result.

  This technique closely parallels that used by the Internet Database Connector (IDC) of IIS, and was the only available technique in the first release of Index Server. Although it is the best-performing technique, it is the least flexible.

- SQL queries can be used in applications to query Index Server. Since an OLE DB provider is supplied for Index Server, other applications can use ActiveX Data Objects (ADO) to query Index Server. The SQL used with Index Server consists of extensions to the subset of SQL-92 and SQL3 that is detailed in the Windows NT Option Pack Online Help.

  For example, in an ASP page, you can use the SQL Extensions to form the query, use ADO to retrieve the data, and use a scripting language to display the data.

Using ASP To Query Index Server

ASP pages typically offer the most general and flexible method of integrating Index Server into a Web application. Using this method has several advantages by allowing you to:

- Integrate searching with your ASP applications.
- Create search criteria dynamically.
- Format and manipulate search results before they are presented to the user.

General Procedure for Accessing Index Server through ASP

To enable query processing in an ASP page, follow these steps:

1. Create a query form (an HTML form that allows the Web client to specify the search that should be performed). The ACTION parameter of the form should be set to the ASP page created in the next step.

   Note that the intrinsic HTML controls on the query form are typically named after the conventional URL tags recognized by Index Server.

   A simple example of a URL sent by a form might be:

   ```
   http://www.chateau.com/search.htm?qu=availability&mh=50
   ```

2. Create an ASP page to process the request, submit a query to Index Server, and format and return the query results.

   Index Server provides two server-side objects—the query object and the utility object—that can greatly aid you in performing these tasks.

3. As an optional step, store the query and results of the search in Step 2 as session variables so that they can be reused.

The following table lists the conventional tags, recognized by Index Server, used to form a query.

Tag	Description
ae	Allow enumeration. Associated with the AllowEnumeration property. If set to a nonzero digit, enumeration is allowed.
ct	Specify the (nondefault) catalog. Associated with the Catalog property.
mh	Specify the maximum hits returned. Associated with the MaxRecords property.
op	Optimize for. Associated with the OptimizeFor property. The first character of the value can be x for "performance" or r for "recall."
qu	Full text of the query. Associated with the Query property.
sd	Sort down (in descending order). Associated with the SortBy property.
so	Sort in ascending order on this field. Associated with the SortBy property.

Using Server-Side Objects to Perform Queries

Index Server provides two server-side objects (SSO)—the query object and the utility object—for building and enhancing Index Server queries. Both the query and utility objects are COM objects that provide late binding through their support of the IDispatch interface. The query object is used to form and submit the basic query, while the utility object adds miscellaneous functionality (such as query refinement) and helper functions for working with the query and query result.

Processing a Search Request with the Query Object

Typically, an ASP page will perform the following minimum number of steps to satisfy a user search request:

1. Create an instance of the query object. If Index Server has not been properly installed on the Web server, this step will fail.

2. Obtain the QUERY_STRING from the request URL by using the Request.ServerVariables or Request.QueryString methods.

3. Parse the request URL to form a valid Index Server query. The query object provides the SetQueryFromURL method for this purpose.

4. Submit the query to Index Server and accept the returned ADO recordset as provided by the CreateRecordSet method of the query object.

5. Format the results and return them to the user. Optionally, the ASP script can choose to further manipulate the information by filtering it for additional security, usefulness, or user preference reasons.

The following example code shows a simple version of the previous procedure:

```
<!-- Using ASP to process a simple Index Server query. -->
<% ClsQry = Server.CreateObject("IXSSO.Query") %>
<% if IsObject(ClsQry) = FALSE then %>
    The Web server's query support is not working
    correctly. Please contact the StateU Site
    Administrator at webmaster@stateu.edu .
<% else
    iRequest = Request.ServerVariables("QUERY_STRING")
    ClsQry.SetQueryFromURL(iRequest)
    RS=ClsQry .CreateRecordSet("nonsequential")
%>
<% end if %>
<!-- Now Format and return results -->
<%NextRecordNumber = 1%>
<% Do While Not RS.EOF%>
<%=NextRecordNumber %> <%=RS("FileName")%>
<A HREF="http::<%=RS("vpath")%>"><%=RS("vpath")%></A><BR>
<% RS.MoveNext NextRecordNumber = NextRecordNumber+1 Loop%>
```

The query object contains several properties and methods to aid the script writer in processing a request. In addition, there are numerous search properties, such as vpath and FileName shown in the previous example code, that you can use to refine and format the search request. To see a complete list of search properties, see "List of Property Names" in the Windows NT Option Pack Help.

Administering Index Server

Like other new Windows NT and BackOffice servers and services, Index Server can be administered through the use of the Index Server Manager, a snap-in program to the Microsoft Management Console (MMC). Common administrative functions that can be performed using the Index Server Manager include:

- Obtaining status and statistics on the current index.
- Specifying the index operation behavior—for example, whether unknown file types are included in the content index, whether document summaries are created, and so on.
- Specifying which directories, if any, under virtual roots to exclude from indexing.
- Stopping or starting the Index Server service.

Once Index Server has been installed, it typically requires minimum day-to-day administration. In addition, you can further customize how Index Server works by changing settings for Registry parameters. For more information about individual Registry parameters and their settings, see "Main Registry Parameters" in Windows NT Option Pack Help.

Updating the Content Index

You might occasionally need to change and update your Web site's content, so it is important that users obtain current results when querying an index on a Web server. Index Server enables indices to be refreshed in the following ways:

■ Automatically

Index server automatically updates the content index in two different scenarios:

- Index Server's content index is updated as a background system process as the result of automatic change notification by the Windows NT file system. Index Server might not index the document right away, but waits until there are sufficient computer resources available to do the indexing without adversely affecting overall system performance.

- When you add a new virtual root to IIS through the Internet Service Manager, Index Server is notified of the change and adds the new directory to its corpus. Consequently, Index Server will immediately index the files in this new virtual directory.

■ Administratively

If a site undergoes a large structural change (for example, if content is replaced, a new content filter is added, or a backup version is used for restoration), you will want to force a manual updating of the content index. This can be accomplished through the Index Server Manager. You can use the procedure shown at the end of this list to manually update a content index.

■ Programmatically

You can produce special administrative scripts to obtain service status, force index merges, and update virtual roots. These administrative scripts are similar to .idq queries, except that they use the .ida file extension. For more information on administrative scripts, see "Writing IDA Scripts" in the Windows NT Option Pack.

➤ **To force Index Server to rescan (update) a directory**

1. In the left pane of MMC, under the catalog where the virtual directory is located, double-click Directories.

2. In the right frame, right-click the directory you want to scan.

3. Select Rescan.

4. In the Full Rescan dialog box, click Yes for a full rescan, or click No for an incremental rescan.

Lesson Summary

Index Server 2.0 is a component of IIS that can add powerful searching and indexing capabilities to your IIS Web site. You can create Web sites that contain a wide range of document formats, which can then be indexed and queried by users. Visual InterDev uses a FrontPage 98 WebBot component to provide a default search form that enables users to search a Web site

Index Server is a standard extension component of IIS that indexes the content of a Web site and allows for users to submit queries against that content. Index Server allows any client using an HTML browser to search a Web site by using a normal HTML form.

Like other Windows NT and BackOffice servers and services, you can administer Index Server through the use of the Index Server Manager, a snap-in program to the MMC. Some common administrative functions that Index Server Manager performs include:

- Obtaining status and statistics on the current index.
- Specifying the index operation behavior—for example, whether unknown file types are included in the content index, whether document summaries are created, and so on.
- Specifying which directories, if any, under virtual roots to exclude from indexing.
- Stopping or starting the Index Server service.

Lesson 3: Adding Multimedia Delivery Capabilities

You can communicate much more efficiently by incorporating multimedia into your Web site. Implementing sound and video are also much more effective in delivering your intended message than simple text and static graphics. In this lesson, you will learn how to offer rich, high-quality interactive content over the Internet or an intranet.

After this lesson, you will be able to:

- Describe the features of Microsoft Netshow
- Define multimedia streaming
- Explain the differences between unicast and multicast

Estimated lesson time: 45 minutes

Using Multimedia on Your Web Site

Graphics and multimedia, if used effectively, can greatly enhance the user's experience. Media elements can instruct, as well as attract the user's attention to important areas of the screen. Using streaming audio and streaming video, like that available through Microsoft NetShow, you can broadcast special events as they happen, or use pre-recorded video to train employees in complex technical operations.

However, because of the speed limitations of modems used for most Internet connections, you should be careful not to add too much multimedia to your site. Low-resolution graphics, if designed correctly, not only download more quickly but also may actually look better than high-resolution graphics on most computer monitors. You may also want to consider implementing multimedia streaming onto your Web site.

Multimedia Streaming and Multicasting

Normally when you access networked multimedia content, you have to wait for the entire file to be transferred before you can use the information. The process of copying a file can take a long time. For example, a 3.15-second audio clip can be 30 kilobytes in size, but take 40 seconds to download over a 28.8 kilobit per second (Kbps) connection. Video is significantly more expensive in terms of storage and download time. For example, a 1/4-screen, 41.67-second video clip takes up 2.4 megabytes of storage space and takes over 18 minutes to download over a 28.8 Kbps connection. With streaming multimedia, the application begins playing while the rest of the application is still being downloaded. You can see or hear the information as it arrives without having to wait.

Using multimedia streaming greatly reduces the amount of format-specific programming needed. Typically, an application that must obtain media data from a file or hardware source must know everything about the data format and the hardware device. The application must handle the connection, the transfer of data, the necessary data conversion, and the actual data rendering or file storage. Because each format and device is slightly different, this process is often complex and cumbersome. Multimedia streaming, however, automatically negotiates the transfer and conversion of data from the source to the application. The streaming interfaces provide a uniform and predictable method of data access and control, which makes it easy for an application to play back the data, regardless of its original source or format.

Multicasting is an open, standards-based method of simultaneously distributing identical information to many users. This contrasts with regular TCP/IP (IP unicast), where the same information can be sent to many clients, but the sender must transmit an individual copy to each. To take full advantage of multicasting, the routers and other infrastructure components that make up intranets and the Internet must be multicast-enabled. Multicasting will be further explained later in this lesson.

Multimedia and Microsoft Internet Explorer

The Web allows you to utilize multimedia capabilities such as movies, sounds, animations and 3-D effects. Internet Explorer supports all the latest multimedia standards including the virtual reality modeling language (VRML), and makes viewing multimedia over the Internet faster and more enjoyable.

Microsoft has worked with Internet standards organizations and independent software developers to support a wide variety of standards. With Internet Explorer, Web developers can easily use multimedia effects to create compelling, interactive Web pages. Dynamic HTML technology enables you to add filters and transitions to pages, create effects that work on a timer, and alter the surface of a bitmap. Internet Explorer supports the following multimedia:

- Audio Interchange File Format (AIFF), Unix Audio (AU), Musical Instrument Digital Interface (MIDI) and waveform audio data (WAV) formats
- audio-video interleaved (AVI) video format
- In-line (streamed) sound support
- QuickTime video playback
- VRML and 3-D animation
- Additional multimedia formats, such as Motion Pictures Experts Group (MPEG) audio and video
- DirectX and MMX support
- Multimedia controls such as the Microsoft Interactive Music control
- NetShow (discussed later in this lesson) and the ActiveMovie application programming interface (API)

Internet Explorer Multimedia Controls

For content developers that want more than dynamic HTML, Internet Explorer includes animation and multimedia controls that can be used to apply visual effects to an entire Web page or elements in a Web page without scripting. These controls support filters, animation, and transitions. Transitions can be used for elements in a page or for transitions between pages. These multimedia controls utilize Internet Explorer multimedia and animation services. ActiveX control and Java developers can take advantage of these services to implement additional multimedia or animation effects. All of the following controls are transparent, windowless, and can be seamlessly integrated within a Web page.

Control	Description
Behaviors	Applies high-level behaviors to controls and dynamic HTML elements.
Effects	Alters any item on a Web page by applying a graphic filter.
Hot spot	Establishes regions of the screen that can process mouse clicks
Mixer	Mixes multiple WAV files together dynamically.
Path	Easily moves objects across a two-dimensional path.
Sequencer	Easily controls timing of events on pages.
Sprite	Creates animated images.
Sprite buttons	Creates animated multi-state buttons.
Structured graphics	Provides high-quality, lightweight, scalable, rotatable graphics. Internet Explorer provides programmatic access so that content developers can dynamically add new graphic elements through script. For example, content developers can create HTML applications that read values from a data bound control, and then create appropriate graphs.
Transitions	Alters any item on a page, or the page itself, over time.

The Interactive Music Control

The Interactive Music control provides dynamic musical accompaniment and software wavetable synthesis. Interactive Music combines the best of MIDI and WAV technologies to present a lightweight, consistent musical accompaniment solution. Interactive Music provides infinitely flexible musical output. It is more flexible than WAV file output because a WAV file is an encapsulated recording that cannot change, whereas the Interactive Music Control can creates music instantaneously according to whatever is happening at that moment.

The Interactive Music engine provides a constantly evolving, responsive musical soundtrack. It tracks the user's actions and creates a soundtrack accordingly. And unlike standard MIDI playback, the music can assume a nonlinear form and respond to user and programmatic input. Additionally, through the Microsoft Synthesizer, Interactive Music supplies the user with software wavetable synthesis, which ensures consistent and configurable musical playback via any sound card.

Microsoft Liquid Motion

The Microsoft Liquid Motion Web multimedia application tool, illustrated in Figure 10.4, makes it easy for programmers and non-programmers alike to create and publish animation on the World Wide Web. Liquid Motion works on any browser on any platform that supports Java. Animation you create with Liquid Motion can bring your Web site to life for users, attracting their attention, engaging their interest, and communicating your message.

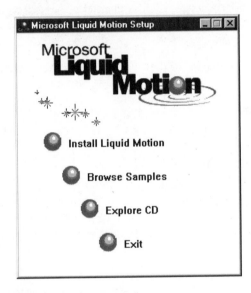

Figure 10.4 Microsoft Liquid Motion

Using NetShow

Web sites attract and retain visitors using the latest technologies in graphics and animation. The integration of audio and video into applications such as online training, corporate communications, customer and sales support, news and entertainment services, and product promotions will provide individuals and organizations with new and exciting ways to communicate.

Integration with Windows NT Server and Internet Information Server (IIS)

NetShow and its streaming services are tightly integrated with Windows NT Server to provide an efficient, reliable, scalable, and secure platform for delivering audio, illustrated audio, and video content over corporate intranets and the Internet.

NetShow is particularly useful in:

- Education and Training

  Multimedia extends the classroom by streaming taped instruction through the Internet and Intranets, and makes it easier for trainers to generate compelling and memorable content and for users to receive training whenever and wherever needed using their PC.

- Corporate Communications

  By delivering multimedia presentations over corporate networks and the Internet, companies save substantially on the costs normally required to distribute training materials, binders, or CD-ROMs. This also provides the opportunity for everyone within the organization to view important organizational briefings live, such as internal presentations or presentations for the press or analysts.

- News and Entertainment

  You can broadcast live or on-demand news and other entertainment, including musical or sporting events, and expand distribution channels beyond a typical broadcast to include international markets via the Web. By charging Internet users or advertisers for the same content delivered through normal channels, news and entertainment organizations significantly expand their revenue potential.

- Advertising and Retailing

  You can use multimedia techniques to advertise products or services on Web sites, which is a more compelling advertising technique than using static Web pages. You can insert advertisements in streamed multimedia broadcasts, providing an alternative method to finance such content over pay-per-view techniques.

- Hospitality and Travel

  You can replace or enhance traditional videotape-based systems in hotels, in-flight systems, cruise ships, hospitals, and connected communities. In addition, you can integrate video rentals and other services, such as Web browsing, e-mail, and games, to enhance revenue potential. Systems may be customized to automate delivery and customer billing, and track usage.

With NetShow, you can stream multimedia over networks that range from low bandwidth dial-up Internet connections to high-bandwidth switched local area networks.

NetShow utilizes all key Windows NT Server manageability features, including a graphical administration console, performance monitoring, an integrated directory and security model, and the Event Log, which records program execution information. NetShow also fully supports Windows NT connectivity, including network environments such as IP, IPX, 14.4/28.8 POTS, ISDN, Ethernet, and others. Sharing the same user interface, APIs, services, and tools means that end users and computer professionals do not have to learn different interfaces or tools. An integrated solution offers easier management, better connectivity, and lower support costs. And because NetShow and IIS are designed to work together, they deliver a high-performance system for broadcasting multimedia.

How NetShow Brings Multimedia to the Internet and Corporate Intranets

NetShow allows users to receive audio and video broadcasts from their personal computers. It uses a client/server architecture and sophisticated compression and buffering techniques to provide the following:

- Powerful broadcast system

  NetShow delivers a complete, high-performance system for broadcasting live and on-demand audio, video, and multimedia.

- Ease of use and reduced cost of ownership

  NetShow reduces the total cost of streaming multimedia because of its tight integration with IIS, Windows NT Server network operating system, and the Internet Explorer browser. Standard multimedia authoring and HTML programming tools can be used to create and host content.

- High-quality audio and video over the Internet

  NetShow enables high-quality content generation and streaming with new, next-generation compression/decompression (codec) technology. Using great compression technology from a variety of companies, including Voxware and Fraunhofer Institut Integrierte Schaltungen (FhG), Microsoft, and Vivo Software, NetShow delivers the best range of codecs for creating content that suits a particular application and bandwidth.

How NetShow Works

NetShow provides a wide variety of features that allow customization of the system. How you use NetShow depends largely on the types of media you want to stream and the characteristics of the network used to deliver the data. Understanding these basic concepts helps determine how to deploy NetShow for your particular application.

Media Streaming

As illustrated in Figure 10.5, NetShow components are distributed across a network. Most of the audio and video content currently hosted on intranets and on Internet sites is downloadable. This means that the multimedia content must be copied to the user's local PC before it can be played. NetShow uses a client/server streaming architecture to deliver multimedia content to clients.

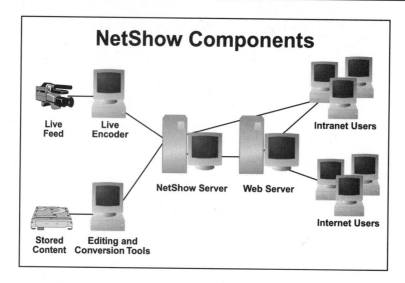

Figure 10.5 How Netshow components are implemented on a network

Streaming content is digitized content that has been compressed or encoded into a format that the server can break down into packets and then stream across a network to a client player, illustrated in Figure 10.6. The content arrives, is buffered briefly, and plays. It is then discarded.

Figure 10.6 Sample.asf playing after being buffered

The content is never actually stored on the user's computer. NetShow users benefit by experiencing instant play, and don't have the frustration of waiting for content to download to determine whether it meets their needs or interests.

Network Bandwidth Issues

Any computer network connection (Internet or intranet) has an upper limit on the amount of data that it can pass in a given second. This data limit is called its bandwidth. The data rate (also called bit rate) of an audio and video file is the amount of data that must transmit in a given second for the whole file to be heard or viewed in its entirety. To transmit a content file completely and smoothly, its data rate must be less than the available bandwidth of its target network.

Content Compression

Because today's networks are usually bandwidth-constrained, audio and video files must be compressed to reduce their data rates. To compress a file, mathematical compression algorithms called codecs are applied that analyze the audio and video and decide what bits of data can be removed or merged with minimum impact on what the ear will hear or eye will see. However, applying compression to an audio or video clip will result in some loss of quality.

The level of quality and fidelity delivered in sound and video files depends primarily on how much bandwidth is available and whether you have authored the content appropriately for that available bandwidth. For example, compare the bandwidth to an empty pipe. You decide to fill that pipe with audio only. If your pipe is large (that is, you are on a corporate network with a high bandwidth connection), you can author that audio to be only slightly compressed, thus delivering very high quality. If your pipe is small (a user with a 28.8 Kbps dial-up connection), you will have to use a codec to compress the audio to fit in such a small pipe. It will sound worse than the audio authored for higher bandwidths. Now, imagine that you want to add images or video to that audio content. In order to make room in that pipe, you will need to compress the audio even more. You will also need to compress the images or video significantly. The end result will be highly compressed multimedia that can play at bandwidths that could support only still images.

Multimedia Compression/Decompression Algorithms (Codec) Independence

The quality of content is largely determined by codec used to compress it. Advances in codec technology are happening monthly, and for this reason NetShow was developed to be codec independent. This means that a variety of codecs ship with the NetShow product so that content creators can choose which codec to create content with, while the users will be able to decode any application without hassles. Most other streaming media companies today use a proprietary codec (one that can be used only by that particular application, and other codecs cannot be used). NetShow offers the content author and end user a well-rounded suite of bundled and stand-alone third-party codecs for voice, music, images, and video, at a variety of bit rates. This provides more options, more flexibility, higher-quality content, and faster innovation, because the codecs can be upgraded independent of NetShow.

Two Key Delivery Techniques: Unicast and Multicast

Unicast refers to networking in which computers establish two-way, point-to-point connections. Most network operations today work in this fashion—a user requests a file and a server sends the file to that client only. One advantage of unicasting is when multimedia is streamed over a network, the client computer can communicate with the computer supplying the multimedia stream. With NetShow, for example, the NetShow server can provide a unicast video stream to a client, and the client can take advantage of the VCR controls in the NetShow Player to ask the server to pause the stream or to skip backward or forward to a marker in the stream. The disadvantage to unicast is that each client that connects to the server receives a separate stream, which rapidly uses up network bandwidth.

IP Multicast refers to networking in which one computer sends a single copy of the data over the network and many computers receive that data. Unlike a broadcast, routers can control where a multicast travels on the network. An advantage to multicasting is that only a single copy of the data is sent across the network, which preserves network bandwidth. In large companies the bandwidth savings can be substantial. The disadvantage to multicasting is that it is connectionless; clients have no control over the streams they receive, so cannot pause or skip backward or forward in the stream.

To use IP multicast on a network, the network routers must support the IP Multicast protocol. However, whether or not your network routers support multicasts, you can always use NetShow multicasting on the local node of your LAN. In addition, by setting up NetShow servers on each node of your network, you can distribute a single stream to the NetShow server on each node and then multicast to clients on that node. Most routers sold within the last 2 to 3 years are able to handle multicast. You will need router software upgrades in order to multicast-enable them.

NetShow combines the best of these unicasting and multicasting, enabling network managers to choose whether unicast or multicast is most appropriate for their network and best suited for their applications and needs.

Active Streaming Format (ASF)

The foundation for all of the components of NetShow content creation is the Active Streaming format (ASF). ASF is an open, standards-based file format that prepares multimedia content for streaming. ASF is the key format for the future, eventually replacing data types such as WAV and AVI. ASF adds error correction and other features necessary for streaming and content delivery over lossy networks. ASF also enables the synchronization of different data types on a common time line, enabling, for example, JPEG images, bitmaps, or WAV files to be synchronized with each other. Multimedia content must be converted to ASF before delivery over a network. ASF content can be hosted on a local hard drive, on an HTTP server, or on a specialized media server such as NetShow. This provides flexibility to the content creator: the same content can be played locally from a CD-ROM or a hard drive, or it can be played from a remote location hosted on an HTTP server or a specialized media server.

NetShow Channels

When you multicast multimedia or files using NetShow, you first set up a channel. The channel establishes the communication between the server and the multicast clients. Much like a television channel, when users connect to a NetShow channel via the NetShow Player or a Web page that embeds the feed in it, they get whatever is being played at the time. For example, you could tune into a particular channel and get nothing if there are no NetShow programs being played at the time.

NetShow Programs

When multimedia or files are multicast using NetShow, a channel is first set up. The channel can be populated with programs, which are the content for that channel. Programs can be live feeds or on-demand content scheduled to be played at specific times. Much like television, what is seen on your screen could be live, or it could be played from a tape at a specific time. Also like television, you can't skip ahead or back; you get the broadcast and if you don't like it you either turn it off or change channels.

Lesson Summary

Graphics and multimedia enhance the look and feel of an application. Using streaming audio and streaming video, like that available through NetShow, you can broadcast special events as they happen, or use pre-recorded video to train employees in complex technical operations.

Streaming content is digitized content that has been compressed or encoded into a format that the server can break down into packets and then stream across a network to a client player. NetShow and its streaming services are tightly integrated with Windows NT Server to provide an efficient, reliable, scalable, and secure platform for delivering audio, illustrated audio, and video content over corporate intranets and the Internet.

Lab 10: Implementing Additional Server-Side Technologies

In this lab, you will examine the default search capabilities supplied by a Visual InterDev Web project working in conjunction with Microsoft Index Server.

To see a demonstration of this lab, run the Lab10.exe animation located in the Animations folder on the companion CD-ROM that accompanies this book.

Before You Begin

You should have already completed Labs 2, 3, 4, 5, 6, 7, 8, and 9. If you have not, follow the steps in Lab 2 to create the Chateau Web project and use the files in the Labs\Lab09\Partial folder to obtain the necessary files to complete this lab.

Estimated lab time: 30 minutes

Exercise 1: Using Default Search Capabilities

In this exercise, you will first examine the default search capabilities of a Visual InterDev Web application by using the Index Server Manager to explore the indexing service. You will then issue search requests using the project's auto-generated search page, Search.htm. Finally you will examine the code behind this page.

➤ **Verify that the index service is installed and running**

Microsoft Index Server is an optional component of the Windows NT Option Pack that must be installed to perform searches on a Web site.

1. On the Windows NT Web server computer, start the Services Control Panel applet.

2. In the Service list box, locate the Content Index entry.

3. If this entry is not listed, you must rerun the setup for the Windows NT Option Pack to install the Index Server component.

4. Verify that its status is started and that the Startup type is Automatic as illustrated in Figure 10.7. If these properties are not set to these values, change them accordingly.

5. Close the Services applet.

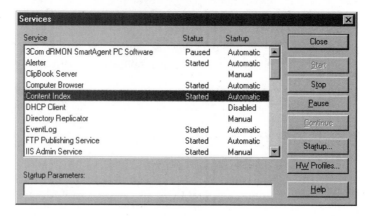

Figure 10.7 The Content Index service

➤ **Examine the indexing service in Index Server Manager**

1. Start the Index Server Manager application.

   On the Start menu, choose Programs, and then Windows NT 4.0 Option Pack.
   Click Microsoft Index Server and Index Server Manager.

2. In the left pane, expand the tree until you see the Web node. Right-click this
   node and click Properties as illustrated in Figure 10.8.

   The Web Properties dialog box is displayed.

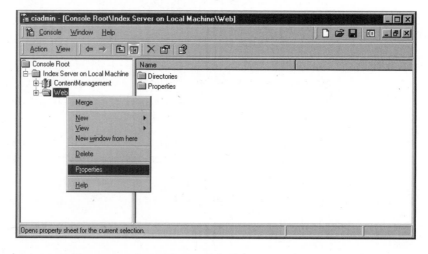

Figure 10.8 Opening the Web Properties dialog

3. Notice that the Web Properties dialog box has three property pages:

   - Location

     Displays the following read-only information: name, location, and number of indexed virtual roots.

   - Web

     Determines which specific directories and directory types will be indexed.

   - Generation

     Allows you to alter the indexing process by choosing whether to index unknown file types and to determine the existence and size of the file characterization (the generated abstract).

4. Click the Directories node in the left pane. All the indexed directories will be displayed in the right pane as illustrated in Figure 10.9.

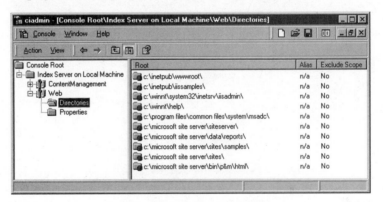

Figure 10.9 A list of indexed directories in MMC

Many of the indexed directories, such as C:\Winnt\Help, support the Find functionality of the online documentation for Windows NT Option Pack components.

Note You can exclude one or more of the listed directories from being indexed through the Internet Information Manager snap-in program. In the Properties dialog box for a directory, click on the Virtual Directory tab, and then clear the Index This Directory option.

---

5. Right-click one of the directories in the right pane, and from the context menu, choose Rescan. This causes Index Server to immediately reindex the content in the selected directory.

➤ **Explore the default search page**

1. Start Internet Explorer and go to the Chateau St. Mark Hotel home page, Default.htm. Expand the Site Services node and click the Search The Site link in the lower left frame to navigate to the default search page.

2. In the Search For text box, type in a word or phrase for which you would like to search in the Chateau St. Mark Hotel Web site (for example "Chateau").

   The returned page will contain all the hits for that text as illustrated in Figure 10.10.

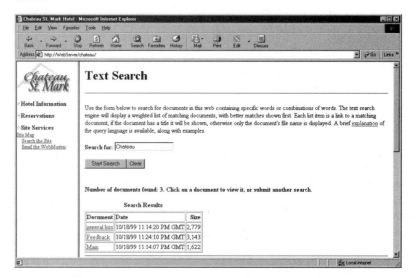

Figure 10.10 Search results for the Chateau St. Mark Hotel Web site

---

Note For the default search page to work properly, you must have FrontPage Server Extensions installed, and your Web project must have generated the _vti_bin and _derived folders for you. (The Web Project Wizard creates the required folders and files when you check the Create search.htm to enable full text searching option in Step 2 of 4.)

---

3. View the source for the search page, Search.htm. Locate the line that contains the string "Webbot".

```
<!--webbot BOT="Search" S-LINK S-FIELDS="TimeStamp,Do cumentK," S-
INDEX="All" S-DSN="default" TAG="FORM" S-TEXT="Search for:" I-
SIZE="20" S-SUBMIT="Start Search" S-CLEAR="Clear" B-
USEINDEXSERVER="1" U-DOC-URL="search.htm" startspan --><form
action="_vti_bin/search.htm0.idq" method="POST"><p><b>Search for:
</b><input type="text" name="UserRestriction" size="20"
value="Chateau"></p><p><input type="submit" value="Start
Search"><input type="reset" value="Clear"></p></form><!--webbot
bot="Search" endspan i-checksum="10629" -->
```

This line is an HTML comment that the FrontPage Server interprets as a request to access the FrontPage Search Component. In the next exercise, you will replace the default search page with an ASP page, to which you will add additional code.

Exercise 2: Integrating Index Server with ASP

In this exercise, you will replace the default search page, Search.htm, which accesses the indexing service through a FrontPage Webbot, with an ASP page, Searchres.asp, which accesses this service though server-side VBScript. You will code the portions of this new page that instantiate and access the COM Query component. You will essentially duplicate the functionality of the Search Webbot. However, scripting allows much more powerful and flexible integration of search capabilities within your Web application.

➤ **Replace the existing search page**

1. Open the Chateau Web project in Visual InterDev if it is not already open.

2. Rename the file Search.htm to OldSearch.htm. Answer No when asked if you want to update the links that refer to this file.

3. Add the files Search.htm and Searchres.asp, located in Labs\Lab10\Partial, to the Chateau project. Search.htm replaces the old file.

4. Open the new files for editing.

➤ **Examine the new project files**

1. Examine the file Search.htm in both Source and Design modes.

Note that the file contains a simple form to take a search string supplied by the user. The action target of this form is the Searchres.asp page. Note that it also contains a simple expanding <DIV> section that explains the query language used to form a search request.

2. Examine SResults.asp in Source mode.

   The body contains two main parts: an initial server-side script section that prepares and executes the query, and a subsequent section that formats the results in a table for return to the user. There are also a number to ToDo comments in the first section.

➤ **Completing the search query script**

In this procedure, you will complete the server-side script that interfaces with the content indexing service.

1. Locate the first ToDo comment. Replace the comment with a line of code that sets the Query property of the query object to the text the user supplied in the Search For text box of the file Search.htm.

2. Replace the next ToDo with a statement that sets the Columns property of the query object to the search properties to be retrieved: filename, vpath, size, and characterization.

3. Replace the next ToDo with a statement that sets the MaxRecords property to 50.

4. Replace the next ToDo comment with a declaration for an Index Server utility object named SUUtil.

5. The next statement, which already exists, calls AddScopeToQuery to limit the scope of the search to the Chateau St. Mark Hotel Web site.

   Your code should look similar to the following:

```
<% Else %>
<% REM then create the recordset object from querystring
    ' Set the query object's properties
    SUQuery.Query = Request("qu")
    SUQuery.Columns = "filename, vpath, size, characterization"
    ' Set maximum return set to 50
    SUQuery.MaxRecords = 50
    ' Restrict the Search scope to Chateau Web Site
    Set SUUtil = Server.CreateObject("IXSSO.Util")
    SUUtil.AddScopeToQuery SUQuery, "/chateau", "deep"
    ' Submit the query and collect results
    Set RS=SUQuery.CreateRecordSet("sequential")%>
<% End If %>
```

➤ **Testing your new search page**

1. View Search.htm in Internet Explorer.

2. Enter Chateau for the search string as you did in the Exercise 1.

   If you did not make any coding errors, the results that are returned should be similar to the results displayed in Exercise 1.

Review

The following questions are intended to reinforce key information presented in this chapter. If you are unable to answer a question, review the appropriate lesson and then try the question again. Answers to the questions can be found in Appendix A, "Questions and Answers."

1. What is CDONTS used for?

2. Describe the process SMTP service goes through when sending mail.

3. Describe the features of the two servers used by Search Bot.

4. What is the difference between unicast and multicast?

APPENDIX A

Questions and Answers

Chapter 1

Review Questions

Page 27

1. Describe the functionality of the three generations of Web servers.

   First-generation Web servers delivered mostly static content—Hypertext Markup Language (HTML) pages with embedded graphics, sound files, and other basic features.

   Second-generation servers supported dynamic content through server-side extensions such as Common Gateway Interface (CGI) and application programming interfaces (APIs). CGI scripts run on the server and return dynamic HTML pages for the Web browser to display

   Third-generation servers support Web-based applications that integrate with other enterprise services. These Web-based applications can be developed in popular programming languages such as Microsoft Visual Basic. With third-generation servers, you can take advantage of component technology and transactions to provide greater scalability and fault tolerance for mission-critical Web applications.

2. What are the main differences between single-tier, two-tier, and three-tier applications?

   In a single-tier application, all three services—user, business, and data—are architecturally combined into a single program. A two-tier application offers significant benefits over single-tier applications because data processing is centralized and becomes a shared resource among potentially many users.

   Three-tier (and multi-tier) applications separate user, business, and data tiers. This can reduce network traffic and balance database server loads more efficiently. The main advantage of a multi-tier architecture is the extraction of business logic from the user and data tiers.

3. Briefly describe the five phases of the Web development process.

   Planning Phase

   - **Identify the project goals. Perform a feasibility study to quantify tradeoffs among time, cost, budget, and benefits. Determine what content will be presented.**

   Analysis and Design Phase

   - **Define the structure of the Web site, navigation, application tasks, and data requirements.**

   Implementation and Testing Phase

   - **Have a working, approved prototype of your Web site. Create HTML pages, COM components, ActiveX controls, scripts, and databases. Create a test plan.**

   Production Phase

   - **Evaluate the result of your work by putting your design into action. Implement a working Web application on a production server.**

   Support Phase

   - **Remove outdated content from the site. Post changes and updates regularly. Make sure updates have consistent style throughout the Web site. Optimize code as you receive feedback from customers.**

4. Currently your organization provides goods and services in the United States. However, your business plan calls for an increase in revenue generated from International customers. In which phase of Web site development should localizing your site to foreign languages be included?

   Planning Phase

5. List the three main benefits of using Visual InterDev to develop a corporate Web site.

   Independence for programmers

   Source code control

   Interoperability with other development tools

6. List three team members typically associated with advanced Web site development.

   Programmer, HTML author, Graphic artist

Chapter 2

Review Questions

Page 80

1. How are conceptual, logical, and a physical designs related to each other?

   Conceptual design is an analysis activity that leads to determining which processes and activities will go into the new system, and how the objectives of those processes and activities will be met. Once the conceptual design is in place, you can derive a logical design that includes the data, user interface, components, and services of the application.

2. List the Visual InterDev version-control tools.

   Server objects, ActiveX controls, design-time controls, HTML general

3. Why is the conceptual design of a solution so important?

   A conceptual design helps you create accurate business requirements. By involving both developers and users you can create business requirements that will effectively address:

   - **The problem**
   - **The needs and technological capabilities of the business and users**
   - **The desired, future state of the work**
   - **Whether upgrading an existing solution is viable**

Chapter 3

Review Questions

Page 122

1. What are the advantages to using scriptlets?

   They allow Web page authors to create reusable user interface components.

   They allow developers using Visual Basic, Visual InterDev, and other development environments that support controls to make use of features built into Web pages.

   They are easy to create and maintain.

   They are small and efficient.

2. What is event bubbling?

   When an event occurs, it fires the source element first. It then fires on the parent of the source element through a process known as bubbling. It continues to fire on successive parent elements until it has reached the top element, the document.

3. What is the Document Object Model (DOM) and how is it used?

   The DOM is an interface that permits script to access and update the content, structure, and style of a document. The DOM includes a model for how a standard set of objects representing documents are combined, and an interface for accessing and manipulating them.

Chapter 4

Review Questions

Page 179

1. What is an ASP page used for?

   Active Server Pages are Web pages that can be customized for each user dynamically, based upon the user's actions or requests. ASP is the server-side technology that allows you to generate Web pages that change each time the page is requested such as returning data from a database.

2. How does an ASP page use a request object?

   An ASP application uses the Request object to interrogate the HTTP request and extract the incoming values. You can use the Request object to retrieve information from or about the current user, and to access all of the information passed in any HTTP request.

3. What is the Browser Capabilities component?

   The Browser Capabilities component determines the capabilities, type, and version of a user's browser.

4. Explain the purpose of using a cookie.

   Cookies are a mechanism by which state can be maintained in a file on the user's computer. They can store user preferences or other personalization information that should be saved between sessions.

Chapter 5

Review Questions

Page 229

1. What is Universal Data Access?

   Universal Data Access is the Microsoft strategy for providing access to all types of information from a variety of sources besides the traditional relational database.

2. What is the purpose of the data environment?

   The data environment is the repository for storing and reusing data connections and data commands in a Visual InterDev project. A data environment contains the information required to access data in a database, and it contains one or more data connections.

3. What are some advantages of using scripting objects?

   Script objects provide certain advantages. These include:
   - **Browser and platform independence**
   - **Support for data binding**
   - **Simplified page navigation**
   - **Support for remote scripting**

4. Define a script object.

   The script object is an object that you can manipulate with code, such as a design-time control. You set its properties, call its methods, and respond to associated events.

Chapter 6

Review Questions

Page 282

1. What is the purpose of SQL?

    SQL is a language used for querying, updating, and managing relational databases. SQL can be used to retrieve, sort, and filter specific data from the database.

2. Explain how a Recordset object is used.

    Once a recordset is retrieved from the database, it is stored in a Recordset object. You can use properties and methods of the Recordset object to manipulate the data in the recordset. You can navigate through the records, or present them to the user, using the Recordset object.

3. Explain how a Connection object is used.

    You can use the Connection object to run commands or queries on the data source. When a recordset is retrieved from the database, it is stored in a Recordset object. To create a Connection object, you supply the name of either an ODBC data source or an OLE DB provider.

4. What are some performance considerations you should remember when implementing remote data service (RDS)?

    RDS is useful in retrieving and displaying records from both small and large recordsets. Your Web site will be easier to maintain and will serve a larger number of users if you isolate the data updates in business objects instead of placing the data update code directly in HTML documents. RDS works only in Internet Explorer 4.0 or later running on an Intel platform in Microsoft Windows 9x or Windows NT 4.0 or later.

Chapter 7

Review Questions

Page 320

1. What are business rules?

    Business rules are self-imposed constraints that companies use to help them operate in their particular business environments. These business rules are used as goals for developers when developing applications.

2. What are some advantages and disadvantages of using in-process components?

    Applications that use in-process servers almost always run faster than those that use out-of-process servers. In-process component is less fault-tolerant so that if the DLL fails, the entire executable fails.

3. Give an example of a business process.

    For the Chateau St. Mark Hotel, a credit card number for a customer must be validated before they can check in to a room.

Chapter 8

Review Questions

Page 366

1. Explain the benefits of using MTS in your Web project.

   Microsoft Transaction Server enables applications to operate efficiently as well as be shared by a large number of users. This lets you focus on building business logic without having to build infrastructure. With MTS, you can use your existing skills with languages such as Visual Basic to build sophisticated n-tier applications. With MTS, you can also:

   - **Access databases and other resources, such as mainframe applications with full transaction protection.**
   - **Use scalability features such as thread pooling, database connection pooling, and just-in-time (JIT) object instantiation.**
   - **Call the same objects from IIS and ASP.**

2. List and describe three services provided by MTS.

   Component Transaction

   - **A component transaction consists of methods running on one or more components. MTS monitors components as they interact with transactional resources, such as databases, and coordinates changes.**

   Object Brokering

   - **MTS acts as an object broker by servicing requests made from various clients for instances of a component. MTS acknowledges requests for object creation from remote clients. MTS then coordinates the creation, maintenance, and destruction of COM component instances and the threads that execute inside them.**

   Just-in-Time (JIT) Activation

   - **With JIT, components consume server resources only while they are actually executing.**

3. What is the ACID test?

   For a transaction to succeed, it must have certain properties described by the ACID test. ACID stands for Atomicity, Consistency, Isolation, and Durability.

Chapter 9

Review Questions

Page 407

1. Describe various security considerations when developing a Web site.

   Security issues on the Web are not much different than security issues that have always been in your organization. You need to:

   - **Keep malicious hackers and careless users from causing problems with your Web servers.**
   - **Determine what data can be accessed through the Web site.**
   - **Determine the ways to access the data.**
   - **Determine how many people need to access each set of data.**

2. Describe the user authentication options in Microsoft SQL Server.

   With the Windows NT Authentication Mode a user connects through a Windows NT user account. SQL Server then verifies that the account name and password were validated when the user logged on to Windows.

   With Mixed Mode users can connect using Windows NT Authentication and SQL Server Authentication.

3. Explain the difference between declarative security and programmatic security.

   With declarative security, security is configured directly with MTS Explorer.

   With programmatic security, security is provided by code. You write in your component to determine if a client is authorized to perform an operation.

Chapter 10

Review Questions

Page 447

1. What is CDONTS used for?

   CDONTS is a subset of the CDO library. It is used for building simple, scalable applications, based on the SMTP mail protocol. CDONTS can run on both IIS and Exchange Server environments.

2. Describe the process SMTP service goes through when sending mail.

   An outbound message that is created as a text file is placed in the Pickup directory. Microsoft SMTP Service then collects and delivers it. It is either placed in the Drop directory, the Queue directory, or the BadMail Directory. The queued messages are transmitted through an outbound TCP port to a receiving mail server for the designated remote domain.

3. Describe the features of the two servers used by Search Bot.

   The Wide Area Information Server (WAIS) search engine the default search engine included with the FrontPage Server Extensions, but is not installed as part of Visual InterDev or the Windows NT Option Pack.

   The Index Server is a content-indexing and search component included with IIS. The Search Bot uses Index Server instead of the WAIS search engine only if Index Server has been installed as part of IIS.

4. What is the difference between unicast and multicast?

   Multicasting is an open, standards-based method of simultaneously distributing identical information to many users. With unicast, the same information can be sent to many clients, but the sender must transmit an individual copy to each.

APPENDIX B

Creating Client Script

Scripting involves creating code that is included on a Web page. The script runs either on the client computer (client-side script) when a user opens the page in his or her browser, or on the Web server (server-side script) before the page is returned to the client. In both cases, you add script to a Web page as ASCII text. This appendix introduces client-side scripting and explains how to implement client-side scripting. It also introduces various scripting languages including Microsoft Visual Basic Script (VBScript), which is the scripting language that will be used in this appendix.

In addition, you will learn about three scripting languages available for most current browsers. You will also learn about the Document Object Model (DOM).

Features of Client-Side Script

Client-side script runs on the client computer. Most Web browsers contain scripting interpreters that can read and run the script. For a client-side script to function, a Web browser must support the scripting language. If it does not, the user will not have full access to the scripted features on the Web page.

Note Client-side script is not compiled, nor is it encrypted on an HTML page. Therefore, if you view the HTML source of a Web page, you will see the script included in the page.

Scripting languages allow you to leverage your existing skills to develop code within your Web pages. Scripting does the following:

- Allows you to make a Web page more active.
- Enables users to interact with your Web site.
- Allows you to determine the type of browser a user has so that you can generate content accordingly.
- Allows you to add forms to your site to gather data.
- Allows you to use Java and Microsoft ActiveX technologies.

You use client-side scripting to enhance the functionality of a Web page by embedding the source code in the page's HTML code. When the Web browser encounters a script embedded in a Web page, the browser calls a scripting interpreter that parses and deciphers the scripting code. The Web browser must also integrate scripting with ActiveX controls or Java applets embedded in the HTML page.

ActiveX Scripting Architecture

Scripting is an easy way to allow your Web pages to interact with the user and other software components. This includes writing code that runs in response to events, invoking object methods, and accessing properties. Script commands can be placed into HTML documents and can be invoked by the browser when the page is loaded or through user interaction.

Microsoft has used ActiveX to provide a flexible architecture for including scripting languages in Web pages as well as in traditional applications. ActiveX Scripting allows *script hosts* to invoke scripting services within *script engines*.

Script hosts and engines are available from different software vendors and can implement different languages. Microsoft Internet Explorer, Active Server Pages (ASP), and Microsoft Visual InterDev are examples of script hosts, but you can easily add scripting to your own applications. VBScript and Microsoft JScript are examples of script languages that come with their own scripting engines, but you can also develop your own scripting language.

A scripting engine is a program that processes commands written in a particular language. ASP comes with two scripting engines: VBScript and JScript. The ActiveX Scripting specifications define the interfaces that a script host and script engine must support, but the vendor of the script engine defines the script language, syntax, and execution rules. All script logic is interpreted at run time by the script engine; there is no requirement for scripts to first be compiled like traditional applications.

One advantage of scripting is its ability to interact with other objects that are accessible within the Web page, within the browser, or through the application. Accessible objects are either:

- Intrinsic (built-in)

  The objects are exposed within the script host and are often referred to as an object model.

- Executable software components

  These are packages of reusable code that usually serve a specific function and don't have to be resident on the browser and can therefore be downloaded when needed.

You can access an object's properties, invoke methods, and detect events through Component Object Model (COM) technology. Creating COM components is covered in Chapter 7 of this course.

Scripting Languages

Any scripting language can be used to develop Web applications so long as there is a script engine, or interpreter, that supports the language. VBScript and JScript are the most common scripting languages.

VBScript

VBScript is a case-insensitive subset of the Visual Basic language that is upwardly compatible with Visual Basic for Applications. Internet Explorer and Internet Information Server (IIS) both support VBScript. However, current versions of Netscape Navigator do not. The VBScript interpreter is fast, portable, and can be freely licensed from Microsoft.

VBScript is intended to be a safe subset of the Visual Basic programming language; therefore it does not include file input/output or direct access to the underlying operating system. However, VBScript does allow you to control the browser, link controls to pages, automate Java applets, and associate forms to databases.

JScript

JScript, Microsoft's version of JavaScript, is compatible with the JavaScript implementation in Netscape Navigator. It is a C-like language that is based on Java, a programming language developed by Sun Microsystems. Both Netscape Navigator and Internet Explorer support JavaScript (and therefore JScript). JScript allows you to link and automate a wide variety of objects in Web pages, including ActiveX controls and applets created using Java. Because the implementations of VBScript and JScript are fairly similar, it is relatively simple to program in both.

However, JScript differs from VBScript in a number of important ways:

- All JScript procedures are declared as functions.
- JScript statements are semi-colon terminated.
- JScript Var statements are used to declare variables.
- Braces are used in JScript to group statements.

Choosing a Client-Side Scripting Language

When choosing a scripting language, consider the following two issues:

- Browser compatibility

  Web browsers must include a scripting interpreter for the language you choose. Internet Explorer 4.0 and later has interpreters for VBScript, JScript, and JavaScript. Netscape Navigator provides an interpreter for JavaScript.

- Programmer familiarity

  Choose a scripting language that is similar to a language you know. If you have Visual Basic experience, you can quickly learn VBScript. If you have Java or C experience, JScript and JavaScript will be more familiar to you.

The following table shows VBScript and JScript code that defines a procedure for displaying a message box:

VBScript	JScript

<pre><SCRIPT LANGUAGE=VBScript>
<!--
Sub SayHello()
    MsgBox "Hello, world!"
End Sub
-->
</SCRIPT></pre>
	<pre><SCRIPT LANGUAGE=JScript>
	<!--
	function SayHello()
	{
	      alert("Hello, world!");
	}
	//-->
	</SCRIPT></pre>

Object-Oriented Programming

Script development is based on the object-oriented programming model. Object-oriented programming enables you to write code that is associated with specific objects in your application.

An object is a combination of code and data that can be treated as a unit. An object can be a piece of an application or Web page, such as a control or the entire page itself. For example, a command button that you place on a form in an HTML page is an object. Objects have the following associated with them:

- Properties
- Methods
- Events

Properties

Properties are the attributes of an object, such as its size, caption, and color. You can set properties of an object when you add the object to a Web page at design time, and you can write script to change properties when a user interacts with the object.

Methods

Methods are the actions an object can perform. For example, a form object has a Submit method.

You can write script to invoke the methods of an object. For example, you can run the following line of code to manually submit the contents of the form to the server:

```
MyForm.Submit
```

Events

Events are procedures that an object invokes in response to user or system actions. For example, a command button has an onclick event procedure that runs when a user clicks the button.

You can add script to event procedures; when the event occurs, the script runs.

Each object has a separate set of event procedures. If you have two command buttons on a Web page, each button has its own onclick event. For example, a Submit button on a form can run code to submit the form's data to the server, while a Reset button can clear all the fields for the user to re-enter the data.

Client-Side vs. Server-Side Scripting

You can write script that runs on the client or on the Web server. Depending on the needs of your Web site, you can use client and server scripts together or independently.

To use client-side script, you embed the source code into the HTML page as ASCII text. When the page is downloaded from the server, the scripting code is not compiled into intermediate code. Consequently, anyone can view or copy your script by viewing your HTML source code. When the Web browser encounters a script, it calls a scripting interpreter, which parses and runs the script code. Therefore, in order for your users to have full access to the features of a Web page that contains script, they must have a browser that supports scripting.

Server-side script runs on the Web server before the page is returned to the user. The script creates standard HTML, and the user never sees the actual script itself. To use server-side script, your Web server must support ASP, which were introduced with IIS 3.0.

When to Use Client-Side or Server-Side Script

Whether to use client-side or server-side script depends on the functionality you want. For example, if you want to validate that the user has entered only digits in a social security field on a form, client-side script is appropriate. The code runs in the browser and submits only valid data to the server.

However, if you are building a Web site for claims agents at an insurance firm where data is retrieved and updated to a live database, you can use server-side script to retrieve the data from the database before returning Web pages to the users. This appendix focuses on writing client-side script. To learn about how to write server-side script, see Chapter 4 in this course.

The <SCRIPT> Tag

Scripting code is contained within the HTML <SCRIPT> tag. The LANGUAGE attribute tells the browser which interpreter to use when running the code. For Visual Basic Scripting Edition, set LANGUAGE to "VBScript"; for JavaScript, set LANGUAGE to "JavaScript". You need to specify the language because some browsers, such as Internet Explorer, can use more than one scripting language.

Note In Internet Explorer, if you don't set the LANGUAGE attribute, the browser assumes that you are running JavaScript. If your code is VBScript, you will receive syntax errors.

When writing scripting code, you should place all of your code for each procedure within the same <SCRIPT> tag. You can have several procedures in the same <SCRIPT> tag, but you can't split the code for one procedure between two <SCRIPT> tags.

Although your HTML page can contain more than one <SCRIPT> tag, maintaining the code is easier when it is contained in the same place. You can place the <SCRIPT> tag in either the BODY or the HEAD sections of the HTML page.

Using Visual Basic Scripting Edition

The following example code is written in VBScript, and runs when the user clicks the corresponding button named btnHello in the Web page:

```
<SCRIPT LANGUAGE="VBScript">
<!--
Sub btnHello_OnClick()
    MsgBox "Hello, world!"
End Sub
-->
</SCRIPT>
<INPUT TYPE=BUTTON NAME=btnHello VALUE="Click Me">
```

> **Note** Browsers that don't understand the <SCRIPT> tag display the code in the HTML page as though it were regular text. Placing script code between comment tags (<!-- and -->) prevents browsers that don't understand the <SCRIPT> tag from displaying the code in the HTML page.

Using JavaScript

The following example code is written in JavaScript, and creates a function procedure that prompts the user to enter his or her ID. The HTML tag for the cmdTest button specifies the procedure to run when a user clicks the button.

```
<SCRIPT Language=JavaScript>
var id
function getid () {
    id = prompt ("Enter your id number");
}
</SCRIPT>
<INPUT TYPE=button NAME=cmdTest OnClick="getid();">
```

Running Script

The location of a script within the <SCRIPT> section of a Web page determines when the script runs. In general, you can add script in the following areas:

- Inline

  If you add script outside a procedure, the script is run when the browser encounters it as the page downloads. This is useful if you want to initialize data or objects on the page.

- Procedures

  If you add script in a procedure, the script runs when the procedure is explicitly invoked.

- Event procedure

  If you add script in an event procedure, the script runs when the event occurs. For example, if you create an onclick event procedure for a button, the script is run when the user clicks the button.

Implementing the VBScript Language

In this practice, you will write VBScript code to calculate the total cost of items selected in the Product table. You will add functionality to the Product List Web page, Products.htm. Use the page provided in the Practice\AppendB directory located on your hard drive or on the companion CD.

You can place script code anywhere on a Web page, but to simplify code maintenance, place all of your code within the same <SCRIPT> section. You can insert the <SCRIPT> tag in either the <BODY> or <HEAD> sections of the

HTML page. Browsers that do not support scripting code will display the code as text in a Web page. To prevent browsers from displaying code, add comment tags (<!-- and -->) around the script code.

Note Netscape Navigator does not natively support VBScript, but you can acquire a plug-in from Netscape at http://www.ncompasslabs.com/Plug-Ins/default.htm.

➤ **To add SCRIPT tags to the products Web page**

1. Start Visual InterDev.

2. If the New Project dialog appears, click Cancel. If it doesn't appear, proceed to step 3.

3. From the File menu, click Open File.

   The Open File dialog appears.

4. In the Open File dialog, click the Existing tab, browse to the Practice\Ch03 folder, and select the Products.htm file.

5. Click Open to edit the Products.htm file.

   The Products.htm file is opened in Design view.

6. Click the Source tab on the HTML Editor window, and enter the following script below the End Sub statement for the Window_onLoad event procedure:

```
Function TotalIt()
    Dim price
    On Error Resume Next
    price = txtQ1.Text * 2.99
    price = price + txtQ2.Text * 75.59
    price = price + txtQ3.Text * 1.75
    price = price + txtQ4.Text * 7.99
    price = price + txtQ5.Text * 4.99
    TotalIt = price
End Function
```

7. Save your changes.

8. From the toolbar, click Preview In Browser.

9. Enter sample values into the quantity textboxes and click Calculate.

   The Products.htm page contains spin controls to allow users to select values by clicking on the control rather than enter values manually. The spin controls do not have script yet, so you must enter the values manually.

➤ **To add an event procedure for the spin controls**

1. Switch to the Source view window.

2. Create a spin1_SpinUp and spin1_SpinDown event procedure by typing the following code in the <script> block:

```
Sub spin1_SpinUp()
    txtq1.text = txtq1.text + 1
End Sub

Sub spin1_SpinDown()
    If txtq1.text > 0 Then txtq1.text = txtq1.text - 1
End Sub
```

3. Repeat this step for each spin button on the Web page. Modify the textbox control names accordingly (txtq2, txtq3, txtq4, and so on).

4. Save your Web page.

5. In the Project Explorer window, right-click the Products.htm file, and then choose View In Browser from the context menu.

   You may need to click the Refresh button to reload the page.

6. Enter sample values for the quantity and use the spin buttons to modify the results.

VBScript Language Syntax

The syntax of VBScript is exactly the same as that of Visual Basic for Applications. However, VBScript is designed to be quickly downloaded over the Internet, so many of the language and run-time elements supported by Visual Basic for Applications are not supported by VBScript. Also, some language elements, such as file input/output (I/0), have been removed for security purposes.

Declaring Variables

A variable is a placeholder that you use to store program information that may change while your script is running. For example, you can create a variable named ClickCount to store the number of times a user clicks an object on a Web page.

Dim Statement

In general, you should declare all variables in your script before you use them. To declare a variable, use the Dim statement, as shown in the following example:

```
Dim MyVar
```

You can declare multiple variables by separating each variable name from the next with a comma. For example:

```
Dim Top, Bottom, Left, Right
```

Option Explicit

Although you can use a variable without declaring it, it is generally not a good practice. You might misspell the variable name in one or more places, causing unexpected results when your script runs.

To ensure that you declare all variables, you can include the Option Explicit statement as the first statement inside the first <SCRIPT> tag in your HTML page. When you use Option Explicit, you will receive an error message if you attempt to use a variable without declaring it. When this code runs, an error will occur when the line myCounter = 5 runs because the variable myCounter is not declared.

```
<Script LANGUAGE = VBScript>
    Option Explicit
    myCounter = 5
</SCRIPT>
```

Naming Variables

Variable names follow the standard rules for naming anything in VBScript. A variable name:

- Must begin with an alphabetic character.
- Cannot contain an embedded period.
- Must not exceed 255 characters.
- Must be unique in the scope in which it is declared.

Constants

A constant is a named value that you set once in script and that cannot change. For example, you can create a constant named TAX_RATE that you set initially and don't change.

To create a constant in VBScript, you use the Const statement. You can create string or numeric constants with meaningful names, and then assign literal values to them.

The following example code uses the Const statement to declare two constants and assigns values to them:

```
Const MYSTRING = "This is my string"
Const MYAGE = 37
```

Note To distinguish constants from variables, name constants with all uppercase letters.

Trying to change the value of a constant in code produces a run-time error. For example, the following code will result in an "Illegal Assignment" error when the line MYAGE = 29 runs.

```
Const MYAGE = 37
MYAGE = 29
MsgBox "I am " & MYAGE & " years old."
```

Working With Arrays

VBScript supports arrays of variables. With arrays, you can refer to a series of variables by the same name and use a number (an index) to tell them apart. This helps you create shorter and simpler code in many situations, because you can set up loops that deal efficiently with any number of cases by using the index number.

Arrays have both upper and lower bounds, and the elements of the array are contiguous within those bounds. Because Visual Basic allocates space for each index number, avoid declaring an array that is larger than necessary.

An array can be a fixed size or dynamically allocated. You use the ReDim statement to change the size of an array at run time. Arrays in VBScript are always zero-based. In the following example, the array MyArray has 13 elements:

```
Dim MyArray(12)
MyArray(0) = 10
MyArray(1) = 20
  .
  .
  .
MyArray(12) = 130
```

Using an array on a Web page can be helpful when gathering information from the user. For example, let's say you design a Web page to generate an order. The form on the page prompts the user to enter the quantity for each item. You can use an array to store the quantity entered for each item. Then, using script code, your Web page can calculate the total number of items ordered. While you can create individual variables for each, an array makes managing a series of related variables easier.

Multidimensional Arrays

Arrays aren't limited to a single dimension—they can have as many as 60 dimensions. To declare an array, include the number of rows and columns in parentheses. The following example code declares the array MyTable as a two-dimensional array consisting of 6 rows and 11 columns:

```
Dim MyTable(5, 10)
```

In a two-dimensional array, the first number is always the number of rows; the second number is the number of columns.

Dynamic Arrays

A dynamic array is an array whose size changes while your script runs. To create a dynamic array, use the Dim statement and don't provide any values for the number of rows and columns, as shown in the following example:

```
Dim MyArray()
```

In script, you use the ReDim statement to change the size of the array.

The Preserve keyword retains the contents of the array as the resizing takes place.

In the following example, the first ReDim statement sets the initial size of the dynamic array to 25 elements. The second ReDim statement resizes the array to 30 elements.

```
ReDim MyArray(24)
MyArray(1) = "first element"
.
.
.
ReDim Preserve MyArray(29)
```

Note There is no limit to the number of times you can resize a dynamic array, but if you make an array smaller than it was, you lose the data in the eliminated elements.

Scope

The scope of a variable defines where in your script you can use the variable. You can declare variables with one of two levels of scope:

- Procedure level (local)
- Script level

Procedure Level

If you only need a variable in a single procedure, you can use the Dim statement to declare the variable in the procedure. This variable is unavailable to any script outside the procedure.

Script Level

If you need a variable to be available to several procedures on your Web page, declare the variable outside a procedure. This creates a script-level variable that all the procedures in your Web page recognize.

In the example below, the variable X is available to the procedure MySub and any other procedures on the page. The variable maintains its value so long as the page is active. The variable Y is recognized only within the procedure MySub and loses its value as soon as the procedure ends.

```
' Script-level variable
Dim X

Sub MySub()
    ' Procedure-level variable
    Dim Y
End Sub
```

Controlling Program Flow

VBScript supports most of the Visual Basic for Applications structures for controlling program flow. The following looping statements are available in VBScript.

- Do...Loop

    Loops while or until a condition is *True*.

- While...Wend

    Loops while a condition is *True*.

- For...Next

    Uses a counter to run statements a specified number of times.

The following example code creates an array and fills it with values:

```
Dim x(10)
For i = 0 to 10
    x(i) = i * 10
Next
```

The following conditional branching statements are available in VBScript.

- If...Then...Else

    Runs code based on a whether a statement is *True* or *False*.

- Select...Case

    Runs code based on the value of a variable.

You can use the If...Then...Else statement to evaluate whether a condition is True or False, and depending on the result, specify one or more statements to run.

For example, the If...Then...Else statement in the following code example calculates a bonus percentage based on the value of the Sales variable. Note the use of the ElseIf statement to specify an action for an additional condition.

```
If Sales > 100000 Then
    Bonus = .10
ElseIf Sales > 50000 Then
    Bonus = .05
Else
    Bonus = .02
End If
```

Select...Case statements are useful when the variable being checked can contain more than two different values. Although your code can use embedded If...Then statements, the Select...Case statement is typically easier to read and maintain. The following sample code demonstrates the Select...Case statement:

```
Select Case Sales
    Case 100000
        Bonus = .10
    Case 50000, 75000
        Bonus = .05
    Case Else
        Bonus = .02
End Select
```

Note Select...Case statements do not support ranges of values or use of the greater-than (>) or less-than (<) signs.

Creating Procedures

In VBScript, there are two kinds of procedures:

- Sub procedures
- Function procedures

You can create your own procedures, which can then be called repeatedly from your Web page without having to copy the code for each instance. For example, you can create a procedure named HelloWorld that runs when a user clicks any one of three push buttons. Instead of having the code copied for each button, you can create one procedure and have each button call that one instance of the code. Procedures must be placed within the <SCRIPT> tag.

Sub Procedures

A Sub procedure is a series of VBScript statements enclosed by the Sub and End Sub statements. It performs actions, but does not return a value. A Sub procedure can take arguments (constants, variables, or expressions that are passed by a calling procedure). The following example code creates a script-level variable, Sales, and a Sub procedure named IncreaseSales:

```
Dim Sales
Sub IncreaseSales(NumSales, CurrentSales)
    Sales = CurrentSales + NumSales
End Sub
```

To call a Sub procedure from another procedure, type the name of the procedure along with values for any required arguments, each separated by a comma as shown in this code sample:

```
IncreaseSales 5, 1000
```

VBScript also provides a number of inherent Sub procedures that are associated with objects on a Web page. For example, a push button on a form has an inherent event named onclick. The onclick event is a Sub procedure that, by default, has no script. You can add VBScript to the onclick event of a button, and that script will run when the user clicks the button. In addition, event procedures can call other existing procedures to make managing script easier.

The following example code could be placed in the onclick event of a button on a Web page. The code calls a Sub procedure named IncreaseSales (created in the previous example) and passes a single argument.

```
Sub ButtonOne_onclick
    Dim NumSales
    NumSales = Inputbox("Enter the number of sales this person made:")
    ' Call an existing procedure outside of the onclick event
    IncreaseSales NumSales
End Sub
```

Function Procedures

A Function procedure is a series of VBScript statements enclosed by the Function and End Function statements. A Function procedure is similar to a Sub procedure, but a Function procedure can return a value. A Function procedure returns a value by assigning a value to its name in the procedure. The return type of a Function procedure is always a Variant data type.

The following example code declares the Function procedure Validate. This procedure accepts a value, determines whether the value is a valid date, and returns True or False.

```
Function Validate(MyDate)
    If IsDate(MyDate) Then
        Validate = True
    Else
        Validate = False
    End If
End Function
```

This following example code invokes the Function procedure from the previous example, by first saving the return value in a new variable and then outputting the return value with the MsgBox function:

```
Result = Validate(Mydate)
Msgbox Validate(MyDate)
```

Data Types

A data type refers to the kind of information that can be stored in a variable. The only data type that VBScript supports is Variant. The Variant data type can contain different kinds of information, depending on how you use it. Because Variant is the only data type in VBScript, it's the data type that functions in VBScript return.

Variant Data Type

At its simplest, a Variant can contain either numeric or string information. A Variant behaves as:

- A number when you use it in a numeric context.

  If you're working with data that looks like numbers, VBScript assumes that it is numbers and performs the operation that is most appropriate for numbers.

- A string when you use it in a string context.

  If you're working with data that can only be string data, VBScript treats it as string data.

  To make a number behave like a string, enclose it in quotation marks (""). In this example the string "5" is first assigned to the variable MyString, then the number 5 is assigned to the same variable.

```
Dim MyString, MyInteger
Rem MyString is a string type that contains the character 5.
MyString = "5"

Rem MyInteger is an integer type that contains the numeric value 5.
MyInteger = 5
```

Subtypes

Beyond the simple numeric or string classifications, a Variant can make further distinctions about the specific nature of numeric information. For example, you can have numeric information that represents a date or a time. When used with other date or time data, the result is always expressed as a date or a time. You can also have a rich variety of numeric information ranging in size from Boolean values to very large, floating-point numbers. These different categories of information that can be contained in a Variant are called subtypes. Most of the time, you can just put the kind of data you want in a Variant, and the Variant behaves in a way that is most appropriate for the data it contains.

You can use conversion functions to convert data from one subtype to another. In addition, the VarType function returns information about how your data is stored within a Variant. The following example code shows a user-defined subroutine that populates a variable named MyVar and displays its subtype:

```
Sub GetDataType()
    Dim MyVar
    MyVar = 32768
    Msgbox "MyVar is currently subtype:" & VarType(MyVar)
End Sub
```

You can also check for a specific data type by using the Is functions, which return *True* or *False*, depending on whether the argument passed to the Is function is of the appropriate type. The available Is functions are:

- IsArray
- IsDate
- IsEmpty
- IsNull
- IsNumeric
- IsObject

For example, the following code prompts the user for a date and uses the IsDate function to verify the data:

```
Dim MyDate
MyDate = Inputbox("Enter a date")
If Not IsDate(MyDate) then
    Msgbox "Not a date."
Else
    Msgbox "Thank you."
End If
```

Writing Script

Through VBScript, you can gain access to objects on a Web page, such as HTML controls, ActiveX controls, Java applets, and other HTML elements. You can change the properties and call the methods of these objects.

Identifying Objects

To control an object by using VBScript, you must:

- Create the object.
- Assign an identifier to the object.

  You use this identifier to:

  - Create event procedures
  - Gain access to the properties and methods of the object.

The way that a name is assigned to an object varies slightly, depending on the type of object.

Form Fields

Every form field has a NAME parameter that assigns a name to the control. The following example code assigns the name "btnValidate" to a button control:

```
<INPUT TYPE=BUTTON NAME="btnValidate" VALUE="Validate Order">
```

Referencing Objects from VBScript

The object model for Internet Explorer determines the syntax requirements for referencing objects and controls within and outside forms in a Web page. If you place a form field in a <FORM> tag, you must put the form name in front of the form field's object name, as in the following example:

```
<FORM NAME=Form1>
<INPUT TYPE=text NAME=txtName>
</FORM>

<SCRIPT LANGUAGE = VBScript>
    Document.Form1.txtName.Value = "Susan"
</SCRIPT>
```

If the HTML control or object is placed outside a <FORM> tag, you reference it directly.

```
<INPUT TYPE=text NAME=txtAge>

<SCRIPT LANGUAGE = VBScript>
    txtAge.Value = "32"
</SCRIPT>
```

Identifying HTML Objects

With Internet Explorer, you are not limited to writing script to control ActiveX controls and Java applets. Internet Explorer supports DHTML, which gives Web authors the ability to write script to change any HTML element, such as a paragraph, font, or hyperlink. You first create an identifier for the HTML element and then you write script to change the element's properties, call methods, and create event procedures.

DHTML gives authors the power to create visually outstanding HTML documents that dynamically change their content and interact with the user—all without relying on server-side programs or complicated sets of HTML pages to achieve special effects:

The following example code assigns the identifier "P1" to a paragraph of text:

```
<P ID="P1">
This is some text.
</P>
```

Initializing a Page

You can write script code that runs each time an HTML page is loaded into the browser. This code is known as initialization code, because you can use it to initialize the variables in your script. You can also use initialization code to set the properties of the controls and other objects on the page. In this way, you can initialize the page dynamically, based on the properties of the environment. You can create initialization code by:

- Writing inline code, embedded in the <SCRIPT> tag pair.
- Using the Window object.

Inline Code

Code in a <SCRIPT> tag that is not contained in a procedure automatically runs when the page loads. For example, the script in the following example displays a message box when the page loads:

```
<SCRIPT LANGUAGE=VBScript>
    Dim X
    X = False
    MsgBox "Hello World!"
</SCRIPT>
```

Note When you write inline code, the position of the code determines when it will run. When the page loads, it is read from the top of the page to the bottom. This is particularly important to remember when writing code that initializes object properties. You must place the initializing code after the tag that defines the object, or the references to the object in the initializing code will not be recognized.

Using the Window Object

The Internet Explorer object model provides a Window object that you can use to initialize a Web page. The onload event of the Window object runs automatically when the HTML page loads. To write script that runs when the page downloads, you can create a Sub procedure for the onload event of the Window object, as shown in the following example:

```
Sub Window_onload()
    MsgBox "Hello World!"
End Sub
```

You can also set the Window onload event procedure in the <BODY> tag. For example:

```
<BODY onload="RunMeFirst">
```

Note Initialization code that you write with inline code always runs before code that is associated with the onload event.

Adding Event Procedures

After you create the objects in your HTML document, you can create event procedures for them. Each object type has a set of events that it recognizes. For example, a command button has an onclick event and a text box has an onchange event.

When creating the event procedure, name the Sub procedure with the convention ObjectName_Event. This is the same method used to define event procedures in Visual Basic. For example, the following procedure runs when the Button1 control is clicked:

```
<INPUT TYPE=BUTTON NAME=Button1>
<SCRIPT LANGUAGE=VBSCRIPT>
Sub Button1_onclick
    Msgbox "Hello World!"
End Sub
</SCRIPT>
```

You can attach script code to an object by specifying the object and the event with attributes in the <SCRIPT> tag. For example, clicking Button1 runs the code contained in the following <SCRIPT> tag:

```
<SCRIPT LANGUAGE=VBScript FOR=Button1 EVENT=onclick>
    Msgbox "Hello World!"
</SCRIPT>
```

If you use this technique, you must create a separate <SCRIPT> section for each event procedure you define, because you can only put executable code between <SCRIPT> tags that are attached to an object. If you put a Sub procedure or Function procedure in the tags, you will get a syntax error.

To assign an event procedure to an object when the object is created, specify in the HTML tag the name of the event procedure to be called. In the following example, the ProcessOrder procedure is called when the RadioGroup control is clicked:

```
<SCRIPT LANGUAGE=VBSCRIPT>
Sub ProcessOrder
    Msgbox "i'll run this code."
End Sub
</SCRIPT>

<INPUT TYPE=RADIO NAME=RadioGroup onclick="ProcessOrder">
```

Using Objects in Visual InterDev

Visual InterDev provides the scripting object model to make Web application development faster and easier. The scripting object model also simplifies Web application development by introducing a familiar object-oriented programming model to HTML and script programming. This model reduces the complexity and quantity of scripting required when creating applications that interact between clients (browsers) and servers.

In addition, the scripting object model defines a set of objects with properties, methods, and events that you can use to create and script your application. You can create the visual interface for your application using design-time controls, and then write script to control the application using familiar object-oriented techniques.

Working with Attributes

The ID attributed in HTML gives a unique name to an element for use when referencing it in code or script. The ID attribute appears inside an opening tag for an element on the page as shown in the following example:

```
<H1 ID="myH1">
```

To use objects on an HTML page, you must first create the object, and then identify it by setting its ID or NAME attributes. You can set an ID attribute for any object, but the NAME attribute applies only to standard HTML controls and Java applets. You use the ID or NAME attribute to create event procedures and to access an object's properties and methods. The syntax for assigning names varies slightly for different types of objects.

The following table lists the standard objects that you can use on a Web page and describes how you identify each in code.

Object Type	ID	Name	Example
ActiveX controls	Y		<OBJECT classid="clsid:99B42120-6EC7-11CF-A6C7-00AA00A47DD2" id=lblOccupation>
Java applets	Y	Y	<APPLET CODE=Outline.class NAME=outline HEIGHT=150 WIDTH=200> </APPLET
Standard HTML objects	Y		<H1 ID="myH1">
Standard HTML controls	Y	Y	<INPUT TYPE="BUTTON" NAME="btnMyButton">

Using Properties and Methods of Objects

When you write script to work with objects, you can set or retrieve property values and invoke methods of an object. In your script, you can reference a script object using the name that you assigned it when you created the design-time control. You read and write most properties using normal Visual Basic syntax. To access the value of an object property of, you use the following syntax:

```
Object.Property = Value
```

To retrieve the values of properties, you use this syntax:

```
Value = Object.Property
```

You call methods for script objects much like you reference a property. For example, you can drag a Listbox control onto the Web page and then populate it by calling its addItem method, as in the following script:

```
<SCRIPT LANGUAGE="VBSCRIPT">
Function LoadNames()
    ListBox1.additem "Jack"
    ListBox1.additem "Nancy"
    ListBox1.additem "Lynn"
End Function
</SCRIPT>
```

In VBScript, you can also use the Call keyword when invoking a method or procedure. However, if you use the Call keyword to call a procedure that requires arguments, the argument list must be enclosed in parentheses. If you omit the Call keyword, you must omit the parentheses around the argument list.

Using the Script Outline for Client Script

Visual InterDev includes a feature to make it easier for you to access and program the various objects that have been included on a Web page. The Script Outline displays the objects that are available in your document and the scripts on the page when you are working in Source view. In Script Outline, you can:

- Display a tree view of all elements on your page that have their ID or NAME attributes set.
- Display events for each element.
- Navigate quickly to any script in the page.
- Quickly create new handlers for events on the page.

In its initial state, the tree view of Script Outline displays the nodes described in the following table:

Node	Description
Client objects and events	The elements that support client script or have client script attached to them with a list of events for the element
Client scripts	The client script for the page with each function or subroutine defined within the script block
Server objects and events	The elements that support server script or have server script attached to them with a list of events for the element
Server scripts	The server script for the page with each function or subroutine defined within the script block

Script Outline generates either VBScript or JavaScript, depending on the default scripting language settings you have made.

➤ **To set the default language for a project**

1. Right-click the project file in the Project Explorer window and choose Properties from the context menu.

2. Click the Editor Defaults tab.

3. Select the default language from the Client drop-down list box in the Default Script Language group.

When you added script to the Products.htm file, you used VBScript. Instead of entering the spinup and spindown event procedures in a script block, you could use the Script Outline window to create the event procedures for you. The spinup event for the spin1 control is highlighted in Figure B.1.

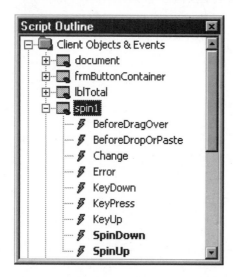

Figure B.1 Viewing controls in the Script Outline window

If you do not see Script Outline when open a window, you can open it manually.

➤ **To open the Script Outline window for a page**

1. From the View menu, click Other Windows.

2. Choose Script Outline from the submenu.

When you add HTML, design-time, or ActiveX controls to a page in your project, the HTML Editor adds the ID for the object and all the events associated with the object to Script Outline.

➤ **To add a Textbox control and an event procedure to a project**

1. Click the HTML tab in the Toolbox.

2. Drag the Textbox control to an appropriate location on the page. The HTML Editor will add the ID for the control to Script Outline under Client Objects And Events.

3. Open the text1 node to display the events associated with the control.

4. Double-click the event procedure that you want to implement. The HTML Editor adds a template for the event procedure to the top of the page. It also adds an item for the script under the Client Scripts node.

Debugging Client Script

Script debugging is integrated into Visual InterDev and Internet Explorer. This debugging functionality allows Web developers to browse, debug, and edit .htm and .asp files. The debugger works with JScript, VBScript, and other scripting languages. All scripting languages can reference the Internet Explorer scripting object model to interact with Web documents, the browser, and the current window. If you are writing client script in an .htm page, debugging is enabled automatically. (Enabling debugging in ASP is covered in Chapter 4.) The following table describes four different techniques for script debugging:

Situation	Technique
In response to an error on a page	If the browser or server encounters a syntax or run-time error in a script, it displays a message that offers you the opportunity to start the debugger at the line where the error occurred.
From Internet Explorer	Choose Script Debugger from the View menu in Internet Explorer, and then select Open Or Break At Next Statement. Script Debugger starts, and then opens the current HTML source file. This starts the Visual InterDev debugger.
From Visual InterDev	From the Debug menu, click Start.
In a script	When writing a script, include a Stop statement (VBScript) or a Debugger statement (JScript) in a script. When script execution reaches that line, the Visual InterDev debugger will start and enter Break mode at that line.

Some of the features of the Visual InterDev debugger include:

- Breakpoints

    You can set breakpoints anywhere in your code. In Break mode, illustrated in Figure B.2, you can single-step through the code. An Immediate window will display the value of variables.

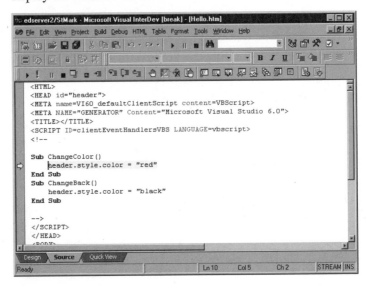

Figure B.2 Debugger in Break mode

- Call Stack

    A Call Stack window displays which procedures have been invoked.

- Syntax coloring

    The HTML and script syntax is displayed with different colors to help you read and debug your script.

Note The debugger opens a copy of a Web page in a temporary Internet cache. Any edits you make while running the debugger will apply only to the cached Web page. To correct an error permanently, you must edit the source file on the Web server.

Handling Run-Time Errors in Client Script

To create a robust Web application, you should anticipate possible script errors and include error-handling code in your Web pages. The error-handling code should resolve the error or return an appropriate message to the user.

On Error Statement

The On Error statement enables an error-handling routine and specifies the location of the routine within a procedure.

The On Error statement syntax can have any of the forms described in the following table:

Statement	Description
On Error Resume Next	Specifies that when a run-time error occurs, control will go to the statement immediately following the statement where the error occurred, and execution will continue. Use this form rather than On Error GoTo when accessing objects.
On Error GoTo 0	Disables any enabled error handler in the current procedure.
On Error GoTo *line*	Enables the error-handling routine that starts at the line specified in the required line argument. The specified line must be in the same procedure as the On Error statement; otherwise, a compile-time error occurs.

Note VBScript does not support the On Error GoTo <*label*> statement, and you cannot write an error handler that is called automatically when an error occurs. Therefore, you must implement inline error handling to check for an error after each statement that can cause an error.

Handling Errors with the Err Object

When an error does occur, Internet Explorer stores the error information in the Err object. The Err object will contain the error information until another error occurs. If a statement runs successfully, the Err object will not be cleared. Therefore, after an error occurs, you should clear the error by invoking the Clear method of the Err object.

You can detect run-time errors by checking the Number property of the Err object after each statement that might cause an error. If Number is zero, an error has not occurred. If it is not zero, an error has occurred. You can also retrieve information about the error by checking the Description property of the Err object.

The following sample code shows how to handle errors in VBScript:

```
' Error Handling Code Sample
Sub cmdSubmit_OnClick
    On Error Resume Next
    ' Statement that might cause an error
    If Err <> 0 Then
        Msgbox "An error occurred. " & Err.Description
        Err.Clear
    End If
    ' Statement that might cause an error
    If Err <> 0 Then
        Msgbox "An error occurred. " & Err.Description
        Err.Clear
    End if
End Sub
```

To test your own error-handling code, you can purposely cause an error by using the Raise method of the Err object.

For example:

```
Err.Raise 65000
```

VBScript does not use all available numbers for its errors. If you want to generate your own errors, begin a numbering scheme with 65535 and work your way down.

It is also common to use this technique when your application needs to raise its own internal errors.

Glossary

A

Activate   Also Activation. A programming process that loads an object into memory, putting the object into an executable or running state. Also, the process of binding an object so as to put the object into its running state.

Active Client   The Active Client is the client-side element of the Active Platform that enables cross-platform content and applications. It includes support for HTML, scripting (VBScript and JScript), Java applets, ActiveX Components, ActiveX Controls, and Active Documents.

Active Document   A Windows-based, non-HTML application embedded in a browser, providing a way for the functionality of these applications to be accessible from within the browser interface.

Active Group, The   A standards organization, under the auspices of The Open Group, an open, customer-driven steering committee responsible for the ongoing development and management of ActiveX technologies and licensing.

Active Platform   An integrated, comprehensive set of client, Active-Client, and server Active-Server component-based development technologies that make it easy for developers to integrate the connectivity of the Internet with the power of the personal computer.

Active Server   The Active Server is the server-side element of the Active Platform, specifically,

a collection of server-side technologies that are delivered with Windows NT, and provide a consistent server-side component and scripting model and an integrated set of system services for component application management, database access, transactions, and messaging.

Active Server Page   The server-side execution environment in Microsoft Internet Information Server 4.0 that executes ActiveX Scripts and ActiveX Components on a server.

ActiveX   A set of language-independent interoperability technologies that enable software components written in different languages to work together in networked environments. The core technology elements of ActiveX are COM and DCOM.

ActiveX Automation   A language-neutral way to manipulate an ActiveX Component's methods from outside an application. ActiveX Automation is typically used to create components that expose methods to programming tools and macro languages.

ActiveX Component   A compiled software component based on the COM that encapsulates a set of business functionality. The functionality in an ActiveX component is accessed through ActiveX Automation interfaces. The ActiveX Component can execute either on a client computer or on a server computer, transparent to the calling application, through DCOM.

ActiveX Controls   Small, reusable objects created using COM technology. Because ActiveX controls are intended to be used as visual programming components, they have additional requirements over standard COM components, such as self-registration, property sheet display, event generation, and so on. ActiveX controls are implemented as in-process dynamically linked libraries (DLLs), usually having an .ocx extension. They can be used in ActiveX control containers, such as Visual Basic or Visual C++ programs, or used within a Web page in Microsoft Internet Explorer.

ActiveX Scripting   The act of using a scripting language to drive ActiveX Components.

ActiveX Server Component   An ActiveX Component designed to run on the server-side of a client/server application. See ActiveX Component.

ADO   ActiveX Data Objects. A set of object-based data access interfaces optimized for Internet-based, data-centric applications.

Aggregation   A programming composition technique for implementing component objects. Using this technique, developers can build a new object using one or more existing objects that support some or all of the new object's required interfaces.

Anonymous FTP   Anonymous File Transfer Protocol. Used in the process of connecting to a remote computer as an anonymous or guest user in order to transfer public files to your local computer.

ANSI   American National Standards Institute. ANSI serves as a quasi-national standards organization. It provides area charters for groups that establish standards in specific fields, such as the Institute of Electrical and Electronics Engineers (IEEE). Also, commonly used to refer to a low-level table of codes used by a computer.

Apartment Model Multi-Threading   The COM supports a form of multi-threading in Windows 95 and Windows NT called the apartment model. Apartment is essentially a way of describing a thread with a message queue that supports COM objects.

Apartment Threaded   A model in which each object "lives in an apartment" (thread) for the life of the object. All calls to that object execute on the apartment thread.

API   Application Programming Interface. A set of routines that an application program uses to request and carry out lower-level services performed by a computer's operating system.

Applet   An HTML-based program built with Java that a browser temporarily downloads to a user's hard disk, from which location it runs when the Web page is open.

Asynchronous Call   A function that enables processing to continue without waiting for the function to return a value.

ATM   Asynchronous Transfer Mode. A communications protocol defined for high-speed data communications.

Automation   *See* ActiveX Automation.

B

Bandwidth   The capacity of the transmission medium stated in bits per second (bps) or as a frequency (Hz). Generally, a higher bandwidth number indicates faster data-transfer capability.

Bind   Also Binding. To put an object into its running state, allowing the operations it supports to be invoked. Objects can be bound at run time, called late binding or dynamic binding, or at compile time, called static binding.

Browser   A program that interprets hypertext markup language (HTML) and displays information on a computer screen.

Bytecode   The executable form of Java code that executes within the Java Virtual Machine. Also called interpreted code, pseudocode, or p-code.

C

Cache   Usually a temporary local store for information, a special memory subsystem where frequently used data values are copied and stored for quick access.

Call   To transfer program execution to some other section of code, usually a subroutine, while saving the necessary information to allow execution to resume at the calling point when the called section has completed execution.

CASE   Computer Aided Software Engineering. Software that aids in application development including analysis, design, and code generation. CASE tools provide automated methods for designing and documenting traditional-structure programming techniques.

Certificate Authority   Certificate Authorities are companies that distribute certificates to software developers. To guarantee a control's authenticity, a Certificate Authority, such as the Verisign Corporation, develops a digital certificate for each developer who uses Authenticode technologies from Microsoft.

CGI   Common Gateway Interface. A server-side interface for initiating software services. A set of interfaces that describes how a Web server

communicates with software on the same computer.

Class   A generalized category in object-oriented programming that describes a group of more specific items called objects. A class provides a template for defining the behavior of a particular type of object.

Class Factory   An object that implements the IClassFactory interface, which allows it to create objects of a specific class.

Class Identifier   Also CLASSID or CLSID. A unique identification tag (UUID) associated with a class object. A class object that is intended to create more than one object registers its CLSID in a task table in the system registration database to enable clients to locate and load the executable code associated with the object(s).

Class Library   A collection of one or more classes that programmers use to implement functionality.

Class Object   A member object within a class.

Client   A program that facilitates a connection to server computers and manages and presents information retrieved from those sources. In a client/server environment, the workstation is usually the client computer. In referring to COM objects, an object that requests services from another object.

Client/Server   A model of computing whereby client applications running on a desktop or personal computer access information on remote servers or host computers.

COM   Component Object Model. The object-oriented programming model that defines how objects interact within a single application or between applications.

COM Component   A compiled software component based on the COM that encapsulates a set of business functionality. The functionality in a COM component is accessed through Automation interfaces. The COM component can execute either on a client computer or on a server computer, transparent to the calling application.

Communications Protocol   A set of rules or standards designed to enable computers to connect with one another and to exchange information with as few errors as possible.

Component   *See* ActiveX Component.

Compound Document   A document that contains data in different formats created by different applications.

Container Application   A container application provides storage for the embedded object, a site for display, access to the display site, and an advisory sink for receiving notification of changes in the object.

Context Object   An object that tracks properties of an MTS server component as it runs within an activity, including its activation state, security information, transaction state (if any), and so on. This frees the component from tracking its own state.

Control   In a graphical user interface, an object on the screen that can be manipulated by a user to perform an action.

Cookies   A means by which, under the HTTP protocol, a server or a script can maintain state or status information on the client workstation.

CORBA   Common Object Request Broker Architecture. An Object Management Group specification for the interface definition between OMG-compliant objects.

Cursor Engine   A mechanism for managing data retrieved from a database, or a full transaction manager that optimizes the retrieval and update of server-based data.

D

DAO   Data Access Objects. DAO includes the full functionality of the Microsoft Jet database engine for local data management.

Data Dictionary   A repository of information about data, such as its meaning, relationships to other data, origin, usage, and format.

DataSpace   An object that creates instances of business objects that reside on a Web server.

DCE   Distributed Computing Environment. An open set of services controlled by the OSF and designed to support performing distributed computing across heterogeneous platforms.

DCOM   Distributed Component Object Model. Additions to the Component Object Model (COM) that facilitate the transparent distribution of objects over networks and over the Internet.

Deadlocks   A situation in which two or more threads of execution are permanently blocked (waiting), with each thread waiting for a resource exclusively held by one of the other threads that are blocked. For example, if thread A locks record 1 and waits to lock record 2, while thread B has locked record 2 and waits to lock record 1, the two threads are deadlocked.

Debugger   A development environment that supports step-by-step execution of application code and viewing the content of code variables.

Default Catalog   A catalog is the directory in which Index Server data is stored. A catalog represents the highest level of organization, and contains information about one or more virtual directories. Catalogs along with other persistent data are stored in a special catalog directory, which by default is named Catalog.wci.

Design-time ActiveX Controls   Visual authoring components that help a developer construct dynamic Web applications by automatically generating standard HTML and/or scripting code. They are analogous to wizards.

Distributed Processing   The physical or logical distribution of software components, processing, data, and management of application software.

DNS   Domain Name Service. A protocol that provides an Internet-wide database of host and domain names. For example, DNS is used to find the IP address of a host name written as microsoft.com.

Domain Name   An entry in an Internet address, such as microsoft.com in the fictitious U.S. address www.example.microsoft.com/.

E

E-commerce   Electronic Commerce. The process of buying and selling over the Web often based on software products such as the Microsoft Merchant Server.

Event   Any action, often generated by a user or an ActiveX Control, to which a program might respond.

Event Handlers   Functions that trap and process events such as keys being pressed, mouse buttons being clicked, menus being opened, and so on.

F

Failfast   A policy of Microsoft Transaction Server (MTS) that facilitates fault containment. When MTS encounters an unexpected failure, it immediately terminates the process and logs a message to the Windows NT event log for details about the failure. MTS will also rollback any transactions affected by the failure.

FAQ   Frequently Asked Questions. Usually a document containing questions and answers that address the basics.

Firewall   A security mechanism such as the Microsoft Proxy Server that provides Internet access from desktops inside an organization, while at the same time preventing access to the corporate LAN by outside Internet users.

FTP   File Transfer Protocol. The Internet standard high-speed protocol for downloading or transferring files from one computer to another.

Function   A general term used for a subroutine. In some programming languages, a subroutine or statement that returns values.

G

GIF   Graphics Interchange Format. A computer graphics file format developed in the mid-1980s by CompuServe for use in photo-quality graphic image display on computer screens.

Gopher   An early Internet protocol and software program designed to search for, retrieve, and display documents from remote computers or sites.

GUI   Graphical User Interface. A user interface that displays graphics and characters and provides an event model for users to control the operating environment.

GUID   Globally Unique Identifier. Identifiers (IDs) assigned to COM objects that are generated through a sophisticated algorithm. The algorithm guarantees that all COM objects are assigned unique IDs, avoiding any possibility of a naming conflict.

H

Home Page   The page that serves as the starting point of a World Wide Web site, sometimes named default.html or index.html.

Host   Any computer that provides services to remote computers or users.

HTML   Hypertext Markup Language. A tag-based notation language used to format documents that can then be interpreted and rendered by an Internet browser.

HTTP   Hypertext Transfer Protocol. A basic communication protocol for Internet or Web server file input and output (I/O).

Hyperlink   A connection to a document or other file on the Internet that generally appears as a highlighted word or image on the screen.

Hypertext   A hypertext document is a document that is structured in chunks of text, marked up (usually using HTML), and connected by links. Hence, the text in the document can properly be named hypertext because of its marked-up and navigable condition.

I

IDC   Internet Database Connector. Provides database connectivity between IIS applications and any ODBC-compliant database.

IEEE   Institute of Electrical and Electronic Engineers.

IETF   Internet Engineering Task Force. A protocol engineering and development organization focused on the Internet.

IIS   Microsoft Internet Information Server.

IMAP   Also IMAP4. A server standard that enables you to maintain e-mail on a server for easy access from different locations and desktops. IMAP4 also allows you to work with your messages on the server, including managing multiple folders on the server.

Impersonate   Also impersonation. The process of allowing a thread to execute in a security context different from that of the process that owns the thread.

In-process   Also in-process component. A COM component that shares the same memory as the container application.

Inheritance   A programming technique that duplicates the characteristics down a hierarchy from one class to another.

Instance   An object for which memory is allocated or persistent.

Instantiate   To create an instance of an object. The process of creating or activating an object based on its class.

Interface   A group of related functions that provide access to COM objects.

Internet   Abbreviation for Internetwork. A set of dissimilar computer networks joined together by means of gateways that handle data transfer and the conversion of messages from the sending network to the protocols used by the receiving networks.

Intranet   Use of Internet standards, technologies, and products within an enterprise to function as a collaborative processing infrastructure. The term intranet is generally used to describe the application of Internet technologies on internal corporate networks.

IP   Internet Protocol. The packet-switching protocol for network communications between Internet host computers.

ISAM   Indexed Sequential Access Method. An indexing mechanism for efficient access to rows of data in a file.

ISAPI   Internet Server Application Program Interface. An application program interface that resides on a server computer for initiating software services tuned for Microsoft Windows NT operating system.

ISDN   Integrated Services Digital Network. An emerging technology that is beginning to be offered by most telephone service providers as a faster alternative to traditional modems.

ISO   International Standards Organization. An organization involved in setting standards worldwide for all fields except electro-technical, which is the responsibility of IEC.

ISP   Internet Service Provider. An organization that provides access to the Internet.

ISV   Independent Software Vendor.

ITU   International Telecommunication Union.

J

Java   A derivative of the C++ language, Java is the Sun Microsystems Corporation distributed programming language, offered as an open standard.

Java Beans   An object model being developed by Sun Microsystems Corporation that is targeted to inter-operate with a variety of other object models, including COM and CORBA.

JavaScript   A scripting language that evolved from Netscape's LiveScript language and was made more compatible with Java. It uses an HTML page as its interface.

JDBC   Java Database Connectivity. Data access interfaces based on ODBC for use with the Java language.

Jet   A Microsoft desktop database engine available in most of Microsoft's development tools and office products, including Microsoft Access, Microsoft Office, and Microsoft Visual Basic.

JPEG   Joint Photographic Experts Group. A widely accepted international standard for compression of color image files, sometimes used on the Internet.

Jscript   The Microsoft open implementation of JavaScript. JScript is fully compatible with JavaScript in Netscape Navigator2.0 and later.

Just-in-Time (JIT) Object Activation   The ability for a Microsoft Transaction Server object to be activated only as needed for executing requests from its client. Objects can be deactivated even while clients hold references to them, allowing otherwise idle server resources to be used more productively.

K

Kerberos   The basis of most of the distributed computing environment (DCE) security services. Kerberos provides the secure use of distributed software components.

L

LAN   Local Area Network. A connection among a set of computers. Computers connected to a LAN can generally share applications or files from a local file server and may be able to connect to other LANs or to the Internet using routers.

Latency   The state of being latent, or to lie hidden; not currently showing signs of existence. Sometimes attributed to the time taken to retrieve pages from the World Wide Web.

LDAP   Lightweight Directory Access Protocol. A standard for updating and searching directories using TCP/IP. LDAP allows you to easily find other Internet users by accessing any LDAP-based directory server, including Internet directories, such as Four11 and Bigfoot, or a company's intranet directory.

Link   See Hyperlink.

M

MAPI   Mail or Messaging Applications Programming Interface. An open and comprehensive messaging interface used by programmers to create messaging and workgroup applications, such as electronic mail, scheduling, calendaring, and document management. In a distributed client/server environment, MAPI provides enterprise messaging services within Windows Open Services Architecture (WOSA).

Marshal   Also Marshaling. The process of packaging and sending interface parameters across process boundaries in computer memory.

Master Index   A persistent on-disk index that contains the indexed data for a large number of documents.

Message Queuing   Server technology developers can use to build large-scale distributed systems with reliable communications between applications that can continue to operate reliably even when networked systems are unavailable.

Method   Member functions of an exposed object that perform some action on an object, such as saving it to disk.

MIME   Multipurpose Internet Mail Extensions. An extension of the Internet mail protocol that enables users to send 8-bit based e-mail messages, which are used to support extended character sets, voice mail, facsimile images, and so on.

Moniker   A name that uniquely identifies a COM object, similar to a directory path name.

MTS   Microsoft Transaction Server. Combines the features of a transaction-processing (TP) monitor and an object-request broker (ORB) in an easy-to-use product.

Multi-Tasking   The ability to simultaneously execute multiple applications within an operating system.

Multi-Threading Running several processes in rapid sequence within a single program, regardless of which logical method of multi-tasking is being used by the operating system.

Multi-T ier Architecture Also known as three-tier, multi-tier is a technique for building applications generally split into user, business, and data services tiers. These applications are built of component services that are based on an object model such as ActiveX.

N

NIST National Institute of Standards and Technology.

NNTP Network News Transfer Protocol. The protocol used to send and receive news messages over the Internet.

Node A computer that is attached to a network; also called a host. Also, a junction of some kind. On a local area network, a device that is connected to the network and is capable of communicating with other network devices.

O

Object A combination of code and data that can be treated as a unit, for example a control, form, or application. Each object is defined by a class. An object is an instance of a class that combines data with procedures.

OCX File extension for an ActiveX control or ActiveX component. Originally used as a file extension for OLE Custom Controls, following the format for a Visual Basic Extension (VBX).

ODBC Open Database Connectivity. A developer can use ODBC to access data in a heterogeneous environment of relational and non-relational databases.

ODBCDirect Technology that makes the full functionality of RDO available from within DAO. Used to bypass the Microsoft Jet database engine for fast, small-memory-footprint access to remote data. *See also* DAO, Jet, and RDO.

OLAP Online Analytical Processing. A multi-dimensional database used for decision support analysis and data warehousing.

OLE Object Linking and Embedding. A set of integration standards to transfer and share information among client applications.

OLE Automation See ActiveX Automation.

OLE Control See ActiveX Control.

OLE DB Data-access interfaces providing consistent access to SQL and non-SQL data sources across the enterprise and the Internet.

OMG Object Management Group. A vendor alliance formed to define and promote CORBA object specifications.

Open Group, The Parent company of a number of standards organizations, including The Active Groupnow managing the core ActiveX technology, X/Open, and OSF.

ORB Object Request Broker. Manages interaction between clients and servers including the distributed computing responsibilities of location referencing as well as coordinating parameters and results.

OSF Open Software Foundation. A vendor alliance that defines specifications, develops software, and makes available an open, portable environment. Now merged with The Open Group.

Out-of-Process   Also out-of-process component. A COM component that runs in its own separate memory space separate from a container application.

P

PKCS   Public Key Certificate Standard. Syntax standards covering a number of security functions, including a standard way of attaching signatures to a block of data, a form for requesting a certificate, and public key encryption algorithms.

Pooling   A performance optimization based on using collections of pre-allocated resources, such as database connections.

POP3   Post Office Protocol version 3. A protocol that permits a workstation to dynamically access a mail drop on a server in a useful fashion. Usually, this means that a POP3 server is used to allow a workstation to retrieve mail that an SMTP server is holding for it. POP3 is specified in RFC 1725.

PPP   Point-to-Point Protocol. The Internet standard for serial communications, PPP defines how data packets are exchanged with other Internet-based systems using a modem connection.

PPTP   Point-to-Point Tunneling Protocol. The Internet can be used for low-cost, secure remote access to a corporate network with virtual private networking support on Windows NT.

Private Communications Technology (PCT) 1.0   Private Communication Technology. Designed to provide secure transactions over the Internet.

ProgID   A string expression that is the programmatic ID of the new object in a component.

Property   A set of characteristics of an object.

Protocol   A mutually determined set of formats and procedures for the exchange of information between computers.

Proxy Server   A proxy server acts as a go-between, converting information from Web servers into HTML to be delivered to a client computer. It also provides a way to deliver network services to computers on a secure subnet without those computers needing to have direct access to the World Wide Web.

R

Race Conditions   A situation where two or more threads of execution are attempting to perform the same action (for example, using the same resource or executing the same code), where the outcome for all the threads is dependent on the (unspecified) order in which they execute.

RAD   Rapid Application Development. An environment that allows developers to quickly and efficiently design, build, debug, and deploy database driven Web applications

RDO   Remote Data Objects. In version 2.0, RDO is a high-level object interface that directly calls ODBC for optimal speed, control, and ease of programming.

Router   An intermediary device on a communications network responsible for deciding by which of several paths message traffic will flow over a network or the Internet.

RPC Remote Procedure Call. A mechanism that extends the notion of a local procedure callmeaning contained in a single memory address space to a distributed computing environment.

RSA A public key cryptography for Internet security. This acronym derives from the last names of the inventors of the technology: Rivest, Shamir, and Adleman.

RTP/RTCP Real-time protocol and real-time control protocol, respectively. A packet format for sending real-time information across the Internet.

S

Scalability The capability to use the same software environment on many classes of computers and hardware configurations.

Script A kind of program that consists of a set of instructions for an application or utility program.

SDK Software Development Kit.

Secure Electronic Transaction (SET) A standard that enables consumers, businesses, and banks and financial institutions to conduct secure, reliable transactions over the Internet. SET encrypts transaction pieces through a strong, exportable 128-bit encryption scheme that creates a three-way trust relationship between seller, buyer, and online bank.

Secure Sockets Layer (SSL) 3.0 Secure Sockets Layer. A standard for providing encrypted and authenticated service over the Internet. Uses RSA public-key encryption for specific TCP/IP ports.

SEPP Secure Electronic Payment Process. A proposed specification that merged with STT, resulting in the SET standard for secure e-commerce transactions.

Server A computer-running administrative software that controls access to all or part of a network and its resources.

Server-side Include A server-side include (SSI) is a directive to include text, graphics, or application information into an HTML page just before sending the HTML page to a user. SSI can be used to include, for example, a time/date stamp, a copyright notice, or a form for a customer to fill out and return.

ServerName A string that identifies the Web server where an instance of the server-side business object is created.

SGML Standard Generalized Markup Language. An original documentation markup standard promulgated by primary defense contractors as a standard for the development and display of documentation. HTML is a subset of SGML.

Signature The return value and parameter data types of a function or method. Also the return values and parameter data types for all methods in an interface.

Single-Threaded A model in which all objects are executed on a single thread.

SMP Symmetric Multiprocessing. A multiprocessor architecture in which all processors are identical, share memory, and execute both user code and operating system code.

SMTP Simple Mail Transfer Protocol. The Internet standard protocol for transferring electronic mail messages from one computer to another.

SQL   Structured Query Language. The international standard language for defining and accessing relational databases.

SQL Access Group (SAG)   A consortium of vendors established in November 1989 to accelerate the Remote Data Access standard and to deliver protocols for interconnectivity among multiple SQL-based software products.

Stored Procedures   Pre-compiled software functions that are managed and that run within a remote database management system (RDBMS).

STT   Secure Transaction Technology. A proposed specification that merged with SEPP, resulting in the SET standard for secure e-commerce transactions.

Synchronous   A function that does not allow further instructions in the processcode to be executed until the function returns a value.

T

TCP/IP   Transmission Control Protocol/Internet Protocol. TCP/IP is a combined set of protocols that perform the transfer of data between two computers.

Telnet   A terminal emulation protocol users can employ to log on to other computers on the Internet. Alternatively, software that can be used to log on to another computer using the telnet protocol.

Three-Tier Architecture   See Multi-tier Architecture.

TP   Transaction Processing. The real-time handling of computerized business transactions as they are received by the system. Also called online transaction processing (OLTP) systems.

Transaction   A group of processing activities that are either entirely completed, or if not completed, that leave the database and processing system in the same state as before the transaction started.

Two-Tier Architecture   *See* Client/Server.

Type Library   A file that contains standard descriptions of data types, modules, and interfaces objects and types that can be used to fully expose objects such as COM components.

U

URL   Uniform Resource Locator. An address that uniquely identifies a World Wide Web site, usually preceded with http:// such as in the fictitious URL http://www.example.microsoft.com/. A URL can contain more detail, such as the name of a page of hypertext, usually identified by the suffix .html or .htm.

V

VBA   Visual Basic, Applications Edition. The development environment and language found in Visual Basic that can be hosted by applications.

VBX   Visual Basic Extension. Custom controls originally designed for 16-bit applications created by Visual Basic.

Virtual Machine   The mechanism the Java language uses to execute Java bytecode on any physical computer. The VM converts the bytecode to the native instruction for the target computer.

Virtual Root   Also Vroot. A virtual tree of Web aliases that points to local, physical directories. This simplifies client URL addresses by presenting an entire set of content directories as a single directory tree.

VRML   Virtual Reality Modeling Language. A language for coding three-dimensional HTML applications.

W

W3C   World Wide Web Consortium.

Web Application   Also Web-based Application. A software program that uses HTTP for its core communication protocol and delivers Web-based information to the user in the HTML language.

Windows Sockets   Also Winsock. Winsock provides a single interface in Microsoft Windows to which multiple network software programs conform.

Working Copy   In a Visual InterDev project, a local, editable copy of a project file that is temporarily owned by the current developer.

World Wide Web   Also the Web or WWW. The Web is a collection of Internet host systems that make these services available on the Internet using the HTTP protocol. Web-based information is usually delivered in the form of hypertext and hypermedia using HTML.

WOSA   Windows Open Services Architecture. An architecture and set of application programming interfaces for Windows that standardized the interfaces developers use in accessing underlying network services.

WYSIWYG   What You See Is What You Get. Authoring software programs that render a document on the computer screen the way it will appear in print, even as it is being edited.

X

X.500 (including DAP)   Directory Access Protocol is a standard for global directory services.

X.509 Certificate   A protocol for a cryptographic certificate that contains a vendor's unique name and the vendor's public key.

XA   A transaction interoperability standard defined by X/Open. The Microsoft Transaction Server uses XA to connect with other transaction processing systems.

X/Open   An independent consortium of international computer vendors created to establish multi-vendor standards based on de facto standards.

Index

S

MICROSOFT LICENSE AGREEMENT
Book Companion CD

IMPORTANT—READ CAREFULLY: This Microsoft End-User License Agreement ("EULA") is a legal agreement between you (either an individual or an entity) and Microsoft Corporation for the Microsoft product identified above, which includes computer software and may include associated media, printed materials, and "online" or electronic documentation ("SOFTWARE PRODUCT"). Any component included within the SOFTWARE PRODUCT that is accompanied by a separate End-User License Agreement shall be governed by such agreement and not the terms set forth below. By installing, copying, or otherwise using the SOFTWARE PRODUCT, you agree to be bound by the terms of this EULA. If you do not agree to the terms of this EULA, you are not authorized to install, copy, or otherwise use the SOFTWARE PRODUCT; you may, however, return the SOFTWARE PRODUCT, along with all printed materials and other items that form a part of the Microsoft product that includes the SOFTWARE PRODUCT, to the place you obtained them for a full refund.

SOFTWARE PRODUCT LICENSE

The SOFTWARE PRODUCT is protected by United States copyright laws and international copyright treaties, as well as other intellectual property laws and treaties. The SOFTWARE PRODUCT is licensed, not sold.

1. **GRANT OF LICENSE.** This EULA grants you the following rights:

   a. **Software Product.** You may install and use one copy of the SOFTWARE PRODUCT on a single computer. The primary user of the computer on which the SOFTWARE PRODUCT is installed may make a second copy for his or her exclusive use on a portable computer.

   b. **Storage/Network Use.** You may also store or install a copy of the SOFTWARE PRODUCT on a storage device, such as a network server, used only to install or run the SOFTWARE PRODUCT on your other computers over an internal network; however, you must acquire and dedicate a license for each separate computer on which the SOFTWARE PRODUCT is installed or run from the storage device. A license for the SOFTWARE PRODUCT may not be shared or used concurrently on different computers.

   c. **License Pak.** If you have acquired this EULA in a Microsoft License Pak, you may make the number of additional copies of the computer software portion of the SOFTWARE PRODUCT authorized on the printed copy of this EULA, and you may use each copy in the manner specified above. You are also entitled to make a corresponding number of secondary copies for portable computer use as specified above.

   d. **Sample Code.** Solely with respect to portions, if any, of the SOFTWARE PRODUCT that are identified within the SOFTWARE PRODUCT as sample code (the "SAMPLE CODE"):

      i. **Use and Modification.** Microsoft grants you the right to use and modify the source code version of the SAMPLE CODE, *provided* you comply with subsection (d)(iii) below. You may not distribute the SAMPLE CODE, or any modified version of the SAMPLE CODE, in source code form.

      ii. **Redistributable Files.** Provided you comply with subsection (d)(iii) below, Microsoft grants you a nonexclusive, royalty-free right to reproduce and distribute the object code version of the SAMPLE CODE and of any modified SAMPLE CODE, other than SAMPLE CODE, or any modified version thereof, designated as not redistributable in the Readme file that forms a part of the SOFTWARE PRODUCT (the "Non-Redistributable Sample Code"). All SAMPLE CODE other than the Non-Redistributable Sample Code is collectively referred to as the "REDISTRIBUTABLES."

      iii. **Redistribution Requirements.** If you redistribute the REDISTRIBUTABLES, you agree to: (i) distribute the REDISTRIBUTABLES in object code form only in conjunction with and as a part of your software application product; (ii) not use Microsoft's name, logo, or trademarks to market your software application product; (iii) include a valid copyright notice on your software application product; (iv) indemnify, hold harmless, and defend Microsoft from and against any claims or lawsuits, including attorney's fees, that arise or result from the use or distribution of your software application product; and (v) not permit further distribution of the REDISTRIBUTABLES by your end user. Contact Microsoft for the applicable royalties due and other licensing terms for all other uses and/or distribution of the REDISTRIBUTABLES.

2. **DESCRIPTION OF OTHER RIGHTS AND LIMITATIONS.**

   - **Limitations on Reverse Engineering, Decompilation, and Disassembly.** You may not reverse engineer, decompile, or disassemble the SOFTWARE PRODUCT, except and only to the extent that such activity is expressly permitted by applicable law notwithstanding this limitation.

   - **Separation of Components.** The SOFTWARE PRODUCT is licensed as a single product. Its component parts may not be separated for use on more than one computer.

   - **Rental.** You may not rent, lease, or lend the SOFTWARE PRODUCT.

- **Support Services.** Microsoft may, but is not obligated to, provide you with support services related to the SOFTWARE PRODUCT ("Support Services"). Use of Support Services is governed by the Microsoft policies and programs described in the user manual, in "online" documentation, and/or in other Microsoft-provided materials. Any supplemental software code provided to you as part of the Support Services shall be considered part of the SOFTWARE PRODUCT and subject to the terms and conditions of this EULA. With respect to technical information you provide to Microsoft as part of the Support Services, Microsoft may use such information for its business purposes, including for product support and development. Microsoft will not utilize such technical information in a form that personally identifies you.

- **Software Transfer.** You may permanently transfer all of your rights under this EULA, provided you retain no copies, you transfer all of the SOFTWARE PRODUCT (including all component parts, the media and printed materials, any upgrades, this EULA, and, if applicable, the Certificate of Authenticity), **and** the recipient agrees to the terms of this EULA.

- **Termination.** Without prejudice to any other rights, Microsoft may terminate this EULA if you fail to comply with the terms and conditions of this EULA. In such event, you must destroy all copies of the SOFTWARE PRODUCT and all of its component parts.

3. **COPYRIGHT.** All title and copyrights in and to the SOFTWARE PRODUCT (including but not limited to any images, photographs, animations, video, audio, music, text, SAMPLE CODE, REDISTRIBUTABLES, and "applets" incorporated into the SOFTWARE PRODUCT) and any copies of the SOFTWARE PRODUCT are owned by Microsoft or its suppliers. The SOFT-WARE PRODUCT is protected by copyright laws and international treaty provisions. Therefore, you must treat the SOFTWARE PRODUCT like any other copyrighted material **except** that you may install the SOFTWARE PRODUCT on a single computer provided you keep the original solely for backup or archival purposes. You may not copy the printed materials accompanying the SOFTWARE PRODUCT.

4. **U.S. GOVERNMENT RESTRICTED RIGHTS.** The SOFTWARE PRODUCT and documentation are provided with RESTRICTED RIGHTS. Use, duplication, or disclosure by the Government is subject to restrictions as set forth in subparagraph (c)(1)(ii) of the Rights in Technical Data and Computer Software clause at DFARS 252.227-7013 or subparagraphs (c)(1) and (2) of the Commercial Computer Software—Restricted Rights at 48 CFR 52.227-19, as applicable. Manufacturer is Microsoft Corporation/One Microsoft Way/Redmond, WA 98052-6399.

5. **EXPORT RESTRICTIONS.** You agree that you will not export or re-export the SOFTWARE PRODUCT, any part thereof, or any process or service that is the direct product of the SOFTWARE PRODUCT (the foregoing collectively referred to as the "Restricted Components"), to any country, person, entity, or end user subject to U.S. export restrictions. You specifically agree not to export or re-export any of the Restricted Components (i) to any country to which the U.S. has embargoed or restricted the export of goods or services, which currently include, but are not necessarily limited to, Cuba, Iran, Iraq, Libya, North Korea, Sudan, and Syria, or to any national of any such country, wherever located, who intends to transmit or transport the Restricted Components back to such country; (ii) to any end user who you know or have reason to know will utilize the Restricted Components in the design, development, or production of nuclear, chemical, or biological weapons; or (iii) to any end user who has been prohibited from participating in U.S. export transactions by any federal agency of the U.S. government. You warrant and represent that neither the BXA nor any other U.S. federal agency has suspended, revoked, or denied your export privileges.

DISCLAIMER OF WARRANTY

NO WARRANTIES OR CONDITIONS. MICROSOFT EXPRESSLY DISCLAIMS ANY WARRANTY OR CONDITION FOR THE SOFTWARE PRODUCT. THE SOFTWARE PRODUCT AND ANY RELATED DOCUMENTATION ARE PROVIDED "AS IS" WITHOUT WARRANTY OR CONDITION OF ANY KIND, EITHER EXPRESS OR IMPLIED, INCLUDING, WITHOUT LIMITA-TION, THE IMPLIED WARRANTIES OF MERCHANTABILITY, FITNESS FOR A PARTICULAR PURPOSE, OR NONINFRINGEMENT. THE ENTIRE RISK ARISING OUT OF USE OR PERFORMANCE OF THE SOFTWARE PRODUCT REMAINS WITH YOU.

LIMITATION OF LIABILITY. TO THE MAXIMUM EXTENT PERMITTED BY APPLICABLE LAW, IN NO EVENT SHALL MICROSOFT OR ITS SUPPLIERS BE LIABLE FOR ANY SPECIAL, INCIDENTAL, INDIRECT, OR CONSEQUENTIAL DAM-AGES WHATSOEVER (INCLUDING, WITHOUT LIMITATION, DAMAGES FOR LOSS OF BUSINESS PROFITS, BUSINESS INTERRUPTION, LOSS OF BUSINESS INFORMATION, OR ANY OTHER PECUNIARY LOSS) ARISING OUT OF THE USE OF OR INABILITY TO USE THE SOFTWARE PRODUCT OR THE PROVISION OF OR FAILURE TO PROVIDE SUPPORT SERVICES, EVEN IF MICROSOFT HAS BEEN ADVISED OF THE POSSIBILITY OF SUCH DAMAGES. IN ANY CASE, MICROSOFT'S ENTIRE LIABILITY UNDER ANY PROVISION OF THIS EULA SHALL BE LIMITED TO THE GREATER OF THE AMOUNT ACTUALLY PAID BY YOU FOR THE SOFTWARE PRODUCT OR US$5.00; PROVIDED, HOWEVER, IF YOU HAVE ENTERED INTO A MICROSOFT SUPPORT SERVICES AGREEMENT, MICROSOFT'S ENTIRE LIABILITY REGARDING SUPPORT SERVICES SHALL BE GOVERNED BY THE TERMS OF THAT AGREEMENT. BECAUSE SOME STATES AND JURISDICTIONS DO NOT ALLOW THE EXCLUSION OR LIMITATION OF LIABILITY, THE ABOVE LIMITATION MAY NOT APPLY TO YOU.

MISCELLANEOUS

This EULA is governed by the laws of the State of Washington USA, except and only to the extent that applicable law mandates govern-ing law of a different jurisdiction.

Should you have any questions concerning this EULA, or if you desire to contact Microsoft for any reason, please contact the Microsoft subsidiary serving your country, or write: Microsoft Sales Information Center/One Microsoft Way/Redmond, WA 98052-6399.

PN 097-0002296

Real-world developer training
for results on the job—and on the exam.

Now you can build the skills and knowledge tested on the MCSD exams—and on the job—with these official Microsoft training kits. Each MCSD TRAINING KIT features a comprehensive training manual, lab exercises, reusable source code, and sample exam questions. Work through the system of self-paced lessons and hands-on labs to gain practical experience with essential development tasks. By the end of the course, you've created a full-featured working application—and you're ready for the corresponding exam!

Desktop Applications with Microsoft® Visual Basic® 6.0 MCSD Training Kit
ISBN: 0-7356-0620-X
U.S.A. $69.99
U.K. £45.99 [V.A.T. included]
Canada $104.99

Desktop Applications with Microsoft Visual C++® 6.0 MCSD Training Kit
ISBN: 0-7356-0795-8
U.S.A. $69.99
U.K. £45.99 [V.A.T. included]
Canada $104.99

Distributed Applications with Microsoft Visual Basic 6.0 MCSD Training Kit
ISBN: 0-7356-0833-4
U.S.A. $69.99
U.K. £45.99 [V.A.T. included]
Canada $104.99

Analyzing Requirements and Defining Solution Architectures MCSD Training Kit
ISBN: 0-7356-0854-7
U.S.A. $69.99
U.K. £45.99 [V.A.T. included]
Canada $104.99

Web Applications with Microsoft Visual InterDev® 6.0 MCSD Training Kit
ISBN: 0-7356-0967-5
U.S.A. $69.99
U.K. £45.99 [V.A.T. included]
Canada $107.99

COMING SOON!
Distributed Applications with Microsoft Visual C++ 6.0 MCSD Training Kit
ISBN: 0-7356-0926-8
U.S.A. $69.99
U.K. £45.99 [V.A.T. included]
Canada $107.99

Microsoft Press® products are available worldwide wherever quality computer books are sold. For more information, contact your book or computer retailer, software reseller, or local Microsoft Sales Office, or visit our Web site at mspress.microsoft.com. To locate your nearest source for Microsoft Press products, or to order directly, call 1-800-MSPRESS in the U.S. (in Canada, call 1-800-268-2222).

Prices and availability dates are subject to change.

mspress.microsoft.com

Get ready for
MCP Exam 70-029.

Learn how to design and implement enterprise database solutions using Microsoft® SQL Server™ 7.0—and prepare for the Microsoft Certified Professional (MCP) exam—with this official Microsoft training kit. Work at your own pace through the modular lessons and hands-on labs to master the procedures for planning, configuring, and deploying a database using SQL Server 7.0. As you gain this work-ready expertise, you'll also be preparing for MCP Exam 70-029—a core credit for the Microsoft Certified Database Administrator certification and an elective for becoming a Microsoft Certified Systems Engineer or Microsoft Certified Solution Developer. The TRAINING KIT includes a 120-day evaluation version of SQL Server 7.0!

U.S.A.	**$99.99**
U.K.	£64.99 [V.A.T. included]
Canada	$149.99
ISBN 1-57231-826-0	

Microsoft®

mspress.microsoft.com

Masterful instruction.
Your pace.
Your place.

Master the tools of your trade with in-depth developer training—straight from the source. The award-winning MICROSOFT MASTERING series is now available in ready-anywhere book format. Work at your own pace through the practical, print-based lessons to master essential development concepts, and advance your technique through the interactive labs on CD-ROM. It's professional-level instruction—when and where you need it—for building real-world skills and real-world solutions.

In-depth. Focused. *And* ready for work.

Get the technical drilldown you need to deploy and support Microsoft products more effectively with the MICROSOFT TECHNICAL REFERENCE series. Each guide focuses on a specific aspect of the technology—weaving in-depth detail with on-the-job scenarios and practical how-to information for the IT professional. Get focused—and take technology to its limits—with MICROSOFT TECHNICAL REFERENCES.

Building Applications with Microsoft® Outlook® 2000 Technical Reference
U.S.A.	$49.99
U.K.	£32.99 [V.A.T. included]
Canada	$74.99
ISBN 0-7356-0581-5	

Microsoft Windows NT® 4.0 Security, Audit, and Control
U.S.A.	$49.99
U.K.	£32.99 [V.A.T. included]
Canada	$71.99
ISBN 1-57231-818-X	

Microsoft Windows NT Server 4.0 Terminal Server Edition Technical Reference
U.S.A.	$49.99
U.K.	£32.99 [V.A.T. included]
Canada	$74.99
ISBN 0-7356-0645-5	

Microsoft Windows® 2000 TCP/IP Protocols and Services Technical Reference
U.S.A.	$49.99
U.K.	£32.99 [V.A.T. included]
Canada	$76.99
ISBN 0-7356-0556-4	

Active Directory™ Services for Microsoft Windows 2000 Technical Reference
U.S.A.	$49.99
U.K.	£32.99 [V.A.T. included]
Canada	$76.99
ISBN 0-7356-0624-2	

Microsoft Windows 2000 Security Technical Reference
U.S.A.	$49.99
U.K.	£32.99 [V.A.T. included]
Canada	$76.99
ISBN 0-7356-0858-X	

Microsoft Windows 2000 Performance Tuning Technical Reference
U.S.A.	$49.99
U.K.	£32.99 [V.A.T. included]
Canada	$76.99
ISBN 0-7356-0633-1	

Microsoft®

mspress.microsoft.com

Web Applications with Microsoft® Visual InterDev® 6.0 MCSD Training Kit

_____

WHERE DID YOU PURCHASE THIS PRODUCT?

_____

CUSTOMER NAME

Microsoft®*Press*

mspress.microsoft.com

Microsoft Press, PO Box 97017, Redmond, WA 98073-9830

OWNER REGISTRATION CARD   *Register Today!*   0-7356-0967-5

Return the bottom portion of this card to register today.

Web Applications with Microsoft® Visual InterDev® 6.0 MCSD Training Kit

_____   _____   _____

FIRST NAME   MIDDLE INITIAL   LAST NAME

_____

INSTITUTION OR COMPANY NAME

_____

ADDRESS

_____

_____   _____   _____

CITY   STATE   ZIP

_____   (   )_____

E-MAIL ADDRESS   PHONE NUMBER

U.S. and Canada addresses only. Fill in information above and mail postage-free.
Please mail only the bottom half of this page.

For information about Microsoft Press®
products, visit our Web site at
mspress.microsoft.com

Microsoft *Press*